D1367423

Black African Literature in English

1977–1981 SUPPLEMENT

Black African Literature in English

1977–1981 SUPPLEMENT

Bernth Lindfors

Africana Publishing Co.
a division of
Holmes & Meier Publishers, Inc.
New York • London

First published in the United States of America 1986 by
Africana Publishing Company
a division of Holmes & Meier Publishers, Inc.
30 Irving Place
New York, N.Y. 10003

Great Britain:
Holmes & Meier Publishers, Ltd.
Pindar Road
Hoddesdon, Hertfordshire EN11 0HF

Library of Congress Cataloging-in-Publication Data

Lindfors, Bernth.
  Black African literature in English. 1977–1981
supplement.

  Includes indexes.
  1. African literature (English)—Black authors—
History and criticism—Bibliography. I. Title.
Z3508.L5L56 Suppl. [PR9340] 016.82 86-1021
ISBN 0-8419-0962-8

Manufactured in the United States of America

CONTENTS

Part II - Individual Authors

Indexes

ACKNOWLEDGMENTS

I wish to express my gratitude to the numerous colleagues and friends who have helped me on this project.

First, a special word of thanks goes to Sondra Brady, who prepared the computerized camera-ready copy of this bibliography, and to Karen Rechnitzer Pope, who did some of the preliminary typing and record-keeping.

I am also extremely grateful to those who provided valuable bibliographical information, especially Stephen Arnold, Ann Biersteker, Rand Bishop, Dan Britz, Biserka Cvjetičanin, William French, Albert Gérard, James Gibbs, Stephen Gray, Lyn Innes, Dan Izevbaye, Vladimír Klíma, Charles Larson, Peter Nazareth, Alastair Niven, Donatus Nwoga, Richard Priebe, Alain Ricard, Dieter Riemenschneider, Reinhard Sander, Ulla Schild, Nancy Schmidt, Ernestyna Skurjat, O-lan Style, Satoru Tsuchiya, Donald Weinstock, Robert Wren, and Hans Zell.

For assistance in translating titles I must acknowledge the cooperation of Ulla Bruun de Neergaard, Frantisek Galan, Bernard Hickey, John Kolsti, André Lefevere, Vera Mark, Gilbert Rappaport, Sandra Shattuck, and Iouri Slezkine.

For locating elusive books and articles I am much obliged to the interlibrary loan staff at the University of Texas at Austin, to Hans Panofsky and Dan Britz of the Melville J. Herskovits Africana Library at Northwestern University, and to numerous librarians at the British Library, the Library of Congress, Harvard University, the University of Ibadan, the University of London School of Oriental and African Studies, the University of Nairobi, New York Public Library, and Yale University.

And for financial help I am very grateful to the University Research Institute at the University of Texas at Austin.

INTRODUCTION

This bibliography is a continuation of BLACK AFRICAN LITERATURE
IN ENGLISH: A GUIDE TO INFORMATION SOURCES (see item 4170, hereafter
cited as BALE) and resumes numbering where that volume left off.
Most of the entries provide information on books and articles
published between 1977 and 1981, but some earlier materials not
listed previously have been recorded here as well. However, nothing
dated later than 1981 has been included.

As before, certain kinds of data have had to be omitted. Brief
reviews of books and stage performances, political biographies of
statesmen, and newspaper reports of the nonliterary activities of
famous authors have been excluded, but not review articles,
biographical materials and newspaper items possessing some literary
significance. No creative works--novels, stories, plays, poems,
anthologies--have been recorded unless prefaced by a substantial
critical introduction. Bibliographies for creative titles are
cited, however, under various genre and topical headings
(bibliographies, fiction, drama, poetry and so forth) in part I,
and, wherever possible, under the appropriate individual author in
part II. The intention has been to provide comprehensive coverage
of major scholarly books and periodicals as well as selective
coverage of other relevant sources of informed commentary.

I have made an effort to examine every item cited and have marked
with an asterisk those not seen. A few inaccurate or possibly bogus
references have been excluded because I have been unable to verify
their existence. Since I intend to continue to update this
bibliography periodically, I would be extremely grateful to anyone
who can provide me with full bibliographical details and a copy of
any materials I may have omitted.

Annotations have been added to some entries, mostly to identify
the authors with whom the article or book is primarily concerned.
The general rule of thumb has been to list all authors who receive
at least a page or two of commentary in a secondary source. If many
authors are mentioned but none discussed at length, the annotation
indicates that the work is a survey. "Et al" (and others) has been
used whenever a work briefly treats additional authors not
identified in the annotation or whenever the discussion includes
African writers using French, Portuguese, or an indigenous language.
In other words, annotations mention by name only those black African
authors who write in English.

The bibliography is divided into two parts, the first organized
by genre or topic, the second by individual author. An effort has
been made to list each item in the bibliography only once and to
provide numbered cross-references to it in all other sections to
which the item belongs. Further, each section and subsection in the
bibliography is followed by a "see also" listing of cross-references
to additional relevant titles. An inventory of periodicals cited
and four indexes--by name, title, subject and geographical area--
should also help users to locate and identify the references they

need.

Some will recognize the bibliographical format employed here as a simplication of standard documentary practice. For instance, it may be assumed that the first number following a journal title is a volume or issue number; if there are two numbers following a journal title, the first is the volume number, the second the issue number.

Also, throughout the bibliography, alphabetization is letter by letter, and when there are multiple references for a given author, or when the sources were published anonymously, the citations are listed in chronological order. English translations have been provided for titles in all languages except French, German, Italian, Spanish and Portuguese.

PERIODICALS CITED: LIST AND ABBREVIATIONS

ABBIA (Yaoundé, Cameroon)

ABPR   AFRICAN BOOK PUBLISHING RECORD (Oxford)

ABRAKA QUARTERLY (Abraka, Nigeria)

ACLALSB   ASSOCIATION FOR COMMONWEALTH LITERATURE AND LANGUAGE
              STUDIES BULLETIN (Mysore, India; from 1978 St. Lucia,
              Australia; from 1981 Lennoxville, Quebec)

ACOLIT (Frankfurt)

ADI   ANUARIO DEL DEPARTAMENTO DE INGLÉS (Barcelona)

AdUA   ANNALES DE L´UNIVERSITÉ D´ABIDJAN (Abidjan, Ivory
              Coast)

AfB   AFRICANA BULLETIN (Warsaw)

AFER (Masaka, Uganda)

AFLYSHY   ANNALES DE LA FACULTÉ DES LETTRES ET SCIENCES HUMAINES
              DE YAOUNDÉ (Yaoundé, Cameroon)

AfrA   AFRICAN ARTS (Los Angeles)

AFRAMN   AFRAM NEWSLETTER (Paris)

AFRICA (Lisbon)

AFRICA (Rome)

AFRICA CURRENTS (London)

AFRICA-KENKYU (Tokyo)

AFRICA NEWS (Durham, NC)

AFRICA PERSPECTIVE (Johannesburg)

AFRICA WOMAN (London)

AFRICAN COMMUNIST (London)

AFRICAN HORIZON (Zaria, Nigeria)

AFRICAN PERSPECTIVES (Leiden)

AFRICAN PERSPECTIVES (Nairobi)

AFRICAN STUDIES NEWSLETTER (Waltham, MA; from 1981 Los Angeles)

AFRICANA N&N   AFRICANA NOTES AND NEWS (Johannesburg)

AfricaR   AFRICA REPORT (Washington, DC)

AFRIKA (Munich)

AFRIKA HEUTE (Bonn)

AFRIKA-POST (Pretoria, South Africa)

AFRIKA SPECTRUM (Hamburg)

AFRIQUE CONTEMPORAINE (Paris)

AFRISCOPE (Yaba, Nigeria)

AfrLJ   AFRICANA JOURNAL (New York)

AfrQ   AFRICA QUARTERLY (New Delhi)

AIBEPM   AFRICA: AN INTERNATIONAL BUSINESS, ECONOMIC AND
               POLITICAL MONTHLY (London)

AKZENTE (Munich)

ALA   L´AFRIQUE LITTÉRAIRE ET ARTISTIQUE (Paris)

ALA NEWSLETTER   AFRICAN LITERATURE ASSOCIATION NEWSLETTER
               (University Park, PA; from 1978 Edmonton, Alberta)

ALT   AFRICAN LITERATURE TODAY (London and New York)

ANNALES DE L´UNIVERSITÉ DE TOULOUSE: LE MIRAIL (Toulouse)

ANTHROPOLOGY AND HUMANISM QUARTERLY (Tallahassee, FL)

ANVIL (Nairobi, Kenya)

AR   ANTIOCH REVIEW (Yellow Springs, OH)

ArielE   ARIEL: A REVIEW OF INTERNATIONAL ENGLISH LITERATURE

(Calgary, Alberta)

ArO   ARCHIV ORIENTÁLNÍ (Prague)

ARTS RHODESIA (Salisbury, Rhodesia)

ASAWIB   AFRICAN STUDIES ASSOCIATION OF THE WEST INDIES
             BULLETIN (later CARJAS; Kingston, Jamaica)

ASEMKA (Cape Coast, Ghana)

ASH MAGAZINE (Adelaide, Australia)

AT   AFRICA TODAY (Denver, CO)

ATCALN   ASSOCIATION FOR THE TEACHING OF CARIBBEAN AND AFRICAN
             LITERATURE NEWSLETTER (London)

AUBTL   ANNALES DE L'UNIVERSITÉ DE BENIN, TOGO: LETTRES (Lomé,
             Togo)

AZIA I AFRIKA SEGODNÎA (Moscow)

BA SHIRU (Madison, WI)

BACKGROUND NOTES (Dar es Salaam, Tanzania)

BALF   BLACK AMERICAN LITERATURE FORUM (Terre Haute, IN)

BANANAS (London)

BBB   BLACK BOOKS BULLETIN (Chicago)

BBT   BULLETIN OF BLACK THEATRE (Washington, DC)

BDB   BÖRSENBLATT FÜR DEN DEUTSCHEN BUCHHANDEL (Frankfurt)

BIM (Christ Church, Barbados)

BINGO (Dakar, Senegal)

BLAC (Cape Town)

BLACK COLLEGIAN (New Orleans, LA)

BLACK PERSPECTIVES IN MUSIC (Cambria Heights, NY)

BLACK PHOENIX (London)

BLACK SCHOLAR (San Francisco)

BlackW   BLACK WORLD (Chicago)

BLOODY HORSE (Johannesburg)

BO   BLACK ORPHEUS (Lagos, Nigeria)

BONA (Johannesburg)

BOOKBIRD (Vienna)

BOOK FORUM (Rhinecliff, NY)

BRITISH BOOK NEWS (London)

BSAA   BULLETIN OF THE SOUTHERN ASSOCIATION OF AFRICANISTS
                (Gainesville, FL)

BUDONIAN (Kampala, Uganda)

BULLETIN (Lusaka, Zambia)

BUSARA (Nairobi)

BUSINESS SOUTH AFRICA (Marshalltown, South Africa)

CAHIERS DES RELIGIONS AFRICAINES (Kinshasa, Zaire)

CAHIERS ROUMAINS D´ÉTUDES LITTÉRAIRES (Bucharest)

CALABAR STUDIES IN MODERN LANGUAGES (Calabar, Nigeria)

CALLALOO (Lexington, KY)

CAMBRIDGE REVIEW (Cambridge, England)

CAMEROON STUDIES IN ENGLISH AND FRENCH (Yaoundé, Cameroon)

CANADIAN DRAMA (Waterloo, Ontario)

CARIB (Kingston, Jamaica)

CARIBBEAN CONTACT (Port of Spain, Trinidad)

CARJAS   CARIBBEAN JOURNAL OF AFRICAN STUDIES (Kingston,
                 Jamaica)

CBAA   CURRENT BIBLIOGRAPHY ON AFRICAN AFFAIRS (Washington,
                 DC)

CEDAR RAPIDS GAZETTE (Cedar Rapids, IA)

CENTREPOINT (Ilorin, Nigeria)

CHANDRABHĀGĀ (Orissa, India)

CHILDREN´S LITERATURE (New Haven, CT)

CHIMO (Lennoxville, Quebec)

CHRISTIANITY AND LITERATURE (University Park, PA)

CHRONICLE OF HIGHER EDUCATION (Baltimore, MD)

CJAS   CANADIAN JOURNAL OF AFRICAN STUDIES (Ottawa)

CJVS   CIZI JAZYKY VE ŠKOLE (Prague)

CLAJ   COLLEGE LANGUAGE ASSOCIATION JOURNAL (Baltimore, MD)

CLASSIC (Johannesburg)

CLQ   COLBY LIBRARY QUARTERLY (Waterville, ME)

CLS   COMPARATIVE LITERATURE STUDIES (Urbana, IL)

CNLQWR   COUNCIL ON NATIONAL LITERATURES/WORLD QUARTERLY REPORT
              (formerly CNLR; Jamaica, NY)

CNLR   COUNCIL ON NATIONAL LITERATURES REPORT (Jamaica, NY)

COMMONWEALTH (London)

COMMONWEALTH NEWSLETTER (Aarhus, Denmark)

COMMUNICATOR (Washington, DC)

COMMUNIQUÉ (Pietersburg, South Africa)

COMPARATIST (Raleigh, NC)

COMPARATIVE DRAMA (Kalamazoo, MI)

ComQ   COMMONWEALTH QUARTERLY (Mysore, India)

ConP   CONTEMPORARY POETRY (Teaneck, NJ)

CONTRAST (Cape Town)

CRCL   CANADIAN REVIEW OF COMPARATIVE LITERATURE (Toronto)

CREATIVE DRAMA (London)

CREATIVE MOMENT (Sumter, SC)

CREPLA BULLETIN OF INFORMATION (Yaoundé, Cameroon)

CRESSET (Valparaiso, IN)

CRevB   CONCH REVIEW OF BOOKS (Buffalo, NY)

CRIT   CRITIQUE: STUDIES IN MODERN FICTION (Atlanta, GA)

CRITICAL ARTS (Grahamstown, South Africa)

CRUX (Pretoria, South Africa)

DAI   DISSERTATION ABSTRACTS INTERNATIONAL (Ann Arbor, MI)

DAILY IOWAN (Iowa City, IA)

DAILY NATION (Nairobi, Kenya)

DAILY TIMES (Lagos, Nigeria)

DAS GUTE JAGENBUCH (Frankfurt)

DÉCENNIE 2 (Abidjan, Ivory Coast)

DEMAIN L'AFRIQUE (Paris)

DENGA (Zomba, Malawi)

DEUTSCHE WELLE TRANSKRIPTION (Cologne)

DHANA (Nairobi, Kenya)

DIALOGW   DIALOG (Warsaw)

DONGA (Pretoria, South Africa)

DR   DALHOUSIE REVIEW (Halifax, Nova Scotia)

DRUM (Johannesburg)

DRUM (Lagos)

DRUM (Nairobi)

DU   DEUTSCHUNTERRICHT (Stuttgart)

EAST AFRICAN LIBRARY ASSOCIATION BULLETIN (Nairobi, Kenya)

EAST-WEST REVIEW (Kyoto, Japan)

EBURNÉA (Abidjan, Ivory Coast)

ECHOS DU COMMONWEALTH (Pau, France)

ECONOMIST (London)

EDUCATION BENINOISE (Porto Novo, Benin)

EDUCATION IN EASTERN AFRICA (Nairobi, Kenya)

EDUCATIONAL FORUM (Menasha, WI)

EDUCATOR (Nsukka, Nigeria)

EJ   ENGLISH JOURNAL (Urbana, IL)

ELTIC REPORTER (Johannesburg)

EMOTAN (Ibadan, Nigeria)

ENGLISH IN AFRICA (Grahamstown, South Africa)

ENGLISH IN NEW GUINEA (Port Moresby, Papua New Guinea)

ENGLISH TEACHERS´ JOURNAL (Lusaka, Zambia)

ENGLISH WORLD-WIDE (Heidelberg)

ES   ENGLISH STUDIES (Amsterdam)

ESA   ENGLISH STUDIES IN AFRICA (Johannesburg)

ESSENCE (New York)

ETHIOPIQUES (Dakar, Senegal)

ETHNOLOGISCHE ABSICHTEN (West Berlin)

EUROPE (Paris)

EVE´S WEEKLY (New Delhi)

FBSLL   FOURAH BAY STUDIES IN LANGUAGE AND LITERATURE
            (Freetown, Sierra Leone)

FEMINA (Bombay)

FIRST WORLD (Atlanta, GA)

FJS   FU JEN STUDIES (Taipei)

FOLIO: PAPERS ON FOREIGN LANGUAGES AND LITERATURE (Brockport, NY)

FOLKET I BILD (Stockholm)

FOLKLORE ANNUAL (Austin, TX)

FRONTLINE (Braamfontein, South Africa)

GAf   GENÈVE-AFRIQUE (Geneva)

GANGA (Maiduguri, Nigeria)

GAR (Austin, TX)

GHANA BOOK WORLD (Accra, Ghana)

GREENFIELD REV   GREENFIELD REVIEW (Greenfield Center, NY)

GUARDIAN (London)

HALGAN (Mogadishu, Somalia)

HEKIMA (Nairobi, Kenya)

HELIKON (Budapest)

HERESY (Johannesburg)

HERITAGE (Gaberone, Botswana)

HISTORY TODAY (London)

HORN OF AFRICA (Summit, NJ)

HUMANITAS (Pretoria, South Africa)

IAF   INTERNATIONALES AFRIKA-FORUM (Bad Godesberg, Germany)

IFR   INTERNATIONAL FICTION REVIEW (Fredericton, New
            Brunswick)

IKORO (Nsukka, Nigeria)

ILANGA LASE NATAL (Durban, South Africa)

INDEX ON CENSORSHIP (London)

INDIANA ENGLISH JOURNAL (Terre Haute, IN)

INDIGO (Lagos, Nigeria)

INSPAN (Johannesburg)

INTERLINK (Lagos, Nigeria)

INTERNATIONAL DEFENCE & AID FUND FACT PAPER ON SOUTHERN AFRICA
            (London)

INTERNATIONAL JOURNAL OF WOMEN'S STUDIES (Montreal)

INTERNATIONAL LIBRARY REVIEW (New York)

INTERNATIONAL THEATRE INFORMATION (Paris)

INTERRACIAL BOOKS FOR CHILDREN (New York)

ISSUE (Waltham, MA)

JAAAA   JOURNAL OF AFRICAN-AFRO-AMERICAN AFFAIRS (Flint, MI)

JACL   JOURNAL OF AFRICAN AND COMPARATIVE LITERATURE (Ibadan,
            Nigeria)

JAfrS   JOURNAL OF AFRICAN STUDIES (Los Angeles)

JANUS (Cape Town)

JCL   JOURNAL OF COMMONWEALTH LITERATURE (London; from 1979
                Oxford, England)

JEn   JOURNAL OF ENGLISH (San´ā´, Yemen)

JeuneA   JEUNE AFRIQUE (Paris)

JLSN   JOURNAL OF THE LITERARY SOCIETY OF NIGERIA (Benin
                City, Nigeria)

JMAS   JOURNAL OF MODERN AFRICAN STUDIES (London)

JNALA   JOURNAL OF THE NEW AFRICAN LITERATURE AND THE ARTS
                (Stanford, CA; later New York)

JNESA   JOURNAL OF THE NIGERIAN ENGLISH STUDIES ASSOCIATION
                (Ibadan, Nigeria)

JOE (Nairobi, Kenya)

JOE HOMESTEAD (formerly JOE; Nairobi, Kenya)

JOURNAL OF AFRO-AMERICAN ISSUES (Washington, DC)

JOURNAL OF LANGUAGE ARTS AND COMMUNICATION (Ibadan, Nigeria)

JOURNAL OF LITERARY STUDIES (Maiduguri, Nigeria)

JOURNAL OF LITERARY STUDIES (Orissa, India)

JOURNAL OF SOUTHERN AFRICAN AFFAIRS (College Park, MD)

JOURNAL OF THE KARNATAK UNIVERSITY: HUMANITIES (Dharwar, India)

JOURNAL OF THE PERFORMING ARTS (Accra, Ghana)

JPC   JOURNAL OF POPULAR CULTURE (Bowling Green, OH)

JSAS   JOURNAL OF SOUTHERN AFRICAN STUDIES (London)

KAAFA (Monrovia, Liberia)

KAKAKI (Kano, Nigeria)

KALALU (Zomba, Malawi)

KENYA JOURNAL OF ADULT EDUCATION (Nairobi, Kenya)

KENYA WEEKLY NEWS (Nairobi, Kenya)

KIABÀRÀ (Port Harcourt, Nigeria)

KNJI (Belgrade)

KOMPARATISTISCHE HEFTE (Bayreuth)

KONTYNENTY (Warsaw)

KREATIEF (Wevelgem, Belgium)

KRISTO (Gwelo, Zimbabwe)

KRITERIUM (Copenhagen)

KUCHA (Nairobi, Kenya)

KUKA (Zaria, Nigeria)

KUNAPIPI (Aarhus, Denmark)

KWANZA JOURNAL (Pretoria, South Africa)

LAAW   LOTUS: AFRO-ASIAN WRITINGS (Cairo)

LANTERN (Pretoria, South Africa)

LARES   LAGOS REVIEW OF ENGLISH STUDIES (Lagos, Nigeria)

LCrit   LITERARY CRITERION (Mysore, India)

LEGACY (Legon, Ghana)

LEGON OBSERVER (Legon, Ghana)

LHY   LITERARY HALF-YEARLY (Mysore, India)

LIBERIA: POLITICAL, ECONOMIC AND SOCIAL MONTHLY (Monrovia, Liberia)

LIBRARY WORLD (London)

LIBRI (Copenhagen)

LISTENER (London)

LITERATURA NA ŚWIECIE (Warsaw)

LitR   LITERARY REVIEW (Madison, NJ)

LJH   LEGON JOURNAL OF THE HUMANITIES (Legon, Ghana)

LO   LITERATURNOE OBOZRENIE (Moscow)

LONDON MAGAZINE (London)

LOOKOUT (Zomba, Malawi)

LORE&L   LORE AND LANGUAGE (Sheffield, England)

LRN   LITERARY RESEARCH NEWSLETTER (Brockport, NY)

MAKTABA (Nairobi, Kenya)

MANA (Suva, Fiji)

MANAS (Los Angeles)

MARANG (Gaberone, Botswana)

MD   MODERN DRAMA (Toronto)

MEANJIN Q   MEANJIN QUARTERLY (Melbourne)

MINORITY VOICES (University Park, PA)

MIRROR (Zaria, Nigeria; superseded by KUKA)

MOSTOVI (Belgrade)

MOULD (Yaoundé, Cameroon)

MR   MASSACHUSETTS REVIEW (Amherst, MA)

MS. (New York)

MUNDO NEGRO (Madrid)

MUSE (Nsukka, Nigeria)

NAIROBI TIMES (Nairobi, Kenya)

NAMES (Youngstown, OH)

NATION (New York)

NATIONAL STUDENT (Grahamstown, South Africa)

NATIVE TEACHERS´ JOURNAL (Pietermaritzburg, South Africa)

NDAANAN (Bathurst, Gambia)

NDL   NEUE DEUTSCHE LITERATUR (Berlin)

NEGRO HISTORY B   NEGRO HISTORY BULLETIN (Washington, DC)

NEOHELIKON (Budapest)

NEW AFRICAN (London)

NEWBREED (Lagos, Nigeria)

NEW CLASSIC (formerly CLASSIC; Johannesburg)

NEW CULTURE (Ibadan, Nigeria)

NEW DAWN (Manchester, England)

NEW OUTLOOK (Durban, South Africa)

NEW REPUBLIC (New York)

NEW SOCIETY (London)

NEW WORLD QUARTERLY (Kingston, Jamaica)

NEW YORKER (New York)

NGAM (Yaoundé, Cameroon)

NIGERBIBLIOS (Lagos, Nigeria)

NIGERIAN CHRISTIAN (Ibadan, Nigeria)

NIGERIAN CHRONICLE (Calabar, Nigeria)

NIGERIAN OBSERVER (Benin City, Nigeria)

NIGERIAN OPINION (Ibadan, Nigeria)

NIGERIAN STUDENT'S VOICE (Washington, DC)

NigM   NIGERIA MAGAZINE (Lagos, Nigeria)

NIGRIZIA (Verona, Italy)

NJH   NIGERIAN JOURNAL OF THE HUMANITIES (Benin City,
            Nigeria)

NLRev   NEW LITERATURE REVIEW (Canberra)

NOTRE LIBRARIE (Paris)

NOWE KSIAŹKI (Warsaw)

NSAL   NSUKKA STUDIES IN AFRICAN LITERATURE (Nsukka, Nigeria)

NSUKKA LIBRARY NOTES (Nsukka, Nigeria)

NSUKKASCOPE (Nsukka, Nigeria)

NYRB   NEW YORK REVIEW OF BOOKS (New York)

NYTBR   NEW YORK TIMES BOOK REVIEW (New York)

OBSERVER (London)

OBSIDIAN (Fredonia, NY; from 1980 Detroit, MI)

ODI (Zomba, Malawi)

OJES   OSMANIA JOURNAL OF ENGLISH STUDIES (Hyderabad, India)

OKIKE (Nsukka, Nigeria)

OMABE (Nsukka, Nigeria)

OPON IFA (Ibadan, Nigeria)

ORACLE (Calabar, Nigeria)

ORITA (Ibadan, Nigeria)

PA   PRÉSENCE AFRICAINE (Paris)

PACE (Johannesburg)

PACIFIC COAST AFRICANIST ASSOCIATION OCCASIONAL PAPER (Pleasant
          Hill, CA)

PAIDEUMA (Frankfurt)

PAN AFRICAN BOOK WORLD (Enugu, Nigeria)

PanA   PAN-AFRICANIST (Evanston, IL)

PAPERS IN EDUCATION AND DEVELOPMENT (Dar es Salaam, Tanzania)

PAPUA NEW GUINEA WRITING (Port Moresby, Papua New Guinea)

PARABOLA (Mt. Kisko, NY)

PELCULEF NEWSLETTER (Gaberone, Botswana)

PENN-TEXAS WORKING PAPERS IN SOCIOLINGUISTICS (Austin, TX)

PERMANENT PRESS (Gothenburg)

PEUPLES NOIRS/PEUPLES AFRICAINES (Paris)

PFr   PRESENCE FRANCOPHONE (Sherbrooke, Quebec)

PHYLON (Atlanta, GA)

PIONEER (Nsukka, Nigeria)

POÉSIE (Basel)

POETRY VENTURE (St. Petersburg, FL)

POSITIVE REVIEW (Ile-Ife, Nigeria)

PQM   PACIFIC QUARTERLY MOANA (Hamilton, New Zealand)

PRZEGLAD INFORMACJI O AFRYCE (Warsaw)

PRZEGLAD ORIENTALISTYCZNY (Warsaw)

PrzS   PRZEGLAD SOCJOLOGICZNY (Łódź, Poland)

PsyculR   PSYCHOCULTURAL REVIEW (Pleasantville, NY)

PUBW   PUBLISHERS WEEKLY (New York)

PULA (Gaberone, Botswana)

QUARTERLY YEKATIT (Addis Ababa, Ethiopia)

QUEST (Calabar, Nigeria)

RADCLIFFE QUARTERLY (Cambridge, MA)

RADIO-TV TIMES (Lagos, Nigeria)

RAL   RESEARCH IN AFRICAN LITERATURES (Austin, TX)

RCR   RED CEDAR REVIEW (East Lansing, MI)

REALITY (Pietermaritzburg, South Africa)

REFLECTOR (Oyo, Nigeria)

RENAISSANCE WEEKLY (Enugu, Nigeria)

RESTANT (Antwerp)

REVIEW OF AFRICAN POLITICAL ECONOMY (London)

REVUE DE L'UNIVERSITÉ DE MONCTON (Moncton, New Brunswick)

REVUE DES LANGUES (Oran, Algeria)

RHODES REVIEW (Grahamstown, South Africa)

RIKKA (Toronto)

RLENA   REVUE DE LITTÉRATURE ET D'ESTHÉTIQUE NÉGRO-AFRICAINES
              (Abidjan, Ivory Coast)

ROYAL COMMONWEALTH SOCIETY LIBRARY NOTES (London)

RPC   RECHERCHE, PÉDAGOGIE ET CULTURE (Paris)

S AFRICAN OUTLOOK   SOUTH AFRICAN OUTLOOK (Lovedale, South Africa)

SARP   SOUTHERN AFRICAN RESEARCH IN PROGRESS: COLLECTED
              PAPERS (York, England)

SATURDAY REVIEW (New York)

SBL   STUDIES IN BLACK LITERATURE (Fredericksburg, VA)

SCENARÍA (Johannesburg)

SCHOOL LEAVER (Kampala, Uganda)

SCIENTIA (Ijebu Ode, Nigeria)

SECHABA (London)

SHUTTLE (Lagos, Nigeria)

SIERRA LEONE LIBRARY JOURNAL (Freetown, Sierra Leone)

S´KETSH´ (Johannesburg)

SNARL (Braamfontein, South Africa)

SOCIETY OF MALAWI JOURNAL (Blantyre, Malawi)

LE SOLEIL (Dakar, Senegal)

SOUTH AFRICAN DIGEST (Pretoria, South Africa)

SOUTH AFRICAN LAW JOURNAL (Cape Town)

SOUTH AFRICAN LIBRARIES (Potchefstroom, South Africa)

SOUTH AFRICAN PANORAMA (Pretoria, South Africa)

SOUTH DAKOTA REVIEW (Vermillion, SD)

SOUTHERN AFRICA (New York)

SOUTHERN SUDAN MAGAZINE (Juba, Sudan)

SOVIET LITERATURE (Moscow)

SOWETAN (Johannesburg)

SPAN (Brisbane, Australia)

SPEAK (Cape Town)

SPEAR (Lagos, Nigeria)

SPHINX (Regina, Saskatchewan)

SpM   SPICILEGIO MODERNO (Pisa, Italy)

SSF   STUDIES IN SHORT FICTION (Newberry, SC)

STAFFRIDER (Braamfontein, South Africa)

STANDARD (Nairobi, Kenya)

STANDPUNTE (Cape Town)

STAR (Ibadan, Nigeria)

STAR (Johannesburg)

STUDIA AFRICANA (Cincinnati, OH)

STUDIES IN THE HUMANITIES (Indiana, PA)

SUDANOW (Khartoum, Sudan)

SUNDAY GLEANER (Kingston, Jamaica)

SUNDAY NATION (Nairobi, Kenya)

SUNDAY OBSERVER (Benin City, Nigeria)

SUNDAY POST (Nairobi, Kenya)

SUNDAY TIMES (Lagos, Nigeria)

SVĚTOVÁ LITERATURA (Prague)

TEMPO (Maputo, Mozambique)

THÉÂTRE EN POLOGNE (Warsaw)

THEATRE Q   THEATRE QUARTERLY (London)

THEORIA (Pietermaritzburg, South Africa)

THIRD WORLD FIRST (Lagos, Nigeria)

TIDSKRIFT FÖR LITTERATURVETENSKAP (Lund, Sweden)

TIMES OF MALTA (Valletta, Malta)

TLS   TIMES LITERARY SUPPLEMENT (London)

TO THE POINT (Johannesburg)

TOPIC (Washington, DC)

TRANSITION (Accra, Ghana)

TRANSLATION (New York)

TRIVENI (Machilipatnam, India)

TRUST (Nairobi, Kenya)

TYGODNIK KULTURALNY (Warsaw)

UCTSE   UNIVERSITY OF CAPE TOWN STUDIES IN ENGLISH (Cape Town,
              South Africa)

UES   UNIVERSITY OF SOUTH AFRICA ENGLISH STUDIES (Pretoria,
              South Africa)

UFAHAMU (Los Angeles)

UGANDA JOURNAL (Kampala, Uganda)

UMMA (Dar es Salaam, Tanzania)

UMMA-N   UMMA (Nairobi, Kenya)

UMOJA (Boulder, CO)

UNESCO BULLETIN FOR LIBRARIES (Paris)

UNESCO COURIER (Paris)

UNIVERSITAS (Legon, Ghana)

UNIVERSITY OF DENVER NEWS (Denver, CO)

UTAFITI (Dar es Salaam, Tanzania)

VIDYA (Pittsburgh, PA)

VINDUET (Oslo)

VIVA (Nairobi, Kenya)

WA   WEST AFRICA (London)

WACC JOURNAL   WORLD ASSOCIATION FOR CHRISTIAN COMMUNICATION
                JOURNAL (London)

WAJML   WEST AFRICAN JOURNAL OF MODERN LANGUAGES (Ibadan,
                Nigeria)

WAR   WEST AFRICAN REVIEW (Liverpool)

WASHINGTON POST (Washington, DC)

WB   WEIMARER BIETRÄGE (Berlin)

WEEKLY REVIEW (Nairobi, Kenya)

WEEKLY SPECTATOR (Accra, Ghana)

WENDEKREIS

WIETIE (Johannesburg)

WILSON LIBRARY BULLETIN (Washington, DC)

WILSON QUARTERLY (Washington, DC)

WIP   WORK IN PROGRESS (Johannesburg)

WITS STUDENT (Johannesburg)

WLT   WORLD LITERATURE TODAY (Norman, OK)

WLWE   WORLD LITERATURE WRITTEN IN ENGLISH (Arlington, TX;
               from 1979 Guelph, Ontario)

WORLDVIEW (New York)

WP   WORK IN PROGRESS (Zaria, Nigeria)

YCGL   YEARBOOK OF COMPARATIVE & GENERAL LITERATURE
               (Bloomington, IN)

YFS   YALE FRENCH STUDIES (New Haven, CT)

Y/T   YALE/THEATRE (New Haven, CT)

Z-A   ZAÏRE-AFRIQUE (Kinshasa, Zaire)

ZAMBEZIA (Salisbury, Rhodesia; then Harare, Zimbabwe)

ZAMBIA MUSEUM JOURNAL (Livingstone, Zambia)

ZANGO (Lusaka, Zambia)

ZEITSCHRIFT FÜR KULTURAUSTAUSCH (Stuttgart)

ZIMBABWE LIBRARIAN (Bulawayo, Zimbabwe)

ZLAJ   ZAMBIA LIBRARY ASSOCIATION JOURNAL (Lusaka, Zambia)

ZMag   Z MAGAZINE (Lusaka, Zambia)

3 WELT MAGAZIN (Bonn)

Part I

GENRE AND TOPICAL STUDIES

AND REFERENCE SOURCES

A. BIBLIOGRAPHIES

Listed here are the general bibliographical resources most useful
for the study of African literature in English. Bibliographies on
specific genres and topics (e.g., fiction, drama, children's
literature, the role of the writer) and on individual authors can be
found in subsequent sections.

3306.   Aboyade, B. Olabimpe. NIGERIAN CONTRIBUTION TO HUMANISTIC
        STUDIES 1948-1975: A BIBLIOGRAPHIC SURVEY. Ibadan: Dept. of
        Library Studies, University of Ibadan, 1978.

3307.   Andersson, Carita. ÖST-AFRIKANSKA BERÄTTARE [East African
        Narrators]. Boras, Sweden: Bibliotekshogskolan Boras, 1980.

            Brief, annotated bibliography.

3308.   Anon. WOMEN AND WOMEN WRITERS IN THE COMMONWEALTH:
        COMMONWEALTH BOOK FAIR 1975. London: Commonwealth Institute
        and The National Book League, 1975.

            Catalog of an exhibition.

3309.   Anon. "Bibliography: Literature, Literary Criticism." AfrLJ
        8 (1977), 68-69, 165-66, 264-66, 357-58; 9 (1978), 76,
        169-71, 365-66; 10 (1979), 70-71, 161-63.

3310.   Anon. INDEX TO SOUTH AFRICAN PERIODICALS. Johannesburg:
        Public Library, 1977-81. Annual.

            Continuation of BALE 6.

3311.   Anon. THE DEVELOPMENTS AND ACHIEVEMENTS OF COMMONWEALTH
        LITERATURE. London: National Book League and Commonwealth
        Institute, 1978.

            Catalog of an exhibition. Africa, pp. 6-15.

3312.   Anon. "750 titres de littérature négroafricaine." NOTRE
        LIBRARIE, 45 (1978), 35-111.

            Mainly francophone, but includes French translations of
            anglophone literary works.

3313.   Anon. THE COMMONWEALTH IN PRINT: CATALOGUE OF AN EXHIBITION
        FIRST SHOWN AT THE COMMONWEALTH INSTITUTE 3-23 SEPTEMBER 1979
        AS THE COMMONWEALTH BOOK EXHIBITION. Commonwealth
        Bibliographies, 1. London: Commonwealth Institute, 1979.

            Includes section on literature, pp. 29-34.

3314.   Anon. COMMONWEALTH WRITERS: SOME OF THE BEST-KNOWN WRITERS
        AND THEIR WORKS. London: Working Party on Library Holdings

of Commonwealth Literature and the Commonwealth Secretariat, 1980.

3315. Anon. DIE FUNKTION MODERNER AFRIKANISCHER LITERATUREN: AFRIKANISCHES LITERATURSYMPOSIUM: AUSWAHLBIBLIOGRAPHIE ZU AFRIKANISCHEN AUTHOREN. Frankfurt am Main: Stadt- und Universitätsbibliothek Frankfurt am Main, 1980.

> Bio-bibliographies on Achebe, Angira, Armah, Bart-Williams, Egbuna, Ekwensi, Emecheta, Farah, Ike, Irele, Madubuike, Matthews, Ngugi, Nkosi, Obiechina, Sepamla, Wanjala, Worku, et al.

3316. Beeton, D.R. A PILOT BIBLIOGRAPHY OF SOUTH AFRICAN ENGLISH LITERATURE (FROM THE BEGINNINGS TO 1971). Pretoria: University of South Africa, 1976.

3317. Berrian, Brenda F. "Bibliographies of Nine Female African Writers." RAL, 12 (1981), 214-36.

> Aidoo, Adelaide Casely-Hayford, Gladys Casely-Hayford, Emecheta, Nwapa, Ogot, Jolaosa Segun, Sutherland, Zirimu.

3318. Chakava, Henry. "East and Central Africa." JCL, 12, 3, (1978), 13-23; 13, 3 (1979), 10-17.

> Annual JCL bibliography; continued by Luvai, 3330, and Ndegwa, 3336.

3319. Cordor, S. Henry. THE BIBLIOGRAPHY OF LIBERIAN LITERATURE: A BIBLIOGRAPHICAL REVIEW OF LITERARY WORKS BY LIBERIANS, SUPPLEMENT ONE. Liberian Literature Studies Series, 4. Monrovia: Liberian Literature Studies Programme, 1971. Typescript.

3320. Couzens, Tim. "Appendix 2: South Africa." JCL, 11, 3 (1977), 40-49; 12, 3 (1978) 57-66; 13, 3 (1979), 21-27.

> Annual JCL bibliography; continued by Driver and Smith, 3322.

3321. Driver, Dorothy. "Appendix II: South Africa." JCL, 15, 2 (1980), 157-64; 16, 2 (1981), 157-71.

> Continuation of list by Driver and Smith, 3322.

3322. Driver, Dorothy, and Judy Smith. "Appendix II: South Africa." JCL, 14, 2 (1979), 113-20.

> Annual JCL bibliography; continuation of lists by Couzens, 3320.

3323. Easterbrook, David L. "Bibliography of Africana Bibliographies, 1975-1976." AfrLJ, 8 (1977), 232-42.

3324.   Fabre, Michel, and Danielle Quet. "A Checklist of Mauritian Creative Writing in English (1920-80)." WLWE, 19 (1980), 138-43.

3325.   Gamble, David P., and Louise Sperling. A GENERAL BIBLIOGRAPHY OF THE GAMBIA (UP TO 31 DECEMBER 1977). Boston: G.K. Hall, 1979.

Literature, pp. 200-203.

3326.   Hall, David, et al., ed. INTERNATIONAL AFRICAN BIBLIOGRAPHY. London: Mansell, 1977-1981. Quarterly.

Continuation of BALE 7. Often contains a section titled "Literature" listing critical articles.

3327.   House, Amelia. BLACK SOUTH AFRICAN WOMEN WRITERS IN ENGLISH: A PRELIMINARY CHECKLIST. Evanston, IL: Program on Women, Northwestern University, 1980.

Includes Boitumelo, 5636, pp. 19-21; Gray, 5403, pp. 22-32.

3328.   Jeppesen, Bent Haugaard. "Litteraturhistorie, kulturproblemer, kunst [Literary History, Cultural Problems, Art]" and "Skønlitteratur [Fiction]." LITTERATUR OM AFRIKA [Literature of Africa]. Ed. Vagn Plenge and Anna Britta Wallenius. Ms. Bibliographier, 6. Copenhagen: Mellemfolkeligt Samvirke og Nordiska Afrikainstitutet, 1973. Pp. 118-26, 127-35.

Annotated bibliographies.

3329.* Licht, Merete. ET UDVALG AF BIBLIOGRAFIER OG MONOGRAFIER OM COMMONWEALTH LITTERATUR I DET KONGELIGE BIBLIOTEK [A Selection of Bibliographies and Monographs on Commonwealth Literature in the Royal Library]. Copenhagen: Det Kongelige Bibliotek, 1978.

Holdings of Danish Royal Library arranged by geographical area.

3330.   Luvai, A.I. "Africa: East and Central." JCL, 14, 2 (1979), 9-12; 15, 2 (1980), 9-10.

Annual JCL bibliography; continuation of lists by Chakava, 3318. See also Ndegwa, 3336.

3331.   McAfee, Judith L. AFRICAN LITERATURE: A BIBLIOGRAPHIC GUIDE. Evanston, IL: Northwestern University Library, 1975.

Mimeographed guide to Northwestern University Library holdings.

3332.   Maurer, Barbara, and Klaus Schwarz. HOCHSCHULSCHRIFTEN ZU

SCHWARZAFRIKA 1960-1978: DEUTSCHLAND, ÖSTERREICH, SCHWEIZ. Fribourg: Schwarz, 1979.

3333. Modern Language Association. MLA INTERNATIONAL BIBLIOGRAPHY OF BOOKS AND ARTICLES ON THE MODERN LANGUAGES AND LITERATURES. New York: Modern Language Association, 1977-81.

Continuation of BALE 30.

3334. Musiker, Reuben. SOUTH AFRICAN BIBLIOGRAPHY. 2nd ed. Cape Town: David Philip, 1980.

3335. Mzee, Said, and Rosemarie Rauter. PUBLISHED AND PRINTED IN AFRICA. Frankfurt am Main: German Booksellers´ and Publishers´ Association, Exhibit Department, 1980.

Catalog for 32nd Frankfurt Book Fair, 1980. See also Rauter, 3343.

3336. Ndegwa, R.N. "Africa: East and Central." JCL, 16, 2 (1981), 9-11.

Continuation of lists by Chakava, 3318, and Luvai, 3330.

3337. Niven, Alastair. "Bibliography of African Literature in English." PROGRESS IN AFRICAN BIBLIOGRAPHY: SCOLMA CONFERENCE, COMMONWEALTH INSTITUTE, 17-18 March 1977 PROCEEDINGS. London: SCOLMA, 1977.

Section 2, pp. 1-12.

3339. Obafemi, B.O. "Africa: Western -- A Note." JCL, 14, 2 (1979), 22-24.

Description of literary activities in 1978.

3340. Ogungbesan, Kolawole. "West Africa: Gambia, Ghana, Nigeria, Sierra Leone." JCL, 11, 3 (1977), 23-39; 12, 3 (1978), 37-42; 13, 2 (1978), 18-28.

Annual JCL bibliography; continued by Sekoni, 3350.

3341. Pala, Francis. "Kenyan Literary Experience." UMMA-N, 5 (1977), 13-14.

Book exhibition catalog.

3342. Pichanick, J., A.J. Chennells, and L.B. Rix, RHODESIAN LITERATURE IN ENGLISH: A BIBLIOGRAPHY (1890-1974/5). Zambeziana Series, 2. Gwelo, Rhodesia: Mambo, 1977.

3343.* Rauter, Rosemarie, and Said Mzee. AFRICANA: AN INTERNATIONAL EXHIBITION OF BOOKS AT THE 32ND FRANKFURT BOOK FAIR/AFRICANA. Frankfurt: Ausstellungs- und Messe-GmbH des Borsenvereins des Deutschen Buchhandels, 1980.

Catalog of Africana exhibition. See also Mzee, 3335.

3344. Ravenscroft, Arthur. "Africa." In COMMONWEALTH LITERATURE:
A HANDBOOK OF SELECT READING LISTS. Ed. C.D. Narasimhaiah.
Delhi: Oxford University Press, 1976. Pp. 23-34.

3345. ____. "Africa: General." JCL, 11, 3 (1977), 2-13; 12, 3
(1978), 2-13; 13, 3 (1979), 3-10.

3346. Rose, Vattel T., Jennifer Jordan, Virginia Barrett, Dorothy
Evans, Enid Bogle, Lorraine Henry, and Leota Lawrence. "An
Annual Bibliography of Afro-American, African, and Caribbean
Literature for the Year, 1976." CLAJ, 21 (1977), 100-57.

3347. Ruuth-Bäcker, Karin. EN LITTERÄR RESA GENOM DET SVARTA
AFRIKA: EN BIBLIOGRAFISK VÄGLEDNING TILL AFRIKANSK
SKÖNLITTERATUR [A Literary Journey around Black Africa: A
Bibliographical Guide to African Fiction]. Uppsala: Nordiska
afrikainstitutet, 1981.

3348. Saint-Andre-Utudjian, Elaine, comp. A BIBLIOGRAPHY OF WEST
AFRICAN LIFE AND LITERATURE. Waltham, MA: African Studies
Association, 1977.

3349. ____. "Bibliographie de la littérature ouest-africaine
d'expression anglaise á l'usage des francophones (Liste des
travaux et traduction en langue française relatifs á la
littérature ouest-africaine d'expression anglaise)." AUBTL,
4, 1 (1977), 105-17.

3350. Sekoni, Oluropo. "Africa: Western." JCL, 15, 2 (1980),
39-42; 16, 2 (1981), 39-42.

Annual JCL bibliography; continuation of lists by
Ogungbesan, 3340.

3351. Simpson, D.H., comp. "Commonwealth: General." JCL, 12, 2
(1977), 3-4; 13, 2 (1978), 2-3; 14, 2 (1979), 7-8; 15, 2
(1980), 7-8; 16, 2 (1981), 7-8.

Annual JCL bibliography.

3352. Style, O-lan. "Southern Africa: Botswana, Lesotho, Rhodesia,
Swaziland." JCL, 11, 3 (1977), 13-23; 12, 3 (1978), 24-36;
13, 2 (1978), 4-18; 14, 2 (1979), 13-21; 15, 2 (1980), 11-38;
16, 2 (1981), 12-31.

Annual JCL bibliography; name of Rhodesia changes to
Zimbabwe in later entries.

3353.* ____. RECENT ZIMBABWEAN LITERATURE. Introd. Alastair Niven.
London: Africa Centre, 1981.

Catalog of exhibition.

3354. Sulzer, Peter, and Verena Müller. DIE AFRICANA-SAMMLUNG IN DER STADTBIBLIOTHEK WINTERTHUR: AFRIKANISCHE LITERATUREN UND SPRACHEN/THE AFRICANA COLLECTION OF THE MUNICIPAL LIBRARY OF WINTERTHUR: AFRICAN LITERATURES AND LANGUAGES, and DER KATALOG DER AFRICANA-SAMMLUNG IN DER STADTBIBLIOTHEK WINTERTHUR. Mitteilungen der Basler Afrika Bibliographien, 17. Basel: Basler Afrika Bibliographien, 1977.

3355. Warwick, Ronald. A HANDBOOK OF LIBRARY HOLDINGS OF COMMONWEALTH LITERATURE: UNITED KINGDOM AND EUROPE. Pref. Alastair Niven. London: British Library Lending Division, 1977.

Revised ed. of BALE 1861.

3356.* Williams, S., and A. Gregory. SOUTH AFRICAN ENGLISH LITERATURE. Pretoria: Unisa Sanlam Library, 1976.

3357.* Williams, S., and E. H. Woolley. A SELECT BIBLIOGRAPHY OF SOUTH AFRICAN ENGLISH LITERATURE 1970-78. Pretoria: Unisa Sanlam Library, n.d.

3358. Wolke, Irmtraud D., FACHKATALOG AFRIKA/SUBJECT CATALOG AFRICA/CATALOGUE-MATIÈRES AFRIQUE: VOL. 3: LITERATUR/LITERATURE/LITTÉRATURE. Munich: K.G. Saur, 1979.

Frankfurt Municipal and University Library's collection on Africa.

3359. ____. "Hilfsmittel zum Studium der afrikanischen Literatur aus den Beständen der Stadt- und Universitätsbibliothek Frankfurt am Main." ZEITSCHRIFT FÜR KULTURAUSTAUSCH, 29 (1979), 307-32.

3360. ____. "Sammelwerke afrikanischer Autoren." BDB, 22 August 1980, pp. 2082-83.

3361. ____. "Afrikanische Literatur in deutscher Übersetzung." BDB, 22 August 1980, pp. 2078-82.

3362. Wolcke-Renk, Irmtraud D., and Adele Hercsik. LITERATUR SCHWARZAFRIKAS IN DEUTSCHEN ÜBERSETZUNGEN. Frankfurt am Main: Stadt- und Universitätsbibliothek, 1980.

3363. Working Party on Library Holdings of Commonwealth Literature. COMMONWEALTH WRITERS: SOME OF THE BEST-KNOWN WRITERS AND THEIR WORKS. London: Commonwealth Institute and Commonwealth Secretariat, 1980.

3364. Zell, Hans M., ed. THE AFRICAN BOOK WORLD AND PRESS: A DIRECTORY/RÉPERTOIRE DU LIVRE ET DE LA PRESSE EN AFRIQUE. Munich: Verlag Dokumentation; Oxford: Hans Zell (Publishers) Ltd.; Detroit: Gale Research Co., 1977. 2nd ed., 1980.

See additions, 3365.

3365. ____. "The African Book World and Press: Supplementary and Updating Service." ABPR, 3 (1977), 265-69; 4 (1978), 157-61.

See 3364.

3366. ____. AFRICAN BOOKS IN PRINT: AN INDEX BY AUTHOR, SUBJECT AND TITLE/LIVRES AFRICAINS DISPONIBLES: INDEX PAR AUTEURS, MATIÈRES ET TITRES. 2nd ed. London: Mansell; Westport, CT: Meckler; Paris: Eds. France Expansion; Ile-Ife, Nigeria: University of Ife Bookshop, 1978. 2 vols.

2nd ed. of BALE 48. Includes 4860.

3367. ____. "Bibliography." ABPR, 3 (1977), 26-70, 101-29, 152-249, 270-314; 4 (1978), 24-71, 113-46, 188-217, 258-90; 5 (1979), 33-71, 106-41, 179-228, 255-88; 6 (1980), 33-88, 115-56, 265-91; 7 (1981), 23-97, 124-79, 207-55.

Books published in Africa.

See also 3368, 3386, 3715-18, 3845-51, 4060, 4169-71, 4273-82, 4322, 4469, 4537-44, 4697-98, 4748-51, 4775, 4804, 4812, 4942, 5080-85, 5525, 5776, 5797, 5822, 5858, 5951-53.

B. BIOGRAPHIES

Listed here are biographical resources that deal with more than one author or with non-African authors. Biographical material on individual writers can be found under the writer's name in Part II, "Individual Authors."

BIBLIOGRAPHY

3368. Anon. "Bibliography: Biography, Autobiography." AfrLJ, 8 (1977), 63, 161-62, 259, 353; 9 (1978), 69-70, 165-66, 360; 10 (1979), 65, 156.

See also 3374.

BOOKS AND ESSAYS

3369. Ansprenger, Franz. "Janheinz Jahn: Un Enthousiaste de l'Afrique." LE SOLEIL, 19 May 1976, supp., pp. 6-7.

3370. Klein, Leonard S., ed. ENCYCLOPEDIA OF WORLD LITERATURE IN THE 20th CENTURY. Rev. ed. Vol. 1. New York: Frederick Ungar, 1981.

> Rpt. of BALE 56, 62. Includes 3641, Abrahams, Achebe, Armah, Awoonor, Brutus, Clark.

3371. Manganyi, N.C. "Biography: The Black South African Connection." In NEW DIRECTIONS IN BIOGRAPHY. Ed. Anthony M. Friedson. Honolulu: University Press of Hawaii, 1981. Pp. 52-61.

3372. Nordmann-Seiler, Almut. "Janheinz Jahn: Eine Stimme für Afrika." AFRIKA HEUTE, 10-11 (Oct.-Nov. 1973), 47-48.

3373. Orimoloye, S.A. BIOGRAPHIA NIGERIANA: A BIOGRAPHICAL DICTIONARY OF EMINENT NIGERIANS. Boston: G.K. Hall, 1977.

> Achebe, Agunwa, Aluko, Clark, Echeruo, Ekwensi, Henshaw, Ike, Mezu, Munonye, Nwankwo, Nwapa, Okara, Okigbo, Okpaku, Onyeama, Rotimi, Soyinka, Tutuola, Uka, et al.

3374. Philombe, René. LE LIVRE CAMEROUNAIS ET SES AUTEURS; UNE CONTRIBUTION À L'HISTOIRE LITTÉRAIRE DU CAMEROUN AVEC NOTICE BIO-BIBLIOGRAPHIQUE. Yaoundé: Eds. Semences Africaines de Yaoundé, 1977.

> Includes brief bio-bibliographies of Fonlon, Kor, Maimo, et al.

3375. Sadji, Booker W. "Hommage á . . . ou plutôt amitié pour Janheinz Jahn." LE SOLEIL, 19 May 1976, supp., pp. 6-7.

3376.   Senghor, Léopold Sédar.   "Janheinz Jahn: Successeur de Léo
        Frobenius." LE SOLEIL, 19 May 1976, supp., p. 6.

3377.   Vinson, James, and D.L. Kirkpatrick, eds. COMMONWEALTH
        LITERATURE. Introd. William Walsh. Great Writers Student
        Library, 14. London and Basingstoke: Macmillan, 1979.

        Abrahams, Achebe, Clark, Ekwensi, Okara, Okigbo,
        p'Bitek, Soyinka, Tutuola.

See also 3315, 3509, 3514, 3935, 4281, 4368, 4441, 4471, 4535, 5059,
        5082, 5086-94, 5271, 5296, 5323-26, 5350-51, 5367-70,
        5392-96, 5401-02, 5407-08, 5416-20, 5422-28, 5445-55,
        5462-65, 5469-70, 5478, 5480-81, 5483-87, 5501-02, 5511,
        5514-15, 5517, 5522, 5537, 5539-40, 5552, 5566, 5568-73,
        5576-77, 5586-90, 5593-5603, 5621-23, 5631-32, 5637, 5641-89,
        5736-37, 5790, 5804, 5823-24, 5830, 5840, 5844-46, 5850,
        5879, 5886-89, 5903-04, 5915, 5919, 5925, 5927-29, 5933,
        5936, 5940, 5953-64, 6101-06, 6135.

C. INTERVIEWS

Listed here are interviews with more than one African author and interviews with commentators on African literature. Interviews with individual writers can be found under the writer's name in Part II, "Individual Authors."

BIBLIOGRAPHY

See 3386.

BOOKS AND ESSAYS

3378. Agetua, John, ed. INTERVIEWS WITH SIX NIGERIAN WRITERS. Benin City: Bendel Newspapers Corp., 1976.

> Ike, Nwapa, Ojaide, Rotimi, Uka, Wonodi.

3379. Alot, Magaga. "Cultural Conflict is a Fact." SUNDAY NATION, 7 May 1972, p. 31.

> Interview with Andrew Gurr, Head of Literature Department at the University of Nairobi.

3380. Celeste, Marie-Claude. "Léopold Sédar Senghor zum Tod Janheinz Jahn." AFRIKA HEUTE, 10-11 (1973), 46.

3381. Colligan, Paddy. SOWETO REMEMBERED: CONVERSATIONS WITH FREEDOM FIGHTERS. Introd. Larry Holmes. New York, Chicago, Atlanta: World View Publishers, 1981.

> Maredi, Zulu, et al.

3382. Eames, John. "What's Wrong with Our Writers?" SUNDAY NATION, 5 September 1965, pp. 29-30.

> Interview with Kariuki and Mphahlele. See responses by Kariara, 3527, and Indignant East African, 3515, and rejoinder by Mphahlele, 3587.

3383. Egejuru, Phanuel Akubueze. TOWARDS AFRICAN LITERARY INDEPENDENCE: A DIALOGUE WITH CONTEMPORARY AFRICAN WRITERS. Contributions in Afro-American and African Studies, 53. Westport, CT: Greenwood Press, 1980.

> Includes interviews with Achebe, Mphahlele, Ngugi, et al.

3384. Herber, Avril, ed. CONVERSATIONS; SOME PEOPLE, SOME PLACE, SOME TIME, SOUTH AFRICA. Introd. Patrick Cullinan. Johannesburg: Bateleur, 1979.

> Dike, Govender, Kani, Sepamla, Small, et al.

3385. Kovalenko, Yuri. "Mikhail Kurgantsev: Translator of African
       Poems." NEW DAWN, 5 (1978), 17-18.

       Russian translator interviewed.

3386. Lindfors, Bernth. "'On the Carpet': Literary Interviews in
       Nairobi's SUNDAY NATION." WLWE, 17 (1978), 422-26.

3387. ___, ed. MAZUNGUMZO: INTERVIEWS WITH EAST AFRICAN WRITERS,
       PUBLISHERS, EDITORS AND SCHOLARS. Papers in International
       Studies, Africa Series, 41. Athens, OH: University Center
       for International Studies, Africa Program, 1980.

       Chakava, de Graft, Hirst, Kamenju, Liyong, Maillu,
       Mwangi, Nazareth, Ng'weno, Nottingham, Ogot, p'Bitek,
       Wanjala. Rpt. from 4637-38, 5397, 5509, 5542, 5554,
       5625, 5771, 5807, 5864, 6133.

3388. Nichols, Lee. "The Voice of America Series, 'Conversations
       with African Writers': an Adventure in International
       Communication." RAL, 8 (1977), 293-303.

3389. ___, ed. CONVERSATIONS WITH AFRICAN WRITERS: INTERVIEWS
       WITH TWENTY-SIX AFRICAN AUTHORS. Pref. Es'kia (Ezekiel)
       Mphahlele. Washington, DC: Voice of America, 1981.

       Charley, Chimombo, Ekwensi, Head, Jow, Kayper-Mensah,
       Khasu, Maddy, Mbise, Moore, Mulaisho, Mwangi, Ogot,
       Omotoso, Oyono-Mbia, p'Bitek, Sithole, Sofola,
       Sutherland, Wanjala, et al.

3390. Seroke, Jaki. "Black Writers in South Africa." STAFFRIDER,
       4, 3 (1981), 41-42.

       Discussion with Mutloatse, Sepamla, Tlali.

See also 3327, 3868, 3878-79, 3889-90, 3895, 3902, 3932, 3955, 3966,
    3976, 3978, 4019, 4065, 4068, 4417, 4509, 4547, 4572, 4593,
    4608, 4635, 4637-38, 4642, 4655, 4675, 4684, 4689, 4691,
    4712, 4736, 4743, 4798, 4868, 5007, 5058, 5060, 5095-5109,
    5117, 5251, 5327-30, 5347, 5352-55, 5373, 5397, 5403, 5413,
    5421, 5456, 5471-73, 5477, 5479, 5488-89, 5503, 5509, 5512,
    5516, 5518-20, 5523, 5538, 5541-43, 5551, 5553-54, 5559,
    5563-64, 5578-79, 5584-85, 5604-07, 5617, 5619, 5624-25,
    5633-34, 5636, 5638-39, 5690-5702, 5770-72, 5774, 5785-87,
    5794-95, 5805-09, 5838, 5841, 5847, 5851, 5853, 5856,
    5860-66, 5905-06, 5908-09, 5916, 5920, 5924, 5934-35, 5937,
    5945-46, 5948, 5955, 5964-72, 6106, 6132.

D. GENERAL

This section lists sources surveying geographical areas, treating several authors, or viewing the subject of African literature in English from an overall, rather than a particular, perspective. A number of the individual authors treated in Part II of this guide are cited in this section for their general critical contribution to the subject in hand.

3391.* Abrahams, Cecil A. "The Literature of Victims in South Africa." LITERARY CRITERION, 13, 2 (1978), 59-72.

3392.* ____. "The Literature of Apartheid." In LINGUISTIQUE, CIVILISATION, LITTÉRATURE. Ed. Lucien Leclaire. Paris: Didier-Érudition, 1980. Pp. 166-74.

3393. ____. "The Context of Black South African Literature." WLWE, 19 (1979), 8-19.

La Guma, Langa, Mphahlele, Rive, Serote, et al.

3394. Achebe, Chinua. "Contemporary Literature." In THE LIVING CULTURE OF NIGERIA. Ed. Saburi O. Biobaku. Lagos: Nelson, 1976. Pp. 47-51.

Survey of fiction and poetry.

3395. ____. IMPEDIMENTS TO DIALOGUE BETWEEN NORTH AND SOUTH: OPENING ADDRESS AT HORIZONTE FESTIVAL, WEST BERLIN, 22 JUNE 1979. Amsterdam: Anansi Press, 1979. Rpt. in OKIKE, 16 (1979), 8-12; TLS, 1 February 1980, p. 113; WA, 25 February 1980, pp. 341, 343; AFRICA CURRENTS, 21-22 (1980), 29-32. Rpt. in German in ETHNOLOGISCHE ABSICHTEN, 2, 4 (1979), 3-10. Rpt. in French in PEUPLES NOIRS/PEUPLES AFRICAINS, 11 (1979), 9-15.

3396. ____. "Metaphor of the Rain and the Clock." DAILY TIMES, 10 November 1979, p. 7; BDB, 22 August 1980, pp. 2015-17.

Text of Achebe's speech accepting the Nigerian National Merit Award.

3397. ____. "The Truth of Fiction." LHY, 22, 2 (1981), 2-15.

On beneficent and malignant fictions. Tutuola, et al.

3398. Adam, Ian. "Editorial." ArielE, 12, 3 (1981), 3-4.

On special issue on African literature.

3399. Agbaje, Tunde. "Introducing Nigerian Writers." SCIENTIA, December 1961, p. 29.

3400.   Anand, Mulk Raj. "Variety of Ways: Is There a Shared
        Tradition in Commonwealth Literature?" In Narasimhaiah,
        3593, pp. 441-46.

3401.   Anon. "What is African Literature?" NEWBREED, End-December
        1976, p. 23.

        Rpt. from London SUNDAY TIMES.

3402.   Anon. "SA Writing Heads for New Wave." WITS STUDENT, 7
        August 1979, p. 14.

3403.   Anon. COLLOQUE SUR LITTÉRATURE ET ESTHÉTIQUE
        NÉGRO-AFRICAINES. Introd. Christophe Dailly. Dakar:
        Nouvelles Éditions Africaines, 1979.

        Includes 4221, 5147, 5975.

3404.   Anon. "New Writing from Africa." BANANAS, 22 (1980), 21.

        Introduction to special supplement featuring African
        literature.

3405.   Anon. "A Painful Transition." AIBEPM, 122 (1981), 134-35.

        Ngugi and others address new social problems.

3406.   Anyidoho, Kofi. "(Pan-) Africanism and African (?)
        Literature." LEGACY, 3, 1 (1976), 5-10.

3407.   Armstrong, Robert Plant. "African Literature Today." BOOK
        FORUM, 3, 1 (1977), 6, 8, 10, 12.

3408.   Arnhold, Barbara, and Eva Maria Bruchhaus. "Schreibende
        Frauen in Afrika: noch Immer eine Minderheit." BDB, 22
        August 1980, pp. 2024-27.

        Aidoo, Emecheta, Head, Nwapa, et al.

3409.   Arnold, Rainer. "Probleme der Herausbildung und Entwicklung
        des Realismus in afrikanischen Literaturen: Thesen." WB, 26,
        9 (1980), 44-52.

        See dissertation 3723.

3410.   Asein, Samuel O. "The Impact of the New World on Modern
        African Literature." CLS, 14 (1977), 74-93.

        Abrahams, Achebe, Kgositsile, La Guma, Mphahlele, et al.

3411.   Auerbach, Frank. "Einführung." In MODERNE ERZÄHLER DER
        WELT: OSTAFRIKA. Ed. Frank Auerbach and Lennard Okola.
        Tübingen and Basel: Erdmann, 1976. Pp. 21-30.

        Survey.

3412. Awoonor, Kofi. "Caliban Answers Prospero: The Dialogue between Western and African Literature." OBSIDIAN, 7, 2-3 (1981), 75-98.

Achebe, Ngugi, et al.

3413. Balogun, Françoise. "Entre la tradition et un monde nouveau: aspects de la société nigériane à travers trois auteurs." PEUPLES NOIRS/PEUPLES AFRICAINS, 16 (1980), 68-75.

Achebe, Ekwensi, Soyinka.

3414. Balogun, Odun. "The Contemporary Stage in the Development of African Aesthetic." OKIKE, 19 (1981), 15-24.

3415. Banjo, Ayo, Conrad-Benedict Brann, and Henri Evans, eds. WEST AFRICAN STUDIES IN MODERN LANGUAGE TEACHING AND RESEARCH. Lagos: National Language Centre, Federal Ministry of Education, 1981.

Includes 3627, 3833, 4093, 4154, 4493, 6069, 6086.

3416. Barnett, Ursula A., and Lionel Abrahams. "Does the White Writer Belong? (extracts from a correspondence)." In QUARRY '78-'79: NEW SOUTH AFRICAN WRITING. Ed. Lionel Abrahams. Johannesburg: Donker, 1979. Pp. 167-76.

Mphahlele, Mtshali, Sepamla, et al.

3417. Barrett, Lindsay. "Über Künstler in Afrika." In Eckardt, 4995, pp. 12-15.

3418. BBC. "Asking Too Much of African Writers." RADIO-TV TIMES, 6-12 December 1965, p. 18.

Report on radio talk given by de Graft at BBC.

3419. Becker, Jörg. AFRIKANISCHE LITERATUR IN DER ENTWICKLUNGSPOLITISCHEN BILDUNGSARBEIT. Forschungsberichte des Bundesministeriums für wirtschaftliche Zusammenarbeit, 21. Cologne: Weltforum, 1981.

Emecheta, Katiyo, Ngugi, Ogot, et al.

3420. Beer, David F. "The Sources and Content of Ethiopian Creative Writing in English." RAL, 8 (1977), 99-124.

Deressa, Gabre-Medhin, Gubegna, Kebede, Lemma, Sellassie, Worku, et al.

3421. ____. "Somali Literature in European Languages." HORN OF AFRICA, 2, 4 (1979), 27-35.

Farah, Syad, et al.

3422. Beier, Ulli, ed. INTRODUCTION TO AFRICAN LITERATURE: AN
       ANTHOLOGY OF CRITICAL WRITING. London: Longman, 1979.

       New edition of BALE 1255 with updated bibliography.
       Includes BALE 733, 790, 942, 1184, 1223, 1352, 2334,
       3287, and 4171.

3423. Bhatnagar, O.P. "The Search for Identity in Commonwealth
       Literature." In Srivastava, 3677, pp. 158-66.
       Survey.

3424. Blumer, Arnold. "Zur Lage der Literatur in Südafrika."
       AKZENTE, 27 (1980), 418-24.
       Survey.

3425. Bozzoli, Belinda, ed. LABOUR, TOWNSHIPS AND PROTEST: STUDIES
       IN THE SOCIAL HISTORY OF THE WITWATERSRAND. Johannesburg:
       Ravan Press, 1979.

       Includes 3676, 3899, 5409.

3426. Brambilla, Cristina. "Letteratura negro-africana degli anni
       ´70." NIGRIZIA, 98, 8 (1980), 29-37.
       Survey.

3427. Breitinger, Eckhard. "Einleitung: Zum Rahmen einer
       afrikanischen und afroamerikanischen Literatur." In
       Breitinger, 3428, pp. 12-58.
       Survey.

3428. ____. BLACK LITERATURE: ZUR AFRIKANISCHEN UND
       AFROAMERIKANISCHEN LITERATUR. Kritische Information, 73.
       Munich: Fink, 1979.

       Includes 3427, 3660, 4347, 5130, 6110.

3429. Brettell, N. "Rhodesian Poetry of a Decade or So." ARTS
       RHODESIA, 1 (1978), 29-32.
       Survey.

3430. Brietzke, Susan Adams. "The Black Voice: Traditional and
       Contemporary African Literature." CRESSET, 44, 1 (1980),
       14-19.
       Survey.

3431. Brimer, A., ed. THE AUETSA PAPERS. Durban: University of
       Durban-Westville, 1979.

Photocopied papers from 1979 conference of the
Association of University English Teachers of South
Africa. Includes 3487, 3781, 5610, 6049.

3432. Brown, Lloyd W. WOMEN WRITERS IN BLACK AFRICA. Contributions
in Women's Studies, 21. Westport, CT, and London: Greenwood
Press, 1981.

Aidoo, Emecheta, Head, Nwapa, Sutherland, et al.

3433. Bruner, Charlotte, and David Bruner. "First Person Feminine:
African Literature on Iowa Radio." GAR, 34 (1980), 20-21.

3434. Brutus, Dennis. "English and the Dynamics of South African
Creative Writing." In ENGLISH LITERATURE: OPENING UP THE
CANON. SELECTED PAPERS FROM THE ENGLISH INSTITUTE, 1979.
Ed. Leslie A. Fiedler and Houston A. Baker, Jr. New Series,
4. Baltimore and London: The Johns Hopkins University Press,
1981. Pp. 1-14.

3435. Burgess, Anthony. "In Search of an African Pen." SATURDAY
REVIEW, 10 November 1979, pp. 40-41, 44.

3436. Chapman, Michael. "The Year That Was: South Africa."
KUNAPIPI, 3, 1 (1981), 169-71.

3437. Chugunov, Konstantin. "Notes on Contemporary African
Writing." SOVIET LITERATURE, 11 (1975), 166-70.

Reasons for publishing African writing in Russia.
Abrahams, Achebe, Armah, Awoonor, Ngugi, et al.

3438. Cook, David. AFRICAN LITERATURE: A CRITICAL VIEW. London:
Longman, 1977.

Chapters on poetry, Achebe, Ekwensi, Ngugi, Nkosi,
Oculi, Palangyo.

3439. ____. "Words, Words, Words." DHANA, 7, 1 (1977), 1-7.

On the nature of literary experience.

3440. Cook, William W. "What Rough Beast: Neo-African Literature
and the Force of Social Change." ISSUE, 8, 4 (1978), 53-59.

Achebe, Armah, et al.

3441.* Corcoran, Kathleen G. "A Critical Study of Nigerian
Literature in Relation to its Background." Master's thesis,
Marshall University, 1967.

3442. Couzens, Tim. "The Hidden Literature of Black South Africa."
NEW SOCIETY, 5 February 1976, pp. 272-73.

3443. Cullinan, Patrick. "Comment." BLOODY HORSE, 2 (1980), 5-8.

Racial tensions among writers in South Africa.

3444.   Currey, James. "After Wole Soyinka, What Next?" GUARDIAN,
11 August 1980, p. 22.

Nigerian literary scene.

3445.   da Silva, Paul Gaspar. "African Writers of Today." STAR
(Ibadan), 4 (1964), 19.

Brief survey.

3446.* Dathorne, O.R. "A Survey of West African and West Indian
Literature." Ph.D. dissertation, University of Sheffield,
1966.

3447.* Davis, Gail Marie. "The Effect of Islam and Christianity on
Modern African Literature." Master's thesis, Midwestern
University, 1974.

3448.* Dei-Anang, Michael. "Women Writers of the 20th Century in
Ghana, West Africa." FOLIO: PAPERS ON FOREIGN LANGUAGES AND
LITERATURE, 11 (1978), 21-27.

3449.   Dessau, Adalbert. "Zur weltliterarischen Bedingtheit,
Geltung und Wirkung der Literaturen Asiens, Afrikas und
Lateinamerikas." WB, 26, 9 (1980), 5-32.

3450.   Dilais, Liam. "Zambian Voices." NEW AFRICAN, September
1978, pp. 63-64.

3451.   Dizdar, Srebren. "Putevi i raskršća savremene afričke
književnosti [Paths and Crossroads of Contemporary African
Literature]." MOSTOVI, 11 (1980), 216-21.

Survey.

3452.   Dolfe, Mikael. "Kenyansk litteratur: En översikt [Kenyan
literature: An Overview]." PERMANENT PRESS, 13-14 (1980),
69-73.

Survey.

3453.   Dorsey, David. "Introduction." CALLALOO, 8-10 (1980),
72-73.

Special section of issue of CALLALOO devoted to African
literature.

3454.   Duffield, A.C. "Creative Writing and the Arts in Uganda."
KENYA WEEKLY NEWS, 23 August 1968, p. 16.

3455.   Dumila, Faraj. "Literary Talent in Kenya." MAKTABA, 3
(1976), 91-95.

Ngugi, Swahili writers, et al.

3456.   Edmands, Ursula. "Südafrika." In Schäfer, 3661, pp. 123-46.

Survey.

3457.   Edwards, Paul. "West African Literature and English Studies." In AFRICAN STUDIES SINCE 1945: A TRIBUTE TO BASIL DAVIDSON. Ed. Christopher Fyfe. London: Longman, 1976. Pp. 91-95.

3458.   ____. "Black Personalities in Georgian Britain." HISTORY TODAY, 31 (September 1981), 39-43.

Equiano, Sancho, et al.

3459.   Egbulefu, John O. DIE SCHWARZAFRIKANISCHE LITERATUR: IHRE ORGINALITÄT UND DAS PROBLEM IHRER BEZIEHUNG ZU EUROPA. Vergleichende Literaturwissenschaft, 2. Darmstadt: Thesen Verlag, 1981.

3460.   Egudu, R. N. "Uses of the Humanities: The Example of Literature." NJH, 2 (1978), 102-08.

3461.   Ekwensi, Cyprian, ed. FESTAC ANTHOLOGY OF NIGERIAN NEW WRITING. Lagos: Federal Ministry of Information, 1977.

Includes 3795, 3797, 4049, 4213, 5023.

3462.   Enekwe, Ossie Onuora. "An Impression of Creative Activities in Nigeria." GREENFIELD REV, 8, 1-2 (1980), 71-74.

3463.*   Ezike, Chukwuma. "La Classe dirigeante dans la société africaine decolonisée, vue à travers la littérature africaine d´expression française et anglaise." Ph.D. dissertation. 3rd cycle. University of Paris III, 1979.

3464.   Fabre, Michel. "Mauritian Voices: A Panorama of Contemporary Creative Writing in English." WLWE, 19 (1980), 121-37.

Asgarally, Beeharry, Edoo, Fanchette, Mulloo, et al.

3465.   ____. "Publications en créole et en anglais dans l´Océan Indien." AFRAMN, 11 (1980), 35-37.

3466.   ____. "Littérature africaine d´expression anglaise." RPC, 53-54 (1981), 61-65.

Survey.

3467.   Ferres, John H., and Martin Tucker, eds. MODERN COMMONWEALTH LITERATURE. Pref. R.T. Robertson. New York: Frederick Ungar, 1977.

Extracts from selected criticism on Abrahams, Achebe, Aidoo, Aluko, Armah, Awoonor, Brutus, Clark, Easmon, Ekwensi, La Guma, Mphahlele, Ngugi, Nzekwu, Okara, Okigbo, p'Bitek, Peters, Plaatje, Rive, Soyinka, Tutuola.

3468.   Feuser, Willfried F. "Entre a tradição e a modernidade: Impressões sobre a literatura nigeriana." AFRICA (Lisbon), 1, 2 (1978), 117-24.

Survey.

3469.   ____. "A Literatura nigeriana em inglês." AFRICA (Lisbon), 1, 3 (1979), 245-52.

Survey.

3470.   ____. "A guerra civil nigeriana e suas consequências." AFRICA (Lisbon), 1, 4 (1979), 379-85.

Survey.

3471.   ____. "Tradition and Revolt in West African Writing." NSAL, 2, 1 (1979), 95-105.

Survey.

3472.   ____. "Promenades dans la littérature nigériane." EUROPE 618 (1980) 7-19.

Achebe, Soyinka, Tutuola, Onitsha literature, et al.

3473.   Fiebach, Joachim. KUNSTPROZESSE IN AFRIKA: LITERATUR IM UMBRUCH. Berlin: Akademie, 1979. Rpt. as LITERATUR DER BEFREIEUNG IN AFRIKA. Munich: Damnitz, 1979.

Achebe, Armah, Liyong, Mphahlele, Ngugi, p'Bitek, Soyinka, Onitsha literature, et al.

3474.   Fonlon, Bernard. "Approach to History and Literature." THE GENUINE INTELLECTUAL. Yaoundé: Buma Kor, 1978. Pp. 83-95.

3475.   ____. "Education Through Literature." AFLSHY, 9 (1979), 263-91.

3476.   ____. "Editorial." ABBIA, 34-37 (1979), 5-7.

Cameroon literature.

3477.   Fouda, Basile Juléat. "Pour une littérature créative." In LE CRITIQUE AFRICAIN, 4178, pp. 276-97.

3478.   Fröhlich, Birgit. "Zur Rolle der Literatur bei der Herausbildung eines gesamtnationalen, antiimperialistischen Patriotismus in Tansania, Kenia und Uganda." WB, 26, 9

(1980), 53-61.

Githae-Mugo, Mwangi, Ngugi, p´Bitek, et al.

3479. Gacheche, R. "South African Writing--A Brief Survey." In
Gachukia and Akivaga, 4799, pp. 195-200.

3480. Garrison, Len. "The Emergence of an Afro-Caribbean Literary
Tradition in Britain." ATCALN, 2 (1980), 6.

3481. Gérard, Albert S. FOUR AFRICAN LITERATURES: XHOSA, SOTHO,
ZULU, AMHARIC. Berkeley, Los Angeles, London: University of
California Press, 1971.

Includes remarks on Ethiopian writing in English,
especially the works of Abbie Gubenga, Ashenafi Kebede,
and Tsegaye Gabre-Medhin.

3482. ____. "Contribuição da Serra Leoa na literatura de língua
inglesa da África Ocidental." AFRICA (Lisbon), 1, 1 (1978),
89-95.

Survey.

3483. ____. "1500 Years of Creative Writing in Black Africa."
RAL, 12 (1981), 147-61; PQM, 6, 3-4 (1981), 277-85; in
Portuguese in AFRICA (Lisbon), 2, 8 (1980), 281-90.

3484. ____. AFRICAN LANGUAGE LITERATURES: AN INTRODUCTION TO THE
LITERARY HISTORY OF SUB-SAHARAN AFRICA. Washington, DC:
Three Continents Press; London: Longman: 1981.

Also surveys some writing in English.

3485. Glick, Mark. "A Reply to Mativo." UFAHAMU, 8, 2 (1978),
184-93.

See Mativo, 3573.

3486. Gneba Kokora, Michel. "Ein Beispiel der Beziehungen zwischen
westeuropäischer und schwarzafrikanischer Literatur." In
DIALOG WESTEUROPA-SCHWARZAFRIKA: INVENTAR UND ANALYSE DER
GEGENSEITIGEN BEZIEHUNGEN. Ed. Otto Mulden. Vienna: Fritz
Molden, 1979. Pp. 155-62.

3487. Gordimer, Nadine. "From Apartheid to Afrocentrism." S
AFRICAN OUTLOOK, 107 (1977), 181-83; ENGLISH IN AFRICA, 7, 1
(1980), 45-50; rpt. in Brimer, 3431, pp. 46-50.

3488. ____. "Författere i Sør-Afrika [Writers in South Africa]."
VINDUET, 32, 3 (1978), 56-61.

3489. Gowda, H.H. Anniah, ed. ESSAYS IN AFRICAN LITERATURE. Powre
Above Powres, 3. Foreword Michael Thorpe. Mysore: Centre
for Commonwealth Literature and Research, University of

Mysore, 1978. Rpt. of LHY, 19, 1 (1978).

3490.   Grant, Jane. "The Literature of Exile: A Comparative Study
of Exiled Writers from the West Indies and South Africa."
SARP, 3 (1978), 30-57.

>   Brutus, Head, La Guma, Makaza, Matshikiza, Mphahlele,
>   Nakasa, Nkosi, et al.

3491.* ____. "The Literature of Exile: A Comparative Study of
Writers from the West Indies and South Africa." Master's
thesis, Essex University, 1980.

3492.   Graubin, G. "Kogda dalekoe--vblizi: Zametki o poezdke v
Afriku [When the Remote is Near: Notes on a Trip to Africa]."
LO, 12 (1979), 37-41.

>   Soviet-African literary relations; introd. Kirill
>   Koval'dzi.

3493.* Gray, Stephen. "Critical Co-ordinates of South African
English Literature." Ph.D. dissertation, Rand Afrikaans
University, 1977.

>   Abrahams, Mphahlele, H.I.E. Dhlomo, R.R.R. Dhlomo, Head,
>   Plaatje. Rev. and published as 3494.

3494.   ____. SOUTHERN AFRICAN LITERATURE: AN INTRODUCTION. Cape
Town: David Philip; London; Rex Collings; New York: Barnes
and Noble, 1979.

>   Revised dissertation, 3493.

3495.   ____. "The Year That Was: Southern Africa." KUNAPIPI, 2, 1
(1980), 154-59.

>   Literary developments in 1979.

3496.   ____. "Critical Co-ordinates of South African English
Literature." HUMANITAS, 6 (1980), 153.

>   Summary of doctoral dissertation, 3493.

3497.   Greene, Michael Thomas. "Sons of the Fathers: Four Nigerian
Writers." DAI, 40 (1980), 5048A (New York-Buffalo).

>   Achebe, Clark, Ekwensi, Tutuola.

3498.   Gregory, Robert G. "Literary Development in East Africa: The
Asian Contribution, 1955-1975." RAL, 12 (1981), 440-59.

>   Bagchi, Nazareth, Neogy, Patel, Ribeiro, Sondhi, et al.

3499.   Griffiths, Gareth. A DOUBLE EXILE: AFRICAN AND WEST INDIAN
WRITING BETWEEN TWO CULTURES. London: Marion Boyars, 1978.

Achebe, Amadi, Armah, Awoonor, Ngugi, Okigbo, Soyinka, Tutuola, et al.

3500. Grosse-Oetringhaus, Hans-Martin. "´Schrei deinen Zorn hinaus´: Afrikanische Literatur im Erziehungssystem der Schwarzen Südafrikas." ZEITSCHRIFT FÜR KULTURAUSTAUSCH, 29 (1979), 205-12.

3501. Gruner, Fritz, ed. LITERATUREN ASIENS UND AFRIKAS: THEORETISCHE PROBLEME. Studien über Asien, Afrika und Lateinamerika, 26. Berlin: Akademie, 1981.

Includes 3725, 4114, 4387.

3502. Gwala, Mafika. "STAFFRIDER Workshop." STAFFRIDER, 2, 3 (1979), 55-58.

Black writing in South Africa.

3503. Habib, Mohammad. "The Illusion of Independence." SOUTH DAKOTA REVIEW, 17, 3 (1979), 112-20.

In Third World literature; Achebe, et al.

3504.* Hall, Susan Jane. "The Role of Education in African Literature." Master´s thesis, Columbia University, 1967.

3505. Haller, Albert von. "Einführung: Literatur in Afrika." In MODERNE ERZÄHLER DER WELT: NIGERIA. Ed. Cyprian Ekwensi and Albert von Haller. Tübingen and Basel: Erdmann, 1973. Pp. 9-32.

Survey.

3506. Harris, Wilson. EXPLORATIONS; A SELECTION OF TALKS AND ARTICLES, 1966-1981. Mundelstrup, Denmark: Dangaroo Press, 1981.

Includes 4482, 6021.

3507. Heusler, Dagmar. "Über Afrikanische Literatur." In Eckardt, 4995, pp. 100-03.

Achebe, Armah, Soyinka, Tutuola, et al.

3508. Hofer-Gut, Beatrice. "Englische und Swahili-Literatur in Ostafrika." GAf, 19, 2 (1981), 144-52.

Ngugi, p´Bitek, popular literature, et al.

3509. Hofmeyr, Isabel. "Perspectives on Working-Class Life among Black and Afrikaans Writers, 1890-1930." AFRICA PERSPECTIVE, 16 (1980), 24-41.

R.R.R. Dhlomo, Dikobe, et al.

3510. Iheakaram, P.O. "Need for New Horizons in African
       Literature." AFRISCOPE, 3, 8 (1973), 7.

3511. Ikiddeh, Ime. "Literature and the Nigerian Civil War." In
       Gachukia and Akivaga, 4799, pp. 149-62.

           Rpt. of BALE 296. Covers Achebe, Clark, Okigbo, Soyinka,
           et al.

3512. Ilieva, Emilia. "Africa in the Struggle for Literary
       Autonomy." AFRICAN COMMUNIST, 87 (1981), 93-97.

3513. Imfeld, Al. "Politik durch Bücher: Forum der jungen
       Generation." WENDEKREIS, 84, 11 (1979), 28-29.

           Ngugi, Maillu, Ogot.

3514. ____. VISION UND WAFFE: AFRIKANISCHE AUTOREN, THEMEN,
       TRADITIONEN. Zurich: Unionsverlag, 1981.

           Achebe, Aidoo, Armah, Brutus, Farah, Liyong, Marechera,
           Matthews, Mwangi, Ngugi, p´Bitek, Soyinka, Tutuola, et
           al.

3515. Indignant East African. "Haven´t They Heard of Our
       Heritage." SUNDAY NATION, 12 September 1965, p. 11.

           Response to interview with Mphahlele and Kariuki, 3382.
           See rejoinder by Mphahlele, 3587.

3516. Innes, C.L. "Through the Looking Glass: African and Irish
       Nationalist Writing." ALT, 9 (1978), 10-24.

3517. Irele, Abiola. THE AFRICAN EXPERIENCE IN LITERATURE AND
       IDEOLOGY. London and Exeter, NH: Heinemann, 1981.

           Rpts. BALE 1283, 1586, 3146. Discusses research,
           criticism, language, negritude, Soyinka, Tutuola, et al.
           Includes 4216, 4348.

3518. Jagne, H.I. "The Position of Literature in the Gambia."
       NDAANAN, 3, 1 (1973), 24-27.

           Peters, et al.

3519. Jahn, Janheinz. "Einführung." In SÜSS IST DAS LEBEN IN
       KUMANSENU: WESTAFRIKA IN ERZÄHLUNGEN DER BESTEN
       ZEITGENÖSSISCHEN AUTOREN. Ed. Janheinz Jahn. Tübingen and
       Basel: Erdmann, 1971. Pp. 11-18.

           Survey.

3520. Jestel, Rüdiger. LITERATUR UND GESELLSCHAFT NIGERIAS.
       Frankfurt am Main: n.p., 1979.

Achebe, Amadi, Egbuna, Ekwensi, Ike, Mezu, Munonye, Nwankwo, Nwapa, Nzekwu, Okara, Soyinka, et al. See summary in ACOLIT, 4 (1979), 17-19.

3521. Johnson, Lemuel A. "´His Excellency´ and the ´Owner of Book´: Moral Vision in African Politics and Literature." JAfrS, 7 (1980), 11-21.

Achebe, Armah, Soyinka, et al.

3522. ____. "The Middle Passage in African Literature: Wole Soyinka, Yambo Ouologuem, Ayi Kwei Armah." ALT, 11 (1980), 62-84.

3523. ____. "´When the Lizard Eats Pepper´: The World Wars and African literature." CALLALOO, 8-10 (1980), 177-202.

Achebe, Armah, Bediako, Emecheta, Gubegna, Mukasa, Soyinka, et al.

3524. Kalu, Ogbu U., ed. AFRICAN CULTURAL DEVELOPMENT. Foreword J.C. Ezeilo. Enugu: Fourth Dimension, 1978.

Includes 4052, 4378.

3525. Kane, Mohamadou. "Az afrikai irodalom jelenkori problémái [Actual Problems of African Literature]." HELIKON, 23 (1977), 255-62; rpt. in French in Köpeczi et al., 3540, pp. 47-55.

3526. Kapelinski, F. J. "Coming of Age of African Literatures." CALABAR STUDIES IN MODERN LANGUAGES, 1, 1 (1977), 11-15; rpt. in Köpeczi et al., 3540, pp. 253-55.

3527. Kariara, J. "This Debate on Our Writers is Misleading." SUNDAY NATION, 12 September 1965, p. 30.

Letter in response to interview with Mphahlele and Kariuki, 3382. See rejoinder by Mphahlele, 3587.

3528. ____. "Personal Views." SUNDAY NATION, 26 September 1965, p. 11.

Letter clarifying nature of opinions offered earlier, 3527.

3529. ____. "Sincere and Painstaking? No--It Was a Cold and Impersonal View." SUNDAY NATION, 3 October 1965, p. 19.

Response to Mphahlele´s rejoinder, 3587.

3530. Kemoli, Arthur. "Africa and the Caribbean." In Gachukia and Akivaga, 4799, pp. 216-223.

Cultural and literary connections.

3531. Keszthelyi, Tibor. AFRIKANISCHE LITERATUR: VERSUCH EINES
ÜBERBLICKS. Budapest: Akademiai Kiado, 1981.

Survey.

3532. Kgositsile, Keorapetse. "Culture and Liberation in Southern
Africa." UMMA, 6, 2 (1976), 140-46; rpt. in Society of
African Culture, 3675, pp. 138-45.

3533. Kimoni, Iyay. DESTIN DE LA LITTÉRATURE NÉGRO-AFRICAINE OU
PROBLÉMATIQUE D'UNE CULTURE. Kinshasa, Zaire: Presses
Universitaires du Zaire; Ottawa: Naaman, 1975.

Deals mainly with French African writings.

3534. ____. "Littérature et culture africaine." JeuneA, 4 March
1977, pp. 80-82.

3535. King, Bruce. "Varieties of African Literature." LHY, 19, 1
(1978), 1-17; rpt. in Köpeczi et al., 3540, pp. 273-77.

Survey.

3536. ____. THE NEW ENGLISH LITERATURES: CULTURAL NATIONALISM IN A
CHANGING WORLD. London and Basingstoke: Macmillan, 1980.

Achebe, Soyinka, et al.

3537. ____. "African Literature and Aesthetics." PQM, 6, 3-4
(1981), 263-66.

3538. Klíma, Vladimír. "Príběhy z Ugandského Venkova [Stories from
the Ugandan Countryside]." SVĚTOVÁ LITERATURA, 24, 2 (1979),
172-87.

Eyakuze, Oculi, p'Bitek, Sebukima, Waiguru, Zirimu, et
al.

3539. Knipp, Thomas R. "Studies in Black and White: The New
Literature of Africa." EAST-WEST REVIEW, 3, 3 (1967-68),
284-98.

Survey.

3540. Köpeczi, Béla, György M. Vajda, and József Kovács, eds.
ACTES DU VIII^C CONGRÉS DE L'ASSOCIATION INTERNATIONALE DE
LITTÉRATURE COMPARÉE/PROCEEDINGS OF THE 8TH CONGRESS OF THE
INTERNATIONAL COMPARATIVE LITERATURE ASSOCIATION. Vol. 2.
Stuttgart: Kunst und Wissen, Erich Bieber, 1980.

Includes 3525-26, 3535, 3612, 4233, 4353, 4455, 4768,
4898, 5075, 6003.

3541. Kosok, Heinz, and Horst Priessnitz, eds. LITERATUREN IN

ENGLISCHER SPRACHE: EIN ÜBERBLICK ÜBER ENGLISCHSPRACHIGE
NATIONALLITERATUREN AUSSERHALB ENGLANDS. Schriftenreihe
Literaturwissenschaft, 5. Bonn: Bouvier, 1977.

Includes 3660, 4800.

3542. La Guma, Alex. "Was liest man im Lande der Apartheid?" NDL,
26, 7 (1978), 163-68.

3543. Landy, Joseph V. "What is a National Literature?" NSAL, 1, 1
(1978), 108-18.

3544. Larson, Charles R. "Anglophone Writing from Africa and Asia."
WLT, 51 (1977), 235-36, 563-65; 52 (1978), 245-47.

Aidoo, Boateng, Ekwensi, Emecheta, Echewa, Farah, Ike,
Katiyo, Liyong, Mwangi, Ngugi, Ng'weno, Peteni, et al.

3545. ____. "Books in English from the Third World." WLT, 53
(1979), 245-47, 625-26; 54 (1980), 246-48, 395-96.

Amadi, Armah, Brutus, Farah, Marechera, Mutswairo,
Okara, p'Bitek, Samkange, Sankawulo, et al.

3546. ____. "New Writers, New Readers." WILSON QUARTERLY, 4, 1
(1980), 81-85.

Survey of Nigerian literature followed by excerpts, pp.
85-92.

3547. ____. "Writing from the Third World." WLT, 55 (1981),
57-58, 422-23.

M. Kunene, Sallah, et al.

3548. Laubscher, Pete. "Social History and Literature: The
Background to the Role of Liquor in Urban Black Writing."
INSPAN, 1, 2 (1978), 131-36.

3549. Leshoai, B.L. "Current Trends in African Culture." MARANG,
(1978), 64-68.

Comments briefly on literature.

3550. ____. "The Impact of Christianity on 20th Century Black
South African Writing." PULA, 1 (1978), 113-44.

H.I.E. Dhlomo, R.R.R. Dhlomo, et al.

3551. Leveson, Marcia, ed. PHILIP SEGAL: ESSAYS AND LECTURES;
SELECTED LITERARY CRITICISM. Cape Town: David Philip, 1973.

Rpts. BALE 1695 and 2105 and includes "The Place of
South African Writing in the University," pp. 216-21.

3552. Lilburn, Tim. "The Spirit in Ascent: A Look at an Emergent
       African Literature." SPHINX, 6 (1976), 28-37.

3553. Lindfors, Bernth. "Ladies and Gentlemen at Ibadan." BA
       SHIRU, 8, 2 (1977). 33-36.

            Letters by Achebe and Soyinka to the editors of Ibadan
            University student publications.

3554. ____. "´East is East and West is West´: Points of Divergence
       in African Literary History." In Narasimhaiah, 3593, pp.
       42-49.

            Survey of West and East African literatures.

3555. ____. "Politics, Culture and Literary Form in Black Africa."
       CLQ, 15 (1979), 240-51.

            Achebe, Ngugi, p´Bitek, et al.

3556. ____. "Negritude and After: Responses to Colonialism and
       Independence in African Literatures." In PROBLEMS IN
       NATIONAL LITERARY IDENTITY AND THE WRITER AS A SOCIAL CRITIC.
       Ed. Anne Paolucci. Whitestone, NY: Griffon House for the
       Council on National Literatures, 1980. Pp. 29-37.

3557. ____. "A Basic Anatomy of East African Literature in
       English." NLRev, 8 (1980), 8-14; PQM, 6, 3-4 (1981), 45-50.

            Liyong, Maillu, Mangua, Ngugi, p´Bitek, et al.

3558. ____. "African Literature." ACADEMIC AMERICAN ENCYCLOPEDIA.
       Princeton: Arete Publishing Co., 1981. Vol. 1, pp. 167-68.

3559. ____, ed. CRITICAL PERSPECTIVES ON NIGERIAN LITERATURES.
       London: Heinemann, 1979.

            English ed. of BALE 372.

3560. Liyong, Taban lo. "How Long Must We Be Children?" SUNDAY
       NATION, 14 May 1972, p. 7.

            Response to p´Bitek, 3632: see rejoinders by p´Bitek,
            3633, and others, 5546-47.

3561. ____. "How East African literature was Born or, Can We Make
       it in the Sudan Also?" SOUTHERN SUDAN MAGAZINE, 4, 4 (1980),
       35-38.

3562. Lodge, Tom. "Biafran Literature." INSPAN, 1, 1 (1978),
       23-32.

            Achebe, Mezu, Munonye, Okigbo.

3563. ____. "Nigerian Literature and the Civil War." WIP, 5

(1978), 21-58.

Achebe, Clark, Mezu, Munonye, Okigbo, Soyinka.

3564. Macauley, Robie. "African Literature, First Generation."
NEW REPUBLIC, 23 April 1962, pp. 32-35.

Survey.

3565. McLeod, A.L. AFRICAN LITERATURE IN ENGLISH: DEVELOPMENT AND
IDENTITY. [Lawrenceville, NJ]: A.L. McLeod, 1981.

Includes 4159, 4172, 4365.

3566. Maduka, C.T. "Intellectuals and the Drama of Social Change."
KIABÀRÀ, 1, 1 (1978), 40-58.

Intellectual as hero in works by Armah, Ngugi, Okara,
Soyinka, et al.

3567. Máille, Pádraig O. DÚDHÚCHAS [Black Heritage]. Dublin:
Sáirséal Agus Dill, 1972.

Achebe, Clark, Ekwere, Nzekwu, Okara, Okigbo, Soyinka,
Tutuola, et al.

3568. Majid, Husain. "Revivalism in Afro-Asian Literature." REVUE
DES LANGUES, 3 (1980), 41-54.

Achebe, Soyinka, et al.

3569. Manganyi, N. Chabani. "The Violent Reverie: The Unconscious
in Literature and Society." MASHANGU'S REVERIE AND OTHER
ESSAYS. Johannesburg: Ravan Press, 1977. Pp. 53-71.

3570. ____. LOOKING THROUGH THE KEYHOLE: DISSENTING ESSAYS ON THE
BLACK EXPERIENCE. Johannesburg: Ravan, 1981.

Interview with Mphahlele, 5606; essays on censorship,
4728, and South African culture.

3571. Massa, Daniel, ed. INDIVIDUAL AND COMMUNITY IN COMMONWEALTH
LITERATURE. Msida: University of Malta Press, 1979.

Includes 3967, 4222, 4375, 5259, 5293, 5496, 5533, 5739,
6020.

3572. ____. "The Postcolonial Dream." WLWE, 20 (1981), 135-49.

Armah, Ngugi, p'Bitek, et al.

3573. Mativo, Kyalo. "Ideology in African Philosophy and
Literature." UFAHAMU, 8, 1 (1977), 67-94; 8, 2 (1978),
132-81.

M. Kunene, Mbiti, Soyinka, et al. See response by

Glick, 3485.

3574.   Maughan-Brown, David. "The Form of Protest in Kenya: Drama
or the Novel." CRITICAL ARTS, 1, 3 (1980), 47-58.

Kibera, Ngugi.

3575.   Mazrui, Ali. "Aesthetic Dualism and Creative Literature in
East Africa." CAMBRIDGE REVIEW, 23 October 1970, pp. 11-20.

Same as BALE 401. Rpt. in BALE 1500.

3576.   ____. "African Literature and the Imperial Legacy." SUNDAY
NATION, 6 February 1977, pp. 8, 10.

See response by p'Bitek, 4241.

3577.   ____. "The International Context of African Literature:
Liberation and Limitation." PanA, 7 (1977), 23-34.

3578.   ____. "Educated Africans in Politics and Society." In THE
POLITICS OF CHANGE AND LEADERSHIP DEVELOPMENT: THE NEW
LEADERS IN INDIA AND AFRICA. Ed. Alfred de Souza. New Delhi:
Manohar, 1978. Pp. 65-91.

Political themes in African literature.

3579.   Mbele, Majola, ed. VIEWPOINTS: ESSAYS ON LITERATURE AND
DRAMA. Nairobi: Kenya Literature Bureau, 1980.

Includes 3892, 3924, 4025, 4433.

3580.   Mbise, Ismael R. "The Struggle for Identity in Selected East
African Literature and Art." DAI, 40 (1979), 2646A (York,
Canada).

Buruga, Kibera, Mphahlele, Ngugi, Oculi, Okola, p'Bitek.

3581.   Meuer, Gerd. "Wole Soyinka und Ngugi wa Thiong'o: Früher
oder später schreiben wir für jeden etwas..." BDB, 22 August
1980, pp. 2021-22.

3582.   Mnthali, Felix. "Nostalgia, Identity and Culture in Africa."
LOOKOUT, 2 (1975), 27-37.

Liyong, Okara, p'Bitek, et al.

3583.   Momodu, A.G.S., and Ulla Schild, eds. NIGERIAN WRITING:
NIGERIA AS SEEN BY HER OWN WRITERS AS WELL AS BY GERMAN
AUTHORS. Tübingen: Erdmann, 1976.

Includes 4050, 4156, 4325, 6085.

3584.   Moore, Gerald. "Against the Titans in Nigerian Literature."
AFRISCOPE, 7, 7 (1977), 19, 21-22, 25.

Jeyifo, Ofeimun, Omotoso, Osofisan.

3585. ____. TWELVE AFRICAN WRITERS. London: Hutchinson; Bloomington: Indiana University Press, 1980.

Achebe, Awoonor, La Guma, Mphahlele, Ngugi, p´Bitek, Soyinka, et al.

3586. ____. "Dirges of the Delta." AFRISCOPE, 10, 11 (1980), 23-25.

Amadi, Clark, Okara.

3587. Mphahlele, Ezekiel. "On...Kenya Literature--or the Lack of it." SUNDAY NATION, 19 September 1965, p. 19.

Reply to Kariara, 3527, and "Indignant East African," 3515. See responses by Kariara, 3529, and Ng´weno, 5602.

3588. ____. "South Africa: Two Communities and the Struggle for a Birthright." JAfrS, 4 (1977), 21-50.

3589. Mudimbe, V.Y. "Sur la littérature africaine." RPC, 33 (1978), 3-4.

3590. Mulloo, Anand Sawant. FOOTPRINTS: CONTAINING ESSAYS ON MAURITIAN LIFE, LITERATURE, LANGUAGES, CULTURE, SOCIETY, HISTORY AND RANDOM THOUGHTS. Port Louis: Standard Printing Establishment, 1968.

Includes brief survey of writing in English, pp. 48-52.

3591. Mzamane, Mbulelo Vizikhungo. "The 50´s and Beyond: An Evaluation." CLASSIC, 4 (1977), 23-32.

Surveys black prose and poetry in South Africa.

3592. ____. "Review of Black Writing in English in the Last Twenty-five Years." MARANG, 3 (1980-81), 86-101.

3593. Narasimhaiah, C.D., ed. AWAKENED CONSCIENCE: STUDIES IN COMMONWEALTH LITERATURE. New Delhi: Sterling Publishers, 1978.

Proceedings of Fourth Triennial Conference of the Association for Commonwealth Literature and Language Studies, New Delhi, January 1977. Includes 3400, 3554, 3595, 4064, 4356, 4813, 5111, 5257, 5265, 5635, 5901, 6017.

3594. ____. "Why Commonwealth Literature?" In Srivastava, 3677, pp. 1-8.

3595. Nazareth, Peter. "Time in the Third World." MANA, 1, 2
       (1976), 1-14; rpt. in Narasimhaiah, 3593, pp. 195-205.

       Armah, Nazareth, Omotoso, et al.

3596. ____, ed. "African Writing Today." PQM, 6, 3-4 (1981).

       Special issue. "Introduction," pp. 7-8.

3597. Ngugi, [wa Thiong'o], J.T. "The New Voices: Some Emerging
       African Writers." SUNDAY POST, 4 June 1961, p. 11.

       Abrahams, Achebe, Conton, Ekwensi, Jabavu, Tutuola.

3598. ____. "African Writers Need a New Outlook." SUNDAY NATION,
       2 December 1962, p. 29.

       On problems of South African Writers.

3599. ____. "A New Mood Prevails." SUNDAY NATION, 24 November
       1963, p. 14.

       On incipient literary activities in East Africa,
       including a production of Soyinka's THE LION AND THE
       JEWEL.

3600. Nikiforova, Irina D. "Die Herausbildung der realistischen
       Methode in den Literaturen des tropischen Afrika." WB, 26, 9
       (1980), 149-53.

       Survey.

3601. ____. RAZVITIE LITERATURY V NEZAVISIMYKH STRANAKH AFRIKI:
       60-70-E GODY XX VEKA [The Development of Literature in
       Independent African Countries: 1960-70 of the 20th Century].
       Moscow: Nauka, 1980.

       Includes 3691, 3693, 3696.

3602. Niven, Alastair. "Exile and Expatriation in African
       Literature." LHY, 21, 1 (1980), 167-80.

       Brutus, Dipoko, Nkosi, Nortje, Okara, et al.

3603.* ____. "From Empire to Commonwealth: The Birth of
       Literature." In LITTÉRATURE ET SES LIEUX DE PRODUCTION.
       Pref. A. Vermeylen. Publications de l'Institut de Formation
       et de Recherches en Littérature, 5. Louvain-la-Neuve:
       Faculté de Philosophie et Lettres, Université Catholique de
       Louvain, 1980; Paris: Belles lettres, 1980. Pp. 27-40.

       Survey.

3604. Njoroge, Paul Ngige. "The Tradition of Search in West
       African Literature." Master's thesis, University of Nairobi,

1976.

Achebe, Armah, Mezu, Okara, Soyinka, Tutuola, et al.

3605.* Njoroge, S. N. "The Influence of Traditional and Western
Religions on the Cultural and Political Thinking of Ngugi wa
Thiong'o and Okot p'Bitek." Master's thesis, Leeds
University, 1978.

3606. Nkosi, Lewis. "African Literature." In FESTAC, 5018, pp.
88-89, 93.

Survey.

3607. ____. "Art contra Apartheid: South African Writers in Exile."
GAf, 18, 2 (1980), 67-72.

3608. ____. TASKS AND MASKS: THEMES AND STYLES OF AFRICAN
LITERATURE. Harlow, Essex: Longman, 1981.

Abrahams, Achebe, Aidoo, Armah, Armattoe, Brutus, Carim,
Clark, de Graft, Dei-Anang, H.I.E. Dhlomo, Dikobe,
Easmon, Gabre-Medhin, Head, Jolobe, M. Kunene, La Guma,
Mphahlele, Ngugi, Okara, p'Bitek, Serote, Serumaga,
Soyinka, Tutuola, et al.

3609. Ntiru, Richard C. "The Creative Artist in African
Literature." In LE CRITIQUE AFRICAIN, 4178, pp. 298-313.

Mazrui, Ngugi, Okigbo, p'Bitek, Soyinka, et al.

3610.* Nwoga, Donatus I. "Herre, tilgiv det hvide Europe [Lord,
Forgive White Europe]." KRITERIUM, 2, 2 (1967), 26-39.

On disillusionment in modern African literature.

3611. ____, ed. LITERATURE AND MODERN WEST AFRICAN CULTURE. Benin
City: Ethiope Publishing Corp., 1978.

Includes 4135, 4239, 4380, 4404, 4410, 4418, 5438.

3612. ____. "The Conceptual Background to Modern West-African
Literature." In Köpeczi et al., 3540, pp. 279-84.

3613. Nyang, Sulayman S. "Literature and the Cosmic Schizophrenic
Tendencies of Man." BO, 3, 4 (1976), 38-43.

3614. Nys, Mon. "Kultuur onder apartheid [Culture under
apartheid]." KREATIEF, 11, 4-5 (1977), 28-49.

3615. Obuke, Okpure O. "South African History, Politics and
Literature: Mphahlele's DOWN SECOND AVENUE and Rive's
EMERGENCY." ALT, 10 (1979), 191-201.

3616.* Oganessova, Michelle. "Problèmes sud-africains à travers les oeuvres littéraires." Ph.D. dissertation. 3rd cycle. University of Caen, 1979.

3617. Ogungbesan, Kolawole, ed. NEW WEST AFRICAN LITERATURE. London: Heinemann, 1979.

Includes 3809, 4070, 5814, 5880, 5911, 6065.

3618. Ohaegbu, A.U. "Autour de l'évocation du passé dans la littérature africaine." PFr, 23 (1981), 107-17.

3619. Okafor, Clement Abiaziem. "The Historical Background to Modern Literature in Tropical Africa." ZAMBIA MUSEUMS JOURNAL, 3 (1972), 49-67.

Achebe, Ngugi, Samkange, et al.

3620. Okafor, Raymond Nnadozié. "L'Écrivain africain devant l'angoisse d'être nègre." AdUA, 9D (1976), 331-53.

Abrahams, Achebe, et al.

3621. Okai, Atukwei. "Vision, Image, and Symbol in Ghanaian Literature." PQM, 6, 3-4 (1981), 51-61.

Aidoo, Armah, Awoonor, Yeboa-Afari, et al.

3622. Okam, Hilary H. "Oral Art Forms and Literature in Africa." AFRICAN SOCIETY, CULTURE AND POLITICS: AN INTRODUCTION TO AFRICAN STUDIES. Ed. Christopher Chukwuemeka Mojekwu, Victor Chikezie Uchendu and Leo F. Van Hoey. Washington, DC: University Presses of America, 1977. Pp. 242-59.

Survey.

3623. Okola, Lennard. "Moderne Literatur in Ostafrika." In MODERNE ERZÄHLER DER WELT: OSTAFRIKA. Ed. Frank Auerbach and Lennard Okola. Tübingen and Basel: Erdmann, 1976. Pp. 11-20.

Survey.

3624. Okpaku, Joseph. "Zeit, das Lendentuch zu schürzen." BDB, 22 August 1980, pp. 2011-13.

3625. Omotoso, Kole. "African Writers of the Sixties: Where Are They Now?" AFRISCOPE, 11, 4 (1981), 22-24, 37.

Survey of Nigerian writers.

3626. ____. "Civil War: the Most Important Theme." GUARDIAN, 6 October 1981, p. 18.

Survey of recent Nigerian literature.

3627. Osofisan, Femi. "Anubis Resurgent: Chaos and Political

Vision in Recent Literature." In Banjo, 3415, pp. 185-98; rpt. in French in PEUPLES NOIRS/PEUPLES AFRICAINS, 14 (1980), 72-94.

Rpt. of BALE 1518. Considers Clark, Soyinka, et al.

3628. Owomoyela, Oyekan. AFRICAN LITERATURES: AN INTRODUCTION. Waltham, MA: Crossroads Press, 1979.

Chapters surveying poetry, fiction, drama. Includes Achebe, Armah, Clark, Ngugi, Soyinka, et al.

3629. Paoli, Pia. "Introduction." In L´AFRIQUE DES GRANDS LACS: L´AMOUR ET LA GUERRE. Ed. Pia Paoli. Paris: Seghers, 1978. Pp. 9-36.

Survey.

3630. Parker, Carolyn A., Stephen H. Arnold. A. M. Porter, and H. Wylie, eds. WHEN THE DRUMBEAT CHANGES. Washington, DC: Three Continents Press, 1981.

Selected proceedings of the 4th annual meeting of the African Literature Association, Boone, NC, April 1978. Includes 4255, 4324, 5263, 5286, 5365, 5494, 5830.

3631. Parrot, Matthew. "From MHUDI to MINE BOY: The Development of Black South African Writing." AFRICA PERSPECTIVE, 3 (1976), 34-47.

Abrahams, H.I.E. Dhlomo, Plaatje, et al.

3632. p´Bitek, Okot. "What is Culture?" SUNDAY NATION, 30 April 1972, p. 7.

See responses by Liyong, 3560, and others, 5546-47.

3633. ____. "Which Way Are We Headed?" SUNDAY NATION, 28 May 1972, p. 7.

Rejoinder to Liyong, 3560.

3634. Peters, Jonathan A. A DANCE OF MASKS: SENGHOR, ACHEBE, SOYINKA. Washington, DC: Three Continents Press, 1978.

3635. ____. "Senghor, Achebe, Soyinka: Conflicting Perceptions of African Priorities." In FIGURES IN A GROUND: CANADIAN ESSAYS ON MODERN LITERATURE COLLECTED IN HONOR OF SHEILA WATSON. Ed. Diane Bessai and David Jackel. Saskatoon: Western Producer Prairie Books, 1978. Pp. 247-63.

Rpt. of concluding chapter of 3634, pp. 225-37.

3636. Phiri, Masautso. "A General Survey of Creative Writing in Zambia." ZANGO, 6 (1979), 34-42.

3637. Pomonti, Jean-Claude. "L´envers des choses." ALA, 51
       (1979), 2-8.

       Liyong, Ngugi, Oculi, p´Bitek, et al.

3638. Popkin, Michael, ed. MODERN BLACK WRITERS. New York:
       Frederick Ungar, 1978.

       Extracts from selected criticism on Abrahams, Achebe,
       Aidoo, Aluko, Amadi, Armah, Awoonor, Brutus, Clark,
       Ekwensi, M. Kunene, La Guma, Mphahlele, Ngugi, Nzekwu,
       Okara, Okigbo, p´Bitek, Peters, Plaatje, Soyinka,
       Tutuola.

3639. Potekhina, G.I. "Colonial Regimes and Culture (Literatures
       of West Africa)." In AFRICA IN SOVIET STUDIES 1973. Moscow:
       Nauka, 1976. Pp. 150-59.

       Rpt. of BALE 535.

3640. Povey, John. "Education Through the Eyes of African
       Writers." EDUCATIONAL FORUM, 31 (1966), 95-102.

       Survey.

3641. ____. "Botswana Literature." In Klein, 3370, pp. 307-08.

       Survey.

3642. Raghavacharyulu, D.V.K. "Beyond Exile and Homecoming: A
       Preliminary Note." In Srivastava, 3677, pp. 31-39.

       Achebe, Ngugi, et al.

3643. ____. "Metaphors of Identity in Commonwealth Literature."
       THE CRITICAL RESPONSE: SELECTED ESSAYS ON THE AMERICAN,
       COMMONWEALTH, INDIAN AND BRITISH TRADITIONS IN LITERATURE.
       Madras: Macmillan, 1980. Pp. 78-90.

       Survey.

3644. Ramamoorthy, Yashoda. "East African Literature in English."
       AfrQ, 21 (1981), 61-66.

       Ngugi, p´Bitek, et al.

3645. Rensburg, A.P.J. van. "Afrika--die voedingsbron [Africa--the
       Source that Feeds]." DONGA, 3 (1976), 1, 4.

3646. Ricard, Alain. "Sur la périodisation des littératures de
       l´Afrique Noire." In PRODUCTION LITTÉRAIRE ET SITUATIONS DE
       CONTACTS INTERETHNIQUES. Ed. H. Giordan and A. Labarrère.
       Études Preliminaires, 7. Nice: Institut d´Études et de
       Recherches Interethniques et Interculturelles, Université de
       Nice, 1974. Pp. 149-57.

3647. Riemenschneider, Dieter. "Die anglophone Literatur der siebziger Jahre." ZEITSCHRIFT FÜR KULTURAUSTAUSCH, 29 (1979), 167-82.

Survey.

3648. ____. "West- und Ostafrika." In Schäfer, 3661, pp. 147-73.

Survey.

3649. Ripken, Peter. "Literatur in Südafrika: Letzte Bastion der Freiheit." BDB, 22 August 1980, pp. 2022-24.

3650. Rive, Richard. "Afrikaner or Suid-Afrikaner?" DONGA, 1 (1976), 1.

Group identity among South African writers.

3651. ____. "The Black Man and White Literature." CLASSIC, 4 (1977), 61-70.

Surveys South African literature, including black protest writing.

3652. ____. SELECTED WRITINGS: STORIES, ESSAYS, PLAYS. Johannesburg: Donker, 1977.

Essays on South African literature, including 4149 and rpts. of BALE 566, 2058, 2103, 2891. Discussion of Mtshali, Nortje, Rive, Sepamla, Serote, et al.

3653. Rogers, Momo K. "The Liberian Writers: A Case of Misconception." LIBERIA: POLITICAL, ECONOMIC AND SOCIAL MONTHLY, 23-24 (1976). 22-24.

3654. Rollins, J.D. "Why Read African Literature?" INDIANA ENGLISH JOURNAL, 7, 1-3 (1972-73), 6-14.

Achebe, Aidoo, et al.

3655. Roscoe, Adrian. UHURU'S FIRE: AFRICAN LITERATURE EAST TO SOUTH. Cambridge: Cambridge University Press, 1977.

Angira, Brutus, Buruga, Chimombo, Kayira, Kibera, La Guma, Liyong, Mphahlele, Ngugi, Ntiru, Oculi, Ogot, Ogutu, Palangyo, p'Bitek, Serumaga, Watene, et al. Rpts. 4151.

3656. ____. "Writers in South Africa." LISTENER, 100 (1978), 533-34.

Brutus, La Guma, Mphahlele, Mtshali, et al.

3657. Sahle Selassie Berhane-Mariam. "Identification of National Literature." QUARTERLY YEKATIT, 5, 2 (1981), 19.

3658. Saint-Andre-Utudjian, Eliane. "Le thème de la folie dans la
       littérature africaine contemporaine (1960-1975)." PA, 115
       (1980), 118-47.

       Achebe, Aidoo, Armah, Awoonor, Head, Okara, Soyinka, et
       al.

3659. Sam-Kubam, Patrick. "The Paucity of Literary Creativity in
       Anglophone Cameroon." ABBIA, 31-33 (1978), 205-09.

3660. Schäfer, Jürgen. "Englischsprachige Literaturen
       Schwarzafrikas." In Kosok and Priessnitz, 3541, pp. 157-76;
       rpt. in Breitinger, 3428, pp. 103-25.

3661. ____, ed. COMMONWEALTH-LITERATUR. Studienreihe Englisch,
       43. Dusseldorf: Bagel; Bern and Munich: Francke, 1981.

       Includes 3456, 3648, 4369, and bibliography of
       criticism.

3662. Schild, Ulla. "Die afrikanische Literatur." In LITERATUR
       NACH 1945 I. Ed. Jost Hermand. Wiesbaden: Akademische
       Verlagsgesellschaft Athenaion, 1979. Pp. 487-508.

       Survey.

3663. ____. "Editorial." ZEITSCHRIFT FÜR KULTURAUSTAUSCH, 29
       (1979), 140-41.

       Introd. to special issue on "Afrikanische Literatur:
       Perspektiven und Probleme."

3664. ____. "Pulsschläge--afrikanische Literatur Heute."
       ZEITSCHRIFT FÜR KULTURAUSTAUSCH, 30 (1980), 380-82.

       Introd. to anthology of African literature in German
       translation.

3665. ____, ed. THE EAST AFRICAN EXPERIENCE: ESSAYS ON ENGLISH
       AND SWAHILI LITERATURE/2ND JANHEINZ JAHN SYMPOSIUM. Mainzer
       Afrika-Studien, 4. Berlin: Reimer, 1980.

       Includes 3705, 4029, 4338.

3666. Schnurer, Jos. "Afrikanische Gedichte als Zugang zum
       Verstandnis afrikanischer Menschen." DU, 31, 4 (1979),
       94-108.

       Survey.

3667. Sebe, Lennox L. "Some Aspects of African Literature." In
       AFRICAN PERSPECTIVES ON SOUTH AFRICA: A COLLECTION OF
       SPEECHES, ARTICLES AND DOCUMENTS. Ed. Hendrik W. van der
       Merwe, Nancy C.J. Charton, D.A. Kotzé, and Åke Magnusson.
       Stanford, CA: Hoover Institute; Cape Town: David Philip;

London: Rex Collings, 1978. Pp. 29-33.

3668. Serote, Mongane Wally. "The Black Word." BLAC, 1, 2 (n.d.), 4-6.

Literary expression in South Africa.

3669. Skurjat, Ernestyna. "Literatura w dziwnym kraju [Literature in a Strange Land]." TYGODNIK KULTURALNY, 22 (1971), 5.

Survey of South African writing.

3670. _____. "Zderzenie kultur w literaturze Czarnej Afryki [Cultural Conflict in the Literature of Black Africa]." PRZEGLAD INFORMACJI O AFRYCE, 2 (1976), 68-76.

Survey.

3671. _____. "Atrybuty Nowoczesności w literaturze afrykańskiej [Attributes of Modernism in African Literature]." PRZEGLAD ORIENTALISTYCZNY, 3 (1977), 230-33.

Liyong, Munonye, et al.

3672. Small, Adam. "In the Crucible: A Situation of Change for South African Literature." In RACE RELATIONS IN SOUTH AFRICA 1929-1979. Ed. Ellen Hellmann and Henry Lever. New York: St. Martin's Press, 1979. Pp. 249-72.

3673. Snyder, Emile. "Modern Africa in Literature." In AFRICA. Ed. Phyllis M. Martin and Patrick O'Meara. Bloomington and London: Indiana University Press, 1977. Pp. 37-47.

Survey.

3674. _____. "Petit panorama de la littérature africaine anglophone." RPC, 33 (1978), 25-27.

Survey.

3675. Society of African Culture. L'AFRIQUE DU SUD AUJOURD'HUI/SOUTH AFRICA TODAY. Paris: Présence Africaine, 1978.

Includes 3532, 4379, 4390, 4411, 4574.

3676. Sole, Kelwyn. "Class, Continuity and Change in Black South African Literature, 1948-1960." In Bozzoli, 3425, pp. 143-82.

3677. Srivastava, Avadhesh K., ed. ALIEN VOICE: PERSPECTIVES ON COMMONWEALTH LITERATURE. Lucknow: Print House, 1981; Atlantic Highlands, NJ: Humanities Press, 1982.

Includes 3423, 3594, 3642, 5125, 5750, 6079.

3678. Sulzer, Peter. "Einleitung." In MODERNE ERZÄHLER DER WELT:
       SÜDAFRIKA. Ed. Peter Sulzer. Tübingen and Basel: Erdmann,
       1977. Pp. 9-23.

       Survey.

3679. Surovtsev, E. Ia. "Literatury Kenii, Ugandy, Malavi (na
       angliiskom yazyke [Literatures of Kenya, Uganda, Malawi (in
       English)]." In Vavilov and Kudelin, 3692, pp. 249-55.

3680. ____. "O nekotorykh chertakh Ugandiiskogo Modernizma [On
       Several Traits of Ugandan Modernism]." In LITERATURA DVUKH
       KONTINENTOV [Literature of Two Continents]. Ed. V.I.
       Semanov. Moscow: Moscow University Press, 1979. Pp. 175-82.

3681. Švob-Ðokić, Nada. PUTOVI AFRIČKE KNJIŽEVNOSTI [Development
       in African Literature]. Zagreb: Sveučilišna Naklada liber,
       1981.

       Achebe, Awoonor, Ekwensi, la Guma, Mangua, Mphahlele,
       Ngugi, Okara, p'Bitek, Soyinka, Tutuola, et al.

3682. Sweeney, Eileen. ANOTHER COUNTRY: THE LAND OF LITERATURE.
       Enugu: Fourth Dimension, 1979.

       Brief essays on Achebe, Amadi, Armah, Ngugi, Okara,
       Tutuola, et al.

3683. Tejani, Bahadur. "Modern African Literature and the Legacy
       of Cultural Colonialism." WLWE, 18 (1979), 37-54.

       Brutus, Liyong, Mazrui, Ngugi, Oculi, p'Bitek, Rubadiri,
       et al.

3684. Thorpe, Michael. "Current Literature 1975: III.
       Commonwealth Literature." ES, 58 (1977) 43-55, 553-63.

       Survey.

3685. Tibble, Anne. "African-English Writing (South and East
       Africa)." STANDARD ENCYCLOPEDIA OF SOUTHERN AFRICA, Vol. 4
       (1971), pp. 363-65.

       Survey.

3686. Tsuchiya, Satoru. "Modern East African Literature: From
       Uhuru to Harambee." WLT, 52 (1978), 569-74; AFRISCOPE, 8, 4
       (1978), 38, 40.

       Liyong, Mwangi, Ngugi, Ogot, et al.

3687. ____. MODERNIZATION AND AFRICA. Tokyo: Asahi Shinbun Press,
       1978.

Includes section on "Modernization from the Literary
Point of View"; in Japanese.

3688. Updike, John. "African Accents." NEW YORKER, 17 May 1977,
pp. 141-48.

Echewa, Soyinka, et al.

3689. Vansina, Jan. "Literature: Oral and Written." In AFRICAN
HISTORY. Ed. Philip Curtin, Steven Feierman, Leonard Thompson
and Jan Vansina. Boston and Toronto: Little, Brown, 1978.
Pp. 546-51.

Survey.

3690. Vavilov, V.N. "Literatura Nigerii (na angliĭskom ĭazyke)
[Literature of Nigeria (in English)]." In Vavilov and
Kudelin, 3692, pp. 163-83.

3691. ____. "Literatura Gany i Nigerii v 70-ye gody [Literature of
Ghana and Nigeria in the 1970s]." In Nikiforova, 3601, pp.
96-124.

Armah, Munonye, Soyinka, et al.

3692. Vavilov, V.N., and A.B. Kudelin, eds. LITERATURY AFRIKI
[African Literatures]. Moscow: Vysshaĩa Shkola, 1979.

Includes 3679, 3692.

3693. Vavilov, V.N., and E. Ia. Surovtŝev. "Literatura Vostochnoĭ
Afriki v 60-70-ye gody [Literature of Eastern Africa in the
1960s and 1970s]." In Nikiforova, 3601, pp. 71-95.

Angira, Liyong, Mangua, p´Bitek, Ruheni, et al.

3694. Vignal, Daniel. "Une autre Afrique." EUROPE, 618 (1980),
3-5.

Introduction to special issue on Nigerian literature.

3695. Visweswariah, H.S. "Black Orpheus Unveiled: A Note on
African Writing in English." TRIVENI, 45, 4 (1977), 16-19.

Achebe, Soyinka, Tutuola.

3696. Vol´pe, M.L. "Literatura Efiopii v 60-70-ye gody [Literature
of Ethiopia in the 1960s and 1970s]." In Nikiforova, 3601,
pp. 49-70.

Gabre-Medhin, Sellassie, Worku.

3697. Wanjala, Chris. "African Writers are not Know-alls." SUNDAY
NATION, 14 August 1977, pp. 13, 23.

3698.   ____.   "People--the Stuff of which our Literature is Made."
SUNDAY NATION, 4 September 1977, p. 17.

    In Kenya.

3699.   ____.   "Link between Our Literature and the Environment."
SUNDAY NATION, 11 September 1977, p. 15.

    In Kenya.

3700.   ____.   "The Varying Interests of Kenyan Writers." SUNDAY
NATION, 23 October 1977, p. 12.

    Survey.

3701.   ____.   "Base Our Creative Activities on Our Own Societies."
SUNDAY NATION, 4 December 1977, p. 18.

3702.   ____.   THE SEASON OF HARVEST: SOME NOTES ON EAST AFRICAN
LITERATURE.   Introd. Angus Calder. Nairobi: Kenya Literature
Bureau, 1978.

    Buruga, Kibera, La Guma, Liyong, Mangua, Mbiti, Ngugi,
    Ntiru, Oculi, Ogot, p'Bitek, Were, et al.

3703.   ____.   "1977: The Season of Literary Harvest." SUNDAY
NATION, 1 January 1978, p. 16.

    FESTAC, Ngugi, Ng'weno, et al.

3704.   ____.   "Everybody is Rushing into Print These Days." SUNDAY
NATION, 28 October 1979.

3705.   ____.   "Imaginative Writing Since Independence: The East
African Experience." In Schild, 3665, pp. 9-24.

    Ngugi, et al.

3706.   ____.   FOR HOME AND FREEDOM. Nairobi: Kenya Literature
Bureau, 1980.

    On East African literature, mainly works by Liyong,
    Lubwa p'Chong, Maillu, Mangua, Mphahlele, Muruah, Ngugi,
    p'Bitek, Serumaga, et al.

3707.   Wauthier, Claude. THE LITERATURE AND THOUGHT OF MODERN
AFRICA. London: Heinemann, 1978.

    2nd ed. of BALE 649. Includes new chapter, "Postface:
    After Independence," surveying recent writing.

3708.   ____.   MODERN AFRICAN LITERATURE: CHALLENGE AND DIRECTION.
New York: Jeffrey Norton Publishers, n.d.

    Tape-recorded lecture.

3709.   ____.   EARLY AFRICAN LITERATURE.   New York: Jeffrey Norton
         Publishers, n.d.

         Tape-recorded lecture.

3710.   Webb, Hugh Graham.   "Disillusionment and the Way Forward: The
         Forms of Modern Anglophone African Literature."   Ph.D.
         dissertation, Murdoch University, 1977.

         Armah, Awoonor, Mphahlele, Ngugi, Nwoga, Soyinka, et al.

3711.   Wilhelm, Cherry A.   "South African Writing in English: 1976."
         STANDPUNTE, 133 (1978), 44-59.

         Sepamla, et al.

3712.   ____.   "South African Writing in English: 1977,
         I."   STANDPUNTE, 141 (1979), 37-49; "II." 142 (1979), 33-42.

         Head, Manganyi, et al; Gwala, Sepamla, et al.

3713.   Wilkinson, Nick.   "Literature and Boundaries: Outline of a
         Concept."   NSAL, 2, 1 (1979), 48-61.

3714.   Zirimu, P.   "Literature and Life: Revelation of a People's
         Life Through Verbal Art."   DHANA, 7, 1 (1977), 77-84.

E. FICTION

BIBLIOGRAPHY

3715. Dressler, Claus Peter. "Bibliografie afrikanischer Literatur: Prosa." In Eckardt, 4995, pp. 112-15.

3716. Gorman, G.E. THE SOUTH AFRICAN NOVEL IN ENGLISH SINCE 1950: AN INFORMATION AND RESOURCE GUIDE. Boston: G.K.Hall, 1978.

3717. ____. "The Modern South African Novel in English: A Selective Bibliography of Dissertations and Theses." RAL, 10 (1979), 383-93.

3718.* Obasi, John U. AFRICAN BOOK LIST: THE NOVEL IN AFRICA. London: Westminster City Libraries, n.d.

   Annotated list of fiction held in Westminster City Libraries.

See also 3307, 3328, 3347, 4322.

BOOKS AND ESSAYS

3719. Abrahams, Cecil. "African Writing and Themes of Colonialism and Post-Independence Disillusionment." CJAS, 12 (1978), 119-25.

   Djoleto, Kayira, Ngugi, Ruheni, et al.

3720. ____. "No Longer at Ease." CJAS, 14 (1980), 529-31.

   Achebe, Ekwensi, Nwankwo.

3721. Amuzu, Koku. "The Theme of Corruption in A MAN OF THE PEOPLE and THE BEAUTYFUL ONES ARE NOT YET BORN." LEGACY, 3, 2 (1977), 18-23.

3722.* Arab, S.A. "The Novel as a Chronicle of Decolonization in Africa." Ph.D. dissertation, Sussex University, 1979.

3723.* Arnold, Rainer. "Entwicklungsprobleme der Prosaliteratur in Ostafrika: Untersuchungen zu Genesis und Situation des ostafrikanischen Romans." Ph.D. dissertation, University of Leipzig, 1977.

3724. ____. "Notes on the Development of the East African Novel." In AFRICAN STUDIES: DEDICATED TO THE IVTH INTERNATIONAL CONGRESS OF AFRICANISTS IN KINSHASA. Ed. Thea Büttner. African Studies, 38. Berlin: Akademie, 1978. Pp. 127-38.

   Survey.

3725. ____. "Revolutionsgedanke und Revolutionsdarstellung im afrikanischen Roman." In Gruner, 3501, pp. 201-05.

Achebe, Ngugi, Soyinka, et al.

3726.* Ar-Rasheed, M.H. "A Typology of the African Novel:
Celebration to Alienation." Ph.D. dissertation, Lancaster
University, 1978.

3727. Asanbe, Joseph. "The Place of the Individual in the Novels
of Chinua Achebe, T.M. Aluko, Flora Nwapa and Wole Soyinka."
DAI, 40 (1980), 5447A (Indiana).

3728.* Bardolph, Jacqueline. "Le Roman de langue anglaise en
Afrique de l'Est, 1964-1976." Ph.D. dissertation, University
of Caen, 1981.

Katigula, Lubega, Mangua, Mazrui, M'imanyara, Mwangi,
Ngubiah, Ngugi, Njau, Ole Kulet, Palangyo, Serumaga, et
al. See summary in AFRAMN, 14 (1981), 19-22.

3729. Barthold, Bonnie J. BLACK TIME: FICTION OF AFRICA, THE
CARIBBEAN AND THE UNITED STATES. New Haven: Yale University
Press, 1981.

Achebe, Armah, Soyinka, et al.

3730. Berkley, Constance E. "The Contours of Sudanese Literature."
AT, 28 (1981), 109-18.

Short story writing in English.

3731.* Brash, E. "Some Stylistic Responses to Linguistic Diversity
in the English Prose Fiction of Selected West African,
Caribbean and Melanesian Writers." Ph.D. dissertation,
Sussex University, 1977.

Achebe, Armah, Okara, Soyinka, Tutuola, et al.

3732.* Brautigam, Petra. "Die Funktion moderner afrikanischer
Literatur dargestellt an gesellschaftskritischen Romanen
Ghanas." Master's thesis, University of Frankfurt, 1977.

3733. Breitinger, Eckhard. "Girls at War--Girls at Peace:
Heroines in Nigerian Prose." KOMPARATISTISCHE HEFTE, 1
(1980), 67-76.

Achebe, Ekwensi, Tutuola.

3734. Britwum, Kwabena. "La Socialité du texte et/ou le texte du
réel: Pour une socio-critique du roman africain." AFRICAN
PERSPECTIVES (Leiden), 1 (1977), 135-42.

3735. Cham, Baboucar Aliew-Badara. "Language and Style in the West
African and West Indian Novel." DAI, 39 (1978) 3562A
(Wisconsin-Madison).

Achebe, Okara, et al.

3736. Chimombo, Steve Bernard Miles. "Contemporary Malawian
       Novels." DAI, 41 (1980), 1589A (Columbia Teachers College).

3737. Chinweizu. "Beyond European Realism." OKIKE, 14 (1978), 1-3.

       Introduction to issue of OKIKE containing articles on
       Tutuola and Latin American novelists.

3738. Christie, Sarah, Geoffrey Hutchings, and Don Maclennan.
       PERSPECTIVES ON SOUTH AFRICAN FICTION. Johannesburg:
       Donker, 1980.

       Mphahlele, Plaatje, et al.

3739.* Clough, Martha Low. "Black Orpheus in the Underworld: The
       Urban Novels of Cyprian Ekwensi and Chinua Achebe." Master's
       thesis, University of Houston, 1976.

3740. Colmer, Rosemary Margaret. "The Development of the
       Sub-Saharan Black African Novel in English, with Special
       Reference to the Works of Achebe, Awoonor, Soyinka and Armah
       and Their Relevance to the Emergence of New Concepts in
       African Aesthetics." Ph.D. dissertation, Macquarie
       University, 1980.

       Also Abrahams, La Guma, Mwangi, Ngugi, et al.

3741.* Conde, M. "L'envers des mythes: le roman ghanéen," NOTRE
       LIBRARIE, 59 (1981), 35-45.

3742.* Cooper. B.L. "A Survey of Modern Black African Fiction, with
       Reference to Independent African and South African Works."
       Master's thesis, Birmingham University, 1975-76.

3743. Coulon, Virginia. "Les Types sociaux dans le roman nigérian
       anglophone." Ph.D. dissertation, 3rd cycle, University of
       Bordeaux, 1979.

       Achebe, Agunwa, Akpan, Aluko, Amadi, Aniebo, Echewa,
       Egbuna, Ekwensi, Emecheta, Ibukun, Ike, Iroh, Mezu,
       Munonye, Nwala, Nwankwo, Nwapa, Nzekwu, Okara, Okpewho,
       Omotoso, Osahon, Osofisan, Soyinka, Ulasi, Uzodinma.

3744.* Coussy, Denise. "La Prose nigeriane anglophone: Le Roman et
       la nouvelle." Doctorat d'État, Université de la Sorbonne
       Nouvelle, 1980.

       Achebe, Ekwensi, Okara, Soyinka, Tutuola, et al; summary
       in AFRAMN, 11 (1980), 21-25.

3745. Cvjetičanin, Biserka. ROMAN I AFRIČKA ZBILJA [The Novel and
       African Reality]. Zagreb: Školska knjiga, 1981.

Achebe, Ngugi, Okara, Sofola, Soyinka, Tutuola, et al.

3746. Dailly, Christophe. "The Novelist as a Cultural
Policy-Maker." AdUA, 13D (1980), 189-201.

3747.* d'Almeida, Irene Assiba. "Aspects of Commitment in Some West
African Novels of English and French Expression." Master's
thesis, University of Ibadan, 1979.

Armah, Soyinka, et al.

3748. Danquah, Moses. "A Blueprint for African Fiction: Echo of a
Review Controversy Long Forgotten." WAR, January 1948, pp.
16-17.

3749. Davenport, Randall Louis. "The Bourgeois Rebel: A Study of
the Been-to in Selected West African Novels." DAI, 38
(1978), 6712-13A (Northwestern).

Achebe, Armah, Soyinka.

3750. Dieltjens, Louis. "Zwarte Engelstalige prozaliteratuur in
Zuid-Afrika: een eerste verkenning. [Black English Prose in
South Africa: Surveying the Territory]." KREATIEF, 11, 4-5
(1977), 127-35.

Abrahams, La Guma, Mphahlele, et al.

3751. Ejrnaes, Anne Marie. AFRIKA--LITTERATUR OG SAMFUND: INDIVID
OG KOLLEKTIV I FEM SAMFUNDSKRITISKE ROMANER. [African
Literature and Society: Individual and Group in Five Novels
of Social Criticism]. Copenhagen: Medusa, 1977.

Armah, FRAGMENTS; Ngugi, A GRAIN OF WHEAT; Soyinka,
SEASON OF ANOMY; et al.

3752.* Elders, Derek. "West African Fiction for its Own Sake." THE
USE OF ENGLISH, 31, 2 (1980), 52-55.

3753. Emeka, Abanime. "La Beauté féminine chez les romanciers
négro-africains: le problème de l'idéal blanc." RLENA, 3
(1981), 7-14.

Achebe, Ekwensi, et al.

3754. Emenyonu, Ernest N. THE RISE OF THE IGBO NOVEL. Ibadan:
Oxford University Press, 1978.

Rev. of BALE 703. Achebe, Agunwa, Amadi, Ekwensi, Ike,
Munonye, Nwankwo, Nwapa, Nzekwu, Ogali, et al.

3755.* Essien, Ezekiel James. "The Dilemma of the New African in
the Fiction of Chinua Achebe, Cyprian Ekwensi and Margaret
Laurence." Master's thesis, Dalhousie University, 1969.

3756.   February, Vernie. "Little Sorrow Sits and Weeps."
        AFRISCOPE, 9, 2 (1979), 35-40.

        Childhood as a theme in third world literature;
        Matthews, Nicol, et al.

3757.   Forstreuter, Burkhard. "Entwicklungstendenzen in der
        englischsprachigen Kurzprosa Nigerias." WB, 26, 9 (1980),
        144-49.

        Achebe, Okara, Tutuola, et al.

3758.   Gakwandi, Shatto Arthur. THE NOVEL AND CONTEMPORARY
        EXPERIENCE IN AFRICA. London: Heinemann; New York: Africana,
        1977.

        Abrahams, Achebe, Aluko, Armah, Duodu, La Guma, Ngugi,
        Soyinka, et al.

3759.   Githae-Mugo, Micere. VISIONS OF AFRICA: THE FICTION OF
        CHINUA ACHEBE, MARGARET LAURENCE, ELSPETH HUXLEY AND NGUGI WA
        THIONG´O. Nairobi: Kenya Literature Bureau, 1978.

        Same as BALE 714.

3760.   Glinga, Werner. DER UNABHÄNGIGKEITSKAMPF IM AFRIKANISCHEN
        GEGENWARTSROMAN FRANZÖSISCHER SPRACHE (MIT EINEM AUSBLICK AUF
        DEN AFRIKANISCHEN GEGENWARTSROMAN ENGLISCHER UND
        PORTUGIESISCHER SPRACHE). Bonn: Bouvier, 1979.

        Includes discussion of Achebe, Armah, La Guma, et al.

3761.   Goldberg, Phyllis Enid. "From Eden to Utopia: A Sociology of
        the African Novel." DAI, 42, (1981), 700A (New York).

3762.   Gordimer, Nadine. "The Novel and the Nation in South
        Africa." RADCLIFFE QUARTERLY, February 1963, pp. 23-44.

        Abrahams, et al. Rpt. of BALE 717.

3763.   Haresnape, Geoffrey. "English Literature: The Novel and
        Short Story." STANDARD ENCYCLOPEDIA OF SOUTHERN AFRICA, Vol.
        12 (1976), pp. 72-73.

        Survey.

3764.   Ikiddeh, Ime. "Revolutionary Trends in Recent Political
        Fiction from Africa: Armah, Soyinka and Ngugi." LAAW, 42-43
        (1979-80), 14-27.

3765.   Izevbaye, Dan S. "Issues in the Reassessment of the African
        Novel." ALT, 10 (1979), 7-31.

        Achebe, Amadi, Armah, La Guma, Mphahlele, Ngugi,
        Omotoso, Soyinka, et al.

3766. ____. "Naming and the Character of African Fiction." RAL,
       12 (1981), 162-84.

       Achebe, Ngugi, Soyinka, Tutuola, et al.

3767.* Jabbi, Bu-Buakei. "Art of African Fiction: A Study of
       Performance Styles and Uses of Milieu in the Modern African
       Novel." Ph.D. dissertation, Sheffield University, 1981.

       Achebe, Ngugi, Soyinka.

3768. Janmohamed, Abdul Raheman. "The Politics of Literary
       Generation in the African Colonial Situation: An Examination
       of the Works of Joyce Cary, Isak Dinesen, Chinua Achebe and
       Ngugi wa Thiong´o." DAI, 37 (1977), 7742-43A (Brandeis).

3769. Jansen, Karl Heinz. LITERATUR UND GESCHICHTE IN AFRIKA:
       DARSTELLUNG DER VORKOLONIALEN GESCHICHTE UND KULTUR AFRIKAS
       IN DER ENGLISCH- UND FRANZÖSISCHSPRACHIGEN FIKTIONALEN
       AFRIKANISCHEN LITERATUR. Kölner Beitrage zur Afrikanistik,
       8. Berlin: Reimer, 1981.

       Achebe, Aidoo, Amadi, Armah, Asalache, Asare, Awoonor,
       Boateng, Brew, Dipoko, Erapu, Gatheru, Kayira, K´Okiri,
       M. Kunene, Liyong, Mphahlele, Mtshali, Mulikita, Ngugi,
       Okafor-Omali, Okara, Okigbo, Owusu, p´Bitek, Plaatje,
       Soyinka, Tutuola, Vambe, et al.

3770. Jones, Brian. "The Way It Was: Two Themes in the African
       Novel in English." UES, 16, 1 (1978), 16-21.

       "The way it was back home" and "ancestors versus
       missionaries" in novels by Achebe and Ngugi.

3771. K., E.M. "Sprecher ihres Volkes: Afrikanische Prosaliteratur
       in deutscher Sprache." WENDEKREIS, 85, 5 (1980), 42-43.

3772.* Kahari, George Payne. "The Search for Identity amidst
       Conflict and Change: The Dominant Theme in the Black
       Rhodesian Novel." Master´s thesis, Sheffield University,
       1978.

       Published as 3773.

3773. ____. THE SEARCH FOR ZIMBABWEAN IDENTITY: AN INTRODUCTION TO
       THE BLACK ZIMBABWEAN NOVEL. Foreword Marshall W. Murphree.
       Mambo Writers Series, English Section, 5. Gwelo, Zimbabwe:
       Mambo Press, 1980.

       Katiyo, Mungoshi, Mutswairo, Samkange, Sithole, et al.
       Publication of master´s thesis, 3772.

3774. Kiiru, Muchugu. "Pessimism in the East African Novel."
       UMMA-N, 8 (1978), 15-17, 20-21.

Rpt. of BALE 336. Bukenya, Kibera, Mangua, Ngugi.

3775. ____. "Aspects of the Novel in East Africa." In Gachukia and Akivaga, 4799, pp. 91-101.

Kibera, Ngugi, et al.

3776. Klíma, Vladimír. "Sierra Leone; Hledání krásné prózy [Sierra Leone: The Search for Prose Fiction]." ŠVETOVÁ LITERATURA, 21, 2 (1976), 216-53.

3777. ____. "Tři Etapy v Ghanské Próze [Three Phases in Ghanaian Prose]." ŠVETOVÁ LITERATURA, 26, 3 (1981), 151-76.

Aidoo, Armah, Djoleto, Konadu, Obeng.

3778. Knipp, Thomas R. "Hero in African Fiction." VIDYA, 1 (Spring 1967), 31-35.

Achebe, Ngugi, et al.

3779. Konstantinović, Zoran, Eva Kushner and Béla Köpeczi, eds. EVOLUTION OF THE NOVEL. Proceedings of the IXth Congress of the International Comparative Literature Association, Innsbruck, 1979. Innsbruck: Instituts für Sprachwissenschaft der Universität Innsbruck, 1982. Vol. 4.

Includes 3794, 3822, 5215.

3780. Larson, Charles R. PANORAMA DU ROMAN AFRICAIN. Introd. Edris Makward. Trans. Alain Ricard. Paris: Éditions Inter-Nationales, 1974.

Translation of BALE 751.

3781. Maclennan, Don. "Mapping South African Fiction." In Brimer, 3431, pp. 51-58.

3782. Mativo, Kyalo. "The Novel by Any Other Name." UFAHAMU, 7, 3 (1977), 131-49.

Theory and form of the novel.

3783. Mazrui, Ali A. "The Novelist as a Mediator Between Art and Social Philosophy." In Priebe and Hale, 4519, pp. 169-80.

3784. Michelman, Fredric. "The West African Novel Since 1911." YFS, 53 (1976), 29-44.

Survey.

3785. Morris, Patricia. "The Early Black South African Newspaper and the Development of the Novel." JCL, 15, 1 (1980), 15-29.

3786.* Mostert, C.W. "The Native in the South African Novel in
English." Master's thesis, University of the Orange Free
State, 1955.

    Abrahams, R.R.R. Dhlomo, Plaatje, et al.

3787.* Muketa, Fumunzanza, ed. AFRICAN QUEST: AN APPROACH TO THE
AFRICAN ENGLISH NOVELS. Lubumbashi: Faculty of Letters,
National University of Zaire, [1973].

3788. Mzamane, Mbulelo Vizikhungo. "The Short Story Tradition in
Black South Africa." DONGA, 7, (1977), 1, 8; MARANG, 1
(1977), [27-29].

3789.* Naumann, Michel. "Roman et réalité sociale: Chinua Achebe
et James Ngugi." Ph.D. dissertation, 3rd cycle, University
of Paris VII, 1978.

3790. Ndebele, Njabulo. "Three Novelists of the African
Revolution." HERITAGE, 3 (1978), 54-57.

    Abrahams, Ngugi, et al.

3791. Nikiforova, Irina Dmitrievna. AFRIKANSKIĬ ROMAN: GENEZIS I
PROBLEMY TIPOLOGII [The African Novel: Genesis and Problems
of Typology]. Moscow: Nauka, 1977.

3792. ____. "Osobennosti zarozhdeniia romana v literaturakh
tropicheskoĭ Afriki [Particularities of the Emergence of the
Novel in the Literature of Tropical Africa]." In GENEZIS
ROMANA V LITERATURAKH AZII I AFRIKI: NATSIONAL'NYE ISTOKI
ZHANRA [The Genesis of the Novel in Asian and African
Literatures: National Sources of the Genre]. Ed. P.A.
Grintser. Moscow: Nauka, 1980. Pp. 251-62.

    Survey.

3793. Niven. Alastair. "Relishing Some Recent Commonwealth
Fiction--a Personal Choice." BRITISH BOOK NEWS, April 1979,
pp. 298-303.

    Achebe, Ekwensi, Ngugi, et al.

3794. Nwezeh, E.C. "Satire in Post-Independence West-African
Fiction." In Konstantinović et al, 3779, pp. 193-99.

    Achebe, Armah, et al.

3795. Nwoga, D. Ibe. "Alienation in Modern African Fiction." In
Ekwensi, 3461, pp. 145-50.

    Rpt. of BALE 793. Covers Achebe, Armah.

3796. Nzewi, Meki. "Ancestral Polyphony." AfrA, 11, 4 (1978), 74,
92-94.

Achebe, Nwapa.

3797. Obiechina, Emmanuel. "Politics in Some African Novels." In
Ekwensi, 3461, pp. 151-65.

Ekwensi, et al.

3798. ____. "Post-Independence Disillusionment in Three African
Novels." NSAL, 1, 1 (1978), 54-78.

Rpt. of BALE 796. Achebe, Armah, Soyinka.

3799.* Odi Assamoi, Georgette. "Le Problème de l'éducation dans le
roman africain de langue anglaise." Ph.D. dissertation, 3rd
cycle, University of Montpellier III, 1977.

3800. Ogundipe-Leslie, Omolara. "The Poetics of Fiction by Yoruba
Writers: The Case of OGBOJU ODE NINU IGBO IRUNMALE." CLAJ, 22
(1979), 240-53.

Comments on Soyinka and Tutuola.

3801. Ohaegbu, A.U., and E.P. Modum. "The Short Story in PRESENCE
AFRICAINE." In Petersen and Rutherford, 4467, pp. 114-17.

3802. Okafor, Dubem. "The Themes of Disintegration in the West
Indian and West African Novel." BIM, 63 (1978), 158-75.

Achebe, Armah, Awoonor, Soyinka, et al.

3803. Okafor, Raymond Nnadozié. "La Ville dans quelques romans
africains." AdUA, 9D (1976), 319-30.

Abrahams, Achebe, Ekwensi, La Guma, Mphahlele, et al.

3804. ____. "Aspects du monde colonial dans le roman africaine."
AdUA, 9D (1976), 355-79.

Achebe, et al.

3805. Oko, Emelia. "The Language of Comedy in Nigerian Fiction:
Aluko and Achebe." NSAL, 3 (1980), 131-44.

3806. Okonkwo, J.I. "Beyond Disillusion: The Combative Mood in the
African Novel." NSAL, 2, 1 (1979), 117-33; STUDIA AFRICANA,
1, 3 (1979), 219-33.

Armah, Kayira, Ngugi, Serumaga, Soyinka, et al.

3807.* ____. "Visions of Stability: The Novel in the African
Revolution." Ph.D. dissertation, University of Nigeria,
1980.

Armah, Kayira, Ngugi, Serumaga, Soyinka.

3808. Oladitan, Olalere. "Coup d'etat in Recent Nigerian Novels."

AFRISCOPE, 8, 1-2 (1978), 43-44.

Achebe, Egbuna, Munonye, Osofisan.

3809. ____. "The Nigerian Crisis in the Nigerian Novel." In
Ogungbesan, 3617, pp. 10-20.

Achebe, Amadi, Ike, Munonye, Omotoso, Osofisan, Soyinka,
et al.

3810. Olorounto, Samuel Boladji. "The Significance of Growing Up
in Selected Novels of Chinua Achebe, Camara Laye, Cheikh
Hamidou Kane and Ngugi wa Thiong'o." DAI, 41 (1981), 4711A
(Indiana).

3811. Omotoso, Kole. THE FORM OF THE AFRICAN NOVEL: A CRITICAL
ESSAY. Akure, Nigeria: Olaiya Fagbamigbe, 1977.

Achebe, Amadi, Armah, Ngugi, Omotoso, Osofisan, Soyinka,
Tutuola, et al.

3812. Osundare, Oluwaniyi. "Bilingual and Bicultural Aspects of
Nigerian Prose Fiction." DAI, 40 (1979), 2667A (York,
Canada).

Tutuola, et al.

3813. Palmer, Eustace. THE GROWTH OF THE AFRICAN NOVEL. London
and Exeter, NH: Heinemann, 1979.

Achebe, Aluko, Armah, Ekwensi, Mwangi, Ngugi, Soyinka,
Tutuola, et al.

3814. ____. "Towards an African Aesthetic: The Case of African
Fiction." FBSLL, 1 (1980), 1-26.

Expands on his introduction to 3813.

3815. ____. "Negritude Rediscovered: A Reading of the Recent
Novels of Armah, Ngugi, and Soyinka." IFR, 8, 1 (1981),
1-11.

3816. Parker, Kenneth. "The South African Novel in English." In
Parker, 3817, pp. 1-26.

Abrahams, La Guma, Plaatje, et al.

3817. ____, ed. THE SOUTH AFRICAN NOVEL IN ENGLISH: ESSAYS IN
CRITICISM AND SOCIETY. London: Macmillan; New York: Africana
Publishing Co., 1978.

Includes 3816, 5076, 5535, 5890.

3818. Petersen, Kirsten Holst. "The Short Story." In Petersen and
Rutherford, 4467, pp. 61-64.

3819.   Povey, John. "The Political Vision of the West African
        Writer." ENGLISH IN AFRICA, 5, 2 (1978), 51-56.

        Achebe, Armah, Ekwensi.

3820.* Rooyen, Danielle J. van. "English-language Fiction in South
        Africa from 1945 to 1960: A Survey of Trends, Influences and
        Cross-Relationships." Master's thesis, Rand Afrikaans
        University, 1977.

        Abrahams, Mphahlele.

3821.   Schipper-de Leeuw, Mineke. "Perspective narrative et récit
        africain à la première personne." AFRICAN PERSPECTIVES
        (Leiden), 1 (1977), 113-33.

3822.   ____. "Réalisme et roman africain." In Konstantinović et
        al., 3779, pp. 201-05.

3823.   Schmidt, Nancy J. "The Nature of Ethnographic Fiction?: A
        Further Inquiry." ANTHROPOLOGY AND HUMANISM QUARTERLY, 6
        (March 1981), 8-18.

3824.   Singler, John Victor. "The Role of the State in the
        Development of Literature: The Liberian Government and
        Creative Fiction." RAL, 11 (1980), 511-28.

        Cooper, Cordor, Dempster, Henries, Bai T. Moore,
        R. William Jaryenneh Moore, Sankawulo, et al.

3825.   Skurjat, Ernestyna. "Proza nigeryjska a możliwość
        upowszechniania nowego systemu wartości [Nigerian Prose and
        the Possibility of Dissemination of the New System of
        Values]." PRZEGLAD INFORMACJI O AFRYCE, 4 (1975), 93-104.

        Achebe, Aluko, Munonye, Soyinka, et al.

3826.   ____. "Proza Nigeryjska w Poszukiwaniu nowej etyki [Nigerian
        Prose: In Search of New Ethics]." In AFRYKA: GOSPODARKA
        SPOŁECZEŃSTWO [Africa: Society and Economy]. Ed. Antoniego
        Kuklińskiego. Warsaw: Ksiaźka i Wiedza, 1979. Pp. 350-70.

        Aluko, Nwankwo, et al.

3827.* ____. "Social Roles of the New Nigerian Elite--in the light
        of Nigerian Novels Published in the Years 1960-1976." Ph.D.
        dissertation, University of Warsaw, 1979.

        Achebe, Aka, Aluko, Amadi, Aniebo, Ekwensi, Ifejika,
        Ike, Mezu, Munonye, Nwankwo, Okara, Okpewho, Omotoso,
        Osofisan, Soyinka.

3828.   ____. "Angielskojezyczni powieściopisarze nigerii w świetle
        własnej twórczości [English language Nigerian Novelists in
        the Light of Their Own Creative Works]." PrzS, 32, 1 (1980),

119-30, 292-93.

3829. ____. "Social Roles of the New Nigerian Elite in the Light
of Nigerian Novels Published Between 1960 and 1976." AfB, 29
(1980), 157-59.

Summary of doctoral dissertation submitted at the
University of Warsaw, 3827.

3830. Soyinka, Susan. "Family and Fertility in the West African
Novel." In THE PERSISTENCE OF HIGH FERTILITY. Ed. John
C. Caldwell. Canberra: Dept. of Demography, Australian
National University, 1977. Pp. 427-49.

Aluko, Nwapa, Nzekwu, Selormey, et al.

3831.* Spurling, D.J. "The Influence of Christianity on African
Sensibility as Reflected in Selected Novels of Nigeria and
Cameroon." Master's thesis, Leeds University, 1977.

3832.* Sy, Mariene. "Le Thème du nationalisme dans le roman
africain d'expression anglaise: Contribution à l'étude de la
littérature engagée en Afrique noire." Ph.D. dissertation,
3rd cycle, University of Paris III, 1977.

3833. Taiwo, Oladele. "The Woman Novelists of West Africa." In
Banjo, 3415, pp. 199-211.

Aidoo, Nwapa, Ulasi.

3834. ____. "Language and Theme in Three African Novels." LHY,
22, 1 (1981), 29-45.

Amadi's THE SLAVE, La Guma's TIME OF THE BUTCHERBIRD,
Mwangi's CARCASE FOR HOUNDS.

3835.* Tala, K.I. "The African Political Novel in English."
Master's thesis, Leeds University, 1978.

3836. Tejani, Bahadur. "Illusion (Ilussion) and Innocence: The
First Indo-African Novel." GANGA, 2, 4 (1980), 12-14.

Rasik and Chiman's DIVORCE BEFORE MARRIAGE.

3837. Trenz, Günter. DIE FUNKTION ENGLISCHSPRACHIGER
WESTAFRIKANISCHER LITERATUR: EINE STUDIE ZUR
GESELLSCHAFTLICHEN BEDEUTUNG DES ROMANS IN NIGERIA. Mainzer
Ethnologische Arbeiten, Bd. 1. Berlin: Reimer, 1980.

Achebe, Aluko, Amadi, Aniebo, Armah, Awoonor, Conton,
Ekwensi, Equiano, Mezu, Mphahlele, Munonye, Ngugi,
Nwankwo, Nwapa, Nzekwu, Okara, Okigbo, Okpewho, Omotoso,
Soyinka, Tutuola, et al.

3838. Vivan, Itala. INTERPRETI RITUALI: IL ROMANZO DELL'AFRICA

NERA. Bari: Dedalo, 1978.

Achebe, Mphahlele, Ngugi, Soyinka, Tutuola.

3839.   Voss, A.E. "A Generic Approach to the South African Novel in
English." UCTSE, 7 (1977), 110-21.

Survey.

3840.   Webb, Hugh. POLITICAL DISILLUSIONMENT AND MODERN AFRICAN
FICTION: THE QUESTIONS OF DESPAIR. African Studies Working
Papers, 1. Murdoch, Australia: African Studies Seminar,
School of Communication, Murdoch University, 1975.

Survey.

3841.   ____. "The African Historical Novel and the Way Forward."
ALT, 11 (1980), 24-38.

Armah, Mazrui, Mezu.

3842.   Wilson, Richard. "The Novel as Evidence." KWANZA JOURNAL, 4
(1980), 11-21.

Achebe, Ngugi, Soyinka, et al.

3843.   Wittmann, Ulrich. DER KONFLIKT ZWEIER WERTSYSTEME IM
IBO-ROMAN. Studien zur englischen Literatur, Band 15. Bonn:
Bouvier, 1978.

Achebe, Agunwa, Akpan, Amadi, Egbuna, Ekwensi, Ike,
Munonye, Nzekwu, Ulasi.

3844.* Zele, Dieudonné. "Le Thème de la recherche de l'identité
dans le roman nègre anglophone." Ph.D. dissertation, 3rd
cycle, University of Nantes, 1978.

See also 3383, 3387, 3393-94, 3397, 3574, 3586, 3591, 3595, 3608,
3615, 3619, 3628, 3655, 3686, 3710, 3712, 4174, 4180, 4187,
4191, 4202, 4214, 4262, 4303, 4316, 4337, 4345, 4360, 4363,
4365, 4375, 4450, 4476-77, 4483, 4491, 4499, 4509, 4516,
4522-23, 4529, 4531, 4827, 4847, 4921-22, 4972, 5063,
5065-68, 5070, 5073, 5075, 5077, 5079, 5110-43, 5145-56,
5158-62, 5164, 5166-76, 5178-5231, 5233-62, 5264-70, 5279-92,
5295, 5297-5322, 5333, 5336-43, 5346, 5366, 5371-72, 5432,
5485, 5530, 5567, 5703, 5706, 5985, 5995, 5997, 6065, 6090.

F. DRAMA

BIBLIOGRAPHY

3845. Ashaolu, A. Olu. "A Bibliography of Modern Nigerian Drama in English." WLWE, 17 (1978), 372-421.

3846. Dressler, Claus Peter. "Afrikanische Theaterstücke." In Eckardt, 4995, pp. 53-55.

3847. Eyoh, Hansel Ndumbe. "Contemporary Cameroonian Drama: 1959-1979." AFLYSHY, 10 (1981), 5-17.

   Includes list of published and unpublished plays.

3848. Lindfors, Bernth. "Nigerian High School Plays 1950-1972." KIABÀRÁ, 3, 1 (1980), 47-88.

   List of theatrical productions.

3849. Riemenschneider, Dieter. "Westafrika." In Stilz, 4043, pp. 143-45.

3850. Steadman, Ian. "Performance Research: A Select Bibliography." CRITICAL ARTS, 2, 1 (1981), 60-65.

3851. Vandenbroucke, Russell. "A Selected Bibliography of the South African Theatre." THEATRE Q, 7, 28 (1977-78), 94-95.

BOOKS AND ESSAYS

3852. Adedeji, Joel. "The Nigerian Theatre in English and Its Audience." In DAS THEATER UND SEIN PUBLIKUM: REFERATE DER INTERNATIONALEN THEATERWISSENSCHAFTLICHEN DOZENTENKONFERENZEN IN VENEDIG 1975 UND WIEN 1976. Vienna: Österreichischen Akademie der Wissenschaften, 1977. Pp. 238-57.

   Rotimi, Soyinka.

3853. _____. "Theatre Forms: The Nigerian Dilemma." NigM, 128-129 (1979), 26-34.

3854.* _____. THE THEATRE IN AN AFRICAN UNIVERSITY: APPEARANCE AND REALITY. Ibadan: Ibadan University Press, 1980.

   Inaugural lecture.

3855. _____. NATIONALISM AND THE NIGERIAN NATIONAL THEATRE. Munger Africana Library Notes, 54. Pasadena: Munger Africana Library, California Institute of Technology, 1980.

   Soyinka, et al.

3856. _____. "Drama: Art or Way of Life." THIRD WORLD FIRST, 2, 1

(1980), 30-38.

3857.   Adelugba, Dapo. "Wale Ogunyemi, 'Zulu Sofola and Ola Rotimi:
Three Dramatists in Search of a Language." In Ogunba and
Irele, 4005, pp. 201-20.

3858.   Agovi, J.K. "The Ghana Dance Ensemble and the Contemporary
Ghanaian Theatre." LEGON OBSERVER, 12, 9 (1980), 213-15.

3859.   Akerman, Anthony. "Why Must These Shows Go On?: A Critique of
Black Musicals Made for White Audiences." THEATRE Q, 7, 28
(1977-78), 67-69.

3860.   ____. "Refugee Theatre in Tanzania." THEATRE Q, 8, 30
(1978), 36-39.

        South African exiles perform FREEDOM IN OUR LIFETIME.

3861.   Akomolafe, Olu. "Theatre Management in Nigeria: Appraisal
and Challenges." In Ogunbiyi, 4006, pp. 425-32.

3862.   Alot, Magaga. "Nairobi University Theatre Revival." NEW
AFRICAN, February 1979, pp. 110-11.

        Productions by Ruganda et al.

3863.   ____. "Acting on a Shoestring." NEW AFRICAN, July 1979, p.
76.

        Kenya's National Theatre Company and Drama School.

3864.   ____. "Kenyan Players Take Independent Line." NEW AFRICAN,
October 1980, pp. 127-28.

3865.   Amankulor, J.N. "A Propos Stage Productions in Nsukka
Theatre." MUSE, 10 (1978), 54-56.

3866.   Amuka, Peter. "Taking Theatre to the People." SUNDAY NATION,
17 October 1976, p. 15.

        Nairobi University Free Travelling Theatre.

3867.   Angmor, Charles. "Drama in Ghana." In Ogunba and Irele,
4005, pp. 55-72.

        Aidoo, Danquah, de Graft, Sutherland, et al.

3868.   Anon. "I Got My First Part at a Fortnight Old." SUNDAY
NATION, 17 June 1962, p. 35.

        Interview with Donovan Maule, actor, producer and
founder of the Donovan Maule Theatre in Nairobi.

3869.   Anon. "Art for the Sake of What?" NIGERIAN OPINION, 4
(1968), 340-41.

Remarks on television drama in Nigeria.

3870.   Anon.   "The Crisis of African Theatre." BUSINESS SOUTH
AFRICA, 8, 4 (1973), 32-33.

3871.   Anon.   "East African Actor's Workshop." AFRIKA, 17, 2 (1976),
47-48.

Organized in Nairobi by the Goethe Institute.

3872.   Anon.   "Black Theatre in South Africa."   INTERNATIONAL
DEFENCE & AID FUND FACT PAPER ON SOUTHERN AFRICA, 2 (June
1976), 1-12.

Kente, Macu, Mqayisa, et al.

3873.   Anon.   "The Market Theatre and What It Could Mean."   BONA,
July 1977, pp.   66-67, 70.

Johannesburg playhouse.

3874.   .Anon.   "Dramatic Giants: Kani and Ntshona." DRUM
(Johannesburg), August 1977, p.   20.

3875.   Anon.   THEATRE IN MALAŴI 1970-76.   Zomba, Malawi: English
Department, Chancellor College, University of Malawi, n.d.

Collection of documents relating to university theatre.
Includes "travelling theatre critical broadsheets," Nos.
1-19 (1973-76).

3876.   Anon.   "The Role of Theatre in African Cultural Development."
INTERNATIONAL THEATRE INFORMATION, Winter-Spring 1979, pp.
27-29.

3877.   Anon.   "Birth of a Krio Drama." WA, 26 February 1979, p.
347.

Raymond Charley in Sierra Leone.

3878.   Anon.   "Dialogue." NEW CULTURE, 1, 4 (1979), 46-47.

Interview on student drama with 'Jide Malomo, Arts
Fellow and Business Manager of the University of
Ibadan's Arts Theatre.

3879.   Anon.   "In Search of a New Aesthetic Theatre: Liking
Werewere." AFRIKA, 20, 5 (1979), 25-26.

Interview with Cameroonian researcher.

3880.   Anon.   "Über Nairobi University Players." In Eckardt, 4995,
p.   40.

3881.   Anon.   "The Best and the Brightest." WEEKLY REVIEW, 28

December 1979, pp. 28-30.

Nairobi theatre productions in 1979.

3882. Anon. "Roadshow Back from Uganda." WEEKLY REVIEW, 30 January
1981, p. 41.

Nairobi University Players on tour.

3883. Anon. "The Fantastic ´AMANDLA.´" SECHABA, July 1981, pp.
117-22.

ANC concert group on tour in Europe.

3884. Asanga, Siga. "Language in the Drama of Clark and Soyinka."
CANADIAN DRAMA, 6, 1 (1980), 102-33.

3885. Asgill, Edmondson J. "African Adaptations of Greek
Tragedies." FBSLL, 1 (1980), 67-92; ALT, 11 (1980), 175-89.

Rotimi, Soyinka, Sutherland.

3886. Ashaolu, Albert Oluwatuyi. "Modern Nigerian Drama in
English: A Descriptive and Critical Survey." DAI, 40 (1979),
2658-59A (New Brunswick).

Clark, Henshaw, Osofisan, Soyinka, et al.

3887. Baker, Donald. "African Theatre and the West." COMPARATIVE
DRAMA, 11 (1977), 227-51.

Clark, Serumaga, Soyinka, Sutherland.

3888. Barret, Lindsay. "The Popular Arts in Nigeria in the 1980s."
POSITIVE REVIEW, 1, 4 (1981), 24-27.

3889. Barton, Vivienne. "Culture: Actors, Poets, Writers...So Much
Budding Talent Here." SUNDAY NATION, 8 December 1968, pp.
15-16.

Interview with Sam Kenyi, Administrator of Uganda´s
National Theatre.

3890. ____. "Theatre: To Make it More African We Need More Help."
SUNDAY NATION, 23 March 1969, pp. 13-14.

Interview with Seth Adagala, Director of the Kenya
National Theatre.

3891. Begho, Felix O. "The Dance in Contemporary Nigerian Theatre:
A Critical Appraisal." NJH, 2 (1978), 18-33.

Ogunyemi, Rotimi, Soyinka, et al.

3892. Birihanze, James N. "African Theatre: A Call for Change." In

Mbele, 3579, pp. 72-81; UMMA, 7, 1 (1980), 37-47.

    Rpt. of BALE 922.

3893. Bloom, Harry. "Wanted: a REAL National Theatre." SUNDAY
NATION, 10 February 1963, p. 11.

    Advocates multiracial national theatre in Kenya.

3894. Böttcher-Wöbcke, Rita. "Prospero und Caliban." ZEITSCHRIFT
FÜR KULTURAUSTAUSCH, 29 (1979), 213-17.

    Aidoo, Clark, Soyinka, et al.

3895. Breach, Jonathan. "Love of the Theatre." SUNDAY NATION, 6
December 1964, p. 11.

    Interview with Robert Young, actor and director at
Donovan Maule theatre in Nairobi.

3896.* Chifunyise, Stephen J. "The Features of a Truly Zambian
Theatre." ZMag, 110 (1980), 27,32.

3897. Clark, J.P. THE HERO AS A VILLAIN. Lagos: University of
Lagos Press, 1978.

    Inaugural lecture delivered at the University of Lagos
on 19 January 1978. Discusses briefly THE OZIDI SAGA.

3898. Clark, VeVe A. "The Archaeology of Black Theatre." CRITICAL
ARTS, 2, 1 (1981), 34-50.

3899. Coplan, David. "´Sophiatown Ma-Windam´: The African
Performer and the Johannesburg Entertainment Industry."
SPEAK, 1, 5 (1978), 3-6; 1, 6 (1979), 3-11; JSAS, 5 (1979),
135-64, rpt. in Bozzoli, 3425, pp. 183-215.

3900. ____. "The Urbanization of African Performing Arts in South
Africa." DAI, 41 (1981), 4087A (Indiana).

3901. Costello, Maurice Law. "Greek Drama and the African World: A
Study of Three African Dramas in the Light of Greek
Antecedents." DAI, 41 (1981), 5090A (Southern California).

    Clark, Soyinka, Sutherland.

3902. Darling, Peter. "The Part That Our Theatre Must Play."
SUNDAY NATION, 24 August 1969, pp. 11-12.

    Interview with Peter Brown, high school headmaster
active in amateur theatre in Kenya.

3903. Davies, D. "Plays Face Censorship." NEW AFRICAN, January
1980, p. 73.

    In Sierra Leone.

3904. de Graft, J.C. "Roots in African Drama and Theatre." ALT, 8
       (1976), 1-25.

3905. Dhlomo, H.I.E. "Drama and the African." ENGLISH IN AFRICA,
       4, 2 (1977), 3-8.

       Rpt. of BALE 936.

3906. ____. "Language and National Drama." ENGLISH IN AFRICA, 4,
       2 (1977), 9-11.

       Rpt. from NEW OUTLOOK, March 1939, pp. 8-10. Argues
       for use of African languages in dramatic performances.

3907. ____. "African Drama and Poetry." ENGLISH IN AFRICA, 4, 2
       (1977), 13-17.

       Rpt. from AFRICAN OUTLOOK, 1 April 1939, pp. 88-90.
       Urges development of metrical rhythm and parallelism in
       drama and poetry.

3908. ____. "African Drama and Research." ENGLISH IN AFRICA, 4, 2
       (1977), 19-22.

       Rpt. from NATIVE TEACHERS' JOURNAL, 18 (1939), 129-33.

3910. Dieltjens, Louis, and Digby Benn. "Theater en apartheid: Het
       zwart Engelstalig theater in Zuid-Afrika [Theatre and
       Apartheid: The Black English Theatre in South Africa]."
       KREATIEF, 11, 4-5 (1977), 68-93.

       Nkosi, Rive, Pieterse, et al.

3911. Edebiri, Unionmwan. "Toward a Convention of Modern African
       Drama." WLT, 52 (1978), 565-69.

       Rotimi, Soyinka, et al.

3912. Enekwe, Ossie Onuora. "Modern Nigerian Theatre: What
       Tradition?" NSAL, 1, 1 (1978), 26-43.

       Clark, Echeruo, Ekwueme, Ezeokoli, Soyinka, et al.

3913. Enem, Uche. "National Theatre Profile." NigM, 128-129
       (1979), 35-51.

       Nigeria.

3914. Etherton, Michael. "Théâtre du Monde Noir/Théâtre in a Black
       World: The Development of a Radio Theatre Programme in
       Zambia." BULLETIN, 3 (1968), 98-108.

3915. ____. "A Popular Theatre for Zambia: The Kasama Theatre
       Workshop." BULLETIN, 4 (1969), 13-21.

3916. ____. "Trends in African Theatre." ALT, 10 (1979), 57-85.

Wide-ranging survey covering Githae-Mugo, Hevi, Ngugi, Ogunniyi, Rotimi, Sentongo, Soyinka, et al.

3917. Etherton, Michael, and Peter Magyer. "Full Streets and Empty Theatres: The Need to Relate the Forms of Drama to a Developing Society." BO, 4, 1 (1981), 46-60.

Nigeria.

3918. Euba, Femi. "The Nigerian Theatre and the Playwright." In Ogunbiyi, 4006, pp. 381-98.

Rotimi, Soyinka, et al.

3919.* Eyoh, H.N. "The Development of Drama in Cameroon, 1959-1979." Ph.D. dissertation, Leeds University, 1979.

3920. Feichtinger, C. "Emanzipationsprobleme im schwarzamerikanischen und schwarzafrikanischen Drama der Gegenwart." DAI, 39 (1979), 370C (Vienna).

Nkosi, Soyinka, et al.

3921. Fiebach, Joachim. "Nachwort." In STÜCKE AFRIKAS. Ed. Joachim Fiebach. Berlin: Henschel, 1974.

Survey.

3922. ____. "Comments on Methods of Presentation and Communication in Theatres of Europe and the Third World." In THEATRE AND SOCIAL REALITY: INTERNATIONAL COLLOQUY FOR THEATRE PEOPLE FROM COUNTRIES OF THE THIRD WORLD. Ed. Joachim Fiebach and Jutta Hengst. Berlin: GDR Centre of the International Theatre Institute, 1977. Pp. 70-73.

3923. ____. "Theater in Schwarzafrika: Theatertraditionen und importierte Konzeptionen." In Eckardt, 4995, pp. 21-26.

3924. ____. "On the Social Function of Modern African Theatre and Brecht." UMMA, 7, 1 (1980), 79-105, rpt. in Mbele, 3579, pp. 81-101.

Rpt. of BALE 953.

3925. Fiofori, Tam. "Growth of the Film Industry in Nigeria." AFRISCOPE, 11, 9 (1981), 43-45.

3926. Francis, Benjy. "Black Writing: Problems and Prospects of a Tradition: Writing for the Theatre Today." S´KETSH´, Winter 1979, pp. 10-11.

3927. ____. "At this stage..." WIETIE, 1 (n.d.), 19, 23-24; 2 (1980), 24-26.

Contemporary South African theatre.

3928.* Fraser, Robert. "Politics and the Nigerian Theatre." DAILY
       NATION, 22 June 1979.

3929. Gibbs, James. "Theatre in Malawi." ODI, 2, 1 (1977), 13-18;
       AFRISCOPE, 7, 11-12 (1977), 69-71.

       Chimombo, et al.

3930. ____. "Ghanaian Playwrights and Nigerians." LEGON OBSERVER,
       13, 11 (1981), 263.

       de Graft, Sekyi, Sutherland.

3931.* Gilliland, Marion Charlotte. "East African Drama: Folk,
       Popular and Literary." Master's thesis, University of
       Florida, 1971.

3932. Hall, Tony. "Good Taste Hasn't Left the Theatre." SUNDAY
       NATION, 23 July 1967, pp. 15-16.

       Interview with Robert Beaumont, Nairobi theatre critic
       and actor.

3933. Haresnape, Geoffrey. "English Literature: Drama." STANDARD
       ENCYCLOPEDIA OF SOUTHERN AFRICA, Vol. 12 (1976), pp. 73-74.

       Survey.

3934. Harper, Peggy, Karol Jakubowicz and Krzysztof Wolicki. "Czy
       bronić się przed synkretyzmem? [Should One Defend Oneself
       from Syncretism?]." DIALOGW, 25, 9 (1980), 118-26.

       Round table on African theatre.

3935. Harrison, Charles. "Killings in Uganda's National Theatre."
       AFRISCOPE, 8, 1-2 (1978), 38.

       Execution of John Male et al.

3936. Haster, Olivia. "E.D.A. in Ethiopia." CREATIVE DRAMA, 4, 9
       (1977), 7-13.

       International Children's Dance and Drama Centre, Addis
       Ababa.

3937. Hauptfleisch, Temple. "Theatre Research in South Africa."
       CRITICAL ARTS, 1, 3 (1980), 11-22.

3938. Hayne, Mary. "Not Much Basis for 'Foreign Domination'
       Claim." SUNDAY NATION, 14 January 1979, p. 18.

       Response to statement by Ngugi, 3988, on Kenyan theatre.

3939. Horn, Andrew. "Uhuru to Amin: The Golden Decade of Theatre
       in Uganda." LHY, 19, 1 (1978), 22-49.

       Ruganda, Sentongo, Serumaga, Zirimu, et al.

3940. ____. "Uganda's Theatre: The Exiled and the Dead." INDEX ON
       CENSORSHIP, 8, 5 (1979), 12-15.

       p'Bitek, Ruganda, Serumaga, et al.

3941. ____. "African Theatre--Docility and Dissent." INDEX ON
       CENSORSHIP, 9, 3 (1980), 9-15.

       Survey of theatre censorship in Africa.

3942. Hutchinson, P. William. "Theatre Safari in Kenya." BBT, 7
       (1976), 7-10.

3943. Inneh, Ikpowonsa. "The Nigerian National Arts Theatre."
       RADIO-TV TIMES, January 1977, p. 10.

3944. International Defence and Aid Fund. "A New Wave of Cultural
       Energy: Black Theatre in South Africa." THEATRE Q, 7, 28
       (1977-78), 57-63.

3945. Iyi-Eweka, Ademola. "The Development of Dramatic Troupes in
       Benin (Nigeria)." DAI, 40 (1980), 3632A (Wisconsin-Madison).

       Ogieiriaixi, et al.

3946. Jakubowicz, Karol. "Afryka dzisiaj (1): Kenia [Africa Today
       (1): Kenya]." DIALOGW, 25, 7 (1980), 112-18.

3947. ____. "Afryka dzisiaj (2): Ghana [Africa Today (2): Ghana]."
       DIALOGW, 25, 9 (1980), 127-33.

3948. Jeyifo, Biodun. "Literary Drama and the Search for a Popular
       Theatre in Nigeria." NigM, 128-129 (1979), 62-67; rpt. in
       Ogunbiyi, 4006, pp. 411-21.

       Clark, Osofisan, Rotimi, Soyinka, et al.

3949. ____. "Patterns and Trends in Committed African Drama."
       POSITIVE REVIEW, 1, 2 (1979), 23-26; rpt. in French in
       PEUPLES NOIRS/PEUPLES AFRICAINS, 9 (1979), 1-10.

       Imbuga, Omotoso, Osofisan.

3950. Jones, Eldred. "Steps towards the Evaluation on African
       Drama." AFRICAN PERSPECTIVES (Leiden), 1 (1977), 143-50.

       Aidoo, Easmon, Soyinka, et al.

3951. Kalejaiye, Oladipo. THE FATHER OF SECRETS, A PLAY, AND THE
       DEFIANCE OF IMITATION, AN ESSAY ON AFRICAN DRAMA. Palo Alto:

Zikawuna Books, 1978.

Essay, pp. 30-31.

3952.* Kamlongera, Christopher. "Development of Contemporary Theatre in Malawi." Master's thesis, Leeds University, 1977.

3953. Kapumpa, Mumba. "A Renaissance is Necessary." AIBEPM, 84 (1978), 74, 77-78.

In African drama.

3954. ____. "Tikwiza ku Africa." AIBEPM, 87 (1978), 100-02.

Tikwiza Theatre troupe in Zambia.

3955. ____. "Theatre: A New Challenge to Our Women." AFRICA WOMAN, 23 (1979), 52-53; rpt. as "Calling African Women." NEW AFRICAN, January 1980, pp. 72-73.

Interview with Matilda Tutu Malamafumu, Zambian actress and director.

3956. Kasoma, Kabwe. "Trends in African Theatre with Special Emphasis to the Zambia Experience." NEW CLASSIC, 5 (1978), 72-78.

3957. Kerr, David. "Three History Plays from East Central Africa." BA SHIRU, 10, 2 (1979), 58-68.

Chimombo, Masiye, et al.

3958. Khumalo, Vusi. "IPI TOMBI: Is it Just a Musical 'Front' for Apartheid?" PACE, October 1980, pp. 78-79.

3959. Klicker, Jochen R. "Othellos schwarze Bruder." BDB, 22 August 1980, pp. 2064-65.

Survey of African theatrical activity.

3960. Klíma, Vladimír. "Nigerijské drama [Nigerian Drama]." SVETOVÁ LITERATURA, 20, 5 (1975), 229-56.

3961. Kotchy, Barthélémy. "Les Sources du théâtre négro-africain." RLENA, 2 (1979), 91-103.

3962. Kugblenu, John. "The Performing Arts in Africa." WA, 19 June 1978, pp. 1180-81.

UNESCO-sponsored workshops in Accra and Lagos.

3963. Labonne, Daniel. "A Theatrical Experience in Mauritius." INTERNATIONAL THEATRE INFORMATION, Winter-Spring 1979, pp. 44-45.

French text of same article, pp. 43-44.

3964. Lampley, James. "The Unhappy Land of Camelot." AIBEPM, 93 (1979), 80-81.

South African musicals.

3965. Leshoai, B.L. "Black South African Theatre." In Ogunba and Irele, 4005, pp. 115-20.

Survey.

3966. Lindfors, Bernth. A ZULU VIEW OF VICTORIAN LONDON. Munger Africana Library Notes, 48. Pasadena: Munger Africana Library, California Institute of Technology, 1979.

Zulu performer tells of visit to England.

3967. ____. "Indigenous Performance in Alien Communities." In Massa, 3571, pp. 20-27.

South African performances in London, 1853-1977.

3968. Lokko, Sophia D. "Theatre Space: A Historical Overview of the Theatre Movement in Ghana." MD, 23 (1980), 309-19.

3969. Lushkova, T. "Stanovlenie professional'nogo teatra v stranakh Vostochnoĭ Afriki [The Makings of Professional Theatre in the Countries of Eastern Africa]." In Turchin, 4048, pp. 225-32.

3970. L'vov, N. "Teatr Afriki prokladyvaet svoĭ put' [The Theatre of Africa Paves Its Own Way]." In Turchin, 4048, pp. 233-53.

3971. ____. SOVREMENNYĬ TEATR TROPICHESKOĬ AFRIKI [Contemporary Theatre of Tropical Africa]. Moscow: Nauka, 1977.

Cameroon, Kenya, Nigeria, Uganda.

3972. ____. "U istokov afrikanskogo teatra [At the Sources of African Theatre]." In Turchin, 4048, pp. 24-38.

Nigeria, et al.

3973. Macpherson, Margaret. IF IT WORKS IT'S RIGHT: A HANDBOOK OF PLAY PRODUCTION FOR EAST AFRICAN SCHOOLS AND COLLEGES. Nairobi: East African Publishing House, 1979.

Includes discussion of many plays, especially comedies by Soyinka.

3974. ____. THE COOKING PAN AND OTHER PLAYS, WITH NOTES. Nairobi: Heinemann, 1979.

Notes on plays by Bazze-Ssentongo, Kalyegira, Matenjwa,

et al.

3975.   Makano, Roderick C. "Lilongwe Trip: Tour Manager's Report."
        DENGA, June 1977, pp. 85-91.

        University of Malawi's Travelling Theatre tour.

3976.   Manaka, Matsemela. "Theatre of the Dispossessed."
        STAFFRIDER, 3, 3 (1980), 28-30.

        Interviews with actors James Mthoba and Joe Rahube.

3977.   Mangwane, Sam. "The Black Theatre." BONA, June 1977, pp.
        46-47.

        In South Africa.

3978.   Matsix. "The Babalaz People." STAFFRIDER, 4, 3 (1981),
        32-34.

        Interview with black actors in London and discussion of
        the relevance of their experience to black theatre in
        South Africa.

3979.* Mbasela, Marrflain. "People in the Nation: Jeff Sitali."
        ZMag, 98 (1979), 18-21.

        On Zambian theatre and actor Jeff Sitali.

3980.* Melamu, M. "Perspectives on Nigerian Tragedy: A Study of
        Selected Plays by Wole Soyinka, J.P. Clark, and Ola Rotimi."
        Ph.D. dissertation, Sussex University, 1977.

3981.   ____. "Prophets and Women in Nigerian Tragedy." PULA, 1
        (1978), 43-88.

        Clark, Rotimi, Soyinka.

3982.   Mlama, Pennina. "Modern African Theatre with Special
        Emphasis on East Africa." UMMA, 7, 1 (1980), 17-35.

        Rpt. of BALE 1021.

3983.   Mohr, Robert. NO HOMAGE UNTO THE SUN: THE MISSED
        OPPORTUNITIES OF SOUTH AFRICAN THEATRE. Inaugural Lecture
        16. Cape Town: University of Cape Town, 1973.

3984.   Mshengu. "Third World Theatre." SNARL, 6 (1977), 5-7.

3985.   ____. "Tradition and Innovation in the Theatre of Workshop
        '71." THEATRE Q, 7, 28 (1977-78), 63-66.

        Condensation of BALE 1031.

3986.   ____. "After Soweto: People's Theatre and the Political

Struggle in South Africa." THEATRE Q, 9, 33 (1979), 31-38.

3987. Mwagiru, Ciugu. "The Travelling Theatre for the People, by the People." UMMA-N, 3 (1976), 26-29.

University of Nairobi troupe.

3988. Mwangi, Wangethi. "Foreign Actors Blasted." STANDARD, 10 January 1979, p. 1.

Ngugi condemns foreign domination of Kenyan theatre and cultural scene. See responses by Hayne, 3938, and Slade, 4035.

3989. Nasiru, Akanji. "Folk-Lore in Nigerian Drama: An Examination of the Works of Three Nigerian Dramatists." LHY, 19, 1 (1978), 51-63.

Ogunyemi, Rotimi, Sofola.

3990. Nazareth, Peter. "East African Drama." In Ogunba and Irele, 4005, pp. 91-113.

Ngugi, p´Bitek, Ruganda, Serumaga, Sondhi, Zirimu, et al.

3991. Ngugi, [wa Thiong´o], James. "Must We Drag Africanness into Everything?" SUNDAY NATION, 2 September 1962, p. 30.

Advocates formation of African amateur dramatic society in Nairobi.

3992. ____. "I Hope THIS Theatre Group Won´t Die, Too." SUNDAY NATION, 19 July 1964, pp. 6-7.

On performances of plays by Mphahlele and Njau staged by African Theatre Company in Nairobi.

3993. ____. "´For the First Time, the People Could See Themselves.´" GUARDIAN, 11 June 1979, p. 15; rpt. in 4400.

On Kamiriithu Educational and Cultural Centre production of NGAAHIKA NDEENDA [I will marry when I want].

3994. ____. "Entscheidung für Kenia." BDB, 22 August 1980, pp. 2045-47.

Theatre in Kenya.

3995. Ng´weno, Hilary. "How We Can Develop Culture in Kenya." SUNDAY NATION, 18 August 1968, p. 6.

On Kenya National Theatre.

3996. Nkosi, Lewis. "Post-war Drama in Africa." In WORLD DRAMA:

FROM AESCHYLUS TO ANOUILH. Ed. Allardyce Nicoll. London:
Harrap; New York: Barnes and Noble, 1976. Pp. 895-99.

Survey.

3997. Nwoko, Demas. "In Search of a New African Theatre." UNESCO
COURIER, May 1977, pp. 29, 33.

Rpt. of BALE 1039.

3998. ____. "Art and the Artist: The Performing Arts." NEW
CULTURE, 1, 11 (1979), 3-5.

3999. Nzewi, Meki. "Music, Dance, Drama and the Stage in Nigeria."
In Ogunbiyi, 4006, pp. 433-56.

4000.* Obafemi, B.O. "Cultural Heritage and Social Vision in
Contemporary Nigerian Theatre." Ph.D. dissertation, Leeds
University, 1981.

4001. Ochieng, Philip. "´Nationalise´ the National Theatre...!´"
SUNDAY NATION, 23 February 1969, p. 6.

In Kenya.

4002. Oculi, Okello. "Women in Drama at Ahmadu Bello University."
AFRICA WOMAN, 20 (1979), 52-53.

4003. Oduneye, ´Bayo. "New Directions for Theatre in Nigeria."
NEW CULTURE, 1, 6 (1979), 38-46.

4004. Ogunba, O. "Modern Drama in Africa Had to Wait for 1950´s."
RADIO-TV TIMES, 12-18 August 1968, pp. 16, 19.

4005. Ogunba, Oyin, and Abiola Irele, eds. THEATRE IN AFRICA.
Ibadan: Ibadan University Press, 1978.

Includes 3857, 3867, 3965, 3990, 5377, 6072.

4006. Ogunbiyi, Yemi, ed. DRAMA AND THEATRE IN NIGERIA; A CRITICAL
SOURCE BOOK. Foreword Garba Ashiwaju. Lagos: Nigeria
Magazine, 1981.

Rpts. BALE 888, 927, 937, 1039, 1075. Includes 3861,
3918, 3948, 3999, 4007, 4011.

4007. ____. "Nigerian Theatre and Drama: A Critical Profile." In
Ogunbiyi, 4006, pp. 3-53.

Survey covering Clark, Henshaw, Rotimi, Soyinka, et al.

4008.* Oko, A. "The Individual and the Community in Modern Nigerian
Drama: A Changing Relationship." Ph.D. dissertation, Essex
University, 1977.

4009. Olusola, Segun. "TV Drama in Our Society." DRUM (Lagos),
       November 1979, pp. 28, 66.

4010. ____. "How T.V. Drama Can Influence Society." DRUM
       (Lagos), December 1979, pp. 41-42.

4011. ____. "The Advent of Television Drama in Nigeria." In
       Ogunbiyi, 4006, pp. 370-80.

       Soyinka, et al.

4012. O'Malley, P. "Travelling Theatre Lilongwe Trip (April 1977)."
       DENGA, June 1977, pp. 81-84.

       University of Malawi.

4013. Oti, Sonny. "In Search of the Actor in Nigeria." NigM,
       126-127 (1978), 22-34.

4014. Owusu, Martin Okyere. "Drama of the Gods: Myth and Ritual in
       Seven West African Plays." DAI, 40 (1979), 2667-68A
       (Brandeis).

       Clark, Rotimi, Soyinka, Sutherland.

4015. Ozynski, Joyce. "The Market Theatre." SNARL, 4 (1976),
       18-20.

       South Africa.

4016. Pearce, Daniel. "Who IS John Moyo? Thoughts on Black
       Theatre in Zimbabwe." JCL, 11, 3 (1977), 54-58.

       School drama productions.

4017. Pendlebury, Shirley. "Jailbird's Eyeview." SNARL, 5 (1976),
       1-3.

       Interview with cast of SURVIVAL, Workshop 71 Theatre Co.

4018. Phillips, Mike. "Black Actors in Britain." AIBEPM, 117
       (1981), 69-70.

4019. Quarshie, Hugh. "Art and Africans." WA, 22 June 1981, pp.
       1410-11, 1413-15.

       Interview with South African actors John Kani and
       Winston Ntshona.

4020. Ricard, Alain. "Popular Theater in West Africa."
       ZEITSCHRIFT FÜR KULTURAUSTAUSCH, 29 (1979), 262-66.

4021. Riemenschneider, Dieter. "Westafrikanisches Drama in
       englischer Sprache: Ola Rotimi und Wole Soyinka." In Stilz,
       4043, pp. 59-71.

4022. Roberts, Sheila V. "South African Bilingual and Multilingual
       Drama of the ´Seventies.´" CANADIAN DRAMA, 6, 1 (1980),
       134-50.

       Mqayisa, Mtsaka, Mutwa, et al.

4023. Rotimi, Ola. "Drama." In THE LIVING CULTURE OF NIGERIA.
       Ed. Saburi O. Biobaku. Lagos: Nelson, 1976. Pp. 33-37.

       Clark, Soyinka, et al.

4024. Rubadiri, David. "Nairobi--Capital that´s so Full of Drama!"
       SUNDAY NATION, 28 August 1977, p. 6.

       On variety of theatrical fare.

4025. Rugyendo, Mukotani. "Approaches to the Theatre for Children
       and Youths." UMMA, 7, 1 (1980), 1-14; rpt. in Mbele, 3579,
       pp. 59-71.

       Rpt. of BALE 1062.

4026. ____. "Towards a Truly African Theatre." UMMA, 7, 1 (1980),
       49-78.

       Rpt. of BALE 1063.

4027. Salvy, Yves. "Essai d´introduction à l´art dramatique et à
       l´étude du lieu scénique en Afrique." AUBTL, 3, 1 (1976),
       127-34.

4028. Schipper-de Leeuw, Mineke. TONEEL EN MAATSCHAPPIJ IN AFRIKA
       [Theatre and Society in Africa]. Terreinverkenningen in de
       Culturele Antropologie, 8. Assen/Amsterdam: Van Gorcum,
       1977.

       Aidoo, Clark, de Graft, Easmon, Henshaw, Kasoma, Ngugi,
       Njau, Nkosi, Ogunyemi, Owusu, Rotimi, Ruganda, Soyinka,
       Sutherland, Tsaro-Wiwa, Watene, et al.

4029. ____. "Origin and Forms of Drama in the African Context."
       In Schild, 3665, pp. 55-64.

       Survey.

4030. Sentongo, Nuwa. "The Wonders of Theatre in Uganda´s Adult
       Education." SCHOOL LEAVER, 1, 2 (1974), 10-15.

4031. Sepamla, Sipho. "The Urban Cultural Scene--Theatre:
       Extracts from a Winter School Talk." S´KETSH´, Winter 1979,
       pp. 17-19.

4032. Serumaga, Robert. "History of the Abafumi Company." SUNDAY
       NATION, 29 January 1978, p. 20.

       Treatre troupe in Uganda.

4033. Shalash, Ali. AL-DRAMA AL-AFRIQIA. Cairo: Dar al-Maarif, 1979.

Soyinka, et al.

4034. Silvestru, Valentin. "Le théâtre africain en Roumanie." CAHIERS ROUMAINS D´ETUDES LITTÉRAIRES, 1 (1980), 152-53.

4035. Slade, Nigel. "A Reply to Ngugi wa Thiong´o." STANDARD, 13 January 1979, p. 11.

Response to Ngugi, 3988.

4036. Sofola, ´Zulu. "The Theatre in the Search for an African Authenticity." In AFRICAN THEOLOGY EN ROUTE. Ed. Kofi Appiah-Kubi and Sergio Torres. Maryknoll, NY: Orbis, 1979. Pp. 126-36.

Rotimi, Sofola, Soyinka.

4037. ____. "The Playwright and Theatrical Creation." NigM, 128-29 (1979), 68-74.

Soyinka et al.

4038. Sonuga, Gbenga. "The Performing Arts in Contemporary Nigeria." NEW CULTURE, 1, 1 (1978), 35-41; 1,2 (1979), 37-42.

4039.* Sowande, O.O. "Contemporary Dramatic Literature in Nigeria: A Study of Drama as an Agent of Cultural Awareness." Ph.D. dissertation, Sheffield University, 1978.

4040. Soyinka, Wole. "Morality and Aesthetics in the Ritual Archetype." In COLLOQUE SUR LITTÉRATURE ET ESTHÉTIQUE NÉGRO-AFRICAINES. Abidjan and Dakar: Nouvelles Éditions Africaines, 1979. Pp. 67-85.

Representation in drama of hero-gods Ogun, Obatala and Sango.

4041.* Steadman, Ian. "Theatre of Commitment: The Political Made Theatrical in South African Theatre." SCENARÍA, 17 (1980), 3, 47.

4042. ____. "Editorial: Culture and Context: Notes on Performance in South Africa." CRITICAL ARTS, 2, 1 (1981), 1-13.

Manaka, Maponya, et al.

4043. Stilz, Gerhard, ed. DRAMA IM COMMONWEALTH. Tübingen: Narr, 1981.

Includes 3849, 4021, 5459.

4044.   Streicher, Elretha. "From Market to Theatre." SOUTH AFRICAN
PANORAMA, 24, 4 (1979), 36-39.

Market Theatre in Johannesburg.

4045.   Tomaselli, Keyan. "Ways of Seeing." FRONTLINE, 1, 2 (1980),
35.

Manaka.

4046.   ____. "Black South African Theatre: Text and Context."
ENGLISH IN AFRICA, 8, 1 (1981), 51-58.

Manaka, et al.

4047.   ____. "The Semiotics of Alternative Theatre in South
Africa." CRITICAL ARTS, 2, 1 (1981), 14-33.

4048.   Turchin, N.M., ed. PUTI RAZVITIÎA TEATRAL´NOGO ISKUSSTVA
AFRIKI: SBORNIK NAUCHNYKH TRUDOV [The Paths of Development of
the Theatrical Art of Africa: A Collection of Scientific
Works]. Moscow: Gitis, 1981.

Includes 3969-70, 3972.

4049.   Uka, Kalu. "Drama in Nigerian Society." In Ekwensi, 3461,
pp. 177-87.

Rpt. of BALE 1092. Survey.

4050.   ____. "The Place of Drama as Medium of Mass Expression in
Nigeria." In Momodu and Schild, 3583, pp. 137-48.

Rpt. of BALE 1093.

4051.   ____. "Beyond the ´Catharsis´: The Communal Perspective of
Dramatic Appeal." NJH, 1, 1 (1977), 77-90.

Gabre-Medhin, Sofola, Sutherland.

4052.   ____. "Drama and Conscientization." In Kalu, 3524, pp.
189-208.

Soyinka and other Nigerian dramatists.

4053.   Uyovbukerhi, Atiboroko Sikerefe Akpovona. "The Idea of
Tragic Form in Nigerian Drama Written in English." DAI, 37
(1977), 6848A (Wisconsin-Madison).

Clark, Rotimi, Soyinka.

4054.   Vandenbroucke, Russell. "South African Blacksploitation."
Y/T, 8, 1 (1976), 68-71.

IPI-TOMBI.

4055.   ____. "A Brief Chronology of the Theatre in South Africa."
         THEATRE Q, 7, 28 (1977-78), 44-46; rpt. in Polish in
         DIALOGW, 23, 6 (1978), 84-87.

4056.   ____. "Chiaroscuro: A Portrait of the South African
         Theatre." THEATRE Q, 7, 28 (1977-78), 46-54; rpt. in Polish
         in DIALOGW, 23, 6 (1978), 88-98.

4057.   Vincent, Theo. "Theatre and Audience in Nigeria." BO, 4, 1
         (1981), 80-84.

4058.   Wanjala, Chris. "Theatre and Politics." AFRICAN
         PERSPECTIVES (Nairobi), 1 (1977), 30, 38.

         Githae-Mugo, Imbuga, Ngugi, Ruganda, Serumaga.

4059.   ____. "´People´s Theatre´ Must Rely on Local Talent."
         SUNDAY NATION, 20 November 1977, p. 31.

         Free Travelling Theatre in Uganda and Kenya.

See also 3387, 3462, 3574, 3579, 3586, 3608, 3628, 3655, 3710, 4067,
         4208, 4257, 4263, 4320, 4534, 4701, 4722, 4732, 4779, 4781,
         4793, 4798, 4811, 4826, 4831, 4866-67, 4873, 4878, 4880,
         4886, 4918-19, 5004, 5045-57, 5143, 5248, 5272-73, 5344-45,
         5375-77, 5379, 5381, 5388, 5390-91, 5399, 5404-06, 5510-11,
         5519, 5522, 5538, 5551, 5564-65, 5619, 5641, 5644-45, 5656,
         5670-71, 5682, 5707, 5709, 5715, 5724, 5738, 5742, 5853,
         5855, 5885, 5908-09, 5921, 5930-31, 5941-43, 5957, 5961,
         5963-64, 5987, 5996, 6002, 6013, 6051, 6068, 6071-72, 6079,
         6092.

G. POETRY

BIBLIOGRAPHY

4060. Dressler, Claus Peter. "Bibliografie Afrikanischer
Literatur: Poesie." In Eckardt, 4995, pp. 116-20.

See also 4322.

BOOKS AND ESSAYS

4061.* Adey, A.D. "Themes in South African English Poetry Since the
Second World War." Master's thesis, University of South
Africa, 1976.

   Mtshali, et al.

4062.* Alvarez-Péreyre, Jacques. "L'Apartheid et la poésie engagée
sud-africaine de langue anglaise." Doctorat d'État,
University of Grenoble III, 1977.

   Later published as 4063.

4063. ____. LES GUETTEURS DE L'AUBE; POÉSIE ET APARTHEID.
Grenoble: Presses Universitaires de Grenoble, 1979.

   Brutus, Matthews, Mphahlele, Mtshali, Nortje, Pieterse,
   Sepamla, Serote, et al.

4064. Amanuddin, Syed. "Toward a View of Commonwealth Poetic
Tradition." In Narasimhaiah, 3593, pp. 423-32; rpt. in
Amanuddin, 4065.

4065. ____. WORLD POETRY IN ENGLISH: ESSAYS AND INTERVIEWS. New
Delhi: Sterling Publishers, 1981.

   Brutus, Okigbo, et al. Includes 4064, 5357.

4066. Anon. "West African Poetry." NIGERIAN CHRISTIAN, 6, 2
(1972), 16-17.

4067. Anon. "Background Story to the Creation of 'An Anthem to
Liberation.'" PELCULEF NEWSLETTER, 1, 1 (1978), 7-11.

   Poetry reading program staged by Pelandaba Cultural
   Effort in Gaberone.

4068. Anon. "Guy Butler and Chris Mann on A NEW BOOK OF SOUTH
AFRICAN VERSE IN ENGLISH." ENGLISH IN AFRICA, 6, 1 (1979),
1-11.

   Interview.

4069. Anon. "First Interlude: Major New Voices (1)." OPON IFA, 1,

2 (1980), 2-12.

Acholonu, Fatoba, Garuba, Opoku-Agyemang, Osundare.

4070.   Apronti, Jawa. "Ghanaian Poetry in the 1970's." In
Ogungbesan, 3617, pp. 31-44.

Anyidoho, Awoonor, Azasu, de Graft, Egblewogbe,
Kayper-Mensah, Okai, Therson-Cofie, et al.

4071.   Archibong, Francis Mendie. "Poetry in Daily Life." QUEST,
17 (1979), 135-36.

Survey.

4072.   Awoonor, Kofi. "The Poem, the Poet and the Human Condition:
Some Aspects of Recent West African Poetry." ASEMKA, 5
(1979), 1-23.

Anyidoho, Ndu, Odamtten, Opoku-Agyemang, Soyinka, Uka,
et al.

4073.* Balogun, S.I. NOTES AND EXERCISES ON MODERN POETRY FROM
AFRICA. Ibadan: Onibonoje Press, 1967.

Exam notes to Moore and Beier anthology.

4074.* Bornstein, Rita. "Revolutionary Black Poetry, 1960-1970."
Master's thesis, Florida Atlantic University, 1971.

4075.   Bruner, Charlotte H., and David K. Bruner. REVERBERATIONS:
BLACK POETS THERE AND HERE. Ames: Iowa State University
Research Foundation, 1977.

Videotape script with headnotes on individual poets.

4076.   Brutus, Dennis. "Vorwort." In MEIN SCHWARZER BRUDER:
GEDICHTE FÜR AFRIKA. Ed. Barbara Haeger. Schriften für die
Anti-Apartheid-Bewegung, 1. Tübingen: Bernhard Bruscha,
1980. P. 9.

4077.   Bukenya, Austin Lwanga. NOTES ON EAST AFRICAN POETRY.
H.E.B. Student's Guide, 13. Nairobi: Heinemann Educational
Books, 1978.

On selections in POEMS FROM EAST AFRICA, ed. David Cook
and David Rubadiri.

4078.   Burton, S.H., and C.J.H. Chacksfield. AFRICAN POETRY IN
ENGLISH: AN INTRODUCTION TO PRACTICAL CRITICISM. London and
Basingstoke: Macmillan, 1979.

Armattoe, Brew, Clark, Djoleto, Erapu, Kassam, Kayper-
Mensah, Okara, Okigbo, p'Bitek, Soyinka, Tejani,
Wangusa, Wonodi, et al.

4079. Butler, F.G. "English Literature: Poetry, 1970-75."
       STANDARD ENCYCLOPEDIA OF SOUTHERN AFRICA, Vol. 12 (1976),
       pp. 70-72.

       Survey.

4080. Calder, Angus. "Under Zomba Plateau: The New Malawian
       Poetry." KUNAPIPI, 1, 2 (1979), 59-67.

       Chimombo, Mapanje, Mnthali, Mphande, Mvula, Nazombe.

4081. Chapman, Michael. "Voices of Apocalypse: Soweto Poetry, Its
       Origins and Directions." UES, 19, 2 (1981), 17-21.

       Abrahams, H.I.E. Dhlomo, Gwala, Mtshali, Sepamla,
       Serote, et al.

4082. Chinweizu, Onwuchekwa Jemie, and Ihechukwu Madubuike.
       "Soyinka's 'Neo-Tarzanism': A Reply." OKIKE, 14 (1978),
       43-51.

       Response to BALE 1218 with poetry by Markwei and Soyinka
       used as examples.

4083. Chukwu, Vincent Onyema. "Where God and the Poet Meet (Three
       New Nsukka Poets)." MUSE, 13 (1981), 29-34.

       Nwankwor, Obi, Ogbuagu.

4084. Clark, J.P. "The Elite's Great Tangle." RADIO-TV TIMES,
       18-24 January 1965, pp. 8, 19-20.

       Okara, Soyinka.

4085. ____. "Exciting Poets in Black Africa Now." RADIO-TV TIMES,
       25-31 January 1965, pp. 10, 19.

       Awoonor, Okigbo, et al.

4086. Couzens, Tim. "Black Poetry in Africa." In Wilhelm and
       Polley, 4167, pp. 47-59.

       Achebe, Mtshali, et al.

4087. ____. "Politics and Black Poetry in South Afirca 1930-1950."
       AFRICA PERSPECTIVE, 7 (1978), 1-15.

       Abrahams, H.I.E. Dhlomo, Ngubane, et al.

4088. Davis, Hedy I. "Insult to Poets." CONTRAST, 12, 2 (1978),
       88-90.

       Response to Ullyatt, 4161, citing poetry of Motjuwadi
       and Nortje.

4088a. Diakhate, Lamine. "Modern African Poetry." In FESTAC, 5018,
       pp. 80-81, 84-85.

       Rev. of BALE 1144.

4089.* Echeruo, Michael J.C. POETS, PROPHETS AND PROFESSORS.
       Ibadan: Ibadan University Press, 1977.

       Inaugural lecture.

4090. Egudu, R.N. "Social Ataraxia in East African Poetry."
       BUSARA, 8, 1 (1976), 47-57.

       Angira, Hauli, Ntiru, p´Bitek, Ruganda, Tejani, et al.

4091. _____. FOUR MODERN WEST AFRICAN POETS. New York: Nok, 1977.

       Rev. of BALE 1148. Awoonor, Clark, Okigbo, Peters.

4092. _____. MODERN AFRICAN POETRY AND THE AFRICAN PREDICAMENT.
       London and Basingstoke: Macmillan; New York: Barnes and
       Noble, 1978.

       Achebe, Angira, Awoonor, Brutus, Clark, Kgositsile,
       Nortje, Ntiru, Okigbo, p´Bitek, Soyinka.

4093. _____. "Anglophone African Poetry and Vernacular Rhetoric:
       The Example of Okigbo." LARES, 1, 1 (1979), 104-13; rpt. in
       Banjo, 3415, pp. 296-308.

       Principally Okigbo but also Awoonor, p´Bitek, Soyinka,
       Wonodi, et al.

4094. El-Mottalibi, Malek. "Assessment of Poetry in LOTUS 1973."
       LAAW, 29 (1976), 81-83.

       African and Asian poets.

4095. Emmett, Tony. "Oral, Political and Communal Aspects of
       Township Poetry in the Mid-Seventies." ENGLISH IN AFRICA, 6,
       1 (1979), 72-81.

       Sepamla, et al.

4096. Enekwe, Ossie Onuora. "Introduction to Anglophone Poetry of
       West and South Africa." In AFTERMATH: AN ANTHOLOGY OF POEMS
       IN ENGLISH FROM AFRICA, ASIA, AND THE CARIBBEAN. Ed. Roger
       Weaver and Joseph Bruchac. Greenwood Review Press Chapbook,
       22. Greenfield Center, NY: Greenfield Review Press, 1977.
       Pp. 2-4.

4097. Ezeh, J.E. NOTES AND QUESTIONS ON WEST AFRICAN VERSE
       (SELECTED POEMS) FOR W.A.S.C./G.C.E. EXAMINATIONS. Ibadan:
       Aromolaran Publishing Co., Ltd., 1973. Rpt. of 1970 ed.

Awoonor, Brew, Clark, Okara, Peters, Soyinka, et al.

4098. Fraser, Robert. "Poets´ Platform." WA, 27 August 1979, pp. 1556-57.

Poetry in WEST AFRICA.

4099. ____. "Africa´s Subversive Litanies." INDEX ON CENSORSHIP, 9, 5 (1980), 26-29.

Anyidoho, Awoonor, Mapanje, Ofeimun, et al.

4100. Goodwin, Ken. "Past, Present, and Future in African Poetry." SPAN, 13 (1981), 40-55.

Clark, M. Kunene.

4101. Gowda, H.H. Anniah. "Modern Commonwealth Poetry Outside England: A Personal View." LHY, 18, 2 (1977), 41-51.

Survey.

4102. Graham, R. "Poetry in Rhodesia." ZAMBEZIA, 6 (1978), 187-215.

Chimsoro, Kadhani, Marechera, Mungoshi, Zimunya, et al.

4103. Haresnape, Geoffrey. "´A Question of Black and White?´ The Contemporary Situation in South African English Poetry." In Wilhelm and Polley, 4167, pp. 35-46.

Survey.

4104. ____. "The Creative Artist in Contemporary South Africa." ENGLISH IN AFRICA, 8, 1 (1981), 45-50.

Serote, et al.

4105. Horn, Peter. "´When it Rains, it Rains´: U.S. Black Consciousness and Lyric Poetry in South Africa." SPEAK, 1, 5 (1978), 7-11.

Survey.

4106. House, Amelia. "A Matter of Commitment." PA, 109 (1979), 107-15.

South African poetry, especially works by Brutus, Kgositsile, Mtshali, Pieterse, Serote.

4107. Ibitokun, Benedict M. "The Image of the Bird in Modern African Poetry." BA SHIRU, 10, 2 (1979), 69-77.

Awoonor, Clark, Datta, Duodu, Okigbo, et al.

4108.   Ifediba, B.O.   "The Protest Element in West and South African
         Poetry." NIGERBIBLIOS, 3, 3 (1978), 18-20.

4109.* Jabbi, Bu-Buakei.   WEST AFRICAN POEMS (FIFTEEN ANALYSES).
        Freetown: Fourah Bay Bookshop, 1974.

        Clark, Okara, Soyinka.

4110.   Kamin, Wayne. "Politics and Poetry in South Africa." GAR,
         31 (1977) 18-19.

4111.   Kemoli, Arthur. "Music and the Creative Imagination in
         Africa." In Gachukia and Akivaga, 4799, pp. 51-61.

         Oculi, Okigbo, p'Bitek, et al.

4112.   Klíma, Vladimír. "The Progress of Sub-Saharan Poetry." ArO,
         45 (1977), 193-200.

4113.   ____. "Expedice začíná. [An Expedition Begins]." In ČERNÝ
         ORFEUS: MODERNÍ POEZIE TROPICKÉ AFRIKY [Black Orpheus: Modern
         Poetry of Tropical Africa]. Ed. Vladimír Klíma. Prague:
         Klub Přátel Poezie, Československý spisovatel, 1977. Pp.
         11-23.

         Survey serving as introduction to anthology of poems in
         translation.

4114.   ____. "Sub-Saharan Poetry Aiming at Progress." In Gruner,
         3501, pp. 335-39.

4115.   Knipp, Thomas. "Militancy and Irony: The Mood of West
         African Poetry in the Seventies." BA SHIRU, 8, 1 (1977),
         43-55.

         Achebe, Awoonor, Clark, Peters, Soyinka, et al.

4116.   ____. "Traditional Religion in Modern West African Poetry."
         BA SHIRU, 10, 1 (1979), 4-13.

         Awoonor, Okigbo, Soyinka, et al.

4117.   Krampah, D.E.K. HELPING WITH LITERATURE. Tema, Ghana:
         Ghana Publishing Corp., 1979.

         Brew, Clark, Okara, Peters, et al.

4118.* Luvai, Arthur I. "The Unacknowledged Negritude in African
        Anglophone Poets, with Special Reference to Soyinka, Okigbo
        and Achebe." Master's thesis, University of Nairobi, 1975.

4119.   ____. "For Whom Does the African Poet Write? An Examination
         of (Form/Content in) the Poetry of Okigbo and Soyinka."
         BUSARA, 8, 2 (1976), 38-52.

4120.   ____. "Negritude in Schools: Francophone or Anglophone
Poetry: A Short Appraisal of the Problem with West African
Examples." In Gachukia and Akivaga, 4799, pp. 180-94.

Okara, Okigbo, Soyinka, et al.

4121.   Madu, Chika C. GUIDES TO AFRICAN POETRY FOR W.A.S.C. AND
OTHER EXAMINATIONS. Onitsha: University Publishing Co.,
1976.

Brew, Clark, Kariuki, Okara, Rubadiri, Soyinka, et al.

4122.   Maduakor, Hezzy. "Peter Thomas and the Development of Modern
Nigerian Poetry." RAL, 11 (1980), 84-99.

Azuonye, Clark, Ndu, Okigbo, Soyinka, Wonodi, et al.

4123.   Maduakor, Obi. "The Poet and His Inner World: Subjective
Experience in the Poetry of Christopher Okigbo and Wole
Soyinka." UFAHAMU, 9, 3 (1979-80), 23-41.

4124.   Mapanje, Jack. "New Verse in Malawi." ODI, 2, 1 (1977),
24-28.

Survey.

4125.   Mark, Ellen. "STAFFRIDER Poets." GAR, 34 (1980), 22-23.

Gwala, et al.

4126.   Mensah, Augustine Nuamah. "The Black Aesthetic: A
Cross-Cultural Perspective." DAI, 40 (1980), 6272A (Iowa).

Rubadiri, et al.

4127.   Mmadu, C. GUIDE TO AFRICAN POETRY. Onitsha: University
Publishing Co., 1977.

4128.   Mphahlele, Ezekiel. "The Voice of Prophecy in African
Poetry." ENGLISH IN AFRICA, 6, 1 (1979), 33-45.

Rpt. of BALE 1189. Survey.

4129.   Muchemwa, K.Z. "Introduction." In ZIMBABWEAN POETRY IN
ENGLISH: AN ANTHOLOGY. Ed. K.Z. Muchemwa. Mambo Writers
Series, 4. Gwelo: Mambo Press, 1978.

Survey.

4130.   Mzite, David. "Politics in African Poetry." MARANG, (1978),
55-63.

Brutus, de Graft, Hauli, Liyong, p'Bitek.

4131.   Ngandu Nkashama, P. "Méthodologie pour une poétique africaine."   AFRICAN PERSPECTIVES (Leiden), 1 (1977), 55-65.

4132.* Niekerk, A.S. van.   "God, the Powers, and Man in the Works
of Some Black South African Poets of the Seventies."   D.D.
dissertation, University of Pretoria, 1980.

Gwala, Mtshali, Sepamla, Serote, et al.

4133. ____. "Wit op Swart: Gedigte van die Sewentigerjare [White
on Black: Poetry of the Seventies]." BLOODY HORSE, 4 (1981),
73-79.

Gwala, Mtshali, Sepamla, Serote, et al.

4134. Nkondo, Gessler Moses. "The Human Image in South African
English Poetry." AT, 27, 3 (1980), 5-18.

Brutus, et al.

4135. Nwoga, Donatus I. "Religion in Modern West African Poetry."
In Nwoga, 3611, pp. 117-29.

Awoonor, Echeruo, Okigbo.

4136. ____. "Modern African Poetry: The Domestication of a
Tradition." ALT, 10 (1979), 32-56.

Brutus, Chinweizu, Echeruo, Ofeimun, Okigbo, Omotoso,
p´Bitek, et al.

4137. Obiols, Maria Rosa. "Pan-African Poetry in Translation."
DAI, 40 (1980), 5853-54A (Southern California).

Translation into Spanish of poems in English from
Africa, the West Indies, and North America.

4138. Obuke, Okpure O. "The Poetry of Wole Soyinka and J.P. Clark:
A Comparative Analysis." WLT, 52 (1978), 216-23.

4139. Ogungbesan, Kolawole, and David Woolger. IMAGES AND
IMPRESSIONS: AN OXFORD SENIOR POETRY COURSE. Oxford: Oxford
University Press, 1978.

Brief comments on numerous poems.

4140. Ogunniyi, ´Dayo. THE TEACHING OF POETRY: BEING A TEACHERS´
BOOK TO A NEW POETRY BOOK FOR SCHOOLS AND COLLEGES BOOKS I &
II. Ibadan: Onibonoje Press, 1971.

Brief notes on numerous poems.

4141. Okara, Gabriel. "Poetry and Oral English." JNESA, 8, 1
(1976), 41-49.

4142. Okwu, Edward Chukwuemeka.   "The Artist-figure in Modern West

African Poetry: An Approach to the Poetry of Awoonor, Okigbo and Soyinka." DAI, 39 (1979), 5505A (California-Los Angeles).

4143. Onukaogu, Abalogu. "Revising Your Poetry at a Glance: Based on the 1977/78 WASC Syllabus." MUSE, 10 (1978), 45-53.

Clark, Kariuki, Okara, Rubadiri, Soyinka, et al.

4144.* Opali, Fred. "Thematic Patterns in Contemporary East African Poetry." Master's thesis, Makerere University, 1980.

4145. Pauker, John. "Five African Poems." NEW REPUBLIC, 28 April 1973, pp. 28-29.

Brief introduction to samples of verse.

4146. Povey, John F. "I am the Voice -- Three South African Poets: Dennis Brutus, Keorapetse Kgositsile, and Oswald Mbuyiseni Mtshali." WLWE, 16 (1977), 263-80.

4147. ____. "The Role of the African Poet." SARP, 4 (1979), 49-58.

Survey of verse by Angira, Kgositsile, Ntiru, et al.

4148. Ravenscroft, Arthur. "Contemporary Poetry from Black South Africa." LCrit, 12, 4 (1977), 33-52.

Brutus, Mtshali, Sepamla, Serote, et al.

4149. Rive, Richard. "Black Poets of the Seventies." ENGLISH IN AFRICA, 4, 1 (1977), 47-54; rpt. in Rive, 3652.

Mtshali, Sepamla, Serote.

4150. Roberts, Sheila. "The Black South African Township Poets of the Seventies." GAf, 18, 2 (1980), 79-93.

Survey.

4151. Roscoe, A.A. "Comment." ODI, 2, 1 (1977), 5-8.

Poetry in Zambia, Rhodesia and Malawi; rpt. in 3655.

4152. Rushing, Andrea Benton. "Comparative Study of the Idea of Mother in Contemporary African and African-American Poetry." CLQ, 15 (1979), 275-88.

Survey.

4153. Saunders, Walter. "Satire in Contemporary South African English Poetry." In Wilhelm and Polley, 4167, pp. 71-81.

Gwala, Mtshali, Vilakazi, et al.

4154.   Senanu, K.E. "Language in Contemporary African Verse." In
        Banjo, 3415, pp. 212-22.

        Awoonor, Brew, Okara, Okigbo, Soyinka, et al.

4155.   Serote, Mongane. "Preface to Poetry Anthology ´Shaya.´"
        PELCULEF NEWSLETTER, 1, 1 (1978), 3-6.

        Poetry by South African exiles in Botswana.

4156.   Taiwo, Oladele. "Two Incantations to ´Abiku.´" In Momodu
        and Schild, 3583, pp. 166-81.

        Rpt. of BALE 1221. Poems by Clark and Soyinka.

4157.   Tejani, Bahadur. "Nairobi´s Enlightened Conscience?" SUNDAY
        NATION, 18 October 1970, pp. 14-15.

        Survey of urban poetry in Kenya.

4158.   Thomas, Peter. "From the Hills of Nsukka." RCR, 6, 1
        (1969), 7.

        Followed by examples of undergraduate verse from the
        University of Nigeria, pp. 8-15.

4159.   ____. "Poetry from Nsukka Since the Biafran War." In
        McLeod, 3565, pp. 23-29; WLT, 55 (1981), 40-42.

        Egudu, Enekwe, Ndu, Okafor, Okigbo, Udechukwu, Wonodi.

4160.* Ugboma, Paul. CRITICAL NOTES ON SOME WEST AFRICAN POEMS.
        Calabar: Scholars Press, 1980.

4161.   Ullyatt, A.G. "Dilemmas in Black Poetry." CONTRAST, 11, 4
        (1977), 51-62.

        Ineptitude in poetry of Ka-Miya, Motjuwadi, Mtshali, et
        al. See responses by Davis, 4088; Slabbert, 4249; and
        Sole, 4253.

4162.* Umeh, Patrick Okechuku. "Nigerian Traditions and Modern
        Nigerian Poetry." Master´s thesis, University of Nigeria,
        1979.

        Okigbo, Soyinka.

4163.   Wake, Clive. "Poetry of the Last Five Years." ALT, 10
        (1979), 233-42.

        Survey.

4164.   Wanjala, Chris L. "Discovering East African Poets." In
        Gachukia and Akivaga, 4799, pp. 77-90.

Buruga, Mbiti, Ntiru, p´Bitek, et al.

4165. Webb, Hugh. "The Flash of Fire: Poems from Africa." WLWE, 18 (1979), 78-89.

Peters, Soyinka, et al.

4166. Wilhelm, Peter. "Student Poetry at a Dead End." WITS STUDENT, 20 March 1979, p. 8.

In South Africa.

4167. Wilhelm, Peter, and James A. Polley, eds. POETRY SOUTH AFRICA: SELECTED PAPERS FROM POETRY ´74. Johannesburg: Donker, 1976.

Part of proceedings of National Poetry Conference, University of Cape Town, January 1974. Includes 4086, 4103, 4153.

4168. Xihoshi, Mokoena. "Poetry Towards the Revolution." SECHABA, April 1981, pp. 15-18; May 1981, pp. 13-19; June 1981, pp. 12-17; October 1981, pp. 26-29.

Gwala, House, Motjuwadi, Ndebele, Sepamla, et al.

See also 3385, 3387, 3393-94, 3438, 3582, 3586, 3591, 3608, 3628, 3655, 3666, 3710, 3712, 3907, 4187, 4249, 4253, 4383, 4460, 4490, 4496, 4525, 4549, 4597, 4622, 4711, 4803, 4827, 4850, 4852, 4965, 5144, 5149, 5157, 5163, 5179, 5232, 5277, 5293-94, 5327, 5335, 5339, 5348-49, 5356-65, 5373-74, 5387, 5389-90, 5398, 5562, 5575, 5615-16, 5777-84, 5814, 5816-17, 5823, 5827-36, 5849, 5990, 5993, 5998, 6015, 6017, 6037-38, 6050, 6064, 6067, 6078.

H. CRITICISM

BIBLIOGRAPHY

4169. Baldwin, Claudia, comp. NIGERIAN LITERATURE: A BIBLIOGRAPHY OF CRITICISM, 1952-76. Boston: G.K. Hall, 1980.

4170. Lindfors, Bernth. BLACK AFRICAN LITERATURE IN ENGLISH: A GUIDE TO INFORMATION SOURCES. American Literature, English Literature, and World Literature in English Information Guide Series, 23. Detroit: Gale, 1979.

4171. _____. "Selected Bibliography of Scholarship and Criticism." In Beier, 3422, pp. 289-98.

See also 3309, 3661, 3717.

BOOKS AND ESSAYS

4172. Abrahams, Cecil. "Western Literary Criticism and African Creative Writing." In McLeod, 3565, pp. 10-22.

4173. _____. "The African Writer and the Western Critic." WLWE, 18 (1979), 6-7.

> Introduction to special issue on literary criticism.

4174. Adebayo, Grace Aduke. "A crítica do romance da África Ocidental de língua francesa e inglesa: evolução e estado actual." AFRICA (Lisbon), 11 (1981), 10-18.

4175. Ade Ojo, S. "Subjectivity and Objectivity in the Criticism of Neo-African Literature." AFRICAN PERSPECTIVES (Leiden), 1, (1977), 43-54.

4176. Alanté-Lima, Willy. "Le Critique noir et son peuple comme créateur de civilisation." In LE CRITIQUE AFRICAIN, 4176, pp. 135-53.

4177. Amadi-Tshiwala, Regina. "Critical Bearings in African Literature." PA, 115 (1980), 148-55.

4178. Anon. LE CRITIQUE AFRICAIN ET SON PEUPLE COMME PRODUCTEUR DE CIVILISATION/THE AFRICAN CRITIC AND HIS PEOPLE AS PRODUCERS OF CIVILIZATION. Paris: Présence Africaine, 1977.

> Proceedings of 1973 colloquium in Yaoundé organized by Society of African Culture and University of Cameroon. Includes 3477, 3609, 4176, 4189, 4194, 4196, 4201, 4215, 4219-20, 4226, 4229-30, 4232, 4245, 4248, 4258-59, 4261, 4269, 4348, 6041.

4179. Anozie, Sunday O. STRUCTURAL MODELS AND AFRICAN POETICS: TOWARDS A PRAGMATIC THEORY OF LITERATURE. London, Boston and

Henley: Routledge and Kegan Paul, 1981.

4180.   Armah, Ayi Kwei. "Larsony or Fiction as Criticism of
Fiction." ASEMKA, 4 (1976), 1-14; FIRST WORLD, 1, 2 (1977),
50-55; NEW CLASSIC, 4 (1977), 33-45; POSITIVE REVIEW, 1
(1978), 11-14.

On Charles R. Larson, THE EMERGENCE OF AFRICAN FICTION,
BALE 751.

4181.   Ashcroft, W.D. "The Function of Criticism in a Pluralist
World." NLRev, 3 (1977), 3-14.

Achebe, Okara, et al.

4182.   Bailly, Séry Z. "A propos de la revalorisation actuelle de la
forme chez les critiques africaines." RLENA, 3 (1981),
71-78.

4183.   Bishop, Rand. "African Critics and the Western Literary
Tradition." BA SHIRU, 8, 1 (1977), 65-75.

4184.   ____. "African Literature for Whom? The Janus-like Function
of African Literary Criticism." PA, 101-02 (1977), 57-80.

4185.   Breitinger, Eckhard. "Afrikanische Literatur und der
westliche Kritiker/Leser." ZEITSCHRIFT FÜR KULTURAUSTAUSCH,
29 (1979), 280-89.

Amadi, Okara, Tutuola, et al.

4186.   Brown, Lloyd W. "The Black Aesthetic and Comparative
Criticism." In ACTES DU VIIe CONGRÈS DE L'ASSOCIATION
INTERNATIONALE DE LITTÉRATURE COMPARÉE/PROCEEDINGS OF THE 7TH
CONGRESS OF THE INTERNATIONAL COMPARATIVE LITERATURE
ASSOCIATION, I: LITTÉRATURES AMÉRICAINES: DÉPENDANCE,
INDÉPENDANCE, INTERDÉPENDANCE/LITERATURES OF AMERICA:
DEPENDENCE, INDEPENDENCE, INTERDEPENDENCE. Ed. Milan
V. Dimić and Eva Kushner, Stuttgart: Bieber, 1979. Pp.
367-71.

Rpt. of BALE 1260. Mphahlele et al.

4187.   Chinweizu; Onwuchekwa Jemie; and Ihechukwu Madubuike. TOWARD
THE DECOLONIZATION OF AFRICAN LITERATURE, VOLUME I: AFRICAN
FICTION AND POETRY AND THEIR CRITICS. Enugu: Fourth
Dimension, 1980.

Achebe, Anozie, Armah, Awoonor, Clark, Echeruo, Ekwensi,
Irele, Izevbaye, Jones, M. Kunene, Ngugi, Nwoga,
Obiechina, Okigbo, Palmer, p'Bitek, Peters, Soyinka,
Tutuola, et al. Expansion of BALE 1265.

4188.   Condé, Maryse. "Non-spécificité de la critique littéraire
´africaine.´" AFRICAN PERSPECTIVES (Leiden), 1 (1977),

35-41.

4189. ____. "Impasses de la critique africaine." In LE CRITIQUE
        AFRICAIN, 4178, pp. 417-26.

4190. Cope, Jack. "Notes." CONTRAST, 12, 2 (1978), 3, 94-96. On
        criticism of, from and in CONTRAST; see response by
        Maughan-Brown, 4228.

4191. Cornwell, Gareth. "Evaluating Protest Fiction." ENGLISH IN
        AFRICA, 7, 1 (1980), 51-70.

        Boetie, La Guma, Matthews, et al.

4192. Couzens, Tim. "Criticism of South African Literature." WIP,
        2 (1978), 41-52.

        Response to Sole, 4250.

4193. Cullinan, Patrick. "Comment: An Open Letter to the SUNDAY
        TIMES." BLOODY HORSE, 3 (1981), 4, 40.

        On poor book reviewing in the SUNDAY TIMES (S. Africa).

4194. Dabo, S.K. "African Literature and the African Critic." In
        LE CRITIQUE AFRICAIN, 4178, pp. 352-82.

        Achebe, Conton, et al.

4195. Dada, P.O. "Marxist Criticism and African Literature."
        GANGA, 2, 4 (1980), 15-23.

4196. Diagne, Pathé. "La Critique Littéraire africaine." In LE
        CRITIQUE AFRICAIN, 4178, pp. 429-40.

4197. Dogbe, Yves-Emmanuel. "Critique littéraire et tendances
        critiques des littératures africaines." ALA, 50 (1978),
        15-20.

        Followed by discussion, pp. 21-22.

4198. du Plessis, Phil. "Black Cats in Dark Rooms (in Search of
        Useful Critics)." HERESY, 3 (1981), 42-47.

        On Gray, 3494, et al.

4199. Eko, Ebele. "The Problem of Cross-Cultural Reception: Three
        Nigerian Writers in England and America." COMPARATIST, 1
        (1977), 11-15.

        Achebe, Soyinka, Tutuola.

4200. Emeto, Julie. "Critique littéraire: L'Approche sociologique
        est-elle efficace?" PFr, 17 (1978), 31-43.

4201. Etsia, Elate Mike Adolf. "The African Author as a Critic."
       In LE CRITIQUE AFRICAIN, 4178, pp. 402-16.

           Achebe, Soyinka, et al.

4202. Frank, Katherine. "Feminist Criticism and the African
       Novel." FBSLL, 2 (1981), 1-23.

4203. Gérard, Albert. "Sur l'historiographie des littératures
       écrites de l'afrique." ETHIOPIQUES, Special No. (November
       1976), pp. 135-42; CREL, 1 (1979), 58-66.

4204. Gowda, H.H. Anniah. "The Colonial Encounter--Criticism."
       LHY, 21, 2 (1980), 78-81.

4205. Gray, Stephen. "The Need for a History of South African
       English Literature." STANDPUNTE, 129 (1977), 36-45.

4206. ____. "Critical Approach to English South African
       Literature." INSPAN, 1, 1 (1978), 43-52.

4207. ____. "Problems of Historiography of South African English
       Literature from Union to the End of the Commonwealth Period
       (1910-1961)." WLWE, 20, (1981), 181-90.

4208. Hagher, Iyorwuese. "The Aesthetic Problem in the Criticism
       of African Drama." UFAHAMU, 10, 1-2 (1980-81), 156-65.

4209. Healy, Jack. "The Louvre, the Musée de l'Homme and the
       Criticism of African Literature." ACLALSB, 5, 3 (1980),
       13-25.

4210. Hofmeyr, Isabel. "'Problems of Creative Writers': A Reply."
       WIP, 2 (1977), 31-37.

           Reply to Sole, 4250.

4211. ____. "The State of South African Literary Criticism."
       ENGLISH IN AFRICA, 6, 2 (1979), 39-50.

4212. Houbein, Lolo. "An Old Creation Myth Retold: Literary
       Criticism in New Literature in English." NLRev, 3 (1977),
       29-34.

4213. Iheakaram, Paul O. "Criticism of African Literature." In
       Ekwensi, 3461, pp. 142-44.

4214. Ijomah, Chuma P. "La Littérature africaine: renouveau
       romanesque et critique littéraire." PFr, 16 (1978), 11-18.

4215. Ikiddeh, Ime. "Writers and Values: Aesthetic and Ethical
       Questions in the Criticism of African Literature." In LE
       CRITIQUE AFRICAIN, 4178, pp. 80-94.

           Clark, Mphahlele, Ngugi, Okigbo, Soyinka, et al.

4216. Irele, Abiola. "Studying African Literature." AFRICAN PERSPECTIVES (Leiden), 1 (1977), 11-23; NIGERIAN JOURNAL OF THE HUMANITIES, 1, 1 (1977), 5-17; rpt. in Irele, 3517.

4217. Izevbaye, D.S. "Phrase and Paraphrase: Problems and Principles in African Criticism." AFRICAN PERSPECTIVES (Leiden), 1 (1977), 25-34.

        Okigbo, Soyinka, et al.

4218. Jabbi, Bu-Buakei. "Influence and Originality in African Writing." ALT, 10 (1979), 106-23; OBSIDIAN, 6, 1-2 (1980), 7-23.

        Achebe, Mazrui, Palmer, Soyinka, et al.

4219. Jones, Eldred. "The Role of the African Critic." In LE CRITIQUE AFRICAIN, 4178, pp. 189-96.

4220. Kane, Mohamadou. "Sur la critique de la littérature africaine moderne." In LE CRITIQUE AFRICAIN, 4178, pp. 257-75.

4221. Kesteloot, lilyan. "Esthétique africaine et critique littéraire." In COLLOQUE SUR LITTÉRATURE, 3403, pp. 303-09.

4222. Killam, G.D. "A Canadian Critic and Teacher of Commonwealth Literature." In Massa, 3571, pp. 147-52.

4223. Knappert, Jan. "Towards a Literature of Essence in Africa: In Defence of Tradition." PQM, 6, 3-4 (1981), 272-76.

        Discussion of ALT 9.

4224. Kom, Ambroise. "Pour une littérature comparée du monde noir." PFr, 16 (1978), 33-45.

4225. Makouta M'boukou, J.-P. "Tatonnements de la critique des littératures africaines." ALA, 50 (1978), 7-14.

4226. Mariko, N'Tji Idriss. "Le Critique africain et son peuple comme producteur de civilisation." In LE CRITIQUE AFRICAIN, 4178, pp. 166-86.

4227. Mateso, Locha. "Critique littéraire et ressources de l'oralité." ALA, 50 (1978), 64-68.

4228. Maughan-Brown, D.A. "Black Literature Debate: Human Beings Behind the Work." CONTRAST, 12, 4 (1979), 86-95.

        Response to editorial by Cope, 4190.

4229. Maximin, Daniel. "Critique de l'activité critique dans le Tiers-Monde noir." In LE CRITIQUE AFRICAIN, 4178, pp.

314-37.

4230.   Nata, Théophile. "Réflexion critique sur la littérature et
        la critique négro-africaines." In LE CRITIQUE AFRICAIN,
        4178, pp. 481-92.

4231.   Niven, Alastair. "Wars, Skirmishes and Strategies in the
        Criticism of Modern African Literature." WLWE, 19 (1980),
        144-51.

4232.   Nkosi, Lewis. "The African Critic as a Creator of Values."
        In LE CRITIQUE AFRICAIN, 4178, pp. 38-44.

            Achebe, et al.

4233.   Nwezeh, E.C. "The Comparative Approach to Modern African
        Literature." YCGL, 28 (1979), 20-25; rpt. in Köpeczi et
        al., 3540, pp. 321-28.

4234.   Ofeimun, Odia. "Criticism as Homicide: A Reply to Femi
        Osofisan's 'Literacy as Suicide.'" AFRISCOPE, 7, 6 (1977),
        31-32.

            Response to 4442. See reply by Osofisan, 4240.

4235.   Ogude, S.E. "Slavery and the African Imagination: A Critical
        Perspective." WLT, 55 (1981), 21-25.

            Achebe, Equiano, Soyinka, et al.

4236.   Ogunba, Oyin. "The Literary Situation: A Bastard Literature
        and a Bastard Criticism." JLSN, 1 (1981), 1-6.

4237.   Okai, Atukwei. "Literary Criticism and Culture." WA, 14
        July 1980, pp. 1282-85.

4238.   Okpewho, Isidore. "Comparatism and Separatism in African
        Literature." WLT, 55 (1981), 25-31.

4239.   Onoge, Omafume. "The Possibilities of a Radical Sociology of
        African Literature: Tentative Notes." In Nwoga, 3611, pp.
        90-96.

4240.   Osofisan, Femi. "Criticism as Homicide: A Brief Reply."
        AFRISCOPE, 7, 8 (1977), 36, 38.

            Reply to Ofeimun, 4234.

4241.   p'Bitek, Okot. "Mazrui under Fire: What Really Is the
        African Tragedy?" SUNDAY NATION, 20 February 1977, pp. 8-9.

            Reply to Mazrui, 3576.

4242.   Povey, John. "South African Writing: Critical Approaches."
        In Ray, et al, 4900, pp. 152-63.

4243. Ricard, Alain. "Le Mythe de la tradition dans la critique
littéraire africaniste." ALA, 54-55 (1979-80), 18-23.

4244. Richard, R., and J. Sevry. "Socio-critique et littératures
africaines." ALA, 50 (1978), 69-76.

Focuses on Achebe's THINGS FALL APART; followed by
discussion, 77-81.

4245. Rubadiri, David. "An African Looks at His Writers." In LE
CRITIQUE AFRICAIN, 4178, pp. 210-19.

4246. Sabor, Peter. "Palm-wine and Drinkards: African Literature
and Its Critics." ArielE, 12, 3 (1981), 113-25.

On Moore, 3585; Palmer, 3813; Fraser, 5305.

4247. Schipper-de Leeuw, Mineke. "Introduction." AFRICAN
PERSPECTIVES (Leiden), 1 (1977), 7-10.

Special issue devoted to the proceedings of a conference
on methodology in African literature study.

4248. Sine, Babakar. "Le Problème de la formation d'une critique
endogène et introvertie." In LE CRITIQUE AFRICAIN, 4178, pp.
220-31.

4249. Slabbert, Jos. "Dilemmas of Bourgeois Criticism: Open
Letter." CONTRAST, 12, 2 (1978), 85-87.

Response to Ullyatt, 4161.

4250. Sole, Kelwyn. "Problems of Creative Writers in South Africa:
A Response." WIP, 1 (1977), 4-25.

See responses by Couzens, 4192, and Hofmeyr, 4210.

4251. ____. "Footnote on Hofmeyr." WIP, 2 (1977), 38-43.

Reply to Hofmeyr, 4210.

4252. ____. "Criticism, Activism and Rhetoric (or: Armah and the
White Pumpkin)." INSPAN, 1, 1 (1978), 129-41.

4253. ____. "Prejudiced Approach." CONTRAST, 12, 2 (1978), 91-94.

Response to Ullyatt, 4161.

4254. ____. "The Abortion of the Intellect: Literary Circles and
'Change' in South Africa Today." WIP, 9 (1979), 13-28.

4255. Songolo, Aliko. "MUNTU Reconsidered: From Tempels and Kagame
to Janheinz Jahn." ZEITSCHRIFT FÜR KULTURAUSTAUSCH, 29
(1979), 142-46; UFAHAMU, 10, 3 (1981), 92-100; rpt. in
Parker, 3630, pp. 155-68.

4256. Soyinka, Wole. "The Critic and Society; Barthes, Leftocracy, and Other Mythologies." BALF, 15 (1981), 133-46.

   Moore, Ogunbiyi, et al.

4257. Steadman, Ian. "Critical Responses to Contemporary South African Theatre." CRITICAL ARTS, 1, 3 (1980), 40-46.

4258. Tchoungui, Pierre. "Connaissance du peuple comme producteur et analyse de l'art comme produit: Existe-t-il une ethnopsychologie littéraire africaine?" In LE CRITIQUE AFRICAIN, 4178, pp. 247-56.

4259. Tidjani-Serpos, Nouréini. "La Critique africaine: Les Critères de recevabilité." In LE CRITIQUE AFRICAIN, 4178, pp. 232-46.

4260. _____. "Aspects de la critique africaine: Méthodologie et perspectives." PFr, 17 (1978), 97-107.

4261. Topor, Wolor. "The Role of the African Literary Critic as an Instrument of Innovation." In LE CRITIQUE AFRICAIN, 4178, pp. 105-20.

4262. Tremaine, Louis. "Literary Sociology and the African Novel: The Theories of Sunday Anozie and Lucien Goldmann." RAL, 9 (1978), 31-45.

4263. Uka, Kalu. "Approaches to Theatre Reviewing as Art Education (Suggestions to Nigerian Reviewers)." BO, 4, 1 (1981), 84-90.

4264. Wanjala, Chris L. "The Mission of Writing and Humanist Commitment." MAKTABA, 3 (1976), 145-48.

   Achebe, Mphahlele, Tutuola, et al.

4265. _____. "Culture, the African Writer, and Alienation." MAKTABA, 4 (1977), 22-27.

   On Rowland Smith's EXILE AND TRADITION.

4266. _____. "The Critic as Superstar." SUNDAY NATION, 22 January 1978, p. 18.

   On the role of the critic in society.

4267. _____. "A Reply to My Critics." SUNDAY NATION, 16 April 1978, p. 18.

   Reply to Magayu, 4822, and others. Discusses Mphahlele as critic.

4268. Wilkinson, Nick. "A Methodology for the Comparative Study of Commonwealth Literature." JCL, 13, 3 (1979), 33-42.

4269. Zaourou, Bernard Zadi, and Christophe Dailly. "Langue et
       critique littéraire en Afrique Noire." In LE CRITIQUE
       AFRICAIN, 4178, pp. 441-80.

See also 3414, 3517, 3526, 3710, 3734, 3737, 3761, 3765, 3782,
       3911-12, 3950, 4078, 4082, 4088-89, 4094, 4131, 4136, 4161,
       4345, 4360, 4362, 4383, 4455, 4482, 4525, 4762, 4768, 4770,
       4787-88, 4821, 4923, 4938, 4989, 5091, 5165, 5177, 5263,
       5297, 5331-32, 5334, 5385, 5439, 5537, 5549, 5620, 5829,
       5976, 5990, 6014, 6049, 6119, 6123, 6125, 6134.

I. AUTOBIOGRAPHY

BIBLIOGRAPHY

See 3368.

BOOKS AND ESSAYS

4270. Beck, Alice Anita. "I Am Because We Are: Four Versions of
       the Common Voice in African and Afro-American Autobiography."
       DAI, 41 (1980), 2591-92A (New York-Binghamton).

        Mphahlele, et al.

4271. Obiechina, Emmanuel. "Africa´s Lost Generations." WILSON
       QUARTERLY, 5 (1981), 178-87.

        Cuguano, Equiano, et al.

4272. Sandiford, Keith Albert. "The Evolution of Racial and
       Political Consciousness in Three Black Writers of Eighteenth-
       Century England." DAI, 40 (1980), 5455A.

        Cugoano, Equiano, Sancho.

See also 3458, 3615, 3710, 3765, 4585, 5062, 5115, 5363, 5408, 5417,
       5445-55, 5466-67, 5482, 5568, 5577, 5598, 5600, 5609,
       5631-32, 5674, 5840, 5846, 5848, 5903-04, 5962, 5992,
       6090-91, 6131.

J. CHILDREN'S LITERATURE

BIBLIOGRAPHY

4273. Anon. COMMONWEALTH BOOK FAIR 1976: STORIES FOR CHILDREN.
London: Commonwealth Institute, 1976.

Catalog of an exhibition.

4274. Anon. "Bibliography: Children's and Young People's
Literature." AfrLJ, 8 (1977), 63-64, 260, 354; 9 (1978), 70,
166-67, 361; 10 (1979), 66, 157.

4275. Anon. COMMONWEALTH CHILDREN'S LITERATURE. Checklists on
Commonwealth Literature, 1. Introd. Michael Foster.
London: Commonwealth Institute, 1979.

Africa, pp. 7-19.

4276. Bevan, Joan. "Children's Literature in English." In
CATALOGUE FOR THE EXHIBITION OF SOUTH AFRICAN CHILDREN'S AND
YOUTH BOOKS. Ed. M.A.G. Swart. Potchefstroom: South
African Library Association, 1978.

Followed by selection of titles, pp. 52-55.

4277. Mensah, Kofi. "Supplement to Children's Books on Africa."
Madison, WI: African Studies Program, University of
Wisconsin-Madison, 1979. Mimeographed.

Annotated list. Supplements Zekiros, 4282.

4278. Ndei, J. "A Bibliography of Children's Literature in Kenya."
MAKTABA, 6, 1 (1979), 81-114.

4279. Panofsky, Hans E. "Bibliographies of Children's Literature
about Africa, 1970-1975."

CRevB, 3, 2-4 (1975), 2-4.

4280.* Rauter, Rosemarie. PRINTED FOR CHILDREN: WORLD CHILDREN'S
BOOK EXHIBITION. Munich: K.G. Saur, 1978.

4281. Schmidt, Nancy J. SUPPLEMENT TO CHILDREN'S BOOKS ON AFRICA
AND THEIR AUTHORS: AN ANNOTATED BIBLIOGRAPHY. African
Bibliography Series, 5. New York and London: Africana, 1979.

Supplements BALE 1361.

4282. Zekiros, Astair. "Children's Books on Africa." Madison, WI:
African Studies Program, University of Wisconsin-Madison,
1978. Mimeographed.

Annotated list. Supplemented by Mensah, 4277.

See also 4312, 4315, 4317.

BOOKS AND ESSAYS

4283.   Anon. "Children's Literature in Kenya: Literature as an
        Image Forming Force." In Gachukia and Akivaga, 4799, pp.
        40-46.

4284.* Bebbe, Charles Henry. "Problems in Children's Book
        Production." CREPLA BULLETIN OF INFORMATION, 2, 2-3 (1979),
        20-23.

4285.* Breitinger, Eckhard. "Kinder- und Jugendliteratur in
        Afrika." BDB, 4 October 1978, pp. 31-35.

4286.* ____. "Zur Situation der Kinder- und Jugendliteratur in
        Afrika." DAS GUTE JUGENDBUCH, 3 (1978), 128-41.

4287.   Dike, Virginia W. "Wanted: African Picture Books for Nigerian
        Children." PAN AFRICAN BOOK WORLD, 1, 1 (1981), 13, 15,
        17-18.

4288.* Fayose, P. Osazee. "A Look at Nigerian Children's
        Literature." BOOKBIRD, 2 (1977), 2-5.

4289.   ____. "Picture Books for African Children." SIERRA LEONE
        LIBRARY JOURNAL, 5, 1-2 (1980), 9-23.

4290.   Holicki, Sabine, and Claudia Mühlfeld. "Alltag, Abenteuer
        und Zauberei." BDB, 22 August 1980, pp. 2068-70.

4291.   Ibru, Enie. "What Should Our Children Read?" AFRICA WOMAN,
        18 (1978), 26.

4292.* Kor, Buma. "The Growth of Children's Literature in Africa."
        In SOUVENIR: INTERNATIONAL CHILDREN'S BOOK FAIR. Ed.
        Children's Book Trust. New Delhi: Children's Book Trust,
        1979. Pp. 93-97.

4293.   Kotei, S.I.A. "Themes for Children's Literature in Ghana."
        ABPR, 4 (1978), 233-39; GHANA BOOK WORLD, 1 (1978), 10-21.

4294.   Lutsky, Judi. "Locating Resources about African Children and
        Children's Books on Africa." CRevB, 3, 2-4 (1975), 5-6.

4295.   Malya, Simoni. "After Literacy, What Next? Tanzania Records
        Its Heritage of Folk Tales in Reading Books for the Newly
        Literate." UNESCO COURIER, 30 (February 1977), 23-27.

4296.* Metzger, Andrew, J.B. "The Place of Literature in the Life
        of the Sierra Leonean Child." Master's thesis, Department of
        Library and Information Studies, University of Technology,
        Loughborough, 1977.

4297.* Moutchia, William. "Problems of Promoting Books for Children." CREPLA BULLETIN OF INFORMATION, 2, 2-3 (1979), 4, 6, 8.

4298. Nyquist, Corinne. "Recent Books for South African Children." CRevB, 3, 2-4 (1975), 97-103.

4299.* Ofori-Atta, Grace. "Notes on Children's Reading in Ghana." LIBRARY WORLD, 64 (1963), 218-21.

4300. Okanlawon, Tunde. "Nigerian Children's Literature: Problems and Goals." JCL, 15, 1 (1980), 30-37.

4301. Omotoso, Kole. "Racist Stereotype in Nigerian Children's Books." AFRISCOPE, 10, 1 (1980), 28-30.

   Okoro, Soyinka, Vatsa, et al.

4302.* ____. "Children's Books in an African Context." In THE SLANT OF THE PEN: RACISM IN CHILDREN'S BOOKS. Ed. Roy Preiswerk. Geneva: World Council of Churches, 1980. Pp. 46-61.

4303.* Osa, Osayimwense. "A Content Analysis of Fourteen Nigerian Young Adult Novels." Ph.D. dissertation, University of Houston, 1981.

4304.* Pala, Francis Otieno. "Children's Literature in Kenya." BOOKBIRD, 13, 2 (1975), 17-21.

4305. Pellowski, Anne. MADE TO MEASURE: CHILDREN'S BOOKS IN DEVELOPING COUNTRIES. Paris: UNESCO, 1980.

4306. Poland, Marguerite. "Books for the Children of Africa: The Need for an Indigenous Literature." CRUX, 15, 1 (1981), 31-33.

4307.* Sackey, Juliana V. "Children's Reading Habits in Ghana." GHANA BOOK WORLD, 1 (1978), 6-9.

4308. Schmidt, Nancy J., ed. "Children's Literature and Audio-Visual Materials in Africa." CRevB, 3, 2-4 (1975), 1-108.

   Special issue of CRevB, also published as book by Conch Magazine Ltd., 1977.

4309. ____. "Resources on African Literature: Children's Literature." In Hale and Priebe, 4810, pp. 198-235.

   Includes bibliography, pp. 222-35.

4310. ____. "African Folklore for African Children." RAL, 8 (1977), 306-26.

   Includes bibliography.

4311. ____. "The Image of the Child in Literature for African
Children." WACC JOURNAL, 24, 4 (1978), 22-25.

Survey.

4312. ____. "African Women Writers of Literature for Children."
WLWE, 17 (1978), 7-21.

Akpabot, Odaga, Sutherland, Waciuma, Were, et al.
Includes bibliography of references cited.

4313. ____. "All Africa Folklore." PROCEEDINGS: CHILDREN'S BOOKS
INTERNATIONAL 4. Boston: Boston Public LIbrary, 1979. Pp.
46-55.

4314. ____. "The Development of Written Literature for Children in
Subsaharan Africa." ZEITSCHRIFT FÜR KULTURAUSTAUSCH, 29
(1979), 267-70.

4315. ____. "Children's Books by Well-Known African Authors."
WLWE, 18 (1979), 114-23.

Achebe, Ekwensi, Kimenye, Lubega, Nwapa, Sutherland, et
al. Includes bibliography.

4316. ____. CHILDREN'S FICTION ABOUT AFRICA IN ENGLISH. Owerri,
New York, London: Conch Magazine Ltd., 1981.

4317. Schmidt, Nancy J., Gustav O. Twerefoo, Daniel S.M. Kamanda,
and John Kennedy, comps. RESOURCES FOR TEACHING CHILDREN
ABOUT AFRICA. Urbana, IL: ERIC Clearinghouse on Early
Childhood Education, 1976.

4318. Vignal, Daniel. "Nigéria: de l'anglais à dix autres
langues." EUROPE, 607-08 (1979), 55-61.

Survey.

4319. Wanjala, Chris. "African Children Need Their Own Literary
Heroes." SUNDAY NATION, 9 October 1977, p. 15.

4320. ____. "Writing for the Child." SUNDAY NATION, 4 March 1979,
p. 10.

4321.* Zell, Hans M. "Children's Book Publishing in Africa Today."
INTERRACIAL BOOKS FOR CHILDREN, 5, 1-2 (1974), 3-5.

See also 4025, 4446, 4896, 4936, 5100, 5199, 5253, 5436, 5457, 5486,
5513.

K. POPULAR LITERATURE

BIBLIOGRAPHY

4322. Lindfors, Bernth. "A Checklist of Prewar Nigerian Chapbook Fiction and Poetry in English." AfrLJ, 11 (1980), 53-63.

See also 4336.

BOOKS AND ESSAYS

4323. Adelman, Sammy. "Debate in the English Dept...: Not Such ´Kissing Couzens.´" WITS STUDENT, 15 May 1979, p. 13.

Comments on controversy between Couzens, 4326, and Marquard, 4334.

4324. Arnold, Stephen H. "Popular Literature in Tanzania: Its Background and Relation to ´East African´ Literature." PA, 115 (1980), 156-77; rpt. in Parker, 3630.

4325. Beier, Ulli. "Public Opinion on Lovers." In Momodu and Schild, 3583, pp. 267-89.

Rpt. of BALE 1376. Onitsha literature.

4326. Couzens. Tim. "Living Culture and the Mortuary Slab." SPEAK, 1, 4 (1978), 13-14.

Popular literature vs. classics. See responses by Marquard, 4334, and Adelman, 4323.

4327. Dodson, Don. "Onitsha Market Literature." In Petersen and Rutherford, 4467, pp. 47-50.

4328. Gikandi, Simon. "Popular Literature in East Africa." AIBEPM, 96 (1979), 83.

Maillu, et al.

4329. Imfeld, Al. "Populärliteratur: Gebrauchsanweisung für den Alltag." BDB, 22 August 1980, pp. 1028-29.

Kenya, Nigeria, South Africa.

4330. Knight, Elizabeth. "Popular Literature in East Africa." ALT, 10 (1979), 177-90.

Maillu, Mangua, et al.

4331. Lepine, Richard. "Spear Books: Pop-Lit Artifacts or You CAN Judge a Book By Its Cover." BA SHIRU, 10, 2 (1979), 36-48.

4332. Lindfors, Bernth. "Popular Literature in English in Black

South Africa." JOURNAL OF SOUTHERN AFRICAN AFFAIRS, 2 (1977), 121-29.

Survey.

4333.   ___. "East African Popular Literature in English." JPC, 13 (1979), 106-15.

Liyong, Maillu, Mangua, Ngugi, p´Bitek, et al.

4334.   Marquard, Jean. "Couzens on Pop Culture: Marquard Replies." SPEAK, 1, 5 (1978), 70.

Response to 4326.

4335.   Obasi, John U. "Printed Nigerian Ephemera Since 1945:   An Investigation into its Acquisition, Organization and Availability within Nigeria with Particular Reference to Socio-historical Studies." Master´s thesis, Polytechnic of North London, 1978.

4336.   Priebe, Richard. "Popular Writing in Ghana: A Sociology and Rhetoric." RAL, 9 (1978), 395-432.

Abbam, Armah, Awoonor, Blay, Donkor, Konadu, Mickson, Ofori, Osae, Quaye, et al. Includes bibliography.

4337.   Ricard, Alain. "Westafrika." In RECLAMS KRIMINALROMANFÜHRER, Ed. Armin Arnold and Josef Schmidt. Stuttgart: Reclam, 1978. Pp. 399-401.

Brief survey of detective fiction.

4338.   Schild, Ulla. "Words of Deception: Popular Literature in Kenya." In Schild, 3665, pp. 25-33.

Afromance pamphlets.

See also 3387, 3472-73, 3508, 3546, 3788, 3866, 3888, 3915, 3931, 3948, 3986-87, 3993, 4020, 4050, 4059, 4320, 4502, 4546, 4574, 4580, 4583, 4637-38, 4659, 4675, 4704, 4733, 4745, 5253, 5439, 5553-58, 5765, 5798, 5852, 6057, 6133.

L. LANGUAGE AND STYLE

BOOKS AND ESSAYS

4339. Achebe, Chinua, Rajat Neogy, Donald Herdeck, Joseph Okpaku, and Mazisi Kunene. "African Writing and the Problems of Translation." TRANSLATION, 3 (1976), 38-43.

    Panel discussion.

4340. Adsanoye, Festus A. "Aspects of Oral Tradition in Nigerian Literary English." BUSARA, 8, 2 (1976), 81-101.

    Achebe, Agunwa, Aluko, Clark, Ike, Munonye, Nwankwo, Nzekwu, Soyinka, Tutuola.

4341.* Agetua, John. "The Role of Pidgin English in Nigerian Literature." NIGERIAN OBSERVER, 28 May 1977.

4342. Angogo, Rachel, and Ian Hancock. "English in Africa: Emerging Standards or Diverging Regionalisms?" ENGLISH WORLD-WIDE, 1, 1 (1980), 67-96.

    Considers "Language and African Writer," pp. 82-93.

4343. Bakari, Mohamed. "Critics of Tribal Literature Agents of Neo-Colonialism." NAIROBI TIMES, 28 November 1979.

    Response to Mzee wa Kiswahili, 4355.

4344. Barbag, Anna. "West African Pidgin English as a Medium of Literary Expression." AfB, 27 (1978), 55-63.

    Achebe, Ekwensi, Ogali, Soyinka, Onitsha literature, et al.

4345. d´Almeida, Irene Assiba. "The Language of African Fiction: Reflections on Ngugi´s Advocacy for an Afro-African Literature." PA, 120 (1981), 82-92.

4346. Duffield, A. C. "When Africans Write in English." KENYA WEEKLY NEWS, 25 April 1969, p. 16.

4347. Hellinger, Marlis. "Creole als Sprache der Schwarzen Literatur." In Breitinger, 3428, pp. 75-102.

4348. Irele, Abiola. "African Literature and the Language Question." In LE CRITIQUE AFRICAIN, 4178, pp. 493-507; rpt. in Irele, 3517.

4349. Johnson, Alex C. "West African Literature and the English Language as a Medium of Wider Communication." FBSSL, 2 (1981), 24-49.

Rotimi, et al.

4350. Kadima-Nzuji, Mukala. "Création littéraire et language en
       Afrique." DÉCENNIE 2, 42 (1979), 47-49.

       Achebe, et al.

4351. Kilanga, Musinde. "Langue et littérature comme moyens
       d´expression de la pensée africaine." RPC, 47-48 (1980),
       24-27.

4352. McLeod, Alan L., and Marian B. McLeod, eds. REPRESENTATIVE
       SOUTH AFRICAN SPEECHES: THE RHETORIC OF RACE AND RELIGION.
       Introd. H.H. Anniah Gowda. Mysore: Centre for Commonwealth
       Literature and Research, University of Mysore, 1980.

       Rpts. Mphahlele on negritude, BALE 431, pp. 223-28.

4353. Mbassi-Manga, Francis. "Language in Literature and Society
       (A Sociolinguistic Approach to the Study of Literature)."
       AFLSHY, 8 (1977), 11-18; rpt. in Köpeczi et al., 3540, pp.
       861-68.

4354. Mphahlele, Ezekiel. "The Impact of African Literature."
       TRANSLATION, 3, (1976), 5-14.

       Surveys impact on the English language.

4355. Mzee wa Kiswahili. "Tribal Literature Doomed." NAIROBI
       TIMES, 30 September 1979.

       Response to Ngugi´s speech at Press Club luncheon
       advocating creative writing in Kenyan languages. See
       5669 and rejoinder by Bakari, 4343.

4356. New, W.H. "New Language, New World." In Narasimhaiah, 3593,
       pp. 360-77.

       Rive, et al.

4357. Ngugi wa Thiong´o. "The Choice for Kenya." GUARDIAN, 11
       June 1979, p. 15; rpt. in 4400.

       On need to develop Kenyan culture and Kenyan languages.

4358. Obilade, Tony. "The Stylistic Function of Pidgin English in
       African Literature: Achebe and Soyinka." RAL, 9 (1978),
       433-44.

4359. Ochieng, William. "Let´s Not Write in Tongues." SUNDAY
       NATION, 4 October 1981, p. 6.

       Advocates that Kenyans write in English.

4360. Ogungbesan, Kolawole. "Simple Novels and Simplistic

Criticism: The Problem of Style in the African Novel."
UMOJA, 1, 3 (1977), 31-41; ASEMKA, 5 (1979), 24-40.

Achebe, Armah, Ekwensi, Soyinka, et al.

4361. ____. "A Cultural Approach to African Languages and
Literatures." UFAHAMU, 7, 2 (1977), 85-95.

4362. Okonkwo, Juliet I. "The Missing Link in African Literature."
ALT, 10 (1979), 86-105.

Urges adoption of African languages for literary
creation.

4363. Okpewho, Isidore. "African Fiction: Language Revisited."
JAfrS, 5 (1978), 414-26.

Achebe, Liyong, Okara, Okpewho, Soyinka, et al.

4364. Porter, Abioseh Michael. "Smohl no bi sik: A Preliminary
Survey of Pidgin Literature in Cameroon." PQM, 6, 3-4
(1981), 62-69.

Survey.

4365. Povey, John. "English Usage in Recent Nigerian Novels." In
McLeod, 3565, pp. 48-67.

Amadi, Aniebo, Iroh, Munonye.

4366. Priebe, Richard K. "An Examination of the Use of Pidgin in
the Works of Three Nigerian Authors." PENN-TEXAS WORKING
PAPERS IN SOCIOLINGUISTICS, 11 (1972), 1-24.

Achebe, Ekwensi, Soyinka.

4367. Ricard, Alain. "Multilinguisme et production littéraire."
WAJML, 3 (1978), 106-12.

4368. Rive, Richard. "What the English Language Means to Me."
CRUX, 15, 3 (1981), 12-17.

4369. Schäfer, Jürgen. "Sprache oder Nation: Zum Problem einer
englischen Nationalliteratur." In Schäfer, 3661, pp. 12-28.

4370. Schild, Ulla. "Die europäischen Sprachen als Vehikel der
Afrikanität: Ein stilanalytischer Beitrag zur ´Negritude.´"
In THEORETISCHE PROBLEME DES SOZIALISMUS IN AFRIKA: NÉGRITUDE
UND ARUSHA-DEKLARATION. Ed. Gerhard Grohs. Hamburg: Buske,
1971. Pp. 89-98.

Achebe, Duodu, Okara, et al.

4371. Simpson, Ekundayo. "Bilinguisme et création littéraire en
Afrique." PA, 111 (1979), 44-60.

Achebe, Oyônô-Mbia, Soyinka, Tutuola.

4372. Soyinka, Wole. "We Africans Must Speak in One Tongue."
AFRIKA, 20, 9 (1979), 22-23.

4373. Tonkin, Elizabeth. "Uses of Pidgin in the Early Literate
English of Nigeria." In READINGS IN CREOLE STUDIES. Ed.
Ian Hancock. Ghent: E. Story-Scientia, 1979. Pp. 303-08.

Duke, et al.

4374. Wren, Robert M. "The Indigenization of English: Rhetoric in
Modern Nigerian Literature." BO, 3, 4 (1976), 44-56.

Achebe, Clark, Ekwensi, Okara, Soyinka, et al.

See also 3434, 3457, 3465, 3517, 3541, 3608, 3650, 3655, 3731, 3735,
3805, 3812, 3834, 3837, 3857, 3884, 3906, 3950, 4022, 4093,
4141, 4154, 4161, 4252, 4269, 4452, 4466, 4509, 4511, 4802,
5129, 5132-34, 5167, 5170, 5186, 5234, 5241, 5244, 5262,
5284, 5306, 5333, 5381, 5624, 5669, 5689, 5714, 5799, 5839,
5854, 5882, 5974, 6040, 6061-62, 6079, 6082, 6093, 6117.

M. LITERATURE AND COMMITMENT

BOOKS AND ESSAYS

4375. Abrahams, Cecil A. "Achebe, Ngugi and La Guma: Commitment and the Traditional Storyteller." MANA, 2, 1 (1977), 11-24; rev. and rpt. in Massa, 3571, pp. 59-68.

4376. ____. "Literature and Politics: The South African Example." CARIB, 2 (1981), 1-8.

Abrahams, Brutus, La Guma, et al.

4377. Achebe, Chinua. "The Uses of African Literature." OKIKE, 15 (1979), 8-17.

Achebe, Ekwere, Equiano, Peters et al.

4378. ____. "Commitment and the African Writer." In Kalu, 3524, pp. 181-88.

Equiano et al.

4379. Alvarez-Péreyre, Jacques. "Le Black Consciousness (La 'Conscience Noire')." In Society of African Culture, 3675, pp. 313-30.

4380. Asein, Samuel O. "Literature as History: Crisis, Violence, and Strategies of Commitment in Nigerian Writing." In Nwoga, 3611, pp. 97-116.

Achebe, Clark, Okigbo, Soyinka, et al.

4381. Asvat, Farouk. "Weapons of Words." WIETIE, 1 (n.d.), 16-17.

South Africa.

4382. Booth, James. WRITERS AND POLITICS IN NIGERIA. London: Hodder and Stoughton; New York: Africana, 1981.

Achebe, Aluko, Okara, Soyinka, Tutuola, et al.

4383. Chinweizu. "Literature and Development." AIBEPM, 98 (1979), 106-07.

Takes issue with Nwoga, BALE 1195.

4384. Dailly, Christophe. "Vers une révaluation idéologique de la littérature négro-africaine." RLENA, 1 (1977), 31-43.

4385. El Sebai, Youssef. "The Writer and Commitment." LAAW, 29 (1976), 6-8.

In Africa and Asia.

4386. Gordimer, Nadine. "Literature and Politics in South Africa."
       TRANSLATION, 3 (1976), 19-35.

       Rpt. of BALE 1485. Discusses censorship and Abrahams,
       La Guma, Mphahlele, Mtshali, Zwelonke, et al.

4387. Gruner, Fritz. "Revolution und Literatur: zu einigen
       Problemen des Wechselverhältnisses von gesellschaftlichen und
       künstlerisch-literarischen Prozessen in den Literaturen
       Asiens und Afrikas." In Gruner, 3501, pp. 183-96.

4388. Jestel, Rüdiger. "Nach der Unabhängigkeit: Nationalismus."
       BDB, 22 August 1980, pp. 2033-35.

       Achebe, Armah, Ngugi, Soyinka, et al.

4389. Johnson, Lemuel A. "Ideology, Art, and Community: African
       Literatures and the Issues." In Priebe and Hale, 4519, pp.
       181-203.

       Achebe, Armah, Soyinka, et al.

4390. Jordan, Z. Pallo. "Literature, Resistance and Revolution."
       In Society of African Culture, 3675, pp. 85-94.

       Survey.

4391. Kembo-Sure. "Literature, Ideology and Liberation." KUCHA,
       1, 1 (1977), 35-37.

4392. La Guma, Alex. "Culture and Liberation." WLWE, 18 (1979),
       27-36.

4393. Martins, Dikobe WaMogale. "Art is Not Neutral: Whom Does it
       Serve?" STAFFRIDER, 4, 2 (1981), 30-31.

4394. Medjigbodo, Nicole. "Dedan Kimathi, héros de la lutte de
       libération kenyanne." PA, 111 (1979), 70-79.

       Githae-Mugo, Ngugi.

4395. Mzamane, Mbulelo Vizikhungo. "Literature and Politics Among
       Blacks in South Africa." NEW CLASSIC, 5 (1978), 42-58; PULA,
       1, 2 (1979), 123-45.

       Abrahams, Kgositsile, La Guma, Mtshali, et al.

4396. ____. "Politics and Literature in Africa: A Review."
       STAFFRIDER, 3, 4 (1980-81), 43-44.

4397. Ngugi wa Thiong'o. "Writers in Politics." BUSARA, 8, 1
       (1976), 1-8; rpt. in 4400.

4398. ____. "Literature and Society." In Gachukia and Akivaga,

4799, pp. 1-29; rpt. in 4400.

    Achebe, et al.

4399. ____. "The National Struggle to Survive." GUARDIAN, 11 June 1979, p. 15; rpt. in 4400.

    Opposition to western domination of Kenyan cultural activities.

4400. ____. WRITERS IN POLITICS: ESSAYS. London: Heinemann, 1981.

    Includes 3993, 4357, 4397-99, and BALE 1506.

4401. Njoroge, Paul. "Literature and Contemporary Relevance: The West African Example." In Gachukia and Akivaga, 4799, pp. 114-26.

    Achebe, Armah, et al.

4402. Nkosi, Lewis. "Literature, Politics and Liberation." AIBEPM, 107 (1980), 116-117; BDB, 22 August 1980, pp. 2013-15.

4403. Ochieng, William. "Writers and Search for a Moral Order." SUNDAY NATION, 12 August 1979, p. 19.

4404. Ogungbesan, Kolawole. "The Modern Writer and Commitment." In Nwoga, 3611, pp. 3-18.

    Abrahams, Achebe, et al.

4405. Omotoso, Kole. "Polityka, propaganda i prostytucja literatury [Politics, propaganda and literary prostitution]." LITERATURA NA ŚWIECIE, 81 (1978), 102-15.

    Rpt. of BALE 1514.

4406. Owomoyela, Oyekan. "Dissidence and the African Writer: Commitment or Dependency?" AfrSR, 24, 1 (1981), 83-98.

    Achebe, Armah, Soyinka, et al.

4407. Reichel, Detlev Theodor. SCHRIFTSTELLER GEGEN APARTHEID: STUDIEN ZUR SÜDAFRIKANISCHEN GEGENWARTSLITERATUR. Berlin: Edition Neue Wege, H.W. Herrmann, 1977.

    La Guma, Mphahlele, Rive, et al.

4408. Rive, Richard. "Non-racialism and Art." CONTRAST, 13, 3 (1981), 19-23.

4409. Schulze, Frank. "Literatur und Antikolonialismus." BDB, 22 August 1980, pp. 2035-39.

Achebe, La Guma, Mphahlele, Ngugi, Soyinka, et al.

4410. Uka, Kalu. "From Commitment to Essence (A View of African
       Writing)." In Nwoga, 3611, pp. 19-31.

       Rpt. of BALE 1527; Achebe, Soyinka, et al.

4411. Vaillant, Florence. "Les Écrivains noirs sud-africains: Du
       témoignage à la révolte." In Society of African Culture,
       3675, pp. 343-50.

       Survey.

4412. Wanjala, Chris. "Literature Written by Africans Can Foster
       Unity." SUNDAY NATION, 6 November 1977, pp. 22, 31.

4413. Wauthier, Claude. "L´Engagement politique de l´écrivain
       africain." JeuneA, 12 July 1978, pp. 193-96, 201-02.

       Survey.

4414. ____. "Inventaire politique de la littérature africaine."
       ZEITSCHRIFT FÜR KULTURAUSTAUSCH, 29 (1979), 146-54.

4415. Webb, Hugh. "Literary Form and Ideology: The African
       Counter-Attack?" NLRev, 3 (1977), 16-22.

See also 3391-93, 3471, 3490, 3516, 3520, 3532, 3555, 3570, 3576-78,
       3607-08, 3615, 3651, 3675, 3725, 3732, 3747, 3764, 3797,
       3832, 3835, 3840, 3949, 4052, 4058, 4062-63, 4074, 4081,
       4087, 4101-02, 4108, 4110, 4115, 4130, 4150, 4161, 4168,
       4264, 4362, 4421-22, 4494, 4577, 4786, 4801, 4920, 5077,
       5095, 5154, 5357, 5471, 5476, 5499, 5534, 5583, 5601, 5640,
       5697, 5708, 5714, 5717, 5722, 5868, 5929, 6059, 6065, 6086,
       6092.

N. THE ROLE OF THE WRITER

BOOKS AND ESSAYS

4416. Agovi, J.K. "The African Writer and His Society." LEGACY, 3, 2 (1977), 4-7.

4417. Anon. "The Role of the African Writer." NEW AFRICAN, November 1979, pp. 54-55.

Interview with Chris Wanjala and Katama Mkangi.

4418. Apronti, E.O. "The Writer in Our Society." In Nwoga, 3611, pp. 77-89.

Armah, et al.

4419. Barrett, Lindsay. "The Artist in Africa: Dilemma of Development." AFRISCOPE, 8, 3 (1978), 21, 24, 27, 29, 44.

4420. Cooper, Brenda. "Some Generalisations about the Class Situation of the Writer-Intellectual from Independent Africa." AFRICA PERSPECTIVE, 16 (1980), 60-79.

Achebe, Aidoo, Aluko, Armah, Mwangi, Ngugi, p´Bitek, Soyinka, et al.

4421. Dhlomo, H.I.E. "The African Artist and Society." ENGLISH IN AFRICA, 4, 2 (1977), 71-72.

Rpt. from ILANGA LASE NATAL, 5 March 1949.

4422. ____. "Masses and the Artist." ENGLISH IN AFRICA, 4, 2 (1977), 61-62.

Rpt. from ILANGA LASE NATAL, 10 April 1943.

4423. Dongala, Emmanuel Boundzéki. "Littérature et société: ce que je crois." PEUPLES NOIRS/PEUPLES AFRICAINS, 9 (1979), 56-64.

4424. Egadu, G.W. "Some Problems of the African Writer." BUDONIAN, 3 (1964), 33.

4425. Ekwensi, Cyprian. "The Dilemma of the African Writer." WAR, July 1956, pp. 701-04, 708.

4426. Essomba, Philippe. "En quête d´auteurs..." BINGO, 319 (1979), 7.

For films.

4427. Jacobson, Dan. TIME OF ARRIVAL AND OTHER ESSAYS. New York: Macmillan, 1963.

Includes BALE 304 and "The Writer in the Commonwealth,"
pp. 157-65, 171-76.

4428. La Guma, A. "O escritor reflecte a consciencia que tem do
povo." TEMPO, 459 (1979), 30-33.

4429. Lopes, Carlos. "Algumas questões sobre a problemática dos
direitos de autor em África." AFRICA (Lisbon), 2 (1980),
347-50.

4430. Maduka, Chukwudi T. "The African Writer and the Drama of
Social Change." ArielE, 12, 3 (1981), 5-18.

4431. Magayu, Magayu K. "East African Literature and the East
African Writer." KUCHA, 1, 1 (1977), 4-8.

4432. Mbatau, R.S.K.N. "The Writer in an Ideological Maze."
BUSARA, 8, 1 (1976), 19-27.

4433. Mbele, Majola. "The Role of the Writer." In Mbele, 3579,
pp. 50-58.

       Revised rpt. of BALE 1555.

4434.* Mbise, Ismael R. "The Writer's Dilemma in East Africa Today."
Master's thesis, University of York, Toronto, 1973.

4435. Nazareth, Peter. THE THIRD WORLD WRITER: HIS SOCIAL
RESPONSIBILITY. Foreword Ime Ikiddeh. Nairobi: Kenya
Literature Bureau, 1978.

       Armah, Mangua, Mazrui, Ngugi, Ntiru, Okigbo, Omotoso,
       p'Bitek, Rubadiri, Ruganda, Sondhi, et al. Rpts. 452,
       2765, 2984.

4436. Ngugi, [wa Thiong'o], J.T. "'The African Personality' is a
Delusion: Do Tigers Have 'Tigritude'?" SUNDAY POST, 7 May
1961, p. 12.

4437. Nwankwo, Patience C. "The Literary Artist in a Changing
Nigeria." MUSE, 13 (1981), 50-56.

4438. Ogot, Grace A. "Welche Leserschaft?" BDB, 22 August 1980, p.
2073.

       Rpt. of BALE 1566.

4439. Ohaegbu, Aloys U. "The African Writer and the Problem of
Cultural Identity." PA, 101-102 (1977), 25-37.

4440. Okai, Atukwei. "The Role of Ghanaian Writers in the
Revolution." WEEKLY SPECTATOR, 14 July 1973, p. 4.

4441. Omotoso, Kole. "An African Belief." PAPUA NEW GUINEA

WRITING, 23 (1976), 19.

On purpose of literature.

4442. Osofisan, Femi. "Literacy as Suicide." AFRISCOPE, 7, 1
(1977), 17-18, 21-23.

See response by Ofeimun, 4234.

4443. Ripken, Peter. "In Search of Identity: The African Author's
Conception of Himself." AFRIKA, 20, 12 (1979), 21.

4444. Riyale, Abdi Yusuf. "The Writer's Role in Society." HALGAN,
21 (1978), 14-16.

4445. Wanjala, Chris. "Come, Let Us Enjoy Our Literature!" SUNDAY
NATION, 7 May 1978, p. 29.

Response to academic paper delivered by Jay Kitsao at
the University of Nairobi.

4446. ____. "Why Writers Must Learn to Support Each Other."
SUNDAY NATION, 29 April 1979, p. 10

Remarks prompted by poorly attended Commonwealth
writers' workshop in Nairobi.

4447. Wolo, Elaine Armour. "The Role of the Young Writer in Nation
Building." KAAFA, 6, 2 (1976), 27-30.

In Liberia.

See also 3405, 3478, 3556, 3627, 3659, 3783, 3924, 4147, 4178, 4219,
4250, 4261, 4266, 4383, 4397, 4400, 4402, 4473, 4480, 4576,
4639, 4654, 4675, 4712, 4771, 4937, 5223, 5328, 5332, 5374,
5601, 5682, 5685, 5749, 5758, 5990, 6058, 6065.

O. FOLKLORE AND LITERATURE

BOOKS AND ESSAYS

4448. Achebe, Christie C. "Literary Insights into the Ogbanje
Phenomenon." JAfrS, 7 (1980), 31-38.

Achebe, Clark, Soyinka, et al.

4449. Adedeji, Joel A. "The Genesis of African Folkloric
Literature." YFS, 53 (1976), 5-18.

Clark, Soyinka, Tutuola, et al.

4450. Agovi, J.E.K. "Traditional Story-Telling and the Modern
Short Story." In OUT OF THE WRITERS' WORKSHOP. Ed. Kwabena
Asiedu. Accra: National Association of Writers, Ghana, 1974.
Pp. 11-25.

4451. Bender, Wolfgang. "Von Oratur zur Literatur." BDB, 22
August 1980, pp. 2030-32.

4452. Chevrier, Jacques. "Conditions et limites de l'oralité dans
l'écriture africaine contemporaine." KOMPARATISTISCHE HEFTE,
1 (1980), 61-66.

4453. Comick, Edward Michael. "Chinua Achebe and Amos Tutuola: A
Study of the Function of Oral Tradition in the English
Language Works of Two African Authors." Honors thesis,
Harvard University, 1974.

4454.* Ebeogu, Afam. "The Igbo Tradition in Nigerian Literature of
English Expression." Ph.D. dissertation, University of
Ibadan, 1980.

4455. Echeruo, Michael J.C. "Influence and Tradition in Modern
Nigerian Literature." In Köpeczi et al., 3540, pp. 313-19.

Achebe, Okigbo, Soyinka, Tutuola.

4456. Gavrysheva, G. "Fol'klornaîà traditŝiîà i tvorchestvo
sovremennykh zapadnoafrikanskikh pisateleî. [The Folklore
Tradition and the Work of Contemporary West African
Writers]." AZIA I AFRIKA SEGODNIÂ, 6 (1979), 56-58.

4457. Hill-Lubin, Mildred A. "'And the Beat Goes On': A
Continuation of the African Heritage in African-American
Literature." CLAJ, 23 (1979), 172-87.

Achebe, Tutuola, et al.

4458.* James, A.A. "The Significance of Oral Tradition in the
Writings of Tutuola, Soyinka and Rotimi." Ph.D.
dissertation, London University, 1979.

4459.   Kunene, Mazisi. "The Relevance of African Cosmological
         Systems to African Literature Today." ALT, 11 (1980),
         190-205.

4460.   Lyonga, Nalova. "Literary Elements of African Oral Tradition
         in Modern Verse: The Structure and Form." NGAM, 3-4 (1978),
         114-33; ABBIA, 34-37 (1979), 232-47.

         Okara, Okigbo, p´Bitek, et al.

4461.*   Mapanje, J.A.C. "The Use of Traditional Literary Forms in
         Modern Malawian Writing in English." Master´s thesis,
         University of London, 1975.

4462.   ___. "The Place of Oral Literature in Literature." KALULU,
         1 (1976), 5-14.

4463.   Mercier, Roger. "Sacré et profane, fonctions et formes du
         mythe dans les littératures africaines." ALA, 54-55
         (1979-80), 24-30.

4464.   Obiechina, E.N. "Africa: Transition from Oral to Literary
         Tradition." LAAW, 36-37 (1978), 34-53.

         Rpt. of BALE 1594.

4465.   Oculi, Okello. "African Women and African Classics." AFRICA
         WOMAN, 7 (1976), 22-23.

4466.   Osundare, Niyi. "From Oral to Written: Aspects of the
         Socio-stylistic Repercussions of Transition." JACL, 1
         (1981), 1-13.

4467.   Petersen, Kirsten Holst, and Anna Rutherford, eds. COWRIES
         AND KOBOS: THE WEST AFRICAN ORAL TALE AND SHORT STORY.
         Introd. Donald Cosentino. Mundelstrup, Denmark: Dangaroo
         Press, 1981.

         Includes 3801, 3818, 4327, 5202, 5276, 5366, 5443, 5773.

4468.   Zirimu, P. "A Critical Note." DHANA, 7, 1 (1977), 76.

         Definition of orature and literature.

See also 3430, 3468, 3486, 3512, 3575, 3622, 3686, 3689, 3904, 3931,
     3989, 4014, 4029, 4040, 4095, 4116, 4118, 4135, 4162, 4227,
     4243, 4295, 4310, 4313, 4340, 4940-41, 5153, 5174, 5213,
     5215, 5218, 5221, 5253-55, 5269, 5335, 5339, 5381, 5716,
     5812, 5914, 5926, 5979, 5988, 6003, 6025, 6042, 6054, 6094,
     6109-10, 6126.

P. IMAGE STUDIES

BIBLIOGRAPHY

4469. Rushing, Andrea Benton. "An Annotated Bibliography of Images
       of Black Women in Black Literature." CLAJ, 21 (1978),
       435-42; 25 (1981), 234-62.

BOOKS AND ESSAYS

4470. Achebe, Chinua. "An Image of Africa." MR, 18 (1977),
       782-94; RAL, 9 (1978), 1-15; rpt. in CHANT OF SAINTS: A
       GATHERING OF AFRO-AMERICAN LITERATURE, ART AND SCHOLARSHIP.
       Ed. Michael S. Harper and Robert B. Stepto. Urbana:
       University of Illinois Press, 1979. Pp. 313-25.

       Rpt. of BALE 93 on Conrad's HEART OF DARKNESS.

4471. Anon. "Ngugi on Karen Blixen." VIVA, March 1981, p. 18.

       Summary of talk given at the Danish Library
       Association's 75th anniversary celebrations. See
       response by Trzebinski, 4500.

4472. Bell, Roseann P., Bettye J. Parker, and Beverly Guy-Sheftall,
       eds. STURDY BLACK BRIDGES: VISIONS OF BLACK WOMEN IN
       LITERATURE. Garden City, NY: Anchor Press/Doubleday, 1979.

       Includes 4485, 4496, 5272.

4473. Bruner, Charlotte. "Been-to or Has-Been: A Dilemma for
       Today's African Woman." BA SHIRU, 8, 2 (1977), 23-31.

       Aidoo, Head, Nwapa, Ogot.

4474. ____. "Child Africa as Depicted by Bessie Head and Ama Ata
       Aidoo." STUDIES IN THE HUMANITIES, 7, 2 (1979), 5-12.

4475. ____. "The Image of Christ Black in Afro-American and
       African Contemporary Art and Poetry." CLAJ, 24 (1981),
       352-68.

       Survey.

4476. Cochrane, Judith. "Some Images of Women in East African
       Fiction." ACLALSB, 5, 1 (1978), 32-47.

       Farah, Ngugi, Oculi, Ogot, Palangyo, p'Bitek, Rubadiri,
       Ruheni.

4477. Coussy, Denise. "L'Image du missionnaire dans le roman
       nigérian." In Richard and Sevry, 4495, pp. 131-33.

       Achebe, Aluko, Akpan, Nwankwo.

4478.* February, V.A. "Flagellated Skin, A Fine Fetish: The
       'Coloured' as a Stereotype in South African Letters." Ph.D.
       dissertation, University of Leiden, 1977.

       Later published as 4479.

4479. ____. MIND YOUR COLOUR: THE 'COLOURED' STEREOTYPE IN SOUTH
       AFRICAN LITERATURE. London and Boston: Kegan Paul
       International, 1981.

       Abrahams, Brutus, La Guma, Matthews, Mphahlele, Nkosi,
       Nortje, Rive, Small, et al. Revised dissertation, 4478.

4480. Githae Mugo, Micere. "Written Literature and the Black
       Image." In Gachukia and Akivaga, 4799, pp. 30-39.

4481. Hammond, Dorothy and Alta Jablow. THE MYTH OF AFRICA. New
       York: Library of Social Science, 1977.

       Rpt. of THE AFRICA THAT NEVER WAS (New York: Twayne,
       1970), a study of British writing on Africa.

4482. Harris, Wilson. "The Frontier on Which HEART OF DARKNESS
       Stands." RAL, 12 (1981), 86-93; rpt. in Harris, 3506, pp.
       134-41.

       Response to Achebe, BALE 93, and 4470.

4483. Kilson, Marion. "Women and African Literature." JAfrS, 4
       (1977), 161-66.

       Aidoo, Ogot.

4484. Lindfors, Bernth. "The Image of the Afro-American in African
       Literature." In ACTES DU VIIe CONGRÈS DE L'ASSOCIATION
       INTERNATIONALE DE LITTÉRATURE COMPARÉE/PROCEEDINGS OF THE 7TH
       CONGRESS OF THE INTERNATIONAL COMPARATIVE LITERATURE
       ASSOCIATION, I: LITTÉRATURES AMÉRICAINES: DÉPENDANCE,
       INDÉPENDANCE, INTERDÉPENDANCE/LITERATURES OF AMERICA:
       DEPENDENCE, INDEPENDENCE, INTERDEPENDENCE. Ed. Milan
       V. Dimić and Eva Kushner. Stuttgart: Bieber, 1979. Pp.
       473-78.

       Rpt. of BALE 1603, covering Aidoo, Clark, Kgositsile,
       Liyong, Soyinka, et al.

4485. Linton-Umeh, Marie. "The African Heroine." In Bell et al.,
       4472, pp. 39-51.

       Abrahams, Achebe, H.I.E. Dhlomo, Tutuola, et al.

4486. Little, Kenneth. "Women in African Literature." WA, 3
       September 1979, pp. 1598-99, 1601; 10 September 1979, pp.
       1650-51; 17 September 1979, pp. 1691-93; 24 September 1979,

pp. 1759-60.

4487.   ____. "Men in African Literature." WA, 22 October 1979, pp.
        1930-31.

        Survey.

4488.   ____. THE SOCIOLOGY OF URBAN WOMEN'S IMAGE IN AFRICAN
        LITERATURE. London: Macmillan; Totowa, NJ: Rowman &
        Littlefield, 1980.

        Achebe, Aidoo, Aluko, Aniebo, Chahilu, Dipoko, Djoleto,
        Ekwensi, Emecheta, Farah, Ike, Kahiga, Mwangi, Ngugi,
        Njau, Nwankwo, Nwapa, Ogot, Okpewho, p'Bitek, Rubadiri,
        Ruheni, Selormey, Soyinka, Zeleza, et al.

4489.   McCaffrey, Kathleen M. "Images of Women in West African
        Literature and Film: A Struggle against Dual Colonization."
        INTERNATIONAL JOURNAL OF WOMEN'S STUDIES, 3, 1 (1980), 76-88.

        Aidoo, Armah, Awoonor, Konadu, et al.

4490.*   Marais, P.S. "The Black Man in English Poetry in South
        Africa." Master's thesis, University of the Orange Free
        State, 1970.

4491.   Milbury-Steen, Sarah L. EUROPEAN AND AFRICAN STEREOTYPES IN
        TWENTIETH-CENTURY FICTION. New York and London: New York
        University Press, 1981.

        Achebe, Aluko, Conton, Echewa, et al. Rev. of BALE
        1605.

4492.   Niven. Alastair. "The Family in Modern African Literature."
        ArielE, 12, 3 (1981), 81-91.

        Survey.

4493.   Nwezeh, Emmanuel. "West African Writers' Response to the
        European Image of Africa." In Banjo, 3415, pp. 172-84.

        Achebe, Armah, et al.

4494.   Porter, Abioseh M. "Ideology and the Image of Women: Kenyan
        Women in Njau and Ngugi." ArielE, 12, 3 (1981), 61-74.

4495.   Richard, René, and Jean Sevry, eds. MISSIONS ET
        MISSIONNAIRES EN AFRIQUE NOIRE. Montpellier: Centre d'Études
        et de Recherches sur les Pays d'Afrique Noire Anglophones,
        Université Paul Valéry de Montpellier, 1981.

        Proceedings of conference held at Montpellier in October
        1980. Includes 4477, 5148, 5561.

4496.   Rushing, Andrea B. "Images of Black Women in Modern African

Poetry: An Overview." In Bell, et al., 4472, pp. 18-24.
Survey.

4497. Sarvan, C.P. "Racism and the HEART OF DARKNESS." IFR, 7 (1980), 6-10.

Responds to Achebe's views on Conrad, 4470.

4498. Skurjat, Ernestyna. "Obraz afryki niepodleglej w twórczości jej pisarzy [The Image of Independent Africa in the Literary Output of Her Writers]." PRZEGLAD INFORMACJI O AFRYCE, 3 (1976), 125-40.

Achebe, Armah, Awoonor, Soyinka, et al.

4499. Staudt, Kathleen. "The Characterization of Women in Soyinka and Armah." BA SHIRU, 8, 2 (1977), 63-69.

Rpt. of BALE 1611.

4500. Trzebinski, Errol. "The Karen Blixen Debate: 'Ngugi's Racist Attitudes.'" VIVA, June 1981, pp. 21, 23.

Response to Ngugi, 4471.

4501. Wachtel, Eleanor. "The Mother and the Whore: Image and Stereotype of African Women." UMOJA, 1, 2 (1977), 31-48.

In East African literature.

See also 3395, 3516, 3566, 3621, 3733, 3743, 3749, 3753, 3759, 3778, 3786, 3897, 3981, 4008, 4107, 4131, 4142, 4152, 4283, 4301, 4311, 4319, 4394, 4609, 4970, 5120, 5145, 5148, 5200, 5204, 5222, 5257, 5268, 5275, 5429, 5459-60, 5500, 5561, 5704, 5718, 5766, 5810-11, 5836, 5883, 6001, 6075.

Q. AUDIENCE

BOOKS AND ESSAYS

4502. Abwoga, S.O. "What are They Reading?" JOE HOMESTEAD, 7, 1 (1980), 12-13.

Kenya high school and university students surveyed.

4503. Anon. "The Fine Literature of Africa and the Germans." AFRIKA, 3 (1962), 155-57.

4504. Balogun, F. Odun. "Who is the Audience of Modern African Literature: A Reply." OBSIDIAN, 7, 2-3 (1981), 29-36.

Response to Egejuru, 4510.

4505. Brambilla, Cristina. "Scrivere per chi?" NIGRIZIA, 94, 23 (1976), 25-28.

4506. ____. "Escriber, ¿Para quien?" MUNDO NEGRO, 186 (1977), 34-38.

4507. Bruner, David. "African Literature by Radio and Cassette." BA SHIRU, 8, 1 (1977), 37-40.

4508. Dressler, Claus Peter. "Der afrikanische Autor und seine Leser." In Eckardt, 4995, pp. 96-99.

4509. Egejuru, Phanuel Akubueze. BLACK WRITERS: WHITE AUDIENCE: A CRITICAL APPROACH TO AFRICAN LITERATURE. Foreword Chukwuemeka Ike. Hicksville, NY: Exposition Press, 1978.

Achebe, Armah, Ekwensi, Nzekwu, Okara, Soyinka, Tutuola, et al; includes interviews with Achebe, Mphahlele, Ngugi, et al. Rev. of BALE 1618.

4510. ____. "Who is the Audience of Modern African Literature?" OBSIDIAN, 5, 1-2 (1979), 51-58.

See respone by Balogun, 4504.

4511. Hale, Thomas A., and Gerard G. Pigeon. "Artist and Audience: The Problems of Africanisms in African Literature of Western Expression." In Priebe and Hale, 4519, pp. 77-83.

4512. Ikiddeh, Ime. "African Literature and the Generation Gap: Aspects of Contemporary Response to West African Anticolonial Literature." In Gachukia and Akivaga, 4799, pp. 127-38.

Rpt. of BALE 1621. Achebe, et al.

4513. Lalande-Isnard, Fanny. "Typology of Readers and of Public Libraries in West Africa." UNESCO BULLETIN FOR LIBRARIES, 31

(1977), 292-97.

4514.   Malya, Simoni.   CREATING LITERACY SURROUNDINGS IN TANZANIA.
Nairobi: Kenya Literature Bureau, 1978.

4515.   Mjöberg, Jöran.   "De afrikanska författarnas vägar till
publiken. [African Writers' Ways to the Public]."   TIDSKRIFT
FÖR LITTERATURVETENSKAP, 2 (1981), 67-78.

Survey.

4516.* Morris, John Douglas.   "A Study of the Responses to Prose
Fiction of Certain Secondary School Students in Uganda
Leading to Proposals for Promoting Creative Reading."
Master's thesis, University of East Africa, 1969.

4517.   Nkwoh, M.U.E.   "Nigerians Should Encourage Their Own."
PIONEER, 2, 2 (1962), 44-46.

Plea for readers and publishing houses.

4518.   Oyewumi, Oladeji.   "The Pleasures of Reading."   REFLECTOR,
14, 1 (1964), 13-14.

4519.   Priebe, Richard K., and Thomas A. Hale, eds.   ARTIST AND
AUDIENCE: AFRICAN LITERATURE AS A SHARED EXPERIENCE.
Washington, DC: Three Continents Press and the African
Literature Association, 1979.

Selected proceedings from the 1977 African Literature
Association Meeting.   Includes 3783, 4389, 4511, 5583.

4520.   Rønning, Helge.   "Forlag publikum og litteratur in Afrika
[Publishing Houses, Audience and Literature in Africa]."
VINDUET, 1 (1975), 49.

4521.   Wanjala, Chris.   "Reading Habit Catching On With Kenyans."
SUNDAY NATION, 29 January 1978, p.   18.

See also 3383, 3534, 3546, 3574, 3581, 3852, 3859, 3918, 3930, 3988,
4057, 4119, 4172-73, 4184-85, 4199, 4259, 4343, 4345,
4348-50, 4355, 4357, 4359, 4421-22, 4438, 4606, 4631, 4675,
4953, 5069, 5278, 5555, 5624, 5841, 6133.

R. CRAFT OF WRITING

BOOKS AND ESSAYS

4522. Abrahams, Lionel. "On Short Story Writing." NEW CLASSIC, 5 (1978), 15-18.

      In South Africa.

4523. Anon. "The Great PACE Short Story Contest: Here Are the Winners, and a Word of Advice from the Judges." PACE, November 1981, p. 114.

4524. Bogi, Ben. "Problems of a Writer." KENYA WEEKLY NEWS, 17 March 1967, p. 7.

4525. Chinweizu, and Onwuchekwa Jemie. "The Hopkins Disease." OKIKE, 12 (1978), 40-46.

      How to write and read "Serious" and "Significant" poetry. Okigbo and Soyinka used as examples.

4526. Fonlon, Bernard. "The Philosophy, the Science and the Art of the Short Story." ABBIA, 34-37 (1979), 427-38.

4527.* Liswaniso, Mufalo. "Do You Want to Write?" ZMag, 94 (1978), 4, 26-28; 95 (1978), 26-27; 98 (1979), 23-27; 99 (1979), 23-25.

4528. Manu, Steven. "Notes on Creative Writing for Young Writers." GHANA BOOK WORLD, 2 (1979), 17-21.

4529. Mphahlele, Es´kia (Zeke). "Workshop I: Some Guidelines for the Short Story." STAFFRIDER, 1, 4 (1978), 58-59.

4530. ____. "Workshop II: More Guidelines for the Short Story." STAFFRIDER, 2, 1 (1979), 50-52.

      Aidoo, Sentso, et al.

4531. ____. "STAFFRIDER Workshop." STAFFRIDER, 2, 2 (1979), 50-51.

      Ngugi, Themba.

4532. ____. LET´S WRITE A NOVEL. Cape Town: Maskew Miller, 1981.

4533.* Odejide, Abiola. "Can Creative Writing Be Taught?" JOURNAL OF LANGUAGE ARTS AND COMMUNICATION, 1, 1 (1980), 101-07.

4534. Roberts, Gabriel J. "A Talk on Drama." NDAANAN, 5, 1-2 (1976), 32-34.

      How to write a play.

4535.   Serote, M.W.   "Shimmers of Writing: An Exploration."   MARANG,
         (1978), 69-73.

4536.   Thesen, Hjalmar.   "Are You a 1st Class Writer?: An
         Examination."   BLOODY HORSE, 5 (1981), 74-78.

              Conditions governing recognition as a writer in South
              Africa.

See also 3915, 3926, 3973, 4037, 4263, 4425, 4450, 4514, 4767,
         4914-16, 5485, 5543.

S. PERIODICALS

BIBLIOGRAPHY

4537. Anon. COMMONWEALTH SPECIALIST PERIODICALS: AN ANNOTATED
DIRECTORY OF SCIENTIFIC, TECHNICAL AND PROFESSIONAL JOURNALS
PUBLISHED IN COMMONWEALTH DEVELOPING COUNTRIES. London:
Commonwealth Secretariat, 1977.

4538. Engeldinger, Eugene A. "Cumulative Author and Subject Indexes
to STUDIES IN BLACK LITERATURE, Vols. 1-6 (1970-1975)."
SBL, 8, 1 (1977), 7-15.

4539. Goode, Stephen H., comp. INDEX TO COMMONWEALTH LITTLE
MAGAZINES, 1974-1975. Troy, New York: Whitston, 1976.

4540. Howlett, Jacques. INDEX ALPHABÉTIQUE DES AUTEURS, ET INDEX
MÉTHODIQUE DES MATIÈRES DE LA REVUE PRÉSENCE AFRICAINE
1947-1976. Paris: Présence Africaine, 1977.

4541. Ojo-Ade, Femi. ANALYTIC INDEX OF PRESENCE AFRICAINE
(1947-1972). Washington, DC: Three Continents Press, 1977.

4542. Travis, Carole, and Miriam Alman, comps. PERIODICALS FROM
AFRICA: A BIBLIOGRAPHY AND UNION LIST OF PERIODICALS
PUBLISHED IN AFRICA. Boston: G.K. Hall, 1977.

4543. Warwick, Ronald, comp. & ed. COMMONWEALTH LITERATURE
PERIODICALS: A BIBLIOGRAPHY, INCLUDING PERIODICALS OF FORMER
COMMONWEALTH COUNTRIES, WITH LOCATIONS IN THE UNITED KINGDOM.
London: Mansell, 1979.

4544. [Zell, Hans M.] "Major Review Media and Publicity Outlets for
African Studies Material." ABPR, 6 (1980), 183-88.

       List of periodical titles and addresses.

See also 3310, 4336, 4697.

BOOKS AND ESSAYS

4545. Abrahams, Lionel. "THE PURPLE RENOSTER: An Adolescence."
ENGLISH IN AFRICA, 7, 2 (1980), 32-49.

4546. Addison, Graeme. "Drum Beat: An Examination of DRUM."
SPEAK, 1, 4 (1978), 4-9.

4547. Anon. "Two Thousand Pounds for a Feature I Refused to Use."
SUNDAY NATION, 10 November 1963, p. 14.

       Interview with Tom Hopkinson, former editor of DRUM.

4548. Anon. "Kate Abbam: OBAA SIMA." WA, 18 April 1977, pp.
764-65.

Ghanaian women's magazine.

4549. Anon. "Notes." CONTRAST, 11, 3 (1977), 3, 94-96.

Writing in MARANG, literary journal of the University of
Botswana, Lesotho and Swaziland at Gaberone.

4550. Anon. "Editorial." PELCULEF NEWSLETTER, 1, 1 (1978), 1-2.

On founding of newsletter by Pelandaba Cultural Effort.

4551. Anon. "Little Mags Speak Out." NATIONAL STUDENT, 4 (1978),
18.

On STAFFRIDER and SPEAK.

4552. Anon. "The Banning of STAFFRIDER, Vol. 2, No. 1--March
1979: Two Letters." STAFFRIDER, 2, 2 (1979), 2-3.

Letters from and to Director of Publications in South
Africa.

4553. Anon. "Consciousness, Class Struggle and 'Black' Periodicals
in South Africa." WIP, 9 (1979), 56-64.

4554. Anon. "WIETIE Banned." WIETIE, 2 (1980), 16.

Letters exchanged with Censorship Board after banning of
WIETIE 1.

4555. Anon. "Up and Up with PACE, the Top Black Magazine." PACE,
September 1980, p. 32.

4556. Chapman, Mike. "Bloody Horse or Sanguinary Equine: An Open
Letter." BLOODY HORSE, 1 (1980), 100-03.

On BLOODY HORSE.

4557. Chinweizu. "Editorial." OKIKE, 20 (1981), 1.

On tenth anniversary of OKIKE.

4558. Coetzee, Ampie. "Kommentaar [Commentary]." BLOODY HORSE, 1
(1980), 6-7.

On BLOODY HORSE.

4559. Coetzee, J.M. "'STAFFRIDER.'" ABPR, 5 (1979), 235-36.

4560. Cope, Jack. "Notes." CONTRAST, 12, 4 (1979), 3, 96.

On CONTRAST.

4561. ____. "The World of CONTRAST." ENGLISH IN AFRICA, 7, 2

(1980), 1-21.

4562. Cullinan, Patrick. "Announcement: THE BLOODY HORSE."
ENGLISH IN AFRICA, 7, 2 (1980), 86-87.

4563. ____. "Comment." BLOODY HORSE, 1 (1980), 5-6.

On BLOODY HORSE.

4564. ____. "Comment." BLOODY HORSE, 6 (1981), 2.

On demise of BLOODY HORSE.

4565. Fugard, Athol, Shiela Fugard, André P. Brink, et al. "The
Banning of STAFFRIDER No. 1." STAFFRIDER, 1, 2 (1978), 2-3.

Letters concerning censorship.

4566. Gordimer, Nadine. "An Unkillable Rabbit-family." CONTRAST,
13, 2 (1980), 25-26.

Notes on anniversary of CONTRAST.

4567. Gordon, Gerald. "Jack Cope and CONTRAST." CONTRAST, 13, 1
(1980), 25-31.

4568. Gray, Stephen. "Death of a Little Magazine." CONTRAST, 11,
2 (1977), 43-49.

IZWI.

4569. Haresnape, Geoffrey. "Notes." CONTRAST, 13, 2 (1980), 3,
96.

50th number of CONTRAST; African Studies Association
Conference.

4570. Jones, Eldred. "Ten Years of AFRICAN LITERATURE TODAY."
ALT, 10 (1979), 1-5.

4571. Kamin, Wayne. "PELCULEF: Pelandaba Cultural Effort." GAR,
32 (1978), 13.

Newsletter of cultural association of South African
refugees living in Botswana.

4572. Kirkwood, Mike. "STAFFRIDER: An Informal Discussion."
ENGLISH IN AFRICA, 7, 2 (1980), 22-31.

Nick Visser interviews Mike Kirkwood.

4573. Kunene, Daniel P. "STAFFRIDER." ALA NEWSLETTER, 6, 3 (1980),
11-12.

4574. Maximin, Daniel. "´Drum´ ou la génération perdue: Les

Intellectuels sud-africains de la revue ´Drum´ dans les
années 50." In Society of African Culture, 3675, pp.
331-42.

Mphahlele, Nakasa, Nkosi, et al.

4575. Morsiani, Jamilè. "BLACK ORPHEUS e la nascita della
letterature nigeriana." SpM, 5 (1976), 132-42.

4576. Nkosi, Lewis. "The Role of the Literary Magazine." TLS, 6
June 1980, p. 640.

4577. Odendaal, Welma. "DONGA: One Angry Voice." ENGLISH IN
AFRICA, 7, 2 (1980), 67-74.

4578. Pepi, Esther. "PRESENCE AFRICAINE: La battaglia degli
intellettuali." NIGRIZIA, 96, 5 (1978), 8.

4579. Rabie, Jan. "CONTRAST, vyftig bloeisels jonk [CONTRAST:
Fifty Flowerings Young]." CONTRAST, 13, 2 (1980), 26-28.

Notes on anniversary of magazine.

4580.* Rabkin, D. "DRUM Magazine (1951-1961) and the Work of Black
South African Writers Associated with It." Ph.D.
dissertation, University of Leeds, 1975.

4581. Ravenscroft, Arthur. "Editorial." JCL, 13, 3 (1979), v-vi.

Valedictory comment by retiring editor.

4582. Rive, Richard. "CONTRAST and the Will to Survive."
CONTRAST, 13, 2 (1980), 28-30.

Notes on anniversary of magazine.

4583. Scholtz, Anton. "Mirror of Real Life: The World of
Photo-Comics." SPEAK, 1, 4 (1978), 25-28.

In South Africa.

4584. Sepamla, Sipho. "A Note on NEW CLASSIC and S´KETSH´."
ENGLISH IN AFRICA, 7, 2 (1980), 81-85.

4585. Simon, Barney. "My Years with THE CLASSIC: A Note." ENGLISH
IN AFRICA, 7, 2 (1980), 75-80.

4586. Strauss, Peter. "Straight Speaking." DONGA, 3 (1976), 1.

On editorial policy of DONGA.

4587. ____. "A Review: STAFFRIDER." REALITY, 10, 6 (1978), 10-11.

See also 3386, 3453, 3502, 3551, 3596, 3663, 3694, 3788, 3801, 4098,
    4150, 4190, 4228, 4523, 4638, 4681, 4699, 4721, 4739, 4743,
    4747, 5638.

T. PUBLISHING

BIBLIOGRAPHY

See also 3364-67, 4273, 4275-76, 4280, 4697.

BOOKS AND ESSAYS

4588. Aje, S.B. "The Role of Publishing in the Dissemination of Knowledge." NIGERBIBLIOS, 3, 1 (1978), 4-6, 19.

4589. Akinleye, Michael. "Publishing Personnel and Management in Developing Countries: A Nigerian View." ABPR, 6 (1980), 215-17.

4590. Altbach, Philip G., and Sheila McVey, eds. PERSPECTIVES ON PUBLISHING. Lexington, MA: Lexington, 1976.

   Includes 4591, 4671-72.

4591. Altbach, Philip G. "Literary Colonialism: Books in the Third World." In Altbach and McVey, 4590, pp. 83-101.

   Review of BALE 1714.

4592. Amadi, Tony. "German Fury at Frankfurt Fair." AIBEPM, 112 (1980), 68.

   Book Fair.

4593. Anon. "On the Carpet." SUNDAY NATION, 17 November 1963, p. 14.

   Interview with Mark Longman, British executive of Longman-Green.

4594. Anon. "African Writing." KENYA WEEKLY NEWS, 19 September 1969, p. 3.

4595. Anon. "The Army of African Authors." WA, 7 March 1977, pp. 459-61; 14 March 1977, pp. 515-16; 21 March 1977, pp. 556-57.

   On increasing output of West African authors. Lists new titles.

4596. Anon. "Publishing: Whose Copyright?" WEEKLY REVIEW, 3 November 1978, p. 12.

   Controversy over East African Publishing House being granted right to print books copyrighted by other publishers.

4597. Anon. "A Place for Poetry." WA, 20 November 1978, pp. 2289-90.

Publication opportunities discussed at Africa Centre in London.

4598.   Anon. "The Sorry Plight of African Writers." STANDARD, 28 November 1978, p. 14.

Publishing in Kenya.

4599.   Anon. "Publishers, Printers in for a Hard Time." WEEKLY REVIEW, 11 April 1980, pp. 27-31.

In Kenya.

4600.   Anon. "The Literature Bureau and National Culture." DAILY NATION, 22 May 1980, p. 6.

On establishment of Kenya Literature Bureau.

4601.   Anon. "Frankfurt Looks Towards Africa." WA, 6 October 1980, p. 1961.

Book Fair.

4602.   Anon. "Matchet's Diary at the Frankfurt Book Fair." WA, 20 October 1980, pp. 2055-57.

4603.   Anon. "Frankfurt Bookfair." SECHABA, January 1981, pp. 27-29.

4604.   Anon. "The Ife Book Fair." WA, 2 February 1981, pp. 224-25.

4605.   Anon. "Achievements at Ile-Ife Book Fair." AIBEPM, 117 (1981), 70-71.

4606.   Anon. "The Challenge to Kenyan Publishers." WEEKLY REVIEW, 26 June 1981, pp. 46-51.

4607.   Barrett, Lindsay. "Promoting Knowledge Through Publishing." WA, 9 March 1981, pp. 500-02.

4608.   Barton, Vivienne. "How We Broke into the Publishing Business and Why." SUNDAY NATION, 20 October 1968, pp. 23-24.

Interview with Bethwell Ogot, then Chairman of the East African Publishing House.

4609.   Bell, Roseann P. "The Absence of the African Woman Writer." CLAJ, 21 (1978), 491-98.

Aidoo, Amadi, Ogot, Sutherland, et al.

4610.   Benoit, Marie, and Gaetan Benoit. "Libraries and Publishing in Mauritius." ABPR, 6 (1980), 225-28.

4611.   Bolze, Louis W. "The Book Publishing Scene in Zimbabwe."
        ABPR, 6 (1980), 229-36.

4612.   Breitinger, Eckhard. "Buchproduktion und Buchmarkt in Ghana:
        eine Fallstudie." BDB, 22 August 1980, pp. 2055-58.

4613.   Brutus, Dennis. "African Publishing Houses: A Proposal."
        AR, 38 (1980), 233-36.

4614.   Chakava, Henry. "Publishing in a Multilingual Situation:
        The Kenya Case." ABPR, 3 (1977), 83-90; UMMA-N, 6 (1977),
        16-17, 20, 24, 29-30.

4615.   Chege, John Waruingi. COPYRIGHT LAW AND PUBLISHING IN KENYA.
        Nairobi: Kenya Literature Bureau, 1978.

4616.   Chirwa, Chris. "Publishing in Zambia: The Work of NECZAM."
        ZLAJ, 12, 2 (1980), 56-63.

4617.   Dean, Elizabeth. "Publishing in Zambia." ZLAJ, 12, 2,
        (1980), 47-55.

4618.   Djoleto, Amu. "The Book Trade of Ghana and the Ghana
        Booksellers Association." GHANA BOOK WORLD, 2 (1979), 1-4.

4619.   Dorsey, David A. "A Preliminary Guide to Publishers and
        Booksellers in Africa." In Hale and Priebe, 4810, pp.
        255-70.

4620.   ____. "Buying African Books in America." CALLALOO, 8-10
        (1980), 203-10.

4621.   Egejuru, Phanuel. "The African Writer and Foreign
        Publishers." OBSIDIAN, 4, 2 (1978), 19-27.

4622.   Fraser, Robert. "Publication Problems Faced By Poets in West
        Africa." WA, 31 July 1978, pp. 1492-93.

4623.* Harrell-Bond, Barbara. AFRICA ASSERTS ITS IDENTITY, PART I:
        THE FRANKFURT BOOK FAIR. Hanover, NH: American Universities
        Field Staff, 1981.

4624.* Hart, Norman. THE LIVELY WORD: CHRISTIAN PUBLISHING AND
        BROADCASTING IN EAST AFRICA. Limbe, Malawi: Popular
        Publications, 1975.

4625.   Hill, Alan. "In Africa: Ex Africa." TLS, 19 September
        1968, pp. 1056-57.

4626.   ____. "Publishing in Africa." TLS, 10 October 1980, p.
        1114.

4627.   Hussain, Iqbal S. "Africa at the Frankfurt Book Fair."
        AFRIKA, 20, 12 (1979), 21-22.

4628. Imfeld, A.C. "Africa Focus at Frankfurt." WA, 26 May 1980,
       pp. 931-32.

       Book Fair.

4629. Imfeld, Al, and Gerd Meuer. "Bauen Bücher Brücken?" BDB, 22
       August 1980, pp. 2007-09.

4630. Jacob, H. "Educational Publishing in Africa." EAST AFRICAN
       LIBRARY ASSOCIATION BULLETIN, 13 (1972), 153-64.

4631. Kadima-Nzuji, Mukala. "Le livre africain et sa diffusion."
       PA, 115 (1980), 97-107.

4632.* Kaungamno, E. E. THE BOOK INDUSTRY IN TANZANIA. Dar es
       Salaam: Tanzania Library Service, 1980.

4633. Kotei, S. I. A. THE BOOK TODAY IN AFRICA. Paris: UNESCO,
       1981.

4634. Kovalenko, Yuri. "Ghanaian Literature in the USSR." LEGON
       OBSERVER, 10, 3 (1978), 65-66.

4635. Kramer-Prein, Gabriele. "Wir haben viel nachzuholen." BDB,
       22 August 1980, pp. 2075-77.

       Interview with Jörg Becker, publisher of Third World
       literature in Germany.

4636. LaSalle, Peter. "Buma Kor & Co." WORLDVIEW, 23, 9, (1980),
       15-16.

       Publisher in Cameroon.

4637. Lindfors, Bernth. "Interview with John Nottingham." ABPR, 5
       (1979), 81-85; rpt. in Lindfors, 3387.

       Nairobi publisher.

4638. ____. "Interview with Terry Hirst." ABPR, 5 (1979), 88-91;
       rpt. in Lindfors, 3387.

       Publisher of JOE MAGAZINE.

4639. ____. "Commerce Versus Creativity in Nigeria." AFRISCOPE,
       10, 5-6 (1980), 34-35.

4640. Mbonde, J. P. "Publishing in East Africa." EAST AFRICAN
       LIBRARY ASSOCIATION BULLETIN, 10 (1969), 38-40.

4641. Mensah, Nana Kwaku. "Bookshops and Bookselling." GHANA BOOK
       WORLD, 2 (1979), 8-10.

       In Ghana.

4642. Meuer, Gerd. "A New Prize for African Book Publishing."
       AFRIKA, 20, 8 (1979), 22-23.

       Interview with Hans Zell.

4643. ____. "Breakthrough for African Literature in West Germany."
       AFRIKA, 20, 12 (1979), 20; rpt. as "African Literature Comes
       to Germany." NEW AFRICAN, February 1980, pp. 48-49.

       New translation series.

4644. ____. "Wir Könnten die Manuskripte auch verschenken." BDB,
       22 August 1980, pp. 2054-55.

4645. Moore, Gerald. "Nigeria." SATURDAY REVIEW, 19 April 1975,
       p. 29.

4646. Mwiyeriwa, Steve S. "Printing Presses and Publishing in
       Malawi." ABPR, 4 (1978), 87, 89-91, 93-97; SOCIETY OF MALAWI
       JOURNAL, 31, 2 (1978), 31-53.

4647. Mzee, Said. "Mehr als nur die Krumen." BDB, 22 August 1980,
       pp. 2058-61.

       Publishing for schools.

4648. Namponya, Clemence R. "History and Development of Printing
       and Publishing in Malawi." LIBRI, 28 (1978), 167-81.

4649. Ndenga, Abner. "Which Way the African Publishers."
       STANDARD, 28 November 1978, pp. 13, 15.

       Kenya publishing industry.

4650. Ngwalla, Mike. "Book Business Can't Be Managed by Phone."
       NAIROBI TIMES, 25 March 1979, p. 10.

       In Kenya.

4651. ____. "The Big Names in Publishing." NAIROBI TIMES, 25
       March 1979, p. 10.

       In Kenya.

4652. Nyarko, Kwame. "Some Aspects of the Book Trade in Ghana."
       ABPR, 6 (1980), 241-46.

4653. Obidike, Egbuna. "Focus on Black Africa: The 32nd Frankfurt
       Book Fair, 8th-13th October 1980." AFRIKA SPECTRUM, 15
       (1980), 211-13.

4654. Ochieng, William. "The Big Dilemma Facing Kenya's Budding
       Writers." SUNDAY NATION, 7 May 1978, p. 29.

       Inadequate publishing opportunities.

4655. Okoli, Enukora Joe. "Afrocentric Publishing." WA, 18 May
       1981, pp. 1098, 1103.

       Interview with Arthur Agwuncha Nwankwo, Chairman of the
       Fourth Dimension Publishing Company.

4656. Okri, Benjamin. "The Problems of Young Writers." DAILY
       TIMES, 10 August 1978, p. 20.

4657. Omotoso, Kole. "The Indigenous Publisher and the Future of
       Culture in Nigeria." In THE INDIGENOUS FOR NATIONAL
       DEVELOPMENT (ESSAYS ON SOCIAL, POLITICAL, EDUCATIONAL,
       ECONOMIC & CULTURAL ISSUES). Ed. G.O. Onibonoje, Kole
       Omotoso, and O.A. Lawal. Ibadan: Onibonoje Press and Book
       Industries, 1976. Pp. 59-70.

4658. ____. "The Year of the Book: Reflections on the New Culture
       of the Book in Nigerian Society." PAN AFRICAN BOOK WORLD, 1,
       1 (1981), 11.

4659. Onyeama, Dillibe. "In Search of Nigeria's James Hadley
       Chase." WA, 14 January 1980, pp. 63-65.

       Publishing scene in Nigeria.

4660. Otieno, Arthur Jones. "Encourage Young Writers." DAILY
       NATION, 2 May 1980, p. 7.

       Letter to editor complaining about absence of publishing
       opportunities in Kenya for young writers.

4661. Paren, Elizabeth. "The Multinational Publishing Firm in
       Africa: The Macmillan Perspective." ABPR, 4 (1978), 15-17.

4662. Plangger, A. B. "Some Observations on Publishing in
       Zimbabwe." ZIMBABWE LIBRARIAN, 11, 3-4 (1979), 41-44.

4663.* ____. "Mambo Press: Neu erstanden." WENDEKREIS, 86, 4
       (1981), 20.

4664. Rathgeber, Eva-Maria McLean. "Nigeria's University Presses:
       Problems and Prospects." ABPR, 5 (1979), 13-17.

4665. Rea, Julian. "Aspects of African Publishing, 1945-74." In
       AFRICAN STUDIES SINCE 1945: A TRIBUTE TO BASIL DAVIDSON. Ed.
       Christopher Fyfe. London: Longman, 1976. Pp. 96-105.

4666. Ripken, Peter. "Frankfurt Book Fair 1980 -- a Success for
       African Publishers?" AFRIKA, 21, 11 (1980), 23-24.

4667. Sabiiti, C. S. "The Work of the East African Literature
       Bureau." EAST AFRICAN LIBRARY ASSOCIATION BULLETIN, 10
       (1969), 144-52.

4668.   Schulz, Hermann. "Aus Negern Afrikaner machen." BDB, 22
        August 1980, pp. 2077-78.

4669.   Skurjat, Ernestyna. "Literatura czarnej afryki w przekladach
        na jezyk polski [The Literature of Black Africa in Polish
        Translation]." PRZEGLAD INFORMATION O AFRYCE, 3 (1976),
        177-88.

4670.   Smidt, Lorna de. "Avoiding the Issues in Frankfurt." NEW
        AFRICAN, November 1980, pp. 50-51.

        Book Fair.

4671.   Smith, Datus C., Jr. "The Bright Promise of Publishing in
        Developing Countries." In Altbach and McVey, 4590, pp.
        117-28.

4672.   Smith, Keith. "Who Controls Book Publishing in Anglophone
        Middle Africa?" In Altbach & McVey, 4590, pp. 129-40.

        Rpt. of BALE 1798.

4673.   Splett, Oskar. "Fürsprache für afrikanische Literatur: Ein
        Versuch der Frankfurter Buchmesse." AFRICA-POST, 27 (1980),
        346-47.

4674.   Ude, Chivuzo. "Publishing African Authors in America."
        TRANSLATION, 3 (1976), 44-47.

        Nok Books.

4675.   Wallace, Milverton, et al. "The Ife Book Fair Conversation."
        OKIKE, 20 (1981), 35-49.

        Discussion with Kole Omotoso, Femi Osofisan, Chinweizu,
        Niyi Osundare, and G. G. Darah on publishing, writing
        and reading in Nigeria and Ghana.

4676.   Wanjala, Chris, and Atieno Odhiambo. "Introduction."
        UMMA-N, 5 (1977), 13-14.

        THE KENYAN LITERARY EXPERIENCE, book exhibition catalog.

4677.   Weidhaas, Peter. "Zum Thema der Buchmesse: Schwarzafrika:
        Auf der Suche nach sich selbst." BDB, 22 August 1980, p.
        2006.

        Frankfurt Bookfair.

4678.   Williams, Geoffrey J. "The Zambian Publishing Scene: A
        Commentary." ABPR, 3 (1977), 15-22.

4679.   Yankey, J. E. K. "A Short History of Printing in Ghana."
        GHANA BOOK WORLD, 1 (1978), 31-33.

4680.   Zell, Hans M. "Publishing Progress in Black Africa
        1973-1977." In Zell, 3366, pp. xi-xxxvi.

4681.   ____. "Publishing Progress in Africa 1975-76: Problems in
        Securing Information and the Role of THE AFRICAN BOOK
        PUBLISHING RECORD." PROGRESS IN AFRICAN BIBLIOGRAPHY:
        SCOLMA CONFERENCE, COMMONWEALTH INSTITUTE, 17-18 MARCH 1977
        PROCEEDINGS. London: SCOLMA, 1977. Section 3, pp. 1-31.

4682.   ____. "African Authors and Publishers." WA, 11 April 1977,
        p. 708.

        Response to SCOLMA conference report, 4942.

4683.   ____. "Ife Book Fair, 1978." WA, 3 April 1978, pp. 650-52;
        ABPR, 4 (1978), 83-86.

4684.   ____. "Interview: ´Wunmi Adegbonmire.´" ABPR, 4 (1978),
        11-14.

        President of Nigerian Booksellers Association and
        Director of Ife Book Fair.

4685.   ____. "The Ife Book Fair, 1979." WA, 2 April 1979, pp.
        583-85; ABPR, 5 (1979), 154-56.

4686.   ____. "Publishing in West Africa: Producing Books Against
        the Odds." WA, 27 August 1979, pp. 1553-56.

4687.   ____. "Multinationals´ Role in Publishing." WA, 3 September
        1979, pp. 1601-02.

4688.   ____. "The Noma Award for Publishing in Africa." RAL, 10
        (1979), 277-78.

4689.   ____. "Interview: James Currey." ABPR, 5 (1979), 237-39.

        Editorial Director of Heinemann Educational Books.

4690.   ____. "African Writers and Their Publishers." ZEITSCHRIFT
        FÜR KULTURAUSTASCH, 29 (1979), 290-301.

4691.   ____. "Interview: Said Mzee." ABPR, 6 (1980), 15-16.

        Coordinator for African focus at Frankfurt Book Fair.

4692.   ____. "Who´s Who of African Publishers at the Frankfurt Book
        Fair 1980." ABPR, 6 (1980), 171-82.

4693.   ____. "Some Dealers in African Books in Europe and the USA."
        ABPR, 6 (1980), 191-93.

4694.   ____. "The First Noma Award for Publishing in Africa."
        ABPR, 6 (1980), 199-203.

4695. ____. "The 6th Ife Book Fair." ABPR, 7 (1981), 105-06.

4696. ____. "Frankfurt Book Fair 1980." ABPR, 7 (1981), 5-8.

See also 3335, 3343, 3383, 3387, 3407, 3437, 3450, 3462, 3495, 4098,
    4284, 4288, 4292, 4297, 4321, 4331, 4338, 4517, 4520-21,
    4753, 4755, 4869, 4948, 5512, 5552, 5554, 5687, 5770-72,
    5844, 5853.

U. CENSORSHIP

BIBLIOGRAPHY

4697. Anon. CATALOGUE OF BANNED BOOKS, PERIODICALS AND RECORDS
       FROM 1st DECEMBER 1967 TO 31st DECEMBER 1976. Salisbury:
       Board of Censors, 1977.

       Rhodesia (now Zimbabwe).

4698. Anon. "Prohibited Publications." 16 January 1978, p. 5.

       List of books and journals banned in Kenya.

BOOKS AND ESSAYS

4699. Achebe, Chinua. "The Annoying Voice of the Artist." INDEX
       ON CENSORSHIP, 10, 6 (1981), 59.

4700. ____. "The Beast of Fanaticism." INDEX ON CENSORSHIP, 10, 6
       (1981), 61.

       Extract from speech given at a conference of Nigerian
       writers held at the University of Nigeria at Nsukka.

4701. Akerman, Anthony. "'Prejudicial to the Safety of the State':
       Censorship and the Theatre in South Africa." THEATRE Q, 7,
       28 (1977-78), 54-57.

4702. Alvarez-Péreyre, Jacques. "Pyramids of Shame: Censorship in
       South Africa." GAf, 16, 2 (1977-78), 7-23.

4703. Anon. "Censorship Legislation: What It Is All About."
       DONGA, 5 (1977), 6.

       On amendment to South Africa's Publications Act of 1974.

4704. Anon. "How to Face Up to Pornography." SUNDAY NATION, 12
       November 1978, p. 6.

4705. Anon. "Another Glimpse of Slavery: A Lawyer's View."
       STAFFRIDER, 3, 3 (1980), 36-37.

       On banning of Matshoba's CALL ME NOT A MAN.

4706. Anon. "Cameroon: New Press Law." INDEX ON CENSORSHIP, 10,
       1 (1981), 62-63.

4707. Brink, André. "Samizdat, Lamizdat." SPEAK, 1, 3 (1978),
       14-15.

       South Africa.

4708. ____. "Censorship and the Author." CRITICAL ARTS, 1, 2
(1980), 16-26.

South Africa.

4709. Coetzee, Ampie. "Kommentaar: Literêre Meriete en Moraliteit
[Commentary: Literary Merit and Morality]." BLOODY HORSE, 2
(1980), 3-5.

4710. Connell, Dorothy. "South Africa: Cultural Boycott -- Yes or
No?" INDEX ON CENSORSHIP, 4, 2 (1975), 5-9.

Followed by opinions on 34 writers, pp. 10-38, including
Lionel Abrahams, Cheney-Coker, Head, La Guma, Sellassie,
et al.

4711. Cope, Jack. "Notes." CONTRAST, 11, 2 (1977), 3, 94-96.

Censorship; teaching of South African literature in
South African universities; poetry competition.

4712. de Villiers, Andre. "South African Writers Talking."
ENGLISH IN AFRICA, 6, 2 (1979), 1-23.

Mphahlele, Nadine Gordimer and André Brink participate
in round table on literature and censorship in South
Africa.

4713. Driver, Dorothy. "Control of the Black Mind is the Main Aim
of Censorship." S AFRICAN OUTLOOK, 110 (1980), 10-13.

South Africa.

4714. Ginwala, Frene. "South Africa's Censorship Laws." INDEX ON
CENSORSHIP, 4, 2 (1975), 38-40.

4715. Goldberg, Melvin. "Anatomy of Melancholy." SPEAK, 1, 3
(1978), 16-17.

South Africa.

4716. Gordimer, Nadine. "98 Kinds of Censorship in South Africa."
HEKIMA, 1 (1980), 115-19.

Rpt. of BALE 1834.

4717. ____. "Censorship and the Word." BLOODY HORSE, 1 (1980),
20-24.

South Africa.

4718. ____. "New Forms of Strategy -- No Change of Heart."
CRITICAL ARTS, 1, 2 (1980) 27-33; INDEX ON CENSORSHIP, 10, 1
(1981), 4-9.

South Africa.

4719.   Gordon, Gerald. "The Right to Write." INDEX ON CENSORSHIP,
        4, 2 (1975), 41-44.

        In South Africa; rpt. of BALE 1836.

4720.   Grant, Jane. "Silenced Generation." INDEX ON CENSORSHIP, 6,
        3 (1977), 38-43.

        Exiled writers unread in South Africa.

4721.   Hachten, William A. "Black Journalists under Apartheid."
        INDEX ON CENSORSHIP, 8, 3 (1979), 43-48.

4722.   Kabeba, Don. "Uganda: No Censors Needed." INDEX ON
        CENSORSHIP, 8, 2 (1979), 18-21.

        Serumaga, et al.

4723.   Karaza-Karumaya. "Burning Books with Idi Amin: A Personal
        Reminiscence of Censorship in Uganda." ZLAJ, 10, 2 (1978),
        45-57.

4724.   Kunene, Daniel P. "Ideas Under Arrest: Censorship in South
        Africa." RAL, 12 (1981), 421-39.

4725.   Larson, Charles R. "African Dissenters." NYTBR, 19 February
        1978, pp. 3, 22.

        Ngugi, et al.

4726.   Laurence, John. "Censorship by Skin Colour." INDEX ON
        CENSORSHIP, 6, 2 (1977), 40-43.

        South Africa.

4727.   McIlwraith, Harriet. "Dr. Banda's Banned Books." INDEX ON
        CENSORSHIP, 8, 6 (1979), 56-58.

4728.   Manganyi, Noel Chabani. "The Censored Imagination." ENGLISH
        IN AFRICA, 6, 2 (1979), 24-32.

        Mphahlele et al.; rpt. in Manganyi, 3570.

4729.   Mathews, A. S. "Censorship, Access to Information and Public
        Debate." THEORIA, 55 (1980), 21-31.

        South Africa.

4730.   Mezgebe, Alem. "Ethiopia -- The Deadly Game." INDEX ON
        CENSORSHIP, 7, 4 (1978), 16-20.

4731.   Mitten, Graham. "Tanzania: A Case Study." INDEX ON
        CENSORSHIP, 6, 5 (1977), 35-46.

On government censorship of the media.

4732. Mustapha, Mukhtar. "Freetown Antics." INDEX ON CENSORSHIP, 9, 5 (1980), 52-54.

Censorship of page and stage in Sierra Leone.

4733. Mutahi, Wahome. "Ban These Books." NAIROBI TIMES, 7 January 1979, p. 4.

Maillu and western popular literature.

4734. Mutloatse, Mothobi. "Statement on Censorship." REALITY, 12, 1 (1980) 9.

On behalf of South African PEN Centre.

4735. Ndifang, David. "Restraining the Word." WA, 21-28 December 1981, pp. 3054-55.

4736. Ndovi, Victor. "Censorship in Malawi. INDEX ON CENSORSHIP, 8, 1 (1979), 22-25.

Interview with journalist Victor Ndovi.

4737. Ngatara, Ludovick. "A Long Way to Go." INDEX ON CENSORSHIP, 10, 3 (1981), 50-51.

Tanzania.

4738. Ngugi [wa Thiong'o], James. "Why Not Let Us be the Judges?" SUNDAY NATION, 29 July 1962, p. 4.

On government censorship in Kenya.

4739. Rajab, Ahmed. "Introduction to Special Issue on Africa." INDEX ON CENSORSHIP, 9, 3 (1980), 3-4.

4740. Rive, Richard. "Black is Banned." SPEAK, 1, 3 (1978), 12-13.

In South Africa.

4741. Silver, Louise. "The Statistics of Censorship." SOUTH AFRICAN LAW JOURNAL, 96 (1979), 120-26.

4742. Sole, Kelwyn. "The Graveyard and the Massacres." SPEAK, 1, 3 (1978), 7-9.

South Africa.

4743. Subramoney, Marimuthu. "I Don't Think I'll Last Much Longer." INDEX ON CENSORSHIP, 10, 3 (1981), 35-38.

Interview with journalist who was national vice-

president of the Media Workers Association of South
Africa.

4744.   Versfeld, Martin. "Pro cui bono." SPEAK, 1, 3 (1978),
10-11.

South Africa.

4745.   Wanjala, Chris. "We Need to Censor Some of Our Literature."
SUNDAY NATION, 21 May 1978, p. 15.

Maillu, Mangua, and popular literature.

4746.   Weiss, Ruth. "Zimbabwe: Black Editors In." INDEX ON
CENSORSHIP, 10, 3 (1981), 27-31.

4747.   Woods, Donald. "South Africa: Black Editors Out." INDEX ON
CENSORSHIP, 10, 3 (1981), 32-34.

See also 3424, 3490, 3542, 3570, 3614, 3903, 3940-41, 4099, 4125,
4324, 4386, 4552, 4554, 4565, 4904-07, 5470, 5510, 5553,
5686, 5698, 5736, 5786.

V. RESEARCH

BIBLIOGRAPHY

4748. Anon. EGYPT, NORTH AFRICA AND SUB-SAHARAN AFRICA: A
DISSERTATION BIBLIOGRAPHY. Introd. Lois A. Aroian. Ann
Arbor: University Microfilms International, 1979.

4749. Anon. "Recent Dissertations." RAL, 8 (1977), 129-32; 9
(1978), 91-94, 449-55; 10 (1979), 279-84; 11 (1980) 373-77.

On oral and written literatures.

4750. Sander, Reinhard W. "B.A. Theses in the Department of
English, University of Nigeria, Nsukka, 1975/76 Academic
Year." RAL, 8 (1977), 343-49.

4751. Sims, Michael, and Alfred Kagan. AMERICAN AND CANADIAN
DOCTORAL DISSERTATIONS AND MASTER'S THESES ON AFRICA,
1886-1974. Waltham, MA: African Studies Association, 1976.

See also 3332, 3717.

BOOKS AND ESSAYS

4752. Arnold, Stephen H. "African Literary Studies: Profile and
Guide to a New Discipline." In Ray, et al., 4900, pp.
128-51.

4753. Boyd, Allen R. "African Imprint Library Services: Bringing
Together the Requirements of Research Libraries." ABPR, 6
(1980) 237-39.

4754. Brindley, D. J. "South African and African Literature."
CRUX, 14, 3 (1980), 25.

On bibliography project designed to assist teachers and
students in South Africa.

4755. Calder, Angus. "The Making of SCHWARZER ORPHEUS: Janheinz
Jahn and George Shepperson." JCL, 15, 1 (1980), 5-14.

4756. Couzens, Tim. "Research in South African Literature."
SNARL, 5 (1976), 15-16.

4757. ____. "Sebokeng, Doories and Bra Jiggs: Research in South
African Literature." In NEW SOUTH AFRICAN WRITING.
Hillbrow, South Africa: Lorton, 1977. Pp. 29-41.

Dikobe, Gwala, et al.

4758. ____. "The ABC of Research: Research in South African
Literature." AFRICA PERSPECTIVE, 4 (1979), 21-26.

4759.   Gérard, Albert S. "New Frontier for Comparative Literature: Africa." ENGLISH IN AFRICA, 6, 2 (1979), 33-38; KOMPARATISTISCHE HEFTE, 1 (1980), 8-13.

4760.   ___. "The Study of African Literature: Birth and Early Growth of a New Branch of Learning." CRCL, 7 (1980), 67-92.

4761.   Grassin, Jean-Marie. "Les littératures africaines modernes devant la documentation encyclopédique internationale." ALA, 50 (1978), 53-61.

   Followed by discussion, 62-63.

4762.   ___. "La littérature africaine comparée: tradition et modernité." ALA, 54-55 (1979-80), 3-10.

4763.* Klíma, Vladimír. "Africké literatury a komparatistika [African literatures and Comparative literature]." CJVŠ, 19 (1975-76), 433-35.

4764.   Lindfors, Bernth. "Researching African Literatures." LRN, 4 (1979), 171-80.

4765.   ___. "Towards a Nigerian Literary Archive." NSAL, 3 (1980), 145-52.

   Tutuola, et al.

4766.   Liyong, Taban lo. "A Tribute to Chief Ulli Beier on the Occasion of his Receiving an Honorary Doctorate of Johannes Gutenberg University at Mainz, 11 May 1979." ACOLIT, 5 (1979), 14-17.

4767.   Makouta-Mboukou, Jean-Pierre. "Suggestions méthodologiques aux candidats au Diplôme d´Études Approfondies (D.E.A.) de Littératures Négro-Africaines." AdUA, 12D (1979), 221-44.

4768.   Nikiforova, I. "Problèmes des études comparées des littératures africaines contemporaines." In Köpeczi et al., 3540, pp. 257-60.

4769.   p´Bitek, Okot. "Parroting of Ideas No Use to Africa." DAILY NATION, 18 July 1972, p. 10.

4770.   Schoeck, R. J. "Towards an Inclusion of Non-Western Views of These Matters." CNLR, 1, 3 (1978), 4-6.

   Cross-cultural perspectives on the humanities needed. Soyinka discussed.

4771.   Soyinka, Wole. "The Scholar in African Society." In COLLOQUIUM PROCEEDINGS, COLLOQUIUM ON BLACK CIVILIZATION AND EDUCATION, SECOND WORLD BLACK AND AFRICAN FESTIVAL OF ARTS AND CULTURE. Ed. A. U. Iwara and E. Mveng. Lagos: Federal Military Government of Nigeria, 1977. Vol. I, pp. 44-53.

4772. Sulzer, Peter. "Die Africana-Sammlung der Stadtbibliothek
       Winterthur." GAf, 19, 2 (1981), 161-62.

2473. Thiry, François, and Michel Fabre. "Inventaire-Répertoire
       des bibliothèques et centres parisiens possédant des
       collections africaines." AFRAMN, Supplement (1979), 1-17.

4774. Wolcke, Irmtraud D. "Afrikanische Literatursammlungen in der
       Bundesrepublik Deutschland und in der Schweiz." ZEITSCHRIFT
       FÜR KULTURAUSTAUSCH, 29 (1979), 306-07.

See also 3331-32, 3354-55, 3359, 3369, 3372, 3375-76, 3380, 3387,
       3415, 3517, 3716, 3908, 3937, 4006, 4027, 4089, 4205, 4216,
       4233, 4247, 4255, 4335, 4511, 4788, 4795-96, 4800, 4821,
       4829, 4833, 4848, 4863, 4898, 5219, 5897-98, 6123.

W. TEACHING

BIBLIOGRAPHY

4775. Stanford, Barbara Dodds, and Karima Amin. BLACK LITERATURE
FOR HIGH SCHOOL STUDENTS. Urbana: National Council of
Teachers of English, 1978. Pp. 169-72, 224-28.

Suggestions for syllabus.

See also 4804, 4812.

BOOKS AND ESSAYS

4776.* Anon. COMMONWEALTH LITERATURE IN SCOTTISH SCHOOLS.
Edinburgh: Commonwealth Institute, Scotland, 1976.

4777. Anon. "SA Stifles its Creative Writers . . . But Af Lit
Dawns on Campuses." NATIONAL STUDENT, 2 (1978), 4.

Talk by Mphahlele.

4778. Anon. "Literature: New Syllabus." WEEKLY REVIEW, 20
February 1981, p. 10.

At Form 4 and Form 6 levels in Kenya.

4779. Bappa, Salihu. "The Maska Project: Drama Workshop for Adult
Educators." WP, 3 (1980), 63-71.

In Zaria, January 1979.

4780. Berrian, Brenda. "Black Literature Component at the
University of Pittsburgh." COMMUNICATOR, 3, 5 (1977), 13-18.

4781. Blecher, Hilary. "Goal Oriented Theatre in the Winterveld."
CREATIVE ARTS, 1, 3 (1980), 23-39.

Workshop in BophutaTswana.

4782. Brash, Elton. "The Relevance of African Literature in
English to Teaching in Papua and New Guinea." ENGLISH IN NEW
GUINEA, 3 (1970), 40-50.

4783.* Breiseth, Jane M. "Contemporary Sub-Sahara Black African
Literature in the Junior High School." Master's thesis,
Cornell University, 1967.

4784. Bruner, David K. "Realistic Goals for the Teaching of African
Literature." In Hale and Priebe, 4810, pp. 3-12.

4785. Butler, Guy. "Some Random Observations on the Teaching of
English in South African Universities Since 1948. UCTSE, 7
(1977), 2-11.

4786. Couzens, T. J. "Ideology and the Teaching of Literature."
       SNARL, 4 (1976), 16-17.

       In South Africa. See reply by Gardiner, 4801.

4787. Croft, Julian. "Nos ancêtres les Anglais: A Reply to
       Daalder." NLRev, 5 (1978), 7-10.

       See Daalder, 4788.

4788. Daalder, Joost. "Studying ´New Literatures in English.´"
       NLRev, 5 (1978), 3-7.

       Response to Docker, 4791. See reply by Croft, 4787.

4789. Datondji, Coovi Innocent. "Literature and Development: How
       the Study of African (English) Literature in Schools and
       Universities Can Help Social Development in African
       Countries." PA, 115 (1980), 61-96.

       Achebe, Amadi, Conton, Ekwensi, Ike, Konadu, Munonye, et
       al.

4790. de Villiers, Andre. "South African Schools and African
       Writing in English." ENGLISH IN AFRICA, 3, 1 (1976), 23-33.

4791. Docker, John. "Commonwealth Literature and the
       Universities." NLRev, 2 (1977), 5-9.

       In Australia. See response by Daalder, 4788.

4792. Dorsey, David. "African Literature in Afro-American Studies
       Programs or: Too Many Indispensables." In Hale and Priebe,
       4810, pp. 108-14.

4793. Douglas, Kirsty. "Drama in Community Education." S AFRICAN
       OUTLOOK, 110 (1980), 111-12.

       Experiment in Western Cape.

4794. Egudu, Romanus N. "What to Teach in Modern African
       Literature." In Hale and Priebe, 4810, pp. 163-75.

4795. Feuser, Willfried F. "The Case for Comparative Literature."
       KIABÀRÀ, 2, 1 (1979), 38-51.

       Includes as appendix, "Comparative Literature Programme
       at Ife University," pp. 52-54.

4796. ____. "The Emergence of Comparative Literature in Nigeria."
       CNLQWR, 3, 1 (1980), 5-10; RAL, 11 (1980), 100-107.

4797. Fraser, Robert. "Boom Time for African Literature." WA, 28
       August 1978, pp. 1693-95.

       Courses in African literature at British universities.

4798. Fullerton, Gary. "Helping the African Child to Explore
       Himself through Drama." NDAANAN, 5, 1-2 (1976), 53-55.

       Interview with Joe de Graft.

4799. Gachukia, Eddah, and S. Kichamu Akivaga, eds. TEACHING OF
       AFRICAN LITERATURE IN SCHOOLS, Vol. I. Nairobi: Kenya
       Literature Bureau, 1978.

       Includes 3479, 3511, 3530, 3775, 4111, 4120, 4164, 4398,
       4401, 4480, 4512, 5536, 5716, 5723, 6016.

4800. Galinsky, Hans. "Entwicklung und Perspektiven der
       literaturwissenschaftlichen Forschung zu den
       englischsprachigen Literaturen ausserhalb Englands." In
       Kosok and Priessnitz, 3541, pp. 239-60.

4801. Gardiner, Michael. "A Reply -- Ideology and South African
       Literature." SNARL, 5 (1976), 16-17.

       Response to Couzens, 4786.

4802. Gerschel, Liz. "Morgan Dalphinis: The Use of Dialect in the
       Classroom." ATCALN, 2 (1980), 3-4.

       Presentation at ATCAL conference.

4803.* Golden, Fay I. "A New Resource: Modern African Poetry in the
       Junior High School Classroom." Master's thesis, Cornell
       University, 1968.

4804. Goodwin, Ken. "Africa: Introductory." In Goodwin, 4805,
       pp. 14-28.

       Includes select bibliography of African Literature, pp.
       23-28.

4805. ____, ed. COMMONWEALTH LITERATURE IN THE CURRICULUM. St.
       Lucia, Australia: South Pacific Association for Commonwealth
       Literature and Language Studies, 1980.

       Includes 4804, 5230.

4806. Gowda, H. H. Anniah. "My African Academic 'Safari': Some
       Highlights of African Academic Life." LHY, 22, 1 (1981),
       2-11.

       Visit to universities in Nairobi, Lagos, Ibadan, Ife,
       Accra, and Freetown. Comments on Clark, p'Bitek,
       Soyinka, et al.

4807. Gray, Stephen. "Teaching South African." UCTSE, 7 (1977),
       104-109; DONGA, 4 (1977) 1, 6.

4808.   ____. "Some Reasons for Including South African and African
         Literature in the English Teaching Syllabus." CRUX, 13, 3
         (1979), 13-19.

         In South Africa.

4809.   Haile-Mariam, Paulos. "English Literature as a Humanistic
         Subject in Ethiopian Secondary Schools." DAI, 40 (1979),
         717A (New York -- Buffalo).

4810.   Hale, Thomas A., and Richard K. Priebe, eds. THE TEACHING OF
         AFRICAN LITERATURE. Austin: University of Texas Press for
         the African Literature Association, 1977.

         Includes 4309, 4619, 4784, 4792, 4794, 4816, 4818, 4824,
         4836, 4840, 4843, 4851-52, 4854, 4859.

4811.*   Imbuga, Francis Davis. "A Study of the Techniques of
         Improvised Drama, with Special Reference to the School
         Situation." Master's thesis, University of Nairobi, 1975.

4812.*   Johnson, Adele Marie. "A Rationale for Teaching African
         Literature and an Introductory Annotated Bibliography of
         African Literature for High School Teachers." Master's
         thesis, Illinois University, 1972.

4813.   Jones, Joseph. "Method or Madness: How May We Expect
         Commonwealth Studies to Affect the Teaching of English?" In
         Narasimhaiah, 3593, pp. 408-12.

4814.   Kenyan Students against Imperial Education. "Education and
         University Must Serve the Majority of Kenyans: A Preliminary
         Critique of the University Education, Culture and Writers in
         Kenya." UTAFITI, 2, 2 (1977), 163-200.

         Liyong, Maillu, Mangua, et al.

4815.   Kinkead-Weekes, Mark. "African Literature in the
         University." OKIKE, 15 (1979), 18-22.

         Achebe, Okara, Soyinka.

4816.   Konrad, Zinta. "A Survey of African Literature in the
         University Curriculum." In Hale and Priebe, 4810, pp.
         271-301; RAL, 9 (1978), 259-81.

4817.   Lakoju, Tunde. "The Kind of Literature to Study at
         A. B. U." MIRROR, 1 (1976-77), 61-63.

         Ahmadu Bello University, Zaria, Nigeria.

4818.   Lindfors, Bernth. "On Disciplining Students in a
         Nondiscipline." In Hale and Priebe, 4810, pp. 41-47.

4819.   ____. "Introduction to the Panel Discussion: 'Emerging and

Neglected Literatures: Their Place in the Traditional
Spectrum of Comparative Literature.´" In ACTES DE VIIe
CONGRÈS DE L´ASSOCIATION INTERNATIONAL DE LITTÉRATURE
COMPARÉE/PROCEEDINGS OF THE 7th CONGRESS OF THE INTERNATIONAL
COMPARATIVE LITERATURE ASSOCIATION, II: LA LITTÉRATURE
COMPARÉE AUJOURD´HUI: THÉORIE ET PRATIQUE/COMPARATIVE
LITERATURE TODAY: THEORY AND PRACTICE. Ed. Eva Kushner and
Roman Struc. Stuttgart: Bieber, 1979.

> Rpt. of BALE 1939.

4820. ____. "Where English Departments Can Go." CNLQWR, 3, 3
(1980), 5-7.

4821. Maduka, Chukwudi T. "Comparative Literature: Concept and
Scope." NSAL, 3 (1980), 115-29.

4822. Magayu, Magayu K. "Culture -- and People´s Right to be Told
the Truth." SUNDAY NATION, 9 April 1978, p. 18.

> Response to Wanjala, 4858, on talk given by Robert
> Green. See rejoinder by Wanjala, 4267.

4823. Manning, Patrick. "Things Fall Together: The Use of
Literature in Teaching African History." BSAA, 8, 3 (1980),
24-31.

4824. Michelman, Fredric. "The Teaching of African Literature and
the Destruction of Stereotypes." In Hale and Priebe, 4810,
pp. 13-17.

4825. Mnthali, Felix, and Omolara Ogundipe-Leslie. "Social
Contexting in the Teaching of African Literature." OKIKE, 20
(1981), 82-90.

4826. Momodu, A.G.S. "A Golden Heritage Left to Decay." RADIO
TIMES, 21 October 1962, pp. 10-11.

> Advocates teaching drama in Nigerian secondary schools.

4827. Mphahlele, Es´kia. "African Prose and Poetry in Schools: An
Introduction." ELTIC REPORTER, 4, 1 (1979), 8-14.

4828.* Msuya, P.A. "The Integration of ´African Literature´ into
the English Language Course: The Situation in Our Tanzanian
Secondary Schools." PAPERS IN EDUCATION AND DEVELOPMENT, 4
(1977), 70-86.

4829. Mzamane, Mbulelo Vizikhungo. "The Study of Literature in
Africa." DONGA, 4 (1977), 1, 5; AFRICA CURRENTS, 10
(1977-78), 7-9; MARANG, (1978), 52-54.

4830. Ngandu Nkashama, P. "L´Enseignement de la littérature
africaine à l´Université Nationale du Zaïre." RAL, 8 (1977),
327-42.

4831. Ngugi, [wa Thiong'o], James. "Why Shakespeare in Africa?"
       DAILY NATION, 22 April 1964, p. 6.

4832. Niven, Alastair, Diana Bailey, John Hardcastle, Charles
       Mungo, and Farrukh Dhondy. "ATCAL Conference Panel." OKIKE,
       15 (1979), 65-91.

       Association for the Teaching of Caribbean and African
       Literature Conference, September 1978.

4833. Nordmann-Seiler, Almut. "Afrikanische Literatur an deutschen
       Universitäten." METHODEN DER AFRIKANISTISCHEN FORSCHUNG UND
       LEHRE IN DER BRD: EINE KRITISCHE BILANZ: 5. JAHRESTAGUNG DER
       VEREINIGUNG VON AFRIKANISTEN IN DEUTSCHLAND (VAD) 1973. Ed.
       Birgitta Benzing and Reinhard Bolz. Schriften der
       Vereinigung von Afrikanisten in Deutschland. Hamburg: Buske,
       1976. Pp. 87-91.

4834. Nunn, A.C. "Some Remarks on the Work of the English
       Department at Fourah Bay College." FBSLL, 1 (1980), 93-97.

4835. Ochieng, Philip. "The University: African Literature Above
       All Others." SUNDAY NATION, 6 April 1969, pp. 6-7.

       On revision of literature syllabus at the University of
       Nairobi.

4836. Ojo-Ade, Femi. "Teaching African Literature to the Black
       Student in Southern United States: Resolution of a Dilemma."
       In Hale and Priebe, 4810, pp. 90-107.

4837. Petersen, K.H. "African Literature in Denmark." OKIKE, 15
       (1979), 48-49.

4838. Phaswana, Koketso. "Teaching African Literature: The Case
       of Zimbabwe." EJ, 66, 3 (1977), 46-48.

4839. Povey, John. "Teaching Literature in South Africa." CRUX,
       14, 2 (1980), 14-19.

4840. Priebe, Richard K. "Teaching African Literature in an Urban
       University." In Hale and Priebe, 4810, pp. 48-89.

       Achebe, Mphahlele, et al.

4841. Profitt, Russell. "Black Studies in the Schools." OKIKE, 15
       (1979), 39-42.

       In England.

4842. Ravenscroft, Arthur, A.R. Gurnah, C.M. Hawkins, and Jane
       W. Grant. "Reports from Workshops: Saturday Morning, 23rd
       September." OKIKE, 15 (1979), 50-56.

       Conference in Canterbury on African and Caribbean
       Literature, September 1978.

4843.   Ricard, Alain. "Afican Literature: A French Perspective."
        In Hale and Priebe, 4810, pp. 125-38.

4844.   Riemenschneider, Dieter. "Zentrales Ziel: schwarze
        Erfahrung." BDB, 22 August 1980, pp. 2039-42.

4845.   Rive, Richard. "Towards a National Literature." SPEAK, 1, 2
        (1978), 37-39, 63; rpt. as "The Right to Teach Students
        Indigenous Literature," ELTIC REPORTER, 5, 3 (1980), 5-8.

        In South Africa.

4846.   Rutherford, Anna. "English in an African Context." BRITISH
        BOOK NEWS, July 1977, pp. 514-16.

        Teaching literature at Ahmadu Bello University, Zaria,
        Nigeria.

4847.* Sanneh, Mohamed Osman. "The Pedagogical Use of the African
        Novel Written in English." Master's thesis, University of
        California at Los Angeles, 1974.

4848.   Schäfer, Jürgen. "Afrikanische Literatur an deutschen
        Universitäten." ZEITSCHRIFT FÜR KULTURAUSTAUSCH, 29 (1979),
        302-05.

4849.   Sifuna, D.N. "Industrial or Literary Training? A History of
        Curriculum Development in East Africa." EDUCATION IN EASTERN
        AFRICA, 7, 1 (1977), 11-18.

4850.   Thomas, Peter. "A Voice for Africa: Creative Writers at
        Nsukka." POETRY VENTURE, 2, 2 (1970), 1-14.

        Teaching poetry at the University of Nigeria.

4851.   Thumboo, Edwin. "Teaching African Literature in a
        Multi-Cultural Society." In Hale and Priebe, 4810, pp.
        139-62.

        Achebe, Armah, Awoonor, Ngugi, Soyinka, et al.

4852.   Tucker, Martin. "Teaching African Poetry." In Hale and
        Priebe, 4810, pp. 186-97.

        Soyinka, et al.

4853.   Van der Water, Mary. "African and Caribbean Literature in
        the Schools." OKIKE, 15 (1979), 27-29.

        Teaching in Scotland.

4854.   Vincent, Theo. "Approaches to the Teaching of African
        Literature: A Consideration of Some Pedagogical Issues." In
        Hale and Priebe, 4810, pp. 176-85.

4855.* ____. "African Literature in Graduate Education in Nigerian Universities: The First Decade." CENTREPOINT, 2, 1 (1981), 84-96.

4856.* Walmsley, Anne. "Literature in Kenyan Education: Problems and Choices in 'The Author as Producer' Strategy." Master's thesis, University of Sussex, 1979.

4857. Wanjala. Chris. "Examining the Teaching of African Literature." SUNDAY NATION, 30 October 1977, p. 20.

4858. ____. "Distorting the True Nature of African Literature." SUNDAY NATION, 26 March 1978, p. 18.

Response to talk by Robert Green on the place of European literature in African studies. See rejoinder by Magayu, 4822.

4859. Warner, Keith Q. "On Teaching African Literature to West Indian Students." CLAJ, 22 (1978), 46-53; rpt. in Hale and Priebe, 4810, pp. 115-24.

4860. Wiley, David. AN EVALUATION OF THE IMPORTANCE OF SOME AFRICAN AUTHORS BY TEACHERS OF AFRICAN LITERATURE IN THE UNITED STATES. East Lansing: African Studies Center, Michigan State University, 1980. Mimeographed.

4861. Wyke, C.H. "The Validity of Courses in Commonwealth Literature." CHIMO, 1 (1980), 12-22.

See also 3379, 3383, 3415, 3457, 3475, 3480, 3504, 3551, 3752, 4030, 4117, 4120-21, 4140, 4143, 4222, 4233, 4267, 4316, 4323, 4326, 4334, 4412, 4507, 4516, 4533, 4630, 4647, 4675, 4689, 4711, 4754, 4759, 4787, 4888, 4908-09, 4926-27, 4977-79, 4988, 5509, 5859, 6097.

X. ORGANIZATIONS AND ASSOCIATIONS

BOOKS AND ESSAYS

4862. Achebe, Chinua. "Why an Association?" OKIKE, 20 (1981), 7-10; WA, 27 July 1981, pp. 1692-94.

> Address at convention of Nigerian authors, 27 June 1981. Photographs of convention on pp. 11-14.

4863. Ali, Z.S. "Centre for Black and African Arts and Civilization." NigM, 128-29 (1979), 55-61.

> In Lagos.

4864. Anon. "Mayibuye: Cultural Weapon of the ANC." SECHABA, March 1977, pp. 41-45.

4865. Anon. "Lit. Bureau to Fall Apart?" JOE, May 1977, pp. 25-26.

> Reorganization of East African Literature Bureau.

4866. Anon. "Kamirithu: Future Looks Dim." WEEKLY REVIEW, 9 January 1978, pp. 11-12.

> Kamirithu Community Educational and Cultural Centre closed down.

4867. Anon. "Federated Union of Black Arts: Prospectus 1979." S´KETSH´, Winter 1979, p. 36.

4868. Anon. "´The Minefield of Culture.´" WA, 19 November 1979, pp. 2138-39.

> Interview with Alastair Niven, Director of the Africa Centre in London.

4869. Anon. "New Showcase for African Books." WA, 1 December 1980, p. 2410.

> Africa Bookcentre at Africa Centre in London.

4870. Cullinan, Patrick. "Comment." BLOODY HORSE, 5 (1981), 3-7.

> On disbanding of the Johannesburg Centre of PEN and establishment of African Writers Association.

4871. de Villiers, Andre. "ISEA: Probing the Problems of English in Africa." RHODES REVIEW, December 1975, pp. 12-13.

> Institute for the Study of English in Africa.

4872. Harrex, S.C. "Letter to the Editor." RAL, 9 (1978), 137-38.

On establishment of the Centre for Research in the New
Literatures in English at Flinders University of South
Australia.

4873. Kahiga, Miriam. "Kamirithu Revisited." DAILY NATION, 19
January 1979, p. 11.

Year after revocation of license to perform Kikuyu play,
NGAAHIKA NDEENDA (I will marry when I want).

4874. Lelyveld, Joseph. "Breakup of a Community." NYTBR, 17 May
1981, pp. 3, 29.

On dissolution of South African PEN.

4875. Mathonsi, Risimati. "Black Writers of South Africa Plan
Their Cultural Revolution." NEW AFRICAN, August 1981, p. 91.

African Writers Association.

4876. Matshoba, Mtutuzeli. "Some Points to Ponder: Thoughts on
the Disbanding of P.E.N." STAFFRIDER, 4, 1 (1981), 45.

4877. Motshumi, Mogorosi. "Dilemmas of a Writers Group."
STAFFRIDER, 3, 3 (1980), 43-44.

Malimu, a group in South Africa.

4878. Munro, Ian H. "The Medu Art Ensemble." WLWE, 18 (1979),
437-38.

South African refugee troupe in Botswana.

4879. ____. "The Medu Art Ensemble: A New Direction for South
African Literature and Art." ACLALSB, 5, 3 (1980), 164-66.

4880. Ngugi wa Mirie. "Kamirithu Literacy Project." KENYA JOURNAL
OF ADULT EDUCATION, 7, 1 (1979), 7-10.

History of Kamirithu Community Educational and Cultural
Centre.

4881. Niven, Alastair. "The Africa Centre in London." RAL, 10
(1979), 274-76; KUNAPIPI, 1, 1 (1979), 173-76.

4882. Omorodion, Arthur. "Melting Pot of Mbari." RADIO-TV TIMES,
18-24 October 1965, p. 19.

4883. Pereira, Ernest. "The English Academy of Southern Africa."
LANTERN, 30, 1 (1980), 57-64.

4884. Sepamla, Sipho. "The Role of FUBA in the Country." REALITY,
11, 6 (1979), 14-15.

Federated Union of Black Arts (South Africa).

4885.   Sonuga, Gbenga. "Nigerian Cultural Centres: Government
Sponsorship of the Arts." NEW CULTURE 1, 10 (1979), 39-52.

4886.   Taylor, Norah. "Pretoria Theatre Organization." ELTIC
REPORTER, 4, 1 (1979), 38-40.

4887.   Wanjala. Chris. "Self-definition Necessary." NAIROBI TIMES,
17 June 1979, p. 4.

On Africanization of Kenya Cultural Centre.

4888.   ____. "The Literature Debate Continues." SUNDAY NATION, 7
September 1980, p. 30

Formation of Kenya Literature Teachers' Association.

See also 3858, 3863, 3871, 3878, 3883, 3889-90, 3893, 3936, 3943,
3954, 3962, 3985, 3991-93, 3995, 4001, 4017, 4032, 4408,
4446, 4550, 4571, 4600, 4618, 4667, 4700, 4902, 4923, 4951.

Y. CONFERENCES

SPECIFIC CONFERENCES: ALPHABETICAL BY LOCATIONS, WITH CHRONOLOGIES

Aarhus, Denmark: 1978

4889. Petersen, Kirsten Holst. "Seminar on Modern African
Literature, Held at Vingsted Conference Centre, Denmark,
15-17 March 1978." KUNAPIPI, 1, 1 (1979), 161-63.

Abidjan, Ivory Coast

See 3403.

Aix-en-Provence: 1978

4890. Stuckert, Klaus. "Report from the FILLM Conference:
Aix-en-Provence, 28 August--2 September 1978." KUNAPIPI, 1,
2 (1979), 188-90.

Algiers: 1969

4891. Berger, Renato. "On the Symposium (A Commentary)." JNALA,
7-8 (1969-70), 129-35.

At First Pan-African Cultural Festival.

Augsburg: 1978

4892. Ramm, Dieter. "Tagung über ´Commonwealth-Literatur in
Deutschland´ vom 24-25 Juli 1978 in Augsburg." ACOLIT, 3
(1978), 1-8.

Bayreuth: 1980

4893. Sander, Reinhard. "Afrikanische Stimmen in der
Weltliteratur: Schriftsteller als Sprecher ihrer Völker."
IAF, 16 (1980), 379-81; ACOLIT, 7 (1980), 13-14.

Bloemfontein, South Africa: 1978

4894. Voss, A.E. "The First Annual Conference of the Association
of University English Teachers of Southern Africa." RAL, 10
(1979), 268-70.

January 10-12, 1978, at the University of the Orange
Free State.

Bonn: 1962

4895. Sosah, Kingsley. "Exhibition of Nigerian Literature,
Sculpture, Paintings and Photographs." AFRIKA, 3 (1962),
157-58.

Boone, North Carolina: 1978

See 3630.

Boston: 1979

4896.   Schmidt, Nancy J. "Fifth Children's Books International,
Boston, 16-18 September 1979." RAL, 11 (1980), 240.

Bremen: 1979

4897.   Martini, Jürgen.   "Tagung uber 'Commonwealth Literatur in
Deutschland' vom 23-24 Juni 1979 in Bremen." ACOLIT, 5
(1979), 5-7.

Budapest: 1976

4898.   Fokkema, Douwe W. "The Comparative Study of Asian and African
Literature." NEOHELIKON, 5, 1 (1977), 283-84; rpt. in
Köpeczi, et al., 3540, pp. 1001-02.

8th Congress of ICLA, 16 August 1976 session.

Calgary: 1981

4899.   Killam, G. Douglas.   "Synthesis and Reflections." In Ray, et
al., 4900, pp. 185-94.

Comments on papers delivered at literature panel by
Arnold, 4752; Povey, 4242, et al.

4900.   Ray, Donald I., Peter Shinnie, and Donovan Williams, eds.
INTO THE 80's: THE PROCEEDINGS OF THE ELEVENTH ANNUAL
CONFERENCE OF THE CANADIAN ASSOCIATION OF AFRICAN STUDIES.
Vol. 2. B.C. Geographical Series, 32. Vancouver: Tantalus
Research Ltd., 1981.

Includes, 4242, 4752, 4899.

Cambridge, Massachusetts: 1979

4901.   Campbell, Elaine.   "Conference on English as a World Language
for Literature." WLWE, 18 (1979), 442-47.

Brutus speaks on South African literature at the English
Institute at Harvard University.

Canterbury: 1978

4902.   Innes, Lyn.   "Editorial." OKIKE, 15 (1979), 1-2.

On publication of the proceedings of the first ATCAL
conference at University of Kent.

4903.   Petersen, Kirsten Holst.   "The University of Kent Conference

on ´The Uses of African and Caribbean Literature: Teaching
and Criticism in the United Kingdom,´ September 22-24, 1978."
RAL, 10 (1979), 271-73; KUNAPIPI, 1, 1 (1979), 166-68.

See also 4832, 4842, 5236.

Cape Town: 1974

See 4167.

Cape Town: 1980

4904. Anon. "Censorship Conference." STAFFRIDER, 3, 2 (1980), 47.

Held at University of Cape Town, 21-25 April.

4905. Beekman, Jan. "Conference Report: Censorship in South
Africa." CRITICAL ARTS, 1, 2 (1980), 42-46.

4906. Driver, Dorothy. "Conference on Censorship." ENGLISH IN
AFRICA, 7, 1 (1980), 97.

4907. j´Mathonsi, Risimati. "A Discussion of Censorship in South
Africa." RAL, 11 (1980), 549-51.

Copenhagen: 1981

See 4471.

Durban: 1979

4908. Gardner, Colin. "University English Evolves: A Review of
the July 1979 Conference of the Association of University
English Teachers of Southern Africa (AUETSA)." ENGLISH IN
AFRICA, 6, 2 (1979), 85-89.

4909. Visser, N.W. "AUETSA 1979." RAL, 11 (1980), 238-39.

Durban: 1979

See also 3431.

Frankfurt: 1980

4910. Farah, Nuruddin. "Germany--and All That Jazz." OKIKE, 18
(1981), 8-12.

Symposium on African Literature at Frankfurt Book Fair.

4911. Nkosi, Lewis. "African Writers at Frankfurt." TLS, 24
October 1980, p. 1200; WA, 3 November 1980, p. 2184.

4912. Riemenschneider, Dieter. "Bericht über das Symposium zur
´Funktion moderner afrikanischer Literaturen´ in Frankfurt
vom 4. bis 6. Oktober 1980." ACOLIT, 7 (1980), 11-12.

See also 3315, 3335, 3343, 4592, 4601-03, 4623, 4627-29, 4653, 4666, 4670, 4673, 4677, 4691-92, 4696.

Frankfurt: 1981

4913. Stummer, Peter. "Konferenz der ´European Association for Commonwealth Literature and Language Studies´ in Frankfurt vom 23 bis 27 März 1981." ACOLIT, 9 (1981), 3-6.

Gaberone, Botswana: 1976

4914. Mothusi, L.G. "Writers´ Workshop, 1976." MARANG 1 (1977), [25-26].

> Summary of papers delivered.

Gaberone, Botswana: 1978

4915. Anon. "Writers´ Workshop: Report of the Workshop Held on the University Campus (Botswana) on the 27th-29th January, 1978." MARANG, (1978), pp. 91-96.

4916. Mothusi, Lloyd G., and Zwide Mbulawa. "Writers´ Workshop: Report of the Workshop Held on the University Campus (Botswana) on the 27th-29th January, 1978." MARANG, (1978), pp. 91-96.

Gainesville, Florida: 1980

4917. Beard, Linda Susan. "Report on the Annual Meeting of the African Literature Association, University of Florida, Gainesville, 9-12 April, 1980: ´Towards Defining the African Aesthetic.´" ENGLISH IN AFRICA, 8, 1 (1981), 94-97.

See also 5090, 5093-94.

Ibadan, Nigeria: 1976

4918. Gibbs, James. "The Ibadan Conference on Drama in Africa." DENGA, June 1977, pp. 33-41.

> Soyinka, et al.

4919. Last, B.W. "African Literature Conference." COMMONWEALTH NEWSLETTER, 11 (1977), 15-16.

> University of Ibadan, 6-10 July 1976.

Ibadan, Nigeria: 1977

4920. Dingomé, J.N. "The Ibadan Workshop on Radical Perspectives of African Literature and Society, University of Ibadan, 18-22 December 1977." KUNAPIPI 1, 2 (1979), 182-84.

Ibadan, Nigeria: 1978

4921. Breitinger, Eckhard. "Third Annual African Literature
        Conference Ibadan 10.-14. Juli 1978." ACOLIT, 3 (1978),
        9-10.

4922. Ilesanmi, Obafemi, and Wole Adamolekun. "On Tutuola,
        Original Manuscripts, and National Literary Archive."
        EMOTAN, 2, 1 (1978), 10-11.

        3rd Annual Literature Conference.

Ile-Ife, Nigeria: 1975

4923. Asein, Samuel O. "Ife Conference Notebook, 1975." RAL, 8
        (1977), 125-28.

        Association of African Literary Critics.

Ile-Ife, Nigeria: 1978

See 4683-84.

Ile-Ife, Nigeria: 1979

See 4685.

Ile-Ife, Nigeria: 1981

See 4604-05, 4675, 4695.

Innsbruck: 1979

See 3779.

Johannesburg: 1975

4924. Greig, Robert. "Changing Mood of Black Writing." STAR
        (Johannesburg), 24 May 1975.

Johannesburg: 1979

4925. Anon. "PEN Conference 1979." STAFFRIDER, 2, 4 (1979), 63.

        Held at University of the Witwatersrand, 8-9 September.

Johannesburg: 1979

4926. Saycell, K.J. "Report on the Symposium." CRUX, 13, 3
        (1979), 18-19.

        Transvaal Association of Teachers of English.

Johannesburg: 1980

4927. Brindley, D.J. "South African and African Literature in
       Schools." ELTIC REPORTER, 5, 2 (1980), 38-39.

       Transvaal Association of English Teachers symposium at
       the University of the Witwatersrand.

Kampala, Uganda: 1962

4928. Ngugi [wa Thiong'o], James. "Here are the Heralds of a New
       Awareness." SUNDAY NATION, 1 July 1962, p. 32.

       On Makerere Writers' Conference

Kampala, Uganda: 1973

See 5091.

Kampala, Uganda: 1981

4929. Anon. "Provocative Debate." WEEKLY REVIEW, 17 April 1981,
       pp. 47-48.

       Creative writers' workshop at Makerere University, 30
       March -- 4 April 1981.

Kinshasa, Zaire: 1978

See 3724.

Lagos, Nigeria: 1977

4930. Anon. "FESTAC Colloquium on Black Civilisation." WA, 31
       January 1977, p. 212.

4931. Anon. "The FESTAC Colloquium." WA, 7 February 1977, pp.
       280-82.

       Soyinka, et al.

4932. Anon. "Festac Brings Together African Genius." WEEKLY
       REVIEW, 7 February 1977, pp. 29-30.

4933. Anon. "Colloquium Round Up: After the Ideological War, a
       Silent Coup." NEWBREED, End-February 1977, pp. 40, 57, 59.

       Soyinka, et al.

4934. Anon. "Colloquium: The Heart of the Matter." SPEAR, April
       1977, p. 22.

4935. Nyangira, Nicholas. "The Colloquium and Culture." UMMA-N, 5
       (1977), 46.

See also 3703, 5966.

Leeds: 1964

See 5088.

Legon, Ghana: 1976

4936. Schmidt, Nancy J. "Legon Seminar on the Writing and
       Production of Literature for Children." RAL, 8 (1977),
       350-52.

Legon, Ghana: 1977

4937. Yamba, Mohamed. "A Symposium: The African Writer and His
       Society." LEGACY, 3, 2 (1977), 8-10.

Leiden: 1976

4938. Ricard, A. "Texte et contexte: Conférence de Leiden sur la
       critique littéraire africaine, 20-25 septembre 1976." RPC,
       28 (1977), 55.

See also 4247.

Leipzig: 1979

4939. Bellmann, D., C. Geisel, R. Karachouli, and E. Taube.
       "Arbeitstagung ´Gesellschaftlicher Fortschritt und die
       Literaturen Asiens, Afrikas und Latinamerikas´ in Leipzig."
       WB, 26, 9 (1980), 164-68.

            6-8 November 1979.

Limoges, France: 1977

4940. Pageard, Robert. "Le colloque de Limoges: Un aperçu.: ALA,
       54-55 (1979-80), 11-17.

            Conference on myth and African literature.

4941. Pageard, Robert. "Mythes et études littéraires." ALA, 54-55
       (1979-80), 115-19.

            Summary of conference.

London: 1975

See 3308.

London: 1977

4942. Anon. "SCOLMA in Session." WA, 28 March 1977, p. 595.

            Bibliographical conference sponsored by Standing
            Committee on Library Materials on Africa. See response

by Zell, 4682.

See also 3337, 4682.

London: 1977

4943.   Sander, Reinhard.   "1977 Symposium of the African Studies
Association of the United Kingdom."   RAL, 9 (1978), 90.

London: 1978

See 3311.

London: 1979

See 3313.

London: 1981

See 3353.

Luanda, Angola: 1979

4944.   Anon.   "VI Conferência dos Escritores Afro-Asiáticos."
AFRICA (Lisbon), 1, 4 (1979), 500-02; 1, 5(1979), 536-40.

26 June - 3 July.

4945.   Anon.   "Escritores Afro-Asiaticos reunidos em Luanda."
TEMPO, 457 (1979), 17-24.

4946.   [La Guma, Alex.]   "Report of the Acting-Secretary General."
LAAW, 42-43 (1979-80), 72-80.

Sixth Conference of Afro-Asian Writers.

4947.   ____.   "Final Speech of Alex La Guma, Secretary General of the
Afro-Asian Writers Association."   LAAW, 42-43 (1979-80),
111-112.

Machakos, Kenya: 1977

4948.   James, O.K.   "´Book Worms, Unite!´"   JOE, September 1977, pp.
25-27.

Conference of writers, publishers and journalists,
including Githae-Mugo, Ngugi, p´Bitek, et al.

Madison, Wisconsin: 1977

4949.   Anon.   "African Writers: The Link to Life."   WEEKLY REVIEW,
11 April 1977, p. 31.

African Literature Association.

4950. Visser, N.W. "The Third ALA Conference." ENGLISH IN AFRICA,
       4, 2 (1977), 77-78.

See 4519.

Mainz, W. Germany: 1975

4951. Best, Bernhard. "Janheinz Jahn Symposium: Tribute by the
       Africanist Association in Germany." AFRIKA, 16, 4 (1975),
       47.

Mainz, W. Germany: 1979

4952. Rutherford, Anna. "Third International Janheinz-Jahn
       Symposium, Johannes Gutenberg University, Mainz, 11-13 May
       1979." KUNAPIPI, 1, 2 (1979), 192-93.

4953. Trenz, Günter. "The Jahn Symposium on Modern East African
       Literature and its Audience." RAL, 9 (1978), 86-89.

4954. Wanjala, Chris. "African Writers Symposium." WEEKLY REVIEW,
       16 May 1977, 31-32; AFRISCOPE, 7, 9 (1977), 50-52.

See also 3665.

Moka, Mauritius: 1979

4955. Sadik, Habib. "The Mauritius International Conference of
       Writers." LAAW, 42-43 (1979-80), 137.

4956. Smith, Angela. "Report of a Conference Held at the Mahatma
       Gandhi Institute, Mauritius." RAL, 11 (1980), 371-72.

Montpellier: 1980

See 4495.

Nairobi, Kenya: 1977

See also 3341.

Nairobi, Kenya: 1979

See 4446.

Nairobi, Kenya: 1980

4957. Anon. "Authors Caught in Cultural Storm." WEEKLY REVIEW, 18
       April 1980, p. 32.

          Dispute over workshop on African literature sponsored by
          Goethe Institute.

4958. Anon. "Festival to Open: Interesting Repertoire Awaits
       Nairobi Audiences." WEEKLY REVIEW, 30 May 1980, p. 39.

Goethe Institute, 2-7 June 1980.

4959. Nation Reporter. "Workshop Plan Enrages Ngugi." DAILY
NATION, 15 April 1980, p. 20.

Writers workshop to be sponsored by Goethe Institute.

4960. Wanjala, Chris. "A Sense of Purpose." WEEKLY REVIEW, 18
July 1980, p. 42.

Writers seminar organized by the Writers' Association of
Kenya.

New Delhi: 1977

4961. Anon. "Magical Mystery Tour: The Delhi Conference."
COMMONWEALTH NEWSLETTER, 11 (1977), 14.

4962. Niven, Alastair. "ACLALS, New Delhi, January 1977." JCL,
11, 3 (1977), 65-67.

4963. ____. "Report on the Fourth Triennial Conference of the
Association for Commonwealth Literature and Language Studies,
New Delhi, India, 2-8 January, 1977." ACLALSB, 4, 5 (1977),
85-87.

4964. Wattie, Nelson. "The Fourth Triennial Conference of the
Association of Commonwealth Literature and Language Studies,
New Delhi, 2-8 January 1977." ACOLIT, 1 (1977), 3-4.

See also 3593.

Newtown, Wales: 1980

4965. Butcher, Margaret. "The Welsh Arts Council International
Writer's Prize 1980 Conference, Gregynog, Newtown, Powys,
17-19 October 1980." KUNAPIPI, 2, 2 (1980), 166-67.

Mbulelo Mzamane on South African poetry.

Nsukka, Nigeria: 1981

4966. Amadike, P.C. "An Address by the Honourable Minister of
Social Development, Youth, Sports and Culture, Chief Paulinus
C. Amadike, at the Convention of Nigerian Authors at Nsukka
on June 27, 1981." OKIKE, 20 (1981), 4-6.

4967. Ndili, F.N. "An Address of Welcome Presented to the
Convention of Nigerian Authors Held at the University of
Nigeria, Nsukka on June 27, 1981, at the Continuing Education
Centre." OKIKE, 20 (1981), 2-3.

See also 4700, 4862, 5097.

Paris: 1976

4968.   Bruner, David and Charlotte.   "C.E.L.A.T.M.A.:   Journées
d´études afro-américaines et africaines."   AFRAMN, 3 (1976),
3-5.

Paris: 1978

4969.   Mounier, Jacques H.   "Résumés des communications du Colloque
sur les Littératures Africaines organisé à Paris III les
10-11 mars 1978."   AFRAMN, 5 (1978), 2-6.

Paris: 1980

4970.   Anon.   "Colloque ´Images de l´Afrique en Occident´
(CERCLEF/CETANLA -- November 1980):   Compte-rendu et résumés
de communications."   AFRAMN, 13 (1981), 7-13.

Philadelphia: 1980

4971.   Roberts, Sheila.   "Report on the Twenty-Third Annual Meeting
of the African Studies Association in Philadelphia 15-18
October, 1980:   ´Changes and Contrasts: New Directions and
Traditional Ties in Africa.´"   ENGLISH IN AFRICA, 8, 1
(1981), 89-94.

See also 4569.

Poitiers, France: 1980

4972.   Bardolph, Jacqueline.   "S.A.E.S. Conference, Poitiers."
AFRAMN, 11 (1980), 1; KUNAPIPI, 2, 1 (1980), 195; RAL, 12
(1981), 237-38.

        Special focus on Ngugi´s PETALS OF BLOOD.   Proceedings
        subsequently published as special issue of ECHOS DU
        COMMONWEALTH, 6 (1980-81).

Rabat, Malta: 1978

4973.   Niven, Alastair.   "European Conference of Commonwealth
Literature and Language Studies Concluded at Rabat."   TIMES
OF MALTA, 1 April 1978, p. 20.

4974.   Stilz, Gerhard.   "ACLALS European Conference in Malta."
ACOLIT, 2 (1978), 6-9.

4975.   Tiffin, Helen.   "EACLALS Conference, Malta."   SPAN, 7 (1978),
37-43.

4976.   Wattie, Nelson.   "The Fifth European Conference of ACLALS,
Malta, 28-31 March 1978."   KUNAPIPI, 1, 1 (1979), 163-66.

182   Conferences

Sheffield, England: 1979

4977. Anon. "Proceedings of the Second National Conference of the
       Association for the Teaching of Caribbean and African
       Literature (ATCAL)." ATCALN, Special No. (1980), 1-10.

4978. Niven, Alastair. "The Second National Conference: Teaching
       Caribbean and African Literature." ATCALN, 2 (1980), 2-3.

4979. Quartermaine, Peter. "Some Thoughts on the Second ATCAL
       Conference at the University of Sheffield." ATCALN, 2
       (1980), 4-5.

See also 4802.

Strasbourg, France: 1979

4980. Rutherford, Anna. "SAES Conference, Strasbourg, 5-7 May
       1979." KUNAPIPI, 1, 2 (1979), 192.

Suva, Fiji: 1980

4981. Beard, Linda Susan. "Association for Commonwealth Literature
       and Language Studies Conference (3-8 January 1980)." RAL, 11
       (1980), 368-70.

4982. Breitinger, Eckhard. "Fünfte Tagung der 'Association of
       Commonwealth Language and Literature Studies': University of
       the South Pacific, Suva, Fiji am 3-8 Jan. 1980." ACOLIT, 7
       (1980), 1-3.

4983. Niven, Alastair. "Fifth Triennial Conference of ACLALS,
       Fiji, January, 1980." SPAN, 10 (1980), 56-58.

4984. Rutherford, Anna. "Suva Conference, 1980." KUNAPIPI 2, 1
       (1980), 189.

Tashkent, USSR: 1978

4985. Anon. "The Road Passed, the Road to Pass. . ." LAAW, 38-39
       (1978-79), 96-108.

       La Guma speaks.

4986. Mukherjee, Subhas. "To and from Tashkent." LAAW, 38-39
       (1978-79), 90-95.

       Meeting of Afro-Asian Writers.

Tübingen, W. Germany: 1980

4987. Bode, Christoph. "Vierte Tagung über Commonwealth Literature
       in Deutschland vom 26-29 Juni in Oberjoch (Allgäu)." ACOLIT,
       7 (1980), 4-8.

Warwick, England: 1980

4988. Anon. "Proceedings of the Third National Conference of the
       Association for the Teaching of Caribbean and African
       Literature (ATCAL): ´African and Caribbean Literature in the
       Classroom,´ University of Warwick, 26-28 September 1980."
       ATCALN, Special No. (1981), 1-10.

Yaoundé, Cameroon: 1977

4989. Bjornson, Richard. "Colloquium on Cameroon Literature and
       Literary Criticism." RAL, 9 (1978), 79-85; ABBIA, 34-37
       (1979), 248-52.

Z. FESTIVALS

SPECIFIC FESTIVALS: ALPHABETICAL BY LOCATION, WITH CHRONOLOGIES

Berlin: 1979

4990. Anon. "Horizons 79: West Berlin." INTERNATIONAL THEATRE
       INFORMATION, Winter-Spring 1979, pp. 37-38.

4991.* Anon. "Africa at the Berlin Cultural Festival." NAIROBI
       TIMES, 29 July 1979, p. 5.

4992. Anon. "Horizonte 79: World Festival of African Arts."
       STAFFRIDER, 2, 3 (1979), 54.

4993. Beti, Mongo. "Choses vues au Festival des arts africains de
       Berlin-Ouest (du 22 juin au 15 juillet 1979)." PEUPLES
       NOIRS/PEUPLES AFRICAINS, 11 (1979), 54-91.

4994. Brutus, Dennis. "The View from Berlin." WA, 27 August 1979,
       pp. 1558-59.

            BILT 79.

4995. Eckhardt, Ulrich, ed. HORIZONTE-MAGAZIN 79. Berlin:
       Berliner Festspiele GmbH, 1979.

            Includes 3417, 3507, 3715, 3846, 3880, 3923, 4060, 4508,
            5086, 5271, 5323, 5351, 5396, 5399, 5469, 5483, 5517,
            5539, 5623, 5642, 5879, 5915, 5919, 5954, 6035.

4996. Egner, Hanno. "Erstes Festival der Weltkulturen: Horizonte
       '79 in Berlin." ACOLIT, 5 (1979), 12-13.

4997. Imfeld, Al, and Gerd Meuer. "The Richness of African
       Literature: Challenges and Rewards." AFRIKA, 21, 4 (1980),
       22-23.

4998. j'Mathonsi, Risimati. "Horizonte 79: World Festival of
       African Arts." STAFFRIDER, 2, 3 (1979), 54; WIETIE, 2
       (1980), 29.

4999. MacNaughton, Robert. "Misunderstanding in Berlin." NEW
       AFRICAN, September 1979, pp. 77-78.

5000. Riemenschneider, Dieter. "Erstes Festival der Weltkulturen:
       Horizonte '79 in Berlin: Berliner Internationale
       Literaturtage." ACOLIT, 5 (1979), 10-11.

5001. ____. "First Festival of World Cultures -- Horizons 79,
       Berlin, 21 June to 15 July 1979." KUNAPIPI, 2, 1 (1980),
       192-94.

5002. Splett, Oskar. "Africa at the Festival of World Cultures in

Berlin." AFRIKA, 20, 8 (1979), 12-13.

5003. Sweetman, David. "Old Horizons." ABPR, 6 (1980), 11-13.

See also 3395, 4996, 5000.

Gwelo, Rhodesia: 1978

5004. Hataguri, L.M. "Henshaw's Play Thrills Hundreds at
       Festival." KRISTO, 4, 8 (1978), 10-11.

       THIS IS OUR CHANCE wins at 6th annual Drama Festival,
       Gwelo Teachers College, Rhodesia.

Lagos: 1977

5005. Abrahams, Alistair. "The Greatest Show on Earth." DRUM
       (Nairobi), April 1977, pp. 20-21.

5006. Adam, Hussein M. "The Heart of FESTAC." HALGAN, 7 (1977),
       40-42; 8 (1977), 42-45, 48.

       Soyinka, et al.

5007. Adewunmi, Bosun. "FESTAC Frustrations." NEWBREED,
       End-February 1977, pp. 42, 44.

       Interviews with participants, including Kgositsile.

5008. Amadi, Tony. "What Really Took Place at the Festival of a
       Life Time." NEWBREED, End-February 1977, pp. 7-8, 11, 13.

5009. Anon. "FESTAC '77 Countdown Hots Up." INDIGO, 3, 12 (1976),
       4-7.

5010. Anon. "The FESTAC Programme." AFRISCOPE, 7, 1 (1977),
       40-41.

5011. Anon. "The Legacy of FESTAC." WA, 21 February 1977, p. 355.

5012. Anon. "Festival Fringe at UNILAG." WA, 7 March 1977, pp.
       453-54.

       FESTAC spin-off at the University of Lagos.

5013. Anon. "FESTAC '77." AIBEPM, 65 (1977), supp. 1-20.

5014. Anon. "FESTAC '77 in Camera." AIBEPM, 67 (1977), 72-79.

5015. Anon. "FESTAC and the Future of the Black Race." INDIGO, 4,
       3-4 (1977), 4, 6-7, 40-41.

5016. Anon. "Festival mondial des arts et de la culture
       négro-africains (Lagos, 15 janvier - 13 février 1977)."
       AFRIQUE CONTEMPORAINE, 90 (1977), 40-41.

5017. Anon. "The FESTAC Question." DRUM (Johannesburg), August
       1977, pp. 66-67.

5018. Anon. FESTAC '77. London: Africa Journal; Lagos:
       International Festival Committee, 1977.

       Includes 3606, 4088a, 5019.

5018. Anon. "Appendix: Basic Facts about FESTAC." In FESTAC,
       5018, pp. 136-37, 140-41, 144-45, 149, 152.

5020. Bebey, Francis. "De Dakar à Lagos." JeuneA, 1 April 1977,
       supp. 6-34.

5021. Boobe. "Reflections on FESTAC '77." HALGAN, 6 (1977),
       39-41.

5022. Chouillou, Clothilde. "FESTAC 77: Succès ou echéc?" BINGO,
       292 (1977), 40-43.

5023. David-West, Fubara. "FESTAC Must be Relevant." In Ekwensi,
       3461, pp. 2-10.

5024. Donaldson, Jeff. "FESTAC 77: A Pan-Afrikan Success." BLACK
       COLLEGIAN, 7, 5 (1977), 32, 64.

5025. Enaharo, Ife. "The Second World Black and African Festival
       of Arts and Culture: Lagos, Nigeria." BLACK SCHOLAR, 9, 1
       (1977), 27-33.

5026. Fuller, Hoyt W. "FESTAC '77: A Footnote." FIRST WORLD, 1, 2
       (1977), 26-27.

5027. Gomez, Daniel G. "El orgullo de ser negro." MUNDO NEGRO, 187
       (1977), 34-37.

5028. Highet, Juliet. "FESTAC: Not Just a Song and Dance Affair."
       NEWBREED, End-February 1977, pp. 17, 19-20.

5029. Horses, Angelo. "Le Olimpiadi della cultura." NIGRIZIA, 95,
       4 (1977), 16-19.

5030. Jordan, Millicent Dobbs. "Durbar at Kaduna." FIRST WORLD,
       1, 2 (1977), 27.

       FESTAC.

5031. Kay, Iris. "FESTAC 1977." AfrA, 11, 1 (1977), 50-51.

5032. Kone, Samba. "FESTAC '77: L'Occasion était trop belle."
       EBURNÉA, 111 (1977), 2-3.

5033. ____. "FESTAC '77: De Dakar . . . à Lagos." EBURNÉA, 111
       (1977), 15-26.

5034. Lumwamu, F. "Civilisation noire et éducation: Lagos: 15
       janvier - 12 février 1977." RPC, 33 (1978), 44-45.

5035. Mana, Kä. "Le Soleil d'un festival." Z-A, 114 (1977),
       197-202.

5036. Meuer, Gerd. "FESTAC 77 -- The Festival of Wonders."
       AFRIKA, 18, 2-3 (1977), 16-21.

5037. Monroe, Arthur. "FESTAC 77 -- The Second World Black and
       African Festival of Arts and Culture: Lagos, Nigeria."
       BLACK SCHOLAR, 9, 1 (1977), 34-37.

5038. Musa, Mamoun el-Baghir. "The Spirit of FESTAC 77." SUDANOW,
       2, 3 (1977), 39-41.

5039. Ndaywell è Nziem. "Les grandes journées africaines de
       Lagos." Z-A, 115 (1977), 303-12.

5040. Njau, Elimo. "Festivals, Petrodollars and Cultural
       Liberation." JOE, February 1977, p. 7.

5041. Opubor, Alfred E. "FESTAC Colloquium: Prolegomena to Black
       Thought?" AFRISCOPE, 7, 3 (1977), 7, 9, 11-12, 15, 17.

5042. Skurjat, Ernestyna. "Festiwal w Lagos: Wezwanie do dyskusji
       [Festival in Lagos: Call to Discussion]." KONTYNENTY, 8
       (1977), 24-28.

5043. Special Correspondent. "FESTAC: One Year After."
       AFRISCOPE, 8, 4 (1978), 10-12.

5044. Wanjala, Chris. "A Re-union of Black Scholars and Artists."
       UMMA-N, 6 (1977), 4-5, 7, 11-12.

See also 3703.

Nairobi, Kenya: 1978

5045. Githae Mugo, Micere. "Where African Drama Fails to Meet the
       Mark." SUNDAY NATION, 9 April 1978, p. 15.

       On adjudicating Schools Drama Festival in Nairobi.

Nairobi, Kenya: 1980

5046. Anon. "Youngsters Show How to Put on a Play." WEEKLY
       REVIEW, 11 April 1980, p. 23.

       National primary school drama festival in Nairobi.

Nairobi, Kenya: 1981

5047. Anon. "Students on the Boards." WEEKLY REVIEW, 27 February
       1981, pp. 42-43.

High school drama festival.

5048.   Anon. "Season for Community Theatre." WEEKLY REVIEW, 20
        March 1981, p. 27.

        Kenya Drama Festival.

5049.   Anon. "Binding Thread of Culture." WEEKLY REVIEW, 10 April
        1981, pp. 42-43.

        Kenya Drama Festival.

5050.   Anon. "School Theatre Hits the Road." WEEKLY REVIEW, 22 May
        1981, pp. 42-43.

        Kenya Schools National Drama Festival winners on tour.

5051.   Anon. "Primary Schools Drama Festival." WEEKLY REVIEW, 16
        October 1981, p. 42.

5052.   Anon. "Colleges Drama Festival." WEEKLY REVIEW, 13 November
        1981, p. 43.

5053.   Anon. "Controversial Drama Awards." WEEKLY RVIEW, 20
        November 1981, pp. 42-43.

        High school drama festival.

Zomba, Malawi: 1977

5054.   Gibbs, James. "The Third University Drama Festival." DENGA,
        June 1977, pp. 42-43.

        Chancellor College, University of Malawi.

5055.   ____. "Chancellor College Drama Festival." DENGA, June
        1977, pp. 44-45.

        University of Malawi.

5056.   ____. "The Ninth Schools´ Drama Festival, March 1977."
        DENGA, June 1977, pp. 109-14.

        Organized by the Association for the Teaching of English
        in Malawi. See response by O´Malley, 5057.

5057.   O´Malley, P. "Drama: Criteria of Excellence." DENGA, June
        1977, pp. 115-17.

        Response to Gibbs on Ninth Schools Drama Festival in
        Malawi, 5056.

PART II

INDIVIDUAL AUTHORS

This section lists books and articles that focus on a single author. The sources are organized into four categories: "Bibliography"; "Biography and Autobiography"; "Interviews"; and "Criticism." Cross-references provide leads into sources cited elsewhere in the bibliography.

ABBAM, KATE

Biography

See 4548.

Interview

5058. Debayo, Jumoke. "Mrs. Kate Abbam: An Extraordinary Woman." AFRICA WOMAN, 8 (1977), 14.

Criticism

See 4336.

ABRAHAMS, PETER

Biography

5059.* Panton, George. "Peter Abrahams: Our Distinguished Immigrant." SUNDAY GLEANER, 23 March 1975, p. 23.

See also 3377.

Interview

5060. Allsop, Kenneth. "The Negro who married a white woman said..." SUNDAY NATION, 19 August 1962.

Criticism

5061.* Aubame, Jean. "Peter Abrahams et le problème de la couleur en Afrique du Sud: 1934-1966." Doctorat d´Université, University of Rouen, 1979.

5062.* Daniels, Russell. PETER ABRAHAMS, TELL FREEDOM. London: Longman, 1981.

5063. Leeman, Clive Philip. "Art and Politics in the Novels of Peter Abrahams: A Study of His Three Political Novels." DAI, 39 (1978), 3600A (California, Santa Barbara).

5064. Lindfors, Bernth. "Abrahams, Peter." In Klein, 3370, pp.

5-6.

5065.   Maduka, Chukwudi T. "Humanism and the South African Writer:
        Peter Abrahams´ A WREATH FOR UDOMO." UMOJA, 1, 1 (1977),
        17-31.

5066.   ____. "Colonialism, Nation-Building and the Revolutionary
        Intellectual in Peter Abrahams´ A WREATH FOR UDOMO.´ JOURNAL
        OF SOUTHERN AFRICAN AFFAIRS, 2, 2 (1977), 245-57.

5067.   Ogungbesan, Kolawole. "Peter Abrahams´s WILD CONQUEST."
        LAAW, 29 (1976), 9-21.

        Rpt. of BALE 2252.

5068.   ____. THE WRITING OF PETER ABRAHAMS. London: Hodder and
        Stoughton; New York: Holmes & Meier, 1979.

5069.   ____. "A Long Way from Vrededorp: The Reception of Peter
        Abrahams´s Ideas." RAL, 11 (1980), 187-205.

5070.   Parasuram, A.N. MINERVA GUIDE TO PETER ABRAHAMS´ MINE BOY.
        Madras: Minerva Publishing House, 1977.

        Rpt. of 1971 ed.

5071.   Rive, Richard. "Writing and the New Society." CONTRAST, 12,
        3 (1979), 60-67.

        Abrahams, Richard Wright, and James Baldwin.

5072.   Rutherford, Anna. "Abrahams, Peter (Henry)." In Vinson and
        Kirkpatrick, 3377, pp. 17-18.

5073.   Scanlon, Paul A. "Dream and Reality in Abrahams´s A WREATH
        FOR UDOMO." OBSIDIAN, 6, 1-2 (1980), 25-32.

5074.   Snow, C.P., et al. "Abrahams, Peter." In Popkin, 3638, pp.
        1-9.

        Extracts from selected criticism.

5075.   Umezinwa, Willy A. "La Voix du silence dans les romans de
        Peter Abrahams et de Mongo Beti." In Köpeczi, et al., 3540,
        pp. 261-65.

5076.   Wade, Michael. "South Africa´s First Proletarian Writer."
        In Parker, 3817, pp. 95-113.

        Rpt. of chapter from BALE 2259.

5077.   Wanjala, Chris. "Literature and Politics in South Africa."
        SUNDAY NATION, 7 August 1977, p. 11.

        A WREATH FOR UDOMO.

5078. Wauthier, Claude, et al. ´Abrahams, Peter." In Ferres and
       Tucker, 3467, pp. 1-4.

       Extracts from selected criticism.

5079. Wynter, Sylvia. "The Instant Novel Now." NEW WORLD
       QUARTERLY, 3, 3 (1967), 78-81.

       THIS ISLAND NOW.

See also 3410, 3437, 3467, 3493-94, 3597, 3608, 3620, 3631, 3638,
       3740, 3750, 3758, 3762, 3786, 3789, 3803, 3817, 3820, 4081,
       4087, 4376, 4386, 4395, 4404, 4479, 4485, 5904.

ACHEBE, CHINUA

Bibliography

5080. Alvarez-Péreyre, J. "Contribution à la bibliographie sur
       Chinua Achebe." ECHOS DU COMMONWEALTH, 5 (1979-80), 196.

5081. Anafulu, Joseph C., comp. "Chinua Achebe: A Preliminary
       Checklist." NSUKKA LIBRARY NOTES, 3 (1978), 1-52.

       Special issue.

5082. Evalds, Victoria K. "Chinua Achebe: Bio-Bibliography and
       Selected Criticism, 1970-1975." AfrLJ, 8 (1977), 101-30;
       CBAA, 10 (1977-78), 67-87.

5083. Lindfors, Bernth. "A Checklist of Works by and about Chinua
       Achebe." OBSIDIAN, 4, 1 (1978), 103-17.

5084. ____. "Recent Scholarship on Achebe." LHY, 21, 1 (1980),
       181-86.

5085. Saint-Andre-Utudjian, E. "Chinua Achebe: A Bibliography."
       AUBTL, 4, 1 (1977), 91-103.

See also 3315.

Biography and Autobiography

5086. Anon. "Chinua Achebe." In Eckardt, 4995, p. 104.

5087. Anon. "Voice of Nigeria." WA, 24 February 1962, p. 201.

5088. Anon. "Chinua Achebe at Leeds Confab." RADIO-TV TIMES,
       19-25 October 1964, p. 17.

       Commonwealth literature conference.

5089. Anon. "Writers ´Doomed to be Free.´" WA, 19 November 1979,

p. 2123.

Achebe receives the Nigerian National Merit Award.   See Achebe, 3396.

5090. Hill-Lubin, Mildred A. "Chinua Achebe and James Baldwin at the African Literature Association Conference in Gainesville." OKIKE, 17 (1980), 1-5.

5091. Kalibbala, V. "´Colonialist Criticism´: Kalibbala Reporting on Chinua Achebe." SCHOOL LEAVER, 1, 2 (1974), 35-37.

Report on address given by Achebe at ACLALS conference in Kampala, 1973. For text of address, see BALE 92.

5092.* Okoro, Anezi. "Who is Afraid of Chinua Achebe?" NSUKKASCOPE, 6 (1978), 31-34.

5093. Povey, John. "Achebe and Baldwin in C.B. Land--10-4 Good Buddy!!! (A Dialogue at the African Literature Association Meeting, Gainesville, Florida, March 1980)." PACIFIC COAST AFRICANIST ASSN. OCCASIONAL PAPER, 3 (1981), [7-9].

5094. Tsuruta, Dorothy Randall. "James Baldwin and Chinua Achebe in Dialogue to Define Aesthetics." BLACK SCHOLAR, 12, 2 (1981), 72-79.

See also 3315, 3373, 3377, 4700, 5082.

Interviews

5095. Agetua, John. "The Need for Dissent." AFRICA CURRENTS, 8 (1977), 27-28.

Portion of interview originally published in SUNDAY OBSERVER, 12 September 1976, and rpt. in Agetua, 5117.

5097. Barrett, Lindsay. "Giving Writers a Voice: An Interview with Chinua Achebe." WA, 22 June 1981, pp. 1405-07.

On conference convened to form a Nigerian Association of Writers.

5098. Chinweizu. "An Interview with Chinua Achebe (Nsukka, 20 January 1981)." OKIKE, 20 (1981), 19-32; PAN AFRICAN BOOK WORLD, 1, 1 (1981), 1-3, 5-7.

5099. Colmer, Rosemary. "The Critical Generation." ASH MAGAZINE, 5 (1980), 5-7.

5100. Cott, Jonathan. "Chinua Achebe: At the Crossroads." PARABOLA, 6, 2 (1981), 30-39.

5101. Davidson, James. "Interview: Chinua Achebe." MEANJIN Q, 39, 1 (1980), 35-47.

5102. Enekwe, Ossie Onuora. "Dialogue--with Chinua Achebe." NEW
       CULTURE, 1, 9 (1979), 37-46.

5103.* ____. "Enekwe Talks to Achebe." NSUKKASCOPE, 7 (1981),
       55-67.

5104. Evalds, Victoria K. "An Interview with Chinua Achebe." SBL,
       8, 1 (1977), 16-20.

5105. Fabre, Michel. "Chinua Achebe on ARROW OF GOD." ECHOS DU
       COMMONWEALTH, 5 (1979-80), 7-17; LHY, 21, 1 (1980), 1-10.

5106. Imfeld, Al. PORTRAITS OF AFRICAN WRITERS: 5. CHINUA ACHEBE.
       Trans. Jan Klingemann. Cologne: Deutsche Welle
       Transkriptionsdienst, [1979].

          Transcript of radio broadcast.

5107. Ogbaa, Kalu. "An Interview with Chinua Achebe." RAL, 12
       (1981), 1-13.

5108. Rensburg, A.P.J. van. "Seeking a Better Place." DONGA, 3
       (1976), 3-4.

5109. Tetteh-Lartey, A. "Chinua Achebe répond aux questions de
       A. Tetteh-Lartey concernant la création littéraire en
       Afrique." ECHOS DU COMMONWEALTH, 5 (1979-80), 181-84.

          Rpt. of BBC African Service interview.

See also 3383, 4509, 5117, 5251.

Criticism

5110. Abanime, Emeka P. "Warfare in the Novels of Chinua Achebe."
       PA, 111 (1970), 90-100.

5111. Abrahams, Cecil A. "George Lamming and Chinua Achebe:
       Tradition and the Literary Chroniclers." In Narasimhaiah,
       3593, pp. 294-306.

5112. ____. "Margaret Laurence and Chinua Achebe: Commonwealth
       Storytellers." ACLALSB, 5, 3 (1980), 74-85.

5113. Adewoye, Samuel Adegboyega. "Ideals and Realities in Chinua
       Achebe's ARROW OF GOD and Thomas Hardy's JUDE THE OBSCURE."
       JOURNAL OF LITERARY STUDIES (Maiduguri), 1, 1 (1977), 49-63.

5114. ____. "City-Life Sophistication as a Destructive Force in
       Wordsworth's 'Michael' and Achebe's NO LONGER AT EASE."
       GANGA, 2, 4 (1980), 38-40.

5115. Agetua, John. NOTES, QUESTIONS AND ANSWERS ON CHINUA
       ACHEBE'S <u>A MAN OF THE PEOPLE</u>. Benin City: P.J. Publications,
       1978.

Includes "Letter from the Author," pp. 4-5.

5116. ____. NOTES ON <u>NO LONGER AT EASE</u> WITH QUESTIONS AND ANSWERS.
Benin City: P.J. Publications, 1978.

5117. ____, ed. CRITICS ON CHINUA ACHEBE 1970-76. Benin City,
Nigeria: Author, 1977.

Rpts. book reviews and brief articles, including BALE
2331, 2444, 2445, and interview with Achebe, 5095, pp.
28-45.

5118.* Ainamon Gannan, Augustin. "Conflit culturel en Afrique et
l'oeuvre de Chinua Achebe." Ph.D. dissertation, 3rd cycle,
University of Caen, 1977.

5119.* Amaïzo, Eliane. "Traditionalisme et modernisme dans les
romans de Chinua Achebe." Ph.D. dissertation, University of
Grenoble, 1973.

5120. ____. "La femme et les changements sociaux et culturels dans
l'oeuvre romanesque de Chinua Achebe." AUBTL, 2, 2 (1975),
101-08.

5121. ____. "ARROW OF GOD et le crépuscule des dieux." ECHOS DU
COMMONWEALTH, 5 (1979-80), 42-49.

5122. Anagbogu, P.W.N. "Titans in Achebe's Trilogy." ABRAKA
QUARTERLY, 1, 1 (1976), 77-81.

5123. Anderson, Martha G., and Mary Jo Arnoldi. ART IN ACHEBE'S
THINGS FALL APART AND ARROW OF GOD. Bloomington: African
Studies Program, Indiana University, 1979. Mimeographed.

Winner of First Annual Graduate Student Paper
Competition, 1978.

5124. Anon. "The Novelist Chinua Achebe." LAAW, 30 (1976),
114-19.

5125. Asnani, Shyam M. "Quest for Identity Theme in Three
Commonwealth Novels." In Srivastava, 3677, pp. 128-36.

NO LONGER AT EASE, et al.

5126.* Babindamana, Joseph. "Critique du colonialisme et de
l'Afrique des indépendances chez Chinua Achebe." Ph.D.
dissertation, 3rd cycle, University of Paris VII, 1979.

5127. Bakalanjwa, Wufela Yaek'Olingo. "Regards sur la conversion
des premiers chrétiens de Mbanta dans LE MONDE S'EFFONDRE de
Chinua Achebe." ALA, 56 (1980), 30-35.

5128. Bashier, Mubarak. "Chinua Achebe: An Individual." SUDANOW,
2, 10 (1977), 56.

5129.   Beckmann, Susan. "Language as Cultural Identity in Achebe,
        Ihimaera, Laurence and Atwood." WLWE, 20 (1981), 117-34.

5130.   Beneke, Jürgen. "Chinua Achebe: THINGS FALL APART -- Der
        Fall in die Geschichte." In Breitinger, 3428, pp. 126-55.

5131.* Biakolo, Anthony. "Achebe et Beti: écriture et réalité en
        Afrique noire." Ph.D. dissertation, 3rd cycle, University of
        Paris XIII, 1979.

5132.   Bonneau, Danielle. "Approaches to Achebe's Language in ARROW
        OF GOD." ECHOS DU COMMONWEALTH, 5 (1979-80), 68-88.

5133.   Brown, Hugh Richard. "Africanized Dialogue and Experience in
        Chinua Achebe's ARROW OF GOD." DAI, 38 (1978), 5430-31A
        (South Carolina).

5134.   ____. "Igbo Words for the Non-Igbo: Achebe's Artistry in
        ARROW OF GOD." RAL, 12 (1981), 69-85.

5135.   Carr, John. "Chinua Achebe." In CRITICAL SURVEY OF SHORT
        FICTION, Vol. 3. Ed. Frank N. Magill. Englewood Cliffs, NJ:
        Salem Press, 1981. Pp. 819-23.

5136.   Carroll, David. CHINUA ACHEBE. 2nd edition. London and
        Basingstoke: Macmillan; New York: St. Martin's Press, 1980.

            Rpt. of BALE 2307.

5137.   ____. NOTES ON ARROW OF GOD. York Notes, 92. London:
        Longman, 1980.

5138.   Cavone, Vito. "Un uomo del popolo nigeriano: La degradazione
        dell'eroe in A MAN OF THE PEOPLE di Chinua Achebe." AFRICA
        (ROME), 35 (1980), 111-24.

5139.   Coirault, Claudine, and Christiane Conturie. "Étude du
        roman: LE MONDE S'EFFONDRE de Chinua Achebe: Compte rendu de
        travaux faits dans les lycées de Côte-d'Ivoire." RPC, 33
        (1978), 32-37.

5140.   Colmer, Rosemary. "'The Start of Weeping is Always Hard':
        The Ironic Structure of NO LONGER AT EASE." LHY, 21, 1
        (1980), 121-35.

5141.   Coulibaly, Yédiéti Edouard. "Weeping Gods: A Study of
        Cultural Disintegration in James Baldwin's GO TELL IT ON THE
        MOUNTAIN and Chinua Achebe's THINGS FALL APART." AdUA, 9D
        (1976), 531-42.

5142.   Coussy, D. "La notion de pouvoir dans ARROW OF GOD." ECHOS
        DU COMMONWEALTH, 5 (1979-80), 50-63.

5143.   Critic. "The Centre Can't Hold." RADIO-TV TIMES, 2-8
        November 1964, pp. 14, 19.

On Eldred Fiberesima's stage adaptation of THINGS FALL
APART.

5144. Croft, Julian. "BEWARE, SOUL BROTHER and the Nigerian Civil
War." LHY, 21, 1 (1980), 92-101.

5145. Dash, J. Michael. "The Outsider in West African Fiction: An
Approach to Three Novels." LHY, 21, 1 (1980), 19-29.

Achebe, et al.

5146. Djangoné-Bi, N. "Cultural Change in Achebe's Novels." LHY,
21, 1 (1980), 156-66.

5147. Djangoné-Bi, N., and R. Okafor. "Chinua Achebe ou la
recherche d'une esthétique négro-africaine." In COLLOQUE SUR
LITTÉRATURE, 3403, pp. 337-56.

5148. Dommergues, André. "Achebe et les Missionnaires." In
Richard and Sevry, 4495, pp. 134-47.

5149. ____. "Le culte du serpent en Afrique noire." PA, 114
(1980), 132-43.

In THINGS FALL APART, ARROW OF GOD, and BEWARE, SOUL
BROTHER.

5150.* Dunn, T.A. NOTES ON CHINUA ACHEBE'S THINGS FALL APART.
London: Longman York Press, 1981.

5151. Echeruo, M.J.C. "Introduction." In Chinua Achebe, THE
SACRIFICIAL EGG AND OTHER STORIES. Onitsha: Etudo Ltd.,
1962. Pp. 3-6.

5152. Egblewogbe, E.Y. FOLKLORE IN THE NOVELS OF CHINUA ACHEBE: AN
ETHNOLINGUISTIC APPROACH. Folklore Preprint Series, Vol. 7,
No. 2. Bloomington: Folklore Publications Group, Indiana
University, 1979.

5153. Egudu, R.N. "Achebe and the Igbo Narrative Tradition." RAL,
12 (1981), 43-54.

5154. Ekaney, Nkwelle. "Corruption and Politics in Chinua Achebe's
A MAN OF THE PEOPLE: An Assessment." PA, 104 (1977), 114-26.

5155. Elias, Mohamed. "Time in Achebe's 'Girls at War': Presence
of Nigerian Past." ComQ, 2, 6 (1978), 17-23.

5156. Emenyonu, Ernest. "Early Fiction in Igbo." RAL, 4 (1973),
7-20; rpt. in BALE 372 and in 3754.

Includes comparison of THINGS FALL APART and Peter
Nwana's OMENUKO.

5157. Esubiyi, Towhé. "'Flying': A Maverick Reading of Achebe's

Festac Poem." PQM, 6, 3-4 (1981), 151-57.

5158. Fido, Elaine. "Time and Colonial History in THINGS FALL
       APART and ARROW OF GOD." LHY, 21, 1 (1980), 64-76.

5159. Firebaugh, Joseph J. "Chinua Achebe and the Plural Society."
       JAAAA, 1, 1 (1977), 66-87.

5160. Fraser, Robert. "A Note on Okonkwo's Suicide." KUNAPIPI, 1,
       1 (1979), 108-13; OBSIDIAN, 6, 1-2 (1980), 33-37.

            See Ogbaa, 5211.

5161. Gale, Steven H. "The Theme of Emasculation in Chinua Achebe's
       NO LONGER AT EASE." PQM, 6, 3-4 (1981), 146-50.

5162. Gillard, G.M. "Centre and Periphery in Achebe's Novels."
       LHY, 21, 1 (1980), 146-54.

5163. Goodwin, K.L. "A Rhetoric of Contraries in Chinua Achebe's
       Poetry." LHY, 21, 1 (1980), 40-49.

5164. Gowda, H.H. Anniah. "Ahmed Ali's TWILIGHT IN DELHI (1940),
       and Achebe's THINGS FALL APART (1958)." LHY, 21, 1 (1980),
       11-18.

5165. ____. "The Colonial Encounter: Achebe's Criticism." LHY,
       22, 2 (1981), 17-22.

5166. Groga-Bada, Emmanuel. "Okonkwo ou la volonté d'un destin
       exemplaire." AdUA, 9D (1976), 521-30; RLENA, 1 (1977),
       83-90.

5167. Guzman, Richard Ramirez. "Bande Mataram: Nationalism,
       Personality and Literary Style in Four Third World Writers."
       DAI, 38 (1978), 4180A (Virginia).

            Achebe, et al.

5168.* Harlech-Jones, Brian. "The Owner Has Noticed: Achebe and
       the Roots of Corruption." COMMUNIQUÉ, 6, 1 (1981), 35-48.

5169. Innes, C.L. "A Source for ARROW OF GOD: A Response." RAL,
       9 (1978), 16-18; rpt. in Innes and Lindfors, 5171.

            Reply to Nnolim, 5205.

5170. ____. "Language, Poetry and Doctrine in THINGS FALL APART."
       In Innes and Lindfors, 5171, pp. 111-25.

5171. Innes, C.L., and Bernth Lindfors, eds. CRITICAL PERSPECTIVES
       ON CHINUA ACHEBE. Washington, DC: Three Continents Press,
       1978; London: Heinemann, 1979.

            Rpts. BALE 795, 2301, 2305, 2327, 2334-36, 2355-56,
            2385, 2393, 2413-14, 2424, 2440, 2443. Also includes

5169-70, 5193, 5205, 5265.

5172.   Iyamabo, Peter. "The Problem of Tragic Responsibility in
ARROW OF GOD." SHUTTLE, 8 (1980), 40-43.

5173.* Jabbi, Bu-Buakei. ACHEBE: THINGS FALL APART (NOTES).
Freetown: Fourah Bay College Bookshop, 1974.

5174.   ____. "Myth and Ritual in ARROW OF GOD." ALT, 11 (1980),
130-48.

5175.   John, Elerius E. "THINGS FALL APART de Chinua Achebe et
SARZAN de Birago Diop: Défaite et triomphe de la civilisation
traditionnelle africaine." NEOHELIKON, 5, 2 (1977), 121-32.

5176.   ____. "Chinua Achebe: THINGS FALL APART." RPC, 33 (1978),
50-52.

5177.   Karanja, J. "The Flies in Our Literary Soup." BUSARA, 8, 1
(1976), 33-38.

Achebe and non-African criticism.

5178.   Kiiru, Muchugu. A STUDY GUIDE TO CHINUA ACHEBE'S NOVEL,
THINGS FALL APART. Nairobi: Oxford University Press, 1978.

5179.   Killam, G.D. THE WRITINGS OF CHINUA ACHEBE. London:
Heinemann, 1977.

Rev. ed. of BALE 2344, now including coverage of poetry
and short stories.

5180.   ____. "Achebe's Aim in ARROW OF GOD." ECHOS DU
COMMONWEALTH, 5 (1979-80), 18-28.

5181.   King, Bruce. "The Revised Edition of ARROW OF GOD." ECHOS
DU COMMONWEALTH, 5 (1979-80), 89-98.

5182.   ____. "Introduction." LHY, 21, 1 (1980), i-ii.

Special issue on Achebe.

5183.   Kothandaraman, Bala. "'Where this Rain Began to Fall...': A
Reading of ARROW OF GOD.' OJES, 17 (1981), 73-81.

5184.   ____. "'Okoli's Death: A Pointer towards the Narrative
Design of Chinua Achebe's THINGS FALL APART'--Another View."
JOURNAL OF LITERARY STUDIES (Orissa), 4, 2 (1981), 77-84.

Response to Pal, 5226.

5185.   Leclaire, Jacques. "L'échange tragique chez Achebe: Destin
et déterminisme dans THINGS FALL APART et ARROW OF GOD."
ECHOS DU COMMONWEALTH, 5 (1979-80), 29-41.

5186. Lee, Mary Hope. "Ethnographic Statement in the Nigerian Novel, with Special Reference to Pidgin." In READINGS IN CREOLE STUDIES. Ed. Ian Hancock. Ghent: E. Story-Scientia, 1979. Pp. 295-302.

5187. Lindfors, Bernth. "Achebe, Chinua." In Klein, 3370, pp. 7-9.

>   Update of BALE 2362.

5188. ____. "Chinua Achebe's Undergraduate Writings." KOMPARATISTISCHE HEFTE, 4 (1981), 103-16.

5189. Macdonald, Bruce F. "Chinua Achebe and the Structure of Colonial Tragedy." LHY, 21, 1 (1980), 50-63.

5190. Machila, Blaise N. "Ambiguity in Achebe's ARROW OF GOD." KUNAPIPI, 3, 1 (1981), 119-33.

5191. Mackay, Mercedes, et al. "Achebe, Chinua." In Popkin, 3638, pp. 9-20.

>   Extracts from selected criticism.

5192. Maduka, Chukwudi. "Irony and Vision in Achebe's A MAN OF THE PEOPLE." BA SHIRU, 8, 1 (1977), 19-30.

5193. Mahood, M. M. THE COLONIAL ENCOUNTER: A READING OF SIX NOVELS. London: Collings, 1977.

>   ARROW OF GOD, et al.; rpt. in Innes and Lindfors, 5171.

5194. Mane, R. "Comment écouter le chant de l'ikolo?" ECHOS DU COMMONWEALTH, 5 (1979-80), 1-6A.

>   ARROW OF GOD.

5195. Mbock, C. G. LE MONDE S'EFFONDRE DE CHINUA ACHEBE: ESSAI CRITIQUE. Yaoundé: Buma Kor, 1978.

5196. Melone, Thomas. "Typologie de l'artiste: Edogo." ECHOS DU COMMONWEALTH, 5 (1979-80), 64-67.

>   Extract on ARROW OF GOD from BALE 2372, pp. 149-56.

5197. Mezu, S. Okechukwu. "The Tropical Dawn: Chinua Achebe." NIGERIAN STUDENT'S VOICE, 2 (January 1965), 2-6.

5198. Middelmann, Michael. "Comments on the Insights Given by Chinua Achebe's Creative Writing into the Last Century of His Society's History." JANUS, (1979), 37-44.

5199. Miller, James. "The Novelist as Teacher: Chinua Achebe's Literature for Children." CHILDREN'S LITERATURE, 9 (1981), 7-18.

5200.   Mojola, Ibiyema. "La femme dans l'oeuvre de Chinua Achebe."
         PEUPLES NOIRS/PEUPLES AFRICAINS, 16 (1980), 48-58.

5201.   Morsiani, Jamilè. "La tetralogia di Chinua Achebe come
         contributo alla decolonizzazione della Nigeria." SpM, 2
         (1973), 84-96.

5202.   Munro, Ian H. "Chinua Achebe, GIRLS AT WAR." In Petersen and
         Rutherford, 4467, pp. 84-88.

5203.   Nandakumar, Prema. "The Theme of Religion in the Fiction of
         Chinua Achebe." JOURNAL OF THE KARNATAK UNIVERSITY:
         HUMANITIES, 20 (1976), 257-64.

5204.   Nasser, Merun. "Achebe and His Women: A Social Science
         Perspective." AT, 27, 3 (1980), 21-28.

5205.   Nnolim, Charles. "A Source for ARROW OF GOD." RAL, 8
         (1977), 1-26; rpt. in Innes and Lindfors, 5171.

             Argues that Achebe made use of Simon Alagbogu Nnolim's
             THE HISTORY OF UMUCHU (1953). See reply by Innes, 5169.

5206.   ____. "Technique and Meaning in Achebe's ARROW OF GOD."
         KIABÀRÀ, 3, 2 (1980), 11-35.

5207.   Nwoga, D. Ibe. "The Igbo World of Achebe's ARROW OF GOD."
         RAL, 12 (1981), 14-42.

5208.   Obiechina, Emmanuel. "Chinua Achebe's NO LONGER AT EASE."
         OKIKE, 13 (1979), 124-44.

5209.   Obumselu, B. "Chinua Achebe's African Aesthetic: A
         Reconsideration of A MAN OF THE PEOPLE." ENGLISH TEACHERS'
         JOURNAL, 1, 2 (1977), 13-20.

5210.   Ogbaa, Kalu. "Names and Naming in Chinua Achebe's Novels."
         NAMES, 28 (1980), 267-89.

5211.   ____. "A Cultural Note on Okonkwo's Suicide." KUNAPIPI, 3,
         2 (1981), 126-34.

             See Fraser, 5160.

5212.   ____. "Death in African Literature: The Example of Chinua
         Achebe." WLWE, 20 (1981), 201-13.

5213.   ____. "Folkways in Chinua Achebe's Novels." Ph.D.
         dissertation, University of Texas at Austin, 1981.

5214.   Ojaide, M. Tanure, and M. Olu Olagoke. NOTES ON NO LONGER AT
         EASE FOR SCHOOL CERTIFICATE/GCE O/L EXAMS. Warri: Nicresay,
         n.d.

5215.   Okafor, Clement A. "Igbo Narrative Tradition and the Novels

of Chinua Achebe: Transition from Oral to Written
Literature." In Konstantinović et al., 3779, pp. 483-87.

5216.   ____. "A Sense of History in the Novels of Chinua Achebe."
JAfrS, 8 (1981), 50-63.

5217.   Okeh, P.I. "Trente arpents et ARROW OF GOD." REVUE DE
L'UNIVERSITÉ DE MONCTON, 5 (1972), 10-17.

5218.   Oko, E.C. "Tradition and History in Achebe's Novels." GANGA,
2, 4 (1980), 24-28.

5219.   Okoli, Godwin Nwili. "Background Information in the Study of
African Fiction." INTERNATIONAL LIBRARY REVIEW, 10 (1978),
205-13.

THINGS FALL APART and ARROW OF GOD.

5220.   Okonkwo, Nelson Chidi. "The Brinks of Knowing: An
Examination of the Oedipal-Quest Motif in ARROW OF GOD."
MUSE, 11 (1979), 49-51.

5221.   Okoye, Chukwuma. "Achebe: The Literary Function of Proverbs
and Proverbial Sayings in Two Novels." LORE&L, 2, 10 (1979),
45-63.

5222.   Ola, V. U. "Aspects of Development in Chinua Achebe's
Treatment of Women." JEn, 7 (1980), 92-119.

5223.   Olafioye, Tayo. "Chinua Achebe: The African Writer as
'Traditional' Social Critic." PACIFIC COAST AFRICANIST
ASSOCIATION OCCASIONAL PAPER, 3 (1981), [5-6].

5224.*   Osinowo, O. NOTES, QUESTIONS/ANSWERS ON THINGS FALL APART.
Ibadan: Aromolaran, 1970.

5225.   Osundahunsi, Dele. AKINNIOLA KEYNOTE REVIEWS ON THINGS FALL
APART (WITH QUESTIONS AND ANSWERS). Ibadan: Akin. Akinniola
Associates, 1981.

5226.   Pal, Dipak. "Okoli's Death: A Pointer toward the Narrative
Design of Chinua Achebe's THINGS FALL APART." JOURNAL OF
LITERARY STUDIES (Orissa), 3, 1 (1980), 29-38.

See response by Kothandaraman, 5184.

5227.   Palangyo, Peter Kishili. "The African Sense of Self with
Special Reference to Chinua Achebe." DAI, 41 (1980),
1589-90A (New York-Buffalo).

5228.   Palmer, Eustace. "Character and Society in Achebe's THINGS
FALL APART." LHY, 22, 1 (1981), 13-27.

5229.   Patterson, Ruth. "ARROW OF GOD by Chinua Achebe." EJ, 66, 3
(1977), 64-65.

5230. Patullo, Patrick J. "Chinua Achebe's THINGS FALL APART." In
       Goodwin, 4805, pp. 29-35.

5231. Peek, Andrew. "Betrayal and the Question of Affirmation in
       Chinua Achebe's NO LONGER AT EASE." LHY, 21, 1 (1980),
       112-20.

5232. Povey, John. "Achebe's War Poetry." LHY, 21, 1 (1980),
       78-90.

5233. Probyn, Clive T. NOTES ON A MAN OF THE PEOPLE. York Notes,
       116. London: Longman, 1981.

5234. Ramamurti, K.S. "Patterns of Distinctiveness in the Language
       of Commonwealth Fiction: A Comparative Study of the Language
       of Achebe, Naipaul, Narayan and Nagarajan." LHY, 22, 2
       (1981), 85-100.

5235. Ravenscroft, Arthur. CHINUA ACHEBE. Writers and Their Work,
       209. 2nd ed. Harlow, Essex: Longman for the British Council,
       1977.

            Rev. ed. of BALE 2410.

5236. ____. "Introducing Chinua Achebe." OKIKE, 15 (1979), 8.

            Before Achebe's talk on "The Uses of African Literature"
       at ATCAL Conference.

5237. Rhodes, H. Winston. "Chinua Achebe and Witi Ihimaera." LHY,
       21, 1 (1980), 104-11.

5238. Rice, Michael. "THINGS FALL APART: A Critical Appreciation."
       CRUX, 10, 2 (1976), 33-40.

5239. Richard, René, ed. "Table ronde sur ARROW OF GOD de Chinua
       Achebe." ECHOS DU COMMONWEALTH, 5 (1979-80), 150-73.

            Followed by excerpts from critical articles and
       interviews, pp. 174-95.

5240. Robertson, P. J. M. "THINGS FALL APART and HEART OF DARKNESS:
       A Creative Dialogue." IFR, 7 (1980), 106-11.

5241. Sabor, Peter. "'Structural Weaknesses' and Stylistic
       Revisions in Achebe's ARROW OF GOD." RAL, 10 (1979), 375-79.

5242. Sarvan, Ponnuthurai. "The Mirror and the Image: Achebe's
       GIRLS AT WAR." SSF, 14 (1977), 277-79.

5243. Séverac, Alain. "Structure causale dans NO LONGER AT EASE de
       Chinua Achebe." UNIVERSITÉ DE DAKAR ANNALES, 7 (1977),
       115-48.

5244. ____. "An Ibo Glossary (of Ibo Words and Phrases Found in

Achebe's ARROW OF GOD)." In DISCOURSE AND STYLE, II. Ed.
J[ean]-P[ierre] Petit. Publications de l'Université Jean
Moulin. Lyon: L'Hermès, 1980. Pp. 51-61.

5245. Sévry, Jean. "Pour une lecture de Achebe (ARROW OF GOD):
Littérature et anthropologie." ECHOS DU COMMONWEALTH, 5
(1979-80), 100-49.

5246. Shelton, Austin J., et al. "Achebe, Chinua." In Ferres and
Tucker, 3467, pp. 4-13.

Extracts from selected criticism.

5247.* Simms, Norman. "Noetics and Poetics: Studying and
Appreciating Chinua Achebe's THINGS FALL APART."
CHANDRABHĀGĀ, 5 (1981), 57-66.

5248. Taylor, Richard. "Japanese Noh Drama in European and African
Dress." KOMPARATISTISCHE HEFTE, 4 (1981), 81-101.

Play based on ARROW OF GOD.

5249. Tidjani-Serpos, Nouréine. "LE MONDE S'EFFONDRE de Chinua
Achebe: Okonkwo, ou du complexe d'Oedipe à la névrose."
EUROPE, 618 (1980), 53-58.

5250. Timberg, Bernard. "Chinua Achebe's THINGS FALL APART and
Chaim Potok's THE CHOSEN." KIABÀRÀ, 2, 1 (1979), 102-28.

5251. Turkington, Kathleen Phyllis. "The Novels of Chinua Achebe."
Master's thesis, University of the Witwatersrand, 1975.

Includes interview with Achebe, pp. 151-57.

5252. ____. CHINUA ACHEBE: THINGS FALL APART. Studies in English
Literature, 66. London: Arnold, 1977.

5253. Ugochukwu, Françoise. "D'OBIADI À LA FLUTE, ou la deuxième
vie des contes populaires au Nigeria." PA, 116 (1980),
159-72.

5254. Umezinwa, Willy A. "La Palabre comme création superposée dans
le roman africain." NEOHELIKON, 5, 2 (1977), 105-19.

5255. ____. "The Idiom of Plastic Figures in Chinua Achebe's
Novels." CAHIERS DES RELIGIONS AFR, 12 (1978), 125-34; NSAL,
3 (1980), 13-22.

5256. Uwajeh, P. N. "Chinua Achebe's Okonkwo: Individual Stasis
versus Social Dynamics." NEOHELICON, 6, 2 (1978), 141-52.

5257. Vargo, Edward P. "Struggling with a Bugaboo: The
Priest-Character in Achebe and Greene and Keneally." FJS, 9
(1976), 1-13; rpt. in Narasimhaiah, 3593, pp. 284-93.

5258. Versinger, Georgette. "Un auteur africain à l'agrégation: Chinua Achebe." PA, 115 (1980), 188-93.

5259. Wattie, Nelson. "The Community as Protagonist in the Novels of Chinua Achebe and Witi Ihimaera." In Massa, 3571, pp. 69-74.

5260. Webb, Hugh. "Drawing the Lines of Battle: A MAN OF THE PEOPLE." LHY, 21, 1 (1980), 136-45.

5261. Winnifrith, T.J. "Achebe, Chinua." In Vinson and Kirkpatrick, 3377, pp. 18-20.

5262. Winters, Marjorie. "An Objective Approach to Achebe's Style." RAL, 12 (1981), 55-68.

5263. ____. "Morning Yet on Judgement Day: The Critics of Chinua Achebe." JLSN, 1 (1981), 26-39; rpt. in Parker, 3630, pp. 169-85.

5264. Wren, Robert M. "From Ulu to Christ: The Transfer of Faith in Chinua Achebe's ARROW OF GOD." CHRISTIANITY AND LITERATURE, 27, 2 (1978), 28-40.

5265. ____. "MISTER JOHNSON and the Complexity of ARROW OF GOD." In Narasimhaiah, 3593, pp. 50-62; rpt. in 5171, 5266.

5266. ____. ACHEBE'S WORLD: THE HISTORICAL AND CULTURAL CONTEXT OF THE NOVELS OF CHINUA ACHEBE. Washington, DC: Three Continents Press, 1980.

        Includes 5265, 5268.

5267. ____. CHINUA ACHEBE, THINGS FALL APART. [London]: Longman, 1980.

5268. ____. "Achebe's Odili: Hero and Clown." LHY, 21, 1 (1980), 30-39; rpt. in 5266.

5269. ____. "Ozo in Chinua Achebe's Novels: The View from the Past." NSAL, 3 (1980), 71-80.

5270. Wynter, Sylvia. "History, Ideology and the Reinvention of the Past in Achebe's THINGS FALL APART and Laye's THE DARK CHILD." MINORITY VOICES, 2, 1 (1978), 43-61.

See also 3410, 3412-13, 3437-38, 3440, 3467, 3472-73, 3497, 3499, 3503, 3507, 3511, 3514, 3520-21, 3536, 3553, 3555, 3562-63, 3567-68, 3585, 3597, 3604, 3608, 3619-20, 3628, 3634-35, 3638, 3642, 3654, 3658, 3681-82, 3695, 3720-21, 3725, 3727, 3729, 3731, 3733, 3735, 3739-40, 3743-45, 3749, 3753-55, 3757-60, 3765-70, 3778, 3789, 3793-96, 3798, 3802-05, 3808-11, 3813, 3819, 3825, 3827, 3837-38, 3842-43, 4086, 4115, 4118, 4181, 4187, 4194, 4199, 4201, 4218, 4232, 4235, 4244, 4264, 4315, 4340, 4344, 4358, 4360, 4363, 4366,

4370-71, 4374-75, 4377, 4380, 4382, 4388-89, 4398, 4401,
4404, 4406, 4409-10, 4420, 4448, 4453, 4455, 4457, 4477,
4482, 4485, 4488, 4491, 4493, 4497-98, 4509, 4512, 4789,
4814, 4840, 4851, 5871.

ACHOLONU, CATHERINE OBIANUJU

Criticism

See 4069.

ADAGALA, SETH

Interview

See 3890.

AGUNWA, CLEMENT

Biography

See 3373, 3743, 3754, 3843, 4340.

AIDOO, AMA ATA

Bibliography

See 3317.

Biography

5271. Anon. "Ama Ata Aidoo." In Eckardt, 4995, p. 104.

Criticism

5272. Chapman, Karen C. "´Introduction´ to Ama Ata Aidoo´s DILEMMA
       OF A GHOST." In Bell et al., 4472, pp. 25-38.
            Rpt. of BALE 2456.

5273. Grant, Jane W. AMA ATA AIDOO: THE DILEMMA OF A GHOST.
       Harlow: Longman, 1980.

5274. Jones, Eldred, et al. "Aidoo, Christina Ama Ata." In Ferres
       and Tucker, 3467, pp. 13-15; Popkin, 3638, pp. 20-23.
            Extracts from selected criticism.

5275. McCaffrey, Kathleen. "Images of the Mother in the Stories of
       Ama Ata Aidoo." AFRICA WOMAN, 23 (1979), 40-41.

5276. Petersen, Kirsten Holst. "Ama Ata Aidoo." In Petersen and
       Rutherford, 4467, pp. 100-03.

See also 3408, 3432, 3467, 3514, 3544, 3608, 3621, 3638, 3654, 3658,
       3769, 3777, 3833, 3867, 3894, 3950, 4028, 4420, 4473,
       4483-84, 4488-89, 4530, 4609.

AKA, SAMUEL M.O.

Criticism

See 3825.

AKPABOT, ANNE

Criticism

See 4312.

AKPAN, NTIEYONG UDO

Criticism

See 3743, 3843, 4477.

AKELLO, GRACE

Criticism

5277. Nazareth, Peter. "Poetic Grace." AFRISCOPE, 11, 1 (1981),
       33-34.

ALI, DUSÉ MOHAMED

Criticism

5278. Duffield, Ian. "Dusé Mohamed Ali: His Purpose and His
       Public." In Niven, BALE 470, pp. 151-73.

ALUKO, TIMOTHY MOFOLORUNSO

Biography

See 3373, 5286.

Criticism

5279. Crowder, Michael, et al. "Aluko, T.M." In Ferres and
       Tucker, 3467, pp. 15-16.

Extracts from selected criticism.

5280. Drayton, Arthur D., et al. "Aluko, T.M." In Popkin, 3638, pp. 27-31.

Extracts from selected criticism.

5281. Dzeagu, S.A. "T.M. Aluko as a Social Critic." LJH, 2 (1976), 28-41.

5282. Ngwaba, Francis E. "T.M. Aluko and the Theme of the Crisis of Acculturation." NSAL, 2, 1 (1979), 3-11.

5283. Obiechina, E.N. "Art and Caricature: A Case of Aborted Vision in Aluko's ONE MAN, ONE WIFE." EDUCATOR, 9 (September 1973), 37-39.

5284. Osundare, Oluwaniyi. "Speech Narrative in Aluko: An Evaluative Stylistic Investigation." JNESA, 8, 1 (1976), 33-39.

5285. Scott, Patrick. "The Cultural Significance of T.M. Aluko's Novels." BSAA, 7, 1 (1979), 1-10.

5286. ____. "A Biographical Approach to the Novels of T.M. Aluko." In Parker, 3630, pp. 215-39.

See also 3467, 3638, 3727, 3743, 3758, 3805, 3813, 3825-27, 3830, 3837, 4340, 4382, 4420, 4477, 4488, 4491.

AMADI, ELECHI

Criticism

5287. Chandar, K.M. "Elechi Amadi's THE CONCUBINE." LHY, 21, 2 (1980), 123-33.

5288.* Ebbatson, Roger. ELECHI AMADI, THE CONCUBINE. York Notes, 139. London: Longman, 1981.

5289. Laurence, Margaret, et al. "Amadi, Elechi." In Popkin, 3638, pp. 32-35.

Extracts from selected criticism.

5290. Niven, Alastair. ELECHI AMADI, THE CONCUBINE: A CRITICAL VIEW. Ed. Yolande Cantù. Nexus Books, 1. London: Rex Collings in association with The British Council, 1981.

5291. Osundare, Niyi. "'As Grasshoppers to Wanton Boys': The Role of the Gods in the Novels of Elechi Amadi." ALT, 11 (1980), 97-109.

5292. Sarr, Ndiawar. "THE CONCUBINE: Roman sur la société

africaine traditionnelle." UNIVERSITÉ DE DAKAR ANNALES, 8 (1978), 139-52.

See also 3499, 3520, 3545, 3586, 3638, 3682, 3743, 3754, 3765, 3769, 3809, 3811, 3827, 3834, 3837, 3843, 4185, 4365, 4609, 4789, 5505.

ANGIRA, JARED

Bibliography

See 3315.

Biography

See 3315.

Criticism

5293.   Calder, Angus. "Jared Angira: Committed Experimental Poet." In Massa, 3571, pp. 36-44.

5294.* Yesufu, Abdur-Rasheed. "Socio-Political Ideology in Poetry: David Diop and Jared Angira." JEn, 8 (1980), 12-27.

See also 3655, 4090, 4092, 4147.

ANIEBO, I.N.C.

Criticism

5295.   Iheakaram, P.O. "Life and Fiction: A Study of Aniebo's THE ANONYMITY OF SACRIFICE." JAfrS, 7 (1980), 180-81.

See also 3743, 3827, 3837, 4365, 4488.

ANOZIE, SUNDAY O

Criticism

See 4187.

ANYIDOHO, KOFI

Criticism

See 4070, 4072, 4099.

ARMAH, AYI KWEI

Bibliography

See 3315.

Biography

5296. Wanjala, Chris. "Re-interpreting African History." SUNDAY
      NATION, 10 December 1978, p. 13.

           Reaction to lecture given by Armah at the University of
           Nairobi.

See also 3315.

Criticism

5297. Abrahams, Cecil. "Perspectives on Africa." CJAS, 11 (1977),
      355-59.

           FRAGMENTS and Rowland Smith's EXILE AND TRADITION.

5298. Adeyemi, N.A. "The Major Artistic Achievements of Armah in
      THE BEAUTYFUL ONES ARE NOT YET BORN." SHUTTLE, 8 (1980),
      46-48.

5299. Amuta, Chidi. "Ayi Kwei Armah, History, and 'The Way': The
      Importance of TWO THOUSAND SEASONS." KOMPARATISTISCHE HEFTE,
      3 (1981), 79-86; rev. and rpt. as "History, Contemporary
      Reality and Social Vision in Ayi Kwei Armah's TWO THOUSAND
      SEASONS." JLSN, 1 (1981), 40-51.

5300. ____. "Ayi Kwei Armah and the Mythopoesis of Mental
      Decolonization." UFAHAMU, 10, 3 (1981), 44-56.

5301. Booth, James. "WHY ARE WE SO BLEST? and the Limits of
      Metaphor." JCL, 15, 1 (1980), 50-64.

5302. Cheatwood, Kiarri T-H. "WHY ARE WE SO BLEST?" BlackW, March
      1974, pp. 85-90.

5303. Colmer, Rosemary. "The Human and the Divine: FRAGMENTS and
      WHY ARE WE SO BLEST?" KUNAPIPI, 2, 2 (1980), 77-90.

5304. Fraser, Robert. "The American Background in WHY ARE WE SO
      BLEST?" ALT, 9 (1978), 39-46.

5305. ____. THE NOVELS OF AYI KWEI ARMAH. London and Exeter, NH:
      Heinemann, 1980.

5306. Goldie, Terry. "A Connection of Images: The Structure of
      Symbols in THE BEAUTYFUL ONES ARE NOT YET BORN." KUNAPIPI 1,

1 (1979), 94-107.

5307.   Kibera, Leonard. "Pessimism and the African Novelist: Ayi
         Kwei Armah's THE BEAUTYFUL ONES ARE NOT YET BORN." JCL, 14,
         1 (1979), 64-72.

5308.*   Lazarus, Neil. "Strategies for Resistance: A Sociological
         Analysis of the Novels of Ayi Kwei Armah and the
         Preconditions of Their Interpretation." Ph.D. dissertation,
         Keele University, 1981.

5309.   Lindfors, Bernth. "Armah's Histories." ALT, 11 (1980),
         85-96.

5310.   Lobb, Edward. "Armah's FRAGMENTS and the Vision of the
         Whole." ArielE, 10, 1 (1979), 25-38.

5311.   ____. "Personal and Political Fate in Armah's WHY ARE WE SO
         BLEST?" WLWE, 19 (1980), 5-19.

5312.   Mensah, A.M. "The Crisis of the Sensitive Ghanaian: A View
         of the First Two Novels of Ayi Kwei Armah." UNIVERSITAS, 2,
         2 (1972), 3-17.

5313.   Miller, Charles, et al. "Armah, Ayi Kwei." In Popkin, 3638,
         pp. 39-47.

              Extracts from selected criticism.

5314.   Nnolim, Charles E. "Dialectic as Form: Pejorism in the Novels
         of Armah." ALT, 10 (1979), 207-23.

5315.*   Pearse, Tokunbo. "Anguish, Alienation and Freedom in the
         Novels of Ayi Kwei Armah." Master's thesis, University of
         Sheffield, 1977.

5316.   Petersen, Kirsten Holst. "Loss and Frustration: An Analysis
         of A.K. Armah's FRAGMENTS." KUNAPIPI, 1, 1 (1979), 53-65.

5317.   Priebe, Richard. "Demonic Imagery and the Apocalyptic Vision
         in the Novels of Ayi Kwei Armah." YFS, 53 (1976), 102-36.

5318.   Shehu, Emman Usman. "A Blessing of Contradictions: A Reading
         of WHY ARE WE SO BLEST?' KAKAKI, 1 (1980-81), 25-52.

5319.   Steele, Shelby, "Existentialism in the Novels of Ayi Kwei
         Armah." OBSIDIAN, 3, 1 (1977), 5-13.

5320.   Tucker, Martin. "Armah, Ayi Kwei." In Klein, 3370, pp.
         118-19.

              Update of BALE 2510.

5321.   Tucker, Martin, et al. "Armah, Ayi Kwei." In Ferres and
         Tucker, 3467, pp. 16-20.

Extracts from selected criticism.

5322. Washington, Clifton. "TWO THOUSAND SEASONS: Essay Review."
       BBB, 7, 1 (1980), 20-24.

See also 3437, 3440, 3460, 3473, 3499, 3507, 3514, 3520-23, 3545,
       3566, 3572, 3595, 3604, 3608, 3621, 3628, 3638, 3658, 3682,
       3691, 3710, 3721, 3729, 3731, 3740, 3747, 3749, 3751, 3758,
       3760, 3764-65, 3769, 3777, 3794-95, 3798, 3802, 3806-07,
       3811, 3813, 3815, 3819, 3837, 3841, 4187, 4252, 4336, 4360,
       4388-89, 4401, 4406, 4418, 4420, 4435, 4489, 4493, 4498-99,
       4509, 4851.

ARMATTOE, RAPHAEL ERNEST GRAIL

Criticism

See 3608.

ASALACHE, KHADAMBI

Criticism

See 3769.

ASARE, BEDIAKO

Criticism

See 3769.

ASGARALLY, AZIZE

Criticism

See 3464.

AWOONOR, KOFI

Biography

5323. Anon. "Kofi Awoonor." In Eckardt, 4995, p. 104.

5324. Bentsi-Enchill, N., and A. Rondos. "The Price of Freedom."
       WA, 20 November 1978, p. 2301.

           Protests Awoonor´s statements on BBC. See response by
           Jantua, 5325.

5325. Jantua, K.P. "Awoonor was Correct." WA, 25 December 1978, p.

2593.

    Defends Awoonor against charges made by Bentsi-Enchill
    and Rondos, 5324.

5326. Wauthier, Claude. "Awoonor, le poète emprisonné." JeuneA,
       25 August 1976, p. 105.

Interviews

5327. Anon. "Kofi Awoonor on Poetry and Prison." WA, 17 April
       1978, pp. 750-51.

5328. Assensoh, A.B. "Interview: Dr. Kofi Awoonor." AFRISCOPE, 8,
       10 (1978), 25, 27, 29: ORACLE, 6, 2 (n.d.), [2]; TO THE
       POINT, 30 June 1978, p. 35.

5329. Bozimo, Willy. "Politics? It's for Scoundrels: Kofi
       Awoonor." SUNDAY TIMES, 6 February 1977, p. 10.

5330. Munro, Ian H., and Wayne Kamin. "Kofi Awoonor: Interview."
       KUNAPIPI, 1, 2 (1979), 76-83.

Criticism

5331. Colmer, Rosemary. "The Restorative Cycle: Kofi Awoonor's
       Theory of African Literature." NLRev, 3 (1977), 23-28.

5332. ____. "Kofi Awoonor: Critical Prescriptions and Creative
       Practice." ACLALSB, 5, 1 (1978), 22-31.

5333. Egharevba, Chris. "Relation of Style and Meaning in Kofi
       Awoonor's THIS EARTH, MY BROTHER..." KUKA, (1978-79), 55-62.

5334. Killam, G.D. "Kofi Awoonor: THE BREAST OF THE EARTH." DR, 56
       (1976), 143-56.

5335. Knipp, Thomas R. "Myth, History and the Poetry of Kofi
       Awoonor." ALT, 11 (1980), 39-61.

5336. Moore, Gerald. "Death, Convergence and Rebirth in Two Black
       Novels." NJH, 2 (1978), 6-17.

       THIS EARTH, MY BROTHER and Wilson Harris's HEARTLAND.

5337. Mphahlele, Ezekiel, et al. "Awoonor, Kofi." In Ferres and
       Tucker, 3467, pp. 20-23.

       Extracts from selected criticism.

5338. Ojo-Ade, Femi. "Madness in the African Novel: Awoonor's
       THIS EARTH, MY BROTHER..." ALT, 10 (1979), 134-52.

5339. Priebe, Richard K. "Kofi Awoonor's THIS EARTH, MY BROTHER as
       an African Dirge." FOLKLORE ANNUAL, 4-5 (1972-73), 78-90.

Same as BALE 2527.

5340. ____. "Awoonor, Kofi." In Klein, 3370, pp. 159-60.

Update of BALE 2528.

5341. Skurjat, Ernestyna. "Kofi Awoonor, THIS EARTH, MY BROTHER."
PRZEGLAD INFORMACJI O AFRYCE, 2 (1976), 131-33.

On Polish translation.

5342. Theroux, Paul, et al. "Awoonor, Kofi." In Popkin, 3638, pp.
50-56.

Extracts from selected criticism.

5343. Tucker, Martin. "Kofi Awoonor: Restraint and Release."
ENGLISH IN AFRICA, 6, 1 (1979), 46-51.

See also 3437, 3460, 3499, 3585, 3621, 3638, 3658, 3681, 3710, 3740,
3769, 3802, 3837, 4070, 4085, 4091-93, 4097, 4099, 4107,
4115-16, 4135, 4142, 4154, 4187, 4336, 4489, 4498, 4851.

AZASU, KWAKUVI

Criticism

See 4070.

AZUONYE, CHUKWUMA

Criticism

See 4122.

BAGCHI, GANESH

Criticism

See 3498.

BALOGUN, OLA

Criticism

5344. Ata, Afum. "BLACK GODDESS: A Critique." NEW CULTURE, 1, 5
(1979), 43-44.

Film.

5345. Sonuga, Gbenga. "'From ALPHA to BLACK GODDESS': Film-maker in Search of an Idiom." NEW CULTURE, 1, 5 (1979), 37-42.

BART-WILLIAMS, GASTON

Bibliography

See 3315.

Biography

See 3315.

BAZZE-SSENTONGO, EMMANUEL

Criticism

See 3974.

BEDIAKO, K.A.

Criticism

See 3523.

BEEHARRY, DEEPCHAND

Criticism

5346. Pollard, Arthur. "Beeharry's THAT OTHERS MIGHT LIVE." WLWE,
       18 (1979), 135-38.

See also 3464.

BESONG, BATE

Interview

5347. Samson-Akpan, Bob. "Nigerian Student Wins African Writers'
       Recognition." NIGERIAN CHRONICLE, 1 December 1979, pp. 8-9.

       Invited to join Union of Writers of the African Peoples.

BLAY, J. BENIBENGOR

Criticism

See 4336.

BOATENG, YAW M.

Criticism

See 3544, 3769.

BOETIE, DUGMORE

Criticism

See 4191.

BOITUMELO

Interview

See 3327.

BREW, KWESI

Criticism

5348. Anon. "´Ancestral Faces´ by Kwesi Brew." OPON IFA, 1, 2
       (1980), 33-35.

5349. Kayper-Mensah, A.W. "Kwesi Brew and His Poetry." LEGACY, 3,
       1 (1976), 28-32.

See also 3769, 4078, 4097, 4117, 4121, 4154.

BRUTUS, DENNIS

Biography

5350. Anon. "Poet Profile: Dennis Brutus." KWANZA JOURNAL, 4
       (1980), 25-26.

5351. Anon. "Dennis Brutus." In Eckardt, 4995, p. 105.

See also 4901, 5363, 5904.

Interviews

5352. Berger, Renato. "Interview with Dennis Brutus." GAf, 18, 2
       (1980), 73-78.

5353. Imfeld, Al. PORTRAITS OF AFRICAN WRITERS: 1. DENNIS BRUTUS.
       Trans. Jan Klingemann. Cologne: Deutsche Welle
       Transkriptionsdienst, [1979].

            Transcript of radio broadcast.

5354. Maunick, Edouard. "Dennis Brutus: l'exil c'est aussi
       lutter." DEMAIN L'AFRIQUE, 27 August 1979, pp. 77-81.

5355. Mezgebe, Alem. "Writers Should Not Live a Lie." NEW
       AFRICAN, November 1978, p. 71.

Criticism

5356. Abasiekong, Daniel, et al. "Brutus, Dennis." In Ferres and
       Tucker, 3467, pp. 25-27; Popkin, 3638, pp. 107-11.

       Extracts from selected criticism.

5357. Amanuddin, Syed. "South African Poetry of Commitment."
       CREATIVE MOMENT, 11-12 (1978), 13-21.

       Rpt. in Amanuddin, 4065.

5358.* De Meester, Ria. "An Introduction to Dennis Brutus' Prison
       Poems." RESTANT, 8, 2 (1980), 47-56.

5359. Nkondo, Gessler Moses. "Nature, God, Man: The Poetry of
       Frances Carey Slater, Roy Campbell, Guy Butler and Dennis
       Brutus." DAI, 41 (1980), 246A (Yale).

5360. ____. "Dennis Brutus: The Domestication of a Tradition."
       WLT, 55 (1981), 32-40.

5361. ____. "Dennis Brutus and the Revolutionary Idea." UFAHAMU,
       10, 3 (1981), 79-91.

5362. Povey, John. "Brutus, Dennis." In Klein, 3370, p. 349.

5363. Ssensalo, Bede M. "The Autobiographical Nature of the Poetry
       of Dennis Brutus." UFAHAMU, 7, 2 (1977), 130-41; 8, 1
       (1977), 130-42.

5364. Thumboo, Edwin. "Dennis Brutus: Apartheid and the
       Troubadour." UMMA-N, 8 (1978), 24-25, 27-32.

       Rpt. of BALE 2562.

5365. Wylie, Hal. "Creative Exile: Dennis Brutus and René
       Depestre." NSAL, 3 (1980), 35-45; rpt. in Parker, 3630, pp.
       279-93.

See also 3467, 3490, 3514, 3545, 3602, 3608, 3638, 3655-56, 3683,
        4063, 4065, 4092, 4106, 4130, 4134, 4136, 4146, 4148, 4376,
        4479, 5353.

BUKENYA, AUGUSTINE S.

Criticism

See 3774.

BURUGA, JOSEPH

Criticism

See 3580, 3655, 3702, 4164.

CANTEY, LAWRENCE OTU

Criticism

5366.   Petersen, Kirsten Holst. "Gyatoso Clinic." In Petersen and
        Rutherford, 4467, pp. 135-36.

CARIM, ENVER

Criticism

See 3608.

CASELY HAYFORD, ADELAIDE

Bibliography

See 3317.

Biography

5367.   Okonkwo, Rina. "Adelaide Casely Hayford: Cultural
        Nationalist and Feminist." PHYLON, 42 (1981), 41-51.

CASELY-HAYFORD, GLADYS

Bibliography

See 3317.

CASELY HAYFORD, JOSEPH EPHRAIM

Biography

5368.   Ofosu-Appiah, L.H. JOSEPH EPHRAIM CASELY HAYFORD: THE MAN OF

VISION AND FAITH. J.B. Danquah Memorial Lectures, 8. Accra: Academy of Arts and Sciences, 1975.

5369. Sampson, Magnus J. "Introduction." WEST AFRICAN LEADERSHIP: PUBLIC SPEECHES DELIVERED BY J.E. CASELY HAYFORD. Foreword L.E.V. M'Carthy. London: Frank Cass, 1969. Pp. 11-36.

Rpt. of 1951 ed.

5370. ____. "Joseph Ephraim Casely Hayford." GOLD COAST MEN OF AFFAIRS (PAST AND PRESENT). Introd. J.B. Danquah. London: Dawsons of Pall Mall, 1969. Pp. 160-73.

Rpt. of 1937 ed.

Criticism

5371. Saint-Andre-Utudjian, E. "Étude d'un écrivain pionnier: Joseph Ephraim Casely-Hayford, premier romancier de l'ouest-african anglophone." AUBTL, 3, 1 (1976), 111-26.

5372. Ugonna, Nnabuenyi. "Casely Hayford: The Fictive Dimension of African Personality." UFAHAMU, 7, 2 (1977), 159-71.

CHAHILU, BERNARD P.

Criticism

See 4488.

CHAKAVA, HENRY M.

Interview

See 3387.

CHARLEY, DELE

Interview

See 3389.

CHENEY-COKER, SYL

Interview

5373. Brown, Stewart. "Syl Cheney-Coker: A Poet in Exile." INDEX ON CENSORSHIP, 10, 6 (1981), 55-57; WA, 21-28 December 1981, pp. 3055-57, 3059.

Criticism

See 4710.

CHIMAN

Criticism

See 3836.

CHIMEDZA, POLYCARP S.

Criticism

5374. Mzamane, Mbulelo. "The People's Mood: The Voice of a
       Guerilla Poet." REVIEW OF AFRICAN POLITICAL ECONOMY, 18
       (1980), 29-41.

CHIMOMBO, STEVE BERNARD MILES

Interviews

See 3389, 3655.

Criticism

See 3929, 3957, 4080.

CHIMSORO, SAMUEL

Criticism

See 4102.

CHINWEIZU

Criticism

See 4136, 4675.

CLARK, JOHN PEPPER

Biography

See 3373, 3377, 4806, 5904.

Criticism

5375. Adulugba, Egbe. "In Defence of J.P. Clark: A Reassessment of

SONG OF A GOAT." KUKA, (1978-79), 31-35.

5376. Ashaolu, Albert Olu. "The Tragic Vision of Life in THE RAFT." OBSIDIAN, 3, 3 (1977), 20-25.

5377. ____. "J.P. Clark: His Significance as Dramatist." In Ogunba and Irele, 4005, pp. 177-99.

5378. Beier, Ulli, et al. "Clark, John Pepper." In Ferres and Tucker, 3467, pp. 30-34; Popkin, 3638, pp. 140-47.

Extracts from selected criticism.

5379. Connor, William. "Diribi's Incest: The Key to J.P. Clark's THE MASQUERADE." WLWE, 18 (1979), 278-86.

5380. Dathorne, O.R. "Clark, John Pepper." In Klein, 3370, pp. 467-68.

5381. Egberike, J.B. "J.P. Clark's Izon-English Translation of the Ozidi Saga." KIABÀRÀ, 2, 1 (1979), 7-35.

5382. Ifie, J.E. "Notes on Ezon Religion and Culture in the Ozidi Saga." ORITA, 12 (1978), 66-81.

5383.* Lipenga, Kenneth. "The Indigenous and the Foreign in the Works of J.P. Clark." M.A. thesis, University of Leeds, 1978.

5384. Okeke-Ezigbo, 'Emeka. "The Drummer is Also a Story Teller." THIRD WORLD FIRST, 2, 4 (1980), 12-14.

5385. O'Malley, Patrick. "J.P. Clark and THE EXAMPLE OF SHAKESPEARE." ODI, 3, 1 (1978), 4-15.

5386. Petersen, Kirsten Holst. "Clark, John Pepper." In Vinson and Kirkpatrick, 3377, pp. 53-54.

5387. ____. JOHN PEPPER CLARK, SELECTED POEMS: A CRITICAL VIEW. Ed. Yolande Cantù. Nexus Books, 3. London: Rex Collings in association with The British Council, 1981.

5388. Saint-Andre-Utudjian, E. "Clark's Use of Local Colour in THE MASQUERADE: A Case of Cultural Ambivalence." AUBTL, 2, 2 (1975), 201-26.

Same as BALE 2591.

5389. Spurling, D. J. "A Critique of 'Night Rain' by John Pepper Clark." CAMEROON STUDIES IN ENGLISH & FRENCH, 1 (1976), 64-70.

5390. Tripathi, Virendra. "John Pepper Clark: Nigerian Poet and Dramatist." AfrQ, 16, 4 (1977), 120-24.

5391.   Uka, Kalu.   "J.P. Clark's OZIDI: A Suggested Teaching
        Approach."   OKIKE, 13 (1979), 84-92.

See also 3467, 3497, 3511, 3563, 3567, 3586, 3608, 3627-28, 3638,
        3884, 3886-87, 3894, 3897, 3901, 3912, 3948, 3980-81, 4007,
        4014, 4023, 4028, 4053, 4078, 4091-92, 4097, 4100, 4107,
        4109, 4115, 4117, 4121-22, 4138, 4143, 4156, 4187, 4215,
        4340, 4374, 4380, 4448-49, 4484, 5904.

CONTON, WILLIAM FARQUHAR

Criticism

See 3597, 3837, 4194, 4491, 4789.

COOPER, CHARLES EDWARD (Varfelli Karlee, pseud.)

Criticism

See 3824.

CORDOR, S. HENRY

Criticism

See 3824.

CUGUOANO, OTTOBAH

Criticism

See 4271-72.

DANQUAH, JOSEPH KWAME KYERETWIE BOAKYE

Biography

5392.   Nyarko, K.   "The Man that Was J.B. Danquah."   LEGON OBSERVER,
        13, 3 (1981), 68-70.

Criticism

See also 3867.

DARAH, G.G.

Interview

See 4675.

DATTA, SAROJ

Criticism

See 4107.

DECKER, THOMAS

Biography

5393. Timothy, Bankolé. "Thomas Decker." WA, 18 September 1978,
       p. 1828.

DE GRAFT, JOSEPH COLEMAN

Biography

5394. Anon. "Joe de Graft." SUNDAY NATION, 12 November 1978, p.
       18.
           Obituary.

5395. Anon. "Joe de Graft (1924-1978)." WA, 1 January 1979, pp.
       16-18.
           Obituary.

5396. Dressler, Claus Peter. "Joe de Graft: Biografische Notiz."
       In Eckardt, 4995, p. 27.

See also 3418.

Interviews

5397. Lindfors, Bernth. "Interview with Joe de Graft." WLWE, 18
       (1979), 314-31; rpt. in Lindfors, 3387.

See also 4798.

Criticism

5398. Awoonor, Kofi. "The Imagery of Fire: A Critical Assessment
       of the Poetry of Joe de Graft." OKIKE, 19 (1981), 70-79.

5399. Klicker, Jochen R. "The School of Performing Arts: Joe C. de
       Graft, MAMBO." In Eckardt, 4995, pp. 28-29.

See also 3608, 3867, 3930, 4028, 4070, 4130.

DEI-ANANG, MICHAEL FRANCIS

Criticism

See 3608.

DEMPSTER, ROLAND TOMBEKAI

Criticism

See 3824.

DERESSA, SOLOMON

Criticism

See 3420.

DHLOMO, HERBERT ISAAC ERNEST

Criticism

5400.   Couzens, Timothy John. "´The New African´: Herbert Dhlomo and
        Black South African Literature in English." DAI, 42 (1981),
        211A(Witwatersrand).

See also 3493-94, 3550, 3608, 3631, 4081, 4087, 4485.

DHLOMO, ROLFUS REGINALD RAYMOND

Criticism

See 3493-94, 3509, 3550, 3786.

DIKE, FATIMA

Biography

5401.   Heyns, Jackie. "Fatima Dike: The Queen of our Stage." DRUM
        (Johannesburg), October 1979, p. 14.

5402.   King, Val, and Paul Alberts. "Fatima Dike--Lady of the
        Theatre." BONA, January 1980, 92-95.

Interviews

5403.   Gray, Stephen. "The Pain of Being Black." CONTRAST, 12, 1
        (1978), 78-83; CALLALOO, 8-10 (1980), 157-64; rpt. in House,

3327, pp. 22-32.

See also 3384.

Criticism

5404. Amato, Rob. "A Xhosa Woman's Serious Optimism." SPEAK, 1, 1 (1977), 14-17.

>   THE FIRST SOUTH AFRICAN.

5405. Meltzer, Lalou. "A Response to This..." SPEAK, 1, 1 (1977), 48-49.

>   Reply to Nicolas-Fanourakis, 5406.

5406. Nicolas-Fanourakis, Dimitri. "Learning from Theatre: An Account of Interpersonal Contact across the Racial Divide." SPEAK, 1, 1 (1977), 46-49.

>   Comments by director of THE FIRST SOUTH AFRICAN. See response by Meltzer, 5405.

DIKOBE, MODIKWE

Biography and Autobiography

5407. Anon. "Profile: Modikwe Dikobe." STAFFRIDER, 3, 1 (1980), 7.

5408. Dikobe, Modikwe. "A Return to the Land--Where Minds Grow Stale." FRONTLINE, October 1980, pp. 3-4.

>   Autobiographical account.

Criticism

5409. Couzens, Tim. "Appendix A. Nobody's Baby: Modikwe Dikobe and Alexandra, 1942-1946.: In Bozzoli, 3425, pp. 90-103.

5410. Deflo, Lionel. "Modikwe Dikobes MARABIDANS: de apartheid van binnen uit [Modike Dikobe's MARABI DANCE: Apartheid from the Inside]." KREATIEF, 11, 4-5 (1977), 116-26.

5411. Hofmeyr, Isabel. "THE MARABI DANCE." AFRICA PERSPECTIVE, 6 (1977), 1-12.

5412. Pinnock, Don. "A Critical Review of THE MARABI DANCE, with Special Attention to the Attitudes and Value Judgements Contained in the Narrative, and Assessing the Value of the Novel to the Historian." JANUS, (1979), 14-21.

See also 3509, 3608, 4757.

DIPOKO, MBELLA SONNE

Criticism

See 3602, 3769, 4488.

DJOLETO, AMY

Criticism

See 3719, 3777, 4078, 4488.

DONKOR, WILLIE

Criticism

See 4336.

DUKE, ANTERA

Criticism

See 4373.

DUODU, CAMERON

Criticism

See 3758, 4107, 4370.

EASMON, RAYMOND SARIF

Interview

5413. Wright, L. "Entretien avec Raymond Sarif Easmon, docteur en
       médecine, romancier, auteur de pièces de théâtre, essayiste."
       RPC, 53-54 (1981), 58-60.

Criticism

5414. Nagenda, John, et al. "Easmon, Sarif R." In Ferres and
       Tucker, 3467, pp. 36-38.
            Extracts from selected criticism.

See also 3467, 3608, 3950, 4028.

EBA, NSANDA

Criticism

5415. Ibrahim, Tala Kashim. "Something New Out of Cameroon: A
       Review of Nsanda Eba's THE GOOD FOOT." NGAM, 5 (1979),
       93-107.

ECHERUO, MICHAEL JOSEPH CHUKWUDALU

Biography

See 3373.

Criticism

See 3912, 4135-36, 4187.

ECHEWA, T. OBINKARAM

Criticism

See 3544, 3688, 3743, 4491.

EDOO, HOSSENJE

Criticism

See 3464.

EGBLEWOGBE, EUSTACE YAWO

Criticism

See 4070.

EGBUNA, OBI BENUE

Bibliography

See 3315.

Biography and Autobiography

5416. Anyanwu, Clement. "There Are Great Writers Like...."
       RENAISSANCE WEEKLY, 22 March 1973, p. 4.
            Response to Egbuna, 5417.

5417. Egbuna, Obi. "I Am No Medusa on Ice." RENAISSANCE WEEEKLY,
       18 March 1973, pp. 8-9, 11.

           Autobiographical statement. See responses by Anyanwu,
           5416; Emeruem, 5418; Obiora, 5419; and Okpanku, 5420.

5418. Emeruem, Godwin. "Let Him Leave the English Alone."
       RENAISSANCE WEEKLY, 22 March 1973, p. 4.

           Response to Egbuna, 5417.

5419. Obiora, John. "I Disagree." RENAISSANCE WEEKLY, 22 March
       1973, p. 4.

           Response to Egbuna, 5417.

5420. Okpanku, Agwu. "Epistle to a Black Power Activist."
       RENAISSANCE WEEKLY, 25 March 1973, pp. 2, 6.

           Response to Egbuna, 5417.

See also 3315.

Interview

5421.* Nwimo, Emma. "My Name is Obi." DRUM (Lagos), October 1974.

Criticism

See 3520, 3743, 3808, 3843.

EGEJURU, PHANUEL AKUBUEZE

Criticism

See 4504.

EGUDU, ROMANUS

Criticism

See 4159.

EKWENSI, CYPRIAN ODIATU DUAKA

Bibliography

See 3315.

Biography and Autobiography

5422. Anon. "Matchet's Diary." WA, 5 February 1955, p. 103.

5423. Anon. "The Chemist and the Author." WAR, June 1956, pp. 553-55.

5424. Anon. "Writer in Fleet Street." WAR, June 1960, p. 37.

5425. Anon. "'Jagua' to be Filmed Soon." DRUM (Lagos), June 1962, pp. 14-15, 33.

5426. Anon. "The Big Film Row: Is the Ban on 'Jagua' Right?" SPEAR, February 1963, pp. 20-21.

        Survey of public opinion.

5427. Anon. "Ekwensi Retains Image of America's Dynamism." INTERLINK, 1, 1 (1965), 16-17.

        After visit to the United States.

5428. Ekwensi, Cyprian. "What Mr. Ekwensi Thinks about Himself." AFRICAN HORIZON, 3 (April-June 1961), p. 30.

        Response to adverse review of THE PASSPORT OF MALLAM ILIA.

See also 3315, 3373, 3377.

Interview

See 3389.

Criticism

5429. Cosentino, Donald. "Jagua Nana: Culture Heroine." BA SHIRU, 8, 1 (1977), 11-17.

5430. Hawkins, Loretta A. "The Free Spirit of Ekwensi's Jagua Nana." ALT, 10, (1979), 202-06.

5431. Ibitokun, B.S. "Prostitution or Neurosis: A Note on Cyprian Ekwensi's JAGUA NANA." NSAL, 3 (1980), 81-87.

5432. Iheakaram, Paul O. "The City as Metaphor: The Short Stories of Cyprian Ekwensi." IFR, 6 (1979), 71-72.

5433. July, Robert W., et al. "Ekwensi, Cyprian O.D." In Ferres and Tucker, 3467, pp. 38-42.

        Extracts from selected criticism.

5434. Linnemann, Russell J. "Structural Weakness in Ekwensi's JAGUA NANA." ENGLISH IN AFRICA, 4, 1 (1977), 32-39.

5435. Morsiani, Jamilè. "Cyprian Ekwensi: Una narrativa
       ´scritta.´" SpM, 11 (1979), 123-55.

5436. Ndu, Pol N. "Urban Modality in Ekwensi´s Juvenile
       Literature." CRevB, 3, 2-4 (1975), 83-86.

5437. Obilade, Anthony. "The Chronicler and the New Generation: A
       Review of Cyprian Ekwensi´s Recent Writings." AfrSR, 20, 1
       (1977), 127-30.

5438. Okonkwo, Juliet I. "Ekwensi and the ´Something New and
       Unstable´ in Modern Nigerian Culture." In Nwoga, 3611, pp.
       130-43.

       Rpt. of BALE 2655.

5439. Osofisan, Femi. "Domestication of an Opiate: Western
       Paraesthetics and the Growth of the Ekwensi Tradition."
       POSITIVE REVIEW, 1, 4 (1981), 1-12.

5440. Petersen, Kirsten Holst. "Ekwensi, Cyprian." In Vinson and
       Kirkpatrick, 3377, pp. 77-78.

5441. Ramsaran, J.A. "Two West African Novelists: A Comparison."
       WAR, August 1958, pp. 683-84.

       Also treats Camara Laye.

5442. Richardson, Maurice, et al. "Ekwensi, Cyprian." In Popkin,
       3638, pp. 182-87.

       Extracts from selected criticism.

5443. Rutherford, Anna. "Cyprian Ekwensi." In Petersen and
       Rutherford, 4467, pp. 65-67.

5444. Skurjat, Ernestyna. "Cyprian Ekwensi: JAGUA NANA." PRZEGLAD
       INFORMACJI O AFRYCE, 4 (1976), 124-26.

       On Polish translation.

See also 3413, 3438, 3467, 3497, 3520, 3544, 3597, 3638, 3681, 3720,
       3733, 3739, 3743-44, 3753-55, 3793, 3797, 3803, 3813, 3819,
       3827, 3837, 3843, 4187, 4315, 4344, 4360, 4366, 4374, 4488,
       4509, 4789, 5505.

EKWERE, JOHN

Criticism

See 3567, 4377.

EKWUEME, L.E.N.

Criticism

See 3912.

EMECHETA, BUCHI

Bibliography

See 3315, 3317.

Biography and Autobiography

5445. Emecheta, Buchi. "To Jog or to Die." WA, 12 March 1978, pp. 444-45.

5446. ____. "Out of the Ditch and Into Print." WA, 3 April 1978, pp. 669, 671-72.

5447. ____. "Another Fear of Flying." WA, 25 June 1978, pp. 1119-20.

5448. ____. "A Time Bomb." WA, 30 October 1978, pp. 2139-40.

5449. ____. "U.S. Longing for Roasted Yams." WA, 27 August 1979, pp. 1560-62.

5450. ____. "U.S. Police Convince Me I Am Lost." WA, 24 September 1979, pp. 1761-62.

5451. ____. "What the Carol Singers Are Missing." WA, 24-31 December 1979, pp. 2385-86.

5452. ____. "Lagos Provides a Warm Welcome." WA, 19 January 1981, pp. 110-13.

5453. ____. "Head Above Water." KUNAPIPI, 3, 1 (1981), 81-90.

5454. ____. "Nigeria: Experiencing a Cultural Lag." WA, 2 November 1981, pp. 2582-83.

5455. ____. "That First Novel." KUNAPIPI, 3, 2 (1981), 115-23.

See also 3315.

Interview

5456. Crichton, S. "PW Interviews Buchi Emecheta." PUBW, 11 June 1979, pp. 10-11.

Criticism

5457. Anon. "Matchet's Diary." WA, 22 January 1979, p. 123.

On her first children's book, TITCH THE CAT.

5458. Dailly, Christophe. "SECOND CLASS CITIZEN et THE BRIDE PRICE de Buchi Emecheta." RLENA, 2 (1979), 145-46.

5459. Stummer, Peter. "Buchi Emecheta und die Erfahrung der schwarzen Frau." In Stilz, 4043, pp. 91-101.

5460. Umeh, Marie. "African Women in Transition in the Novels of Buchi Emecheta." PA, 116 (1980), 190-201.

5461. Wilson, Judith. "Buchi Emecheta: Africa from a Woman's View." ESSENCE, February 1980, pp. 12-13.

See also 3408, 3419, 3432, 3523, 3544, 3743, 4488.

ENEKWE, OSSIE ONUORA E.

Criticism

See 4159.

EQUIANO, OLAUDAH

Biography

5462. Anon. "'Afric's Sun-Burnt Race.'" ROYAL COMMONWEALTH SOCIETY LIBRARY NOTES, N.S. 222 (1977), 4.

On memorial inscription to his daughter Anna, who died at the age of 4.

5463. Edwards, Paul. "Olaudah Equiano." HISTORY TODAY, 31 (September 1981), 44.

5464. Francis, Elman V. "Olaudah Equiano: A Profile." NEGRO HISTORY B, 44 (1981), 31, 43-44.

5465. Killingray, David. OLAUDAH EQUIANO AND THE SLAVE TRADE. Round the World Histories, 31. Amersham: Hulton Educational Publications, 1974.

Book for children.

See also 3458.

Criticism

5466. Abanime, Emeka. "Equiano, précurseur de la littérature nigériane anglophone." ETHIOPIQUES, 19 (1979), 80-84.

5467. Baker, Houston A., Jr. THE JOURNEY BACK: ISSUES IN BLACK LITERATURE AND CRITICISM. Chicago and London: University of Chicago Press, 1980. Pp. 15-21, passim.

5468. Preston, David G. "Olaudah Equiano." EUROPE, 618 (1980), 35-38.

See also 3837, 4235, 4271-72, 4377-78.

ERAPU, LABAN

Criticism

See 3769, 4078.

EYAKUZE, VALENTINE

Criticism

See 3538.

EZEOKOLI, VICTORIA C.

Criticism

See 3912.

FANCHETTE, RÉGIS

Criticism

See 3464.

FARAH, NURUDDIN

Bibliography

See 3315.

Biography

5469. Anon. "Nuruddin Farah." In Eckardt, 4995, p. 106.

5470. Walmsley, Anne. "Nuruddin Farah and Somalia." INDEX ON CENSORSHIP, 10, 2 (1981), 17-19.

See also 3315.

Interviews

5471.   Anon. "Nuruddin Farah: 'Committed Writer.'" NEW AFRICAN,
        January 1979, p. 85.

5472.   Kitchener, Julie. "Author in Search of an Identity." NEW
        AFRICAN, December 1981, p. 61.

5473.   Lampley, James. "A View of Home from the Outside." AIBEPM,
        124 (1981), 81-82.

Criticism

5474.   Cochrane, Judith. "The Theme of Sacrifice in the Novels of
        Nuruddin Farah." WLWE, 18 (1979), 69-77.

5475.   Imfeld, Al, and Gerd Meuer. "Nuruddin Farah: A Modern
        Nomad." AFRIKA, 21, 9 (1980), 23-25.

5476.   Petersen, Kirsten Holst. "The Personal and the Political:
        The Case of Nuruddin Farah." ArielE, 12, 3 (1981), 93-101.

See also 3421, 3514, 3544-45, 4476, 4488.

FATOBA, FEMI

Criticism

See 4069.

FEBRUARY, VERNON

Interview

5477.   Anon. "Interview met Vernie February." KREATIEF, 11, 4-5
        (1977), 13-22.

            On South African literature in English and Afrikaans.

FIBERISIMA, ELDRED

Criticism

See 5143.

FONLON, BERNARD

Biography

5478.   Baratte-Eno Belinga, Thérèsa. ÉCRIVAINS, CINÉASTES ET
        ARTISTES CAMEROUNAIS: BIO-BIBLIOGRAPHIE. Yaoundé: Ministère

de l´Information et de la Culture de la République Unie du
Cameroun, 1978.

Includes Fonlon and francophone writers.

See also 3374.

Interview

5479.   Arnold, S.H.   "An Interview about Literature with Bernard
Fonlon."   WLWE, 20 (1981), 48-62.

GABRE-MEDHIN, TSEGAYE

Criticism

See 3420, 3481, 3608, 3696, 4051.

GARUBA, HARRIE

Criticism

See 4069.

GATHERU, REUEL JOHN MUGO

Criticism

See 3769.

GITHAE-MUGO, MICERE

Biography

5480.   Anon.   "New Dean."   WEEKLY REVIEW, 21 March 1980, pp. 8-9.

5481.   Brittain, Victoria.   "A Heady Mixture in Search of Culture."
GUARDIAN, 2 June 1980, p. 15.

Profile of Dean of Arts at the University of Nairobi.

See also 4948.

Criticism

See 3478, 3916, 4058, 4394, 5709, 5715, 5738, 5742.

GOVENDER, RONNIE

Interview

See 3384.

GRONNIOSAW, JAMES ALBERT UKAWSAW

Criticism

5482. Herring, Maben. "James Gronniosaw, an African Autobiographer
       in England." JOURNAL OF AFRO-AMERICAN ISSUES, 5 (1977),
       143-60.

GUBEGNA, ABBIE

Criticism

See 3420, 3481, 3523.

GWALA, MAFIKA PASCAL

Biography

See 5904.

Criticism

See 3712, 4081, 4125, 4132-33, 4153, 4168, 4757.

HAULI, CRISPIN

Criticism

See 4090, 4130.

HEAD, BESSIE

Biography and Autobiography

5483. Anon. "Bessie Head." In Eckardt, 4995, p. 106.

5484. Head, Bessie. "Witchcraft." MS., 4, 5 (1975), 72-73.

5485. _____. "Some Notes on Novel Writing." NEW CLASSIC, 5 (1978),
       30-32.
              In Botswana and South Africa.

5486. ____. "A Note on RAIN CLOUDS." GAR, 33 (1979), 27.

5487. ____. "Social and Political Pressures that Shape Literature in South Africa." WLWE, 18 (1979), 20-26.

Interviews

5488. Fradkin, Betty McGinnis. "Conversations with Bessie." WLWE, 17 (1978), 427-34.

5489. Imfeld, Al. PORTRAITS OF AFRICAN WRITERS: 3. BESSIE HEAD. Trans. Jan Klingemann. Cologne: Deutsche Welle Transkriptionsdienst, [1979].

      Transcript of radio broadcast.

See also 3389.

Criticism

5490. Abrahams, Cecil A. "The Tyranny of Place: The Context of Bessie Head's Fiction." WLWE, 17 (1978), 22-29.

5491. Beard, Linda Susan. "Bessie Head's A QUESTION OF POWER: The Journey Through Disintegration to Wholeness." CLQ, 15 (1979), 267-74.

5492. Beeton, D.R. "Preserving a Cultural Heritage: A South African Past, Present and Future." COMMUNIQUÉ, 5, 2 (1980), 1-10.

      Head, et al.

5493. Brown, Lloyd W. "Creating New Worlds in Southern Africa: Bessie Head and the Question of Power." UMOJA, 3, 1 (1979), 43-53.

5494. Bruner, Charlotte H. "Bessie Head: Restless in a Distant Land." In Parker, 3630, pp. 261-77.

5495. Grant, Jane W. "Bessie Head: An Appreciation." BANANAS, 22 (1980), 25-26.

5496. Heywood, Christopher. "Traditional Values in the Novels of Bessie Head." In Massa, 3571, pp. 12-19.

5497. Marquard, Jean. "Bessie Head: Exile and Community in Southern Africa." LONDON MAGAZINE, 18, 9-10 (1978-79), 48-61.

5498. ____. "The Farm: A Concept in the Writing of Olive Schreiner, Pauline Smith, Doris Lessing, Nadine Gordimer and Bessie Head." DR, 59 (1979), 293-307.

Botswana: Alienation and Commitment in the Writings of Bessie Head." PA, 109 (1979), 92-106; JAfrS, 6 (1979-80), 206-12.

5500. Ojo-Ade, Femi. "Bessie Head's Alienated Heroine: Victim or Villain?" BA SHIRU, 8, 2 (1977), 13-21.

See also 3408, 3490, 3493-94, 3608, 3658, 3712, 4473, 4710, 5489.

HENRIES, A. DORIS BANKS

Criticism

See 3824.

HENSHAW, JAMES ENE

Biography

See 3373.

Criticism

See 3886, 4007, 4028.

HEVI, JACOB

Criticism

See 3916.

HOLMES-ASHBURN, GENE

Biography

5501. Richardson, Nathaniel R. "Brief Biography of Gene Holmes-Ashburn, Late Liberian Natural Poet." In ANTHOLOGY OF LIBERIAN LITERATURE. Monrovia: Society of Liberian Authors, 1974. Pp. 39-40.

HOUSE, AMELIA

Criticism

See 4168.

IBUKUN, OLU

Criticism

See 3743.

IFEJIKA, SAMUEL U.

Criticism

See 3827.

IJIMERE, OBOTUNDE (pseud. of Ulli Beier)

Biography

5502. Owomoyela, Oyekan. "Obotunde Ijimere, The Phantom of
       Nigerian Theater." AfrSR, 22, 1 (1979), 43-50.
            Reveals that Ulli Beier wrote under this pseudonym.

IKE, VINCENT CHUKWUEMEKA

Bibliography

See 3315.

Biography

See 3315, 3373.

Interviews

5503. Udoakah, Nkereuwem. "Mr. Vincent Ike: The Undergrad is No
       More Sacred." QUEST, 15 (1979), 135-36.

See also 3378.

Criticism

5504. Agetua, John. TOADS FOR SUPPER: NOTES, WITH QUESTIONS AND
       ANSWERS. Benin City: P.J. Publications, [1978].

5505. Amuzu, Koku. "SUNSET AT DAWN: An Artist's View of the
       Biafran War." LEGACY, 3, 2 (1977), 59-62.

5506. Johnson, Alex C. "SUNSET AT DAWN: A Biafran on the Nigerian
       Civil War." ALT, 11 (1980), 149-60.
            Includes comments on civil war writings by Amadi,
            Ekwensi, Mezu, Okpewho.

See also 3520, 3544, 3743, 3754, 3809, 3827, 3843, 4340, 4488, 4789.

IMBUGA, FRANCIS

Criticism

5507. Arden, Richard, and Austin Lwanga Bukenya. FRANCIS
       D. IMBUGA, BETRAYAL IN THE CITY. [London]: Longman, 1978.

5508. Erapu, Laban. NOTES ON FRANCIS IMBUGA´S BETRAYAL IN THE
       CITY. H.E.B. Student´s Guide, 15. Nairobi: Heinemann
       Educational Books, 1979.

See also 3949, 4058.

IRELE, ABIOLA

Bibliography

See 3315.

Biography

See 3315.

Criticism

See 4187.

IROH, EDDIE

Criticism

See 3743, 4365.

IZEVBAYE, DANIEL S.

Criticism

See 4187.

JABAVU, NONI

Criticism

See 3597.

JEYIFO, BIODUN

Criticism

See 3584.

JOLOBE, JAMES JAMES RANISI

Criticism

See 3608.

JONES, ELDRED DUROSIMI

Criticism

See 4187.

JOW, CHARLES

Interview

See 3389.

KADHANI, MUDERERI

Criticism

See 4102.

KAHIGA, SAMUEL

Criticism

See 4488.

KALYEGIRA, JUNDA S.

Criticism

See 3974.

KAMENJU, GRANT

Interview

5509.   Lindfors, Bernth. "Interview with Grant Kamenju."   CHIMO, 3
        (1981), 21-29; rpt. in Lindfors, 3387.

KA-MIYA, THEMBA

Criticism

See 4161.

KANI, JOHN

Biography

See 3874.

Interviews

See 3384, 4019.

KARGBO, KOLLOSA JOHN

Biography

5510.   Anon. "Curtains on Kargbo Play."   NEW AFRICAN, December
        1979, p. 55.
            Closing down of POYOH TON WAHALA.

Criticism

5511.   Stevens, Karwigoko-Roy. "Drama's Historical Backdrop."   NEW
        AFRICAN, June 1979, pp. 74-75.
            LET ME DIE ALONE, a play about Sierra Leone's Poro
            secret society.

KARIARA, JONATHAN

Biography

See 5904.

Interview

5512.   Mulei, Christopher. "Writers Falling Prey to Colonial

Hangover." SUNDAY NATION, 22 August 1971, pp. 13-14.

Criticism

See 3587, 5904.

KARIUKI, JOSEPH

Interviews

See 3382, 3515, 3527.

Criticism

See 4121, 4143.

KARLEE, VARFELLI (See Cooper, Charles Edward)

KASANGA, RHODA

Criticism

5513. Anon. "A Fine New Writing Talent." WEEKLY REVIEW, 23
       October 1981, p. 42.
             Author of children's plays.

KASOMA, KABWE

Criticism

See 4028.

KASSAM, YUSUF O.

Criticism

See 4078.

KATIGULA, BARNABAS

Criticism

See 3728.

KATIYO, WILSON

Autobiography

5514. Katiyo, Wilson. "'The Time it Takes to Struggle is the Time
       to Live.'" COMMONWEALTH, April-May 1981, p. 13.

Criticism

See 3419, 3544, 3773.

KAYIRA, LEGSON

Criticism

See 3655, 3719, 3769, 3806-07.

KAYPER-MENSAH, ALBERT WILLIAM

Interview

See 3389.

Criticism

See 4070, 4078.

KEBEDE, ASHENAFI

Criticism

See 3420, 3481.

KENTE, GIBSON

Biography

5515. Sehume, Leslie. "Their Love, Their Hate--That's His Life."
       BONA, June 1980, pp. 54-60, 62.

Interview

5516. Mponja, Mapula. "Mapula Mponja Interviews Gibson Kente."
       BONA, August-September 1976, pp. 18-19.

Criticism

See 3872.

KENYI, SAM

Interview

See 3889.

KGOSITSILE, KEORAPETSE WILLIAM

Biography

5517. Anon. "Keorapetse William Kgositsile." In Eckardt, 4995, p. 107.

Interviews

5518. Rowell, Charles H. "´With Bloodstains to Testify´: An Interview with Keorapetse Kgositsile." CALLALOO, 2 (1978), 23-41.

See also 5007.

Criticism

See 3410, 4092, 4106, 4146-47, 4395, 4484, 5007.

KHASU, KONA

Interviews

5519. Martin, Carlos. "Blamadon: The Bud of Liberian Theatre." LIBERIA: POLITICAL, ECONOMIC AND SOCIAL MONTHLY, 23-24 (1976), 28-32.

        Interview with organizer of Blamadon Theatre Workshop.

See also 3389.

KIBERA, LEONARD

Criticism

See 3574, 3580, 3655, 3702, 3774-75, 5871.

KIMBUGWE, HENRY SERUMA (Eneriko Seruma, pseud.)

Interview

5520. Mulei, Christopher. "Characters ´Larger Than Life´ to Put Over Message." SUNDAY NATION, 27 June 1971, pp. 14-15.

KIMENYE, BARBARA

Criticism

See 4315.

KITSAO, JAY

Criticism

See 4445.

K´OKIRI, L.G. OGUDA

Criticism

See 3769.

KONADU, SAMUEL ASARE

Criticism

See 3777, 4336, 4489, 4789.

KOR, BUMA

Biography

See 3374.

Criticism

5521.   Butake, Bole.   "SEARCHLIGHT POEMS: Buma Kor´s Apologia."
        NGAM, 5 (1979), 57-75.

See also 4636.

KUMALO, ALTON

Biography

5522.   Anon.   "Alton Kumalo--The Man Who´s Taking Black Theatre to
        Britain." DRUM (Nairobi), December 1979, pp. 44-45.

KUNENE, RAYMOND MAZISI

Biography

See 5904.

Interview

5523. Luchembe, Chipasha, ed. "An Interview with Mazisi Kunene on
       African Philosophy." UFAHAMU, 7, 2 (1977), 3-27.

Criticism

5524. Bulane, Mofolo, et al. "Kunene, Mazisi." In Popkin, 3638,
       pp. 272-75.
           Extracts from selected criticism.

See also 3547, 3573, 3608, 3638, 3769, 4100, 4187.

LA GUMA, ALEX

Bibliography

5525. Green, Robert and Agnes Lonje. "Alex La Guma: A Selected
       Bibliography." WLWE, 20 (1981), 16-22.

Biography

See 4985, 5904.

Criticism

5526. Banham, Martin, et al. "La Guma, Alex." In Popkin, 3638,
       pp. 276-80.
           Extracts from selected criticism.

5527. Bunting, Brian, et al. "La Guma, Alex." In Ferres and
       Tucker, 3467, pp. 54-56.
           Extracts from selected criticism.

5528. Futcha, Innocent. "The Fog in IN THE FOG OF THE SEASON'S
       END." NGAM, 1-2 (1977), 78-92.

5529. Green, Robert. "Alex La Guma's IN THE FOG OF THE SEASON'S
       END: The Politics of Subversion." UMOJA, 3 (1979), 85-93.

5530. ____. "Chopin in the Ghetto: The Short Stories of Alex La
       Guma." WLWE, 20 (1981), 5-16.

5531. Kibera, Leonard. "A Critical Appreciation of Alex La Guma's
       IN THE FOG OF THE SEASON'S END." BUSARA, 8, 1 (1976), 59-66.

5532. Lefevere, André. "Alex La Guma." KREATIEF, 11, 4-5 (1977),
       136-46.

5533. Riemenschneider, Dieter. "The Prisoner in South African
       Fiction: Alex La Guma's THE STONE COUNTRY and IN THE FOG OF
       THE SEASON'S END." In Massa, 3571, pp. 51-58; ACLALSB, 5, 3
       (1980), 144-53.

5534. Scanlon, Paul A. "Alex La Guma's Novels of Protest: The
       Growth of the Revolutionary." OKIKE, 16 (1979), 39-47.

5535. Wade, Michael. "Art and Morality in Alex La Guma's A WALK IN
       THE NIGHT." In Parker, 3817, pp. 164-91.

5536. Wanjala, Chris Lukorito. "Fossilized Black Martyrs." In
       Gachukia and Akivaga, 4799, pp. 201-15.

       On IN THE FOG OF THE SEASON'S END.

See also 3393, 3410, 3467, 3490, 3585, 3608, 3638, 3655-56, 3681,
       3702, 3740, 3750, 3758, 3760, 3765, 3803, 3817, 3834, 4191,
       4375-76, 4386, 4395, 4407, 4409, 4479, 4710.

LANGA, MANDLENKOSI

Criticism

See 3393.

LEMMA, MENGHISTU

Criticism

See 3420.

LESHOAI, BENJAMIN LETHOLOA (Bob)

Biography

5537. Pereira, Ernest. "The Author: Benjamin Letholoa Leshoai."
       In CONTEMPORARY SOUTH AFRICAN PLAYS. Ed. Ernest Pereira.
       Johannesburg: Ravan, 1977. Pp. 252-53.

           Followed by remarks by Leshoai, pp. 253-54, on his play
           LINES DRAW MONSTERS, published on pp. 255-66. Pereira
           comments on the play on pp. 13-14.

Interview

5538. Mulei, Christopher. "Relevance as Key to New Theatre."
SUNDAY NATION, 24 October 1971, pp. 13-14.

LIYONG, TABAN LO

Biography and Autobiography

5539. Anon. "Taban lo Liyong." In Eckardt, 4995, p. 108.

5540. Liyong, Taban lo. MEDITATIONS OF TABAN LO LIYONG. London:
Rex Collings, 1978.

> Expansion of MEDITATIONS IN LIMBO. Shield Series, 1.
> Nairobi: Equatorial Publishers, 1970.

Interviews

5541. Darling, Peter. "Breaking the Shackles of Old Ideas."
SUNDAY NATION, 7 December 1969, pp. 17-18, 42.

5542. Lindfors, Bernth. "Interview with Taban lo Liyong."
ACLALSB, 5, 2 (1979), 1-22; rpt. in Lindfors, 3387.

5543. Yaak, Atem. "The Challenge of Writing." SUDANOW, June 1978,
pp. 44-46.

Criticism

5544. Imfeld, Al. "Taban lo Liyong: Katalysator und Stimulator."
BDB, 22 August 1980, pp. 2017-18.

5545. Imfeld, Al, and Gerd Meuer. "Taban lo Liyong: A Dancer in
Space." AFRIKA, 21, 6 (1980), 24-26.

5546. Jaslie, L.M., and Samson Sika-Oywa. "...and Readers Join the
Fray." SUNDAY NATION, 28 May 1972, p. 7.

> Letters to the editor in response to article by Liyong,
> 3560.

5547. Luzuka, Theo, F.X. Sserunjogi, Chris Wanjala, and Albert
Austine Obuya. "Taban lo Liyong Raises a Storm." SUNDAY
NATION, 21 May 1972, pp. 6, 11.

> Letters to the editor in response to article by Liyong,
> 3560.

5548. Nazareth, Peter. "Bibliyongraphy, or Six Tabans in Search of
an Author." ESA, 21 (1978), 33-49.

5549. Wanjala, Chris. "The True Father of East African Literary

Criticism." SUNDAY NATION, 28 May 1978, pp. 18, 23.

See also 3473, 3514, 3544, 3557, 3582, 3637, 3655, 3683, 3686, 3702, 3706, 3769, 4130, 4333, 4363, 4484, 4814, 5868, 5871.

LUBEGA, BONNIE

Criticism

See 3728, 4315.

LUBWA P´CHONG, CLIFF

Criticism

5550. Wanjala, Chris. "Discovering a Poet in a Pigeon Hole." SUNDAY NATION, 26 February 1978, p. 27.

> Also discusses Omotoso.

See also 3706.

MACU, RIDGEWAY

Criticism

See 3872.

MADDY, YULISA AMADU (Pat)

Interviews

5551. Maddy, Yulisa Amadu. "Creating a Black Theatre in Britain: An Interview." In WHITE MEDIA AND BLACK BRITAIN: A CRITICAL LOOK AT THE ROLE OF THE MEDIA IN RACE RELATIONS TODAY. Ed. Charles Husband. London: Arrow, 1975. Pp. 52-65.

> Interview with Yulisa Amadu Maddy.

See also 3389.

MADUBUIKE, IHECHUKWU

Bibliography

See 3315.

Biography

See 3315.

MAILLU, DAVID

Biography

5552.   Nyamora, Pius. "Maillu Under Fire." DAILY NATION, 19
        December 1979, p. 19.

        Accused of holding manuscripts too long and not
        returning them to authors.

Interviews

5553.   Anon. "Writer Talks of Books Ban." STANDARD, 7 June 1976.

        Banned in Tanzania.

5554.   Lindfors, Bernth. "Interview with David G. Maillu." ABPR, 5
        (1979), 85-88; rpt. in Lindfors, 3387.

Criticism

5555.   Apronti, E.O. "David G. Maillu and His Readers: An Unusual
        Poll of Readers´ Evaluation of a Popular Writer´s Work."
        ABPR, 6 (1980), 219-24; PQM, 6, 3-4 (1981), 162-75.

5556.   Ogbaa, Kalu. "David G. Maillu and the East African Social
        Scene." LHY, 20, 2 (1979), 114-28; UFAHAMU, 10, 3 (1981),
        57-67.

5557.   Wanjala, Chris. "David Maillu Against Ideology in Tanzania."
        UMMA-N, 4 (1976), 23-25, 28, 30-31.

5558.   ____. "Why Maillu is More Popular than Ngugi." ANVIL, 18
        October 1976, p. 3.

See also 3513, 3557, 3706, 4328, 4330, 4333, 4733, 4745, 4814.

MAIMO, A.O. (Sankie)

Biography

See 3374.

Interview

5559.   Anon. "Interview with Sankie Maimo." MOULD, 3 (1978), 1-6.

Criticism

5560.   Butake, Bole. "Sankie Maimo´s SOV-MBANG THE SOOTHSAYER: A
        Spiritual Tragedy." NGAM, 5 (1979), 76-92.

MAKAZA, WEBSTER

Criticism

See 3490.

MALAMAFUMU, MATILDA TUTU

Interview

See 3955.

MALE, JOHN

Biography

See 3935.

MALOMO, ´JIDE

Interview

See 3878.

MANAKA, MATSEMELA

Criticism

See 4042, 4045-46.

MANGANYI, NOEL CHABANI

Criticism

See 3712.

MANGUA, CHARLES

Criticism

5561.   Bardolph, Jacqueline. "Histoire d´un ´Mission-Boy´ dans
         Charles Mangua, A TAIL IN THE MOUTH." In Richard and Sevry,
         4495, pp. 164-69.

See also 3557, 3681, 3702, 3706, 3728, 3774, 4330, 4333, 4435, 4745,
    4814.

MAPANJE, JACK

Criticism

5562.   Calder, Angus. "Jack Mapanje, Malawian Poet: Some Personal
        Reactions." ACLALSB, 5, 3 (1980), 137-43.

See also 4080, 4099.

MAPONYA, MAISHE

Criticism

See 4042.

MARECHERA, DAMBUDZO

Interview

5563.   Imfeld, Al. PORTRAITS OF AFRICAN WRITERS: 9. DAMBUDZO
        MARECHERA. Trans. Jan Klingemann. Cologne: Deutsche Welle
        Transkriptionsdienst, [1979].
            Transcript of radio broadcast.

Criticism

See 3514, 3545, 4102.

MAREDI, SELAELO

Interviews

5564.   Reaves, Malik Stan. "Writing Plays for Freedom's Sake."
        SOUTHERN AFRICA, 12, 3 (1979), pp. 24-26.

See also 3381.

MARKWEI, MATEI

Criticism

See 4082.

MARSHALL, BILL

Criticism

5565.   Yirenkyi, Asiedu. "Bill Marshall and the Ghanaian Theatre of
        the Early Seventies." JOURNAL OF THE PERFORMING ARTS, 1, 1
        (1980), 27-51.

MASIYE, ANDREYA SYLVESTER

Criticism

See 3957.

MATENJWA, CHRISTINE J.

Criticism

See 3974.

MATSHIKIZA, TODD

Biography

5566.   Motsisi, Casey. "Todd Matshikiza." In Mutloatse, 5592, pp.
        90-93.
            Rpt. of BALE 2760.

See also 5904.

Criticism

See 3490.

MATSHOBA, MTUTUZELI

Criticism

5567.   Vaughan, Mike. "The Stories of Mtutuzeli Matshoba: A
        Critique." STAFFRIDER, 4, 3 (1981), 45-47.

See also 4705.

MATTERA, DON

Biography and Autobiography

5568. Alvarez-Péreyre, Jacques. "Does it Matter about Don
       Mattera?" KUNAPIPI, 2, 1 (1980), 1-6.

       Followed by autobiographical writings by Mattera, pp.
       6-9.

5569. ____. "Pour saluer Don Mattera." GAf, 18, 2 (1980), 115-20.

       Followed by "Open Letter to White South Africans," 5571,
       and poems, pp. 121-33.

5570. Mattera, Don. "Scenes from a Banned Life." INDEX ON
       CENSORSHIP, 7, 5 (1978), 3-8.

5571. ____. "Open Letter to South African Whites." INDEX ON
       CENSORSHIP, 9, 1 (1980), 49-50; rpt. in French in GAf, 18, 2
       (1980), 121-23.

MATTHEWS, JAMES

Bibliography

See 3315.

Biography

5572. Alvarez-Péreyre, J. "James Matthews à Grenoble." AFRAMN, 14
       (1981), 25-26.

5573. Stafford, Faith. "Profile: James Matthews." INDEX ON
       CENSORSHIP, 8, 6 (1979), 54-55.

See 3315, 5904.

Criticism

5574. Alvarez-Péreyre, Jacques. "Huis Clos ou impasse? Quelques
       remarques sur ´No Exit.´" GAf, 18, 2 (1980), 105-08.

5575. Anon. "Indomitable James Matthews: Black African Poet."
       THIRD WORLD FIRST, 1, 2-3 (1978), 52.

See also 3514, 3756, 4063, 4191, 4479.

MAZRUI, ALI A.

Biography and Autobiography

5576. Anon. "The Kenyan Who Found Fame in Other Lands." DRUM
       (Nairobi), November 1978, p. 39.

5577. Mazrui, Ali. "The Two Fine Men Who Haunt My Thoughts."
       SUNDAY NATION, 21 November 1971, pp. 29-30.
            On inspiration for THE TRIAL OF CHRISTOPHER OKIGBO.
            Rpt. of BALE 2764.

Interviews

5578. Adam, M. Mlamali. "An ´African Academic Ambassador´ Speaks."
       NEW AFRICAN, June 1980, pp. 39-40.

5579. Mulei, Christopher. "Boredom in the Barracks Can Lead to
       Coups." SUNDAY NATION, 11 July 1971, pp. 13-14.

Criticism

5580. Aboh, Tom. "The Grand Trial of Africa." LEGACY, 2 (1975),
       32-37.
            On THE TRIAL OF CHRISTOPHER OKIGBO.

5581. Duffield, A.C. "How About Trying a Who Dunnit?" SUNDAY
       NATION, 5 December 1971, p. 14.
            On THE TRIAL OF CHRISTOPHER OKIGBO. See response by
            Markham, 5582.

5582. Markham, R.C. "Mazrui´s New Book." SUNDAY NATION, 12
       December 1971, p. 6.
            Response to Duffield, 5581.

See also 4241, 3609, 3683, 3728, 3841, 4218, 4241, 4435.

MBISE, ISMAEL R.

Interview

See 3389.

Criticism

5583. Arnold, Stephen H. "Ismail Mbise´s BLOOD ON OUR LAND:
       Pre-Independence Action Related to Present Ujamaa Policy."
       In Priebe and Hale, 4519, pp. 84-102.

MBITI, JOHN SAMUEL

Interview

5584.   Mulei, Christopher. "God and His Place in African Life."
        SUNDAY NATION, 5 September 1971, pp. 13-14.

Criticism

See 3573, 3702, 4164.

MEZU, SEBASTIAN OKECHUKWU

Biography

See 3373.

Criticism

See 3520, 3562-63, 3604, 3743, 3827, 3837, 3841, 5505.

MICKSON, E.K.

Criticism

See 4336.

M´IMANYARA, ALFRED M.

Criticism

See 3728.

MKANGI, KATAMA

Interview

See 4417.

MNTHALI, FELIX

Criticism

See 4080.

MODISANE, BLOKE WILLIAM

Biography

See 5904.

Interview

5585. Hall, Eve. "South African Soliloquy." SUNDAY NATION, 19
       September 1965, p. 23.

MOORE, BAI TAMIA JOHNSON

Interview

See 3389.

Criticism

See 3824.

MOORE, R. WILLIAM JARYENNEH

Criticism

See 3824.

MOTJUWADI, STANLEY

Criticism

See 4088, 4161.

MOTSISI, MOSES CASEY

Biography

5586. Anon. "Casey: Kid with a Touch of Genius." TRUST, April
       1978, pp. 24-25.

5587. Anon. "Casey Motsisi: Tributes." STAFFRIDER, 1, 2 (1978),
       53-54.

5588. Langa, Dan. "The Passing of Casey ´the Kid.´" BONA,
       November 1977, pp. 62-63. ´

5589. Motjuwadi, ´Black Stan.´ "Kid Brother." In Mutloatse, 5592,
       pp. viii-ix.

5590. Musi, Obed. "Broken Shoe Casey." In Mutloatse, 5592, pp.
       x-xi.

See also 5904.

Criticism

5591. Mutloatse, Mothobi. "Introduction." In Mutloatse, 5592, pp.
       xv-xvi.

5592. ____, ed. CASEY & CO.: SELECTED WRITINGS OF CASEY ´KID´
       MOTSISI. Johannesburg: Ravan Press, 1980.

           Includes 5566, 5589-91, 6099.

MPHAHLELE, ES´KIA [Ezekiel]

Biography and Autobiography

5593.* Anon. "Profile on Professor Ezekiel Mphahlele." ELTIC
        REPORTER, 3, 3 (1978), 3.

5594. Anon. "Zeke Mphahlele: Shouting across the Distances."
       FRONTLINE, March 1981, p. 31.

5595. Anon. "Es´kia Mphahlele: A Man of Two Worlds." UNIVERSITY
       OF DENVER NEWS, August 1981, p. 4.

           Profile done after Mphahlele returned to University of
           Denver to teach during the spring quarter of 1981.

5596. Barnett, Ursula A. "The Legend of Zeke Mphahlele." CONTRAST,
       11, 2 (1977), 20-24.

5597. Cassidy, Peter. "Profile on Professor Ezekiel Mphahlele."
       ELTIC REPORTER, 3, 3 (1978), 3.

5598. Mphahlele, Ezekiel. "My Integrity as a Teacher is Attacked."
       SUNDAY NATION, 3 October 1965, p. 19.

           Response to Ng´weno, 5602.

5599. ____. "A South African Exile´s Return: Back to Ancestral
       Ground." FIRST WORLD, 1, 3 (1977), 13-17.

           Autobiography.

5600. ____. "To the Reader." CHIRUNDU. Westport, CT: Lawrence
       Hill, 1979. Pp. vii-x.

           Explains return to South Africa.

5601. ____. "Exile, the Tyranny of Place and the Literary
       Compromise." UES, 17, 1 (1979), 37-44.

Reflective, partly autobiographical essay.

5602. Ng'weno, Hilary. "Mphahlele Takes Too Much for Granted."
SUNDAY NATION, 26 September 1965, p. 11.

> Criticizes Mphahlele's response to critics, 3587. See
> Mphahlele's rejoinder, 5598.

5603. Zille, Helen. "An Exiled Professor Returns to South Africa."
CHRONICLE OF HIGHER EDUCATION, 8 May 1978, pp. 1, 8.

See also 5904.

Interviews

5604.* Anon. "Zeke Speaks: Interview with the People's Minister of
Education." SOWETAN, 20 November 1981, p. 34.

5605. Manganyi, Noel. "The Early Years...." STAFFRIDER, 3, 3
(1980), 45-46.

> Rpt. in Manganyi, 3570.

5606. Shreeve, Gavin. "A Rebel and His Roots: Interview with Gavin
Shreeve." GUARDIAN, 7 May 1979.

5607. ____. "Exile and Return." NEW AFRICAN, November 1979, p.
55.

See also 3382-83, 4509.

Criticism

5608. Asein, Samuel Omo. "The Humanism of Ezekiel Mphahlele."
JCL, 15, 1 (1980), 38-49.

5609. Gotoh, Tomokuni. "On South African Black Writer Mphahlele's
Autobiography, DOWN SECOND AVENUE." AFRICA-KENKYU, 14
(1974), 52-61.

> In Japanese.

5610. Hodge, Norman. "Mphahlele's 'Mrs. Plum' and the Craft of
Shorter Fiction." In Brimer, 3431, pp. 101-07; rev. and
published as "Dogs, Africans and Liberals: The World of
Mphahlele's 'Mrs. Plum.'" ENGLISH IN AFRICA, 8, 1 (1981),
33-43.

5611. Leepile, Methaetsile. "Artistry in Ezekiel Mphahlele's DOWN
SECOND AVENUE." MARANG, 3 (1980-81), 80-85.

5612. Melamu, M.J. "The Individual Dilemma in Mphahlele's 'A Point
of Identity.'" HERITAGE, 3 (1978), 20-24.

5613. Moore, Gerald, et al. "Mphahlele, Ezekiel." In Ferres and

Tucker, 3467, pp. 71-74.

Extracts from selected criticism.

5614. Plomer, William, et al. "Mphahlele, Ezekiel." In Popkin, 3638, pp. 313-18.

Extracts from selected criticism.

See also 3393, 3410, 3416, 3467, 3473, 3490, 3493, 3515, 3527, 3529, 3580, 3585, 3608, 3615, 3638, 3655-56, 3681, 3706, 3710, 3738, 3750, 3765, 3769, 3803, 3820, 3837-38, 3992, 4063, 4186, 4215, 4264, 4267, 4270, 4352, 4386, 4407, 4409, 4479, 4574, 4728, 4777, 4840.

MPHANDE, LUPENGA.

Criticism

See 4080.

MQAYISA, KHAYALETHU

Criticism

See 3872, 4022.

MTHOBA, JAMES

Criticism

See 3976.

MTSAKA, MAKWEDINI ZWELAKHE JULIUS

Criticism

See 4022.

MTSHALI, OSWALD MBUYSENI

Biography

See 5904.

Criticism

5615. Chainet, Monique. "SOUNDS OF A COWHIDE DRUM/Échos d´un tam-tam en cuir de vache (Extraits)." POÉSIE, 8 (1979), 69.

Brief note followed by French translations of poems, pp.

70-90.

5616.   Igbudu, Igbarumun. "Protest Poetry in South Africa and
Mtshali´s Refuge under ´The Cryptic Mode.´" KUKA, (1979-80),
36-43.

See also 3416, 3652, 3656, 3769, 4061, 4063, 4081, 4086, 4106,
4132-33, 4146, 4148-49, 4153, 4161, 4386, 4395.

MUGO, MICERE (See GITHAE-MUGO, MICERE)

MUKASA, HAM

Criticism

See 3523.

MULAISHO, DOMINIC

Interview

See 3389.

MULIKITA, FWANYANGA MATALE

Criticism

See 3769.

MULLOO, ANAND SAWANT

Criticism

See 3464.

MUNGOSHI, CHARLES

Interview

5617.   Seroke, Jaki. "´We Were Brought Up in a Literary Desert.´"
STAFFRIDER, 3, 4 (1980-81), 18-19.

Criticism

See 3773, 4102.

MUNONYE, JOHN

Biography

See 3373.

Criticism

5618.   Robb, J. Stanhope.   "A DANCER OF FORTUNE by John Munonye."
        LHY, 20, 1 (1979), 106-15.

See also 3520, 3562-63, 3691, 3743, 3754, 3808-09, 3825, 3827, 3837,
        3843, 4340, 4365, 4789.

MURUAH, GEORGE KAMAU

Criticism

See 3706.

MUSINGA, VICTOR ELAME

Interview

5619.   Zang, Meh.   "Interview with Victor Elame Musinga, Founder and
        Director of the Musinga Drama Group, Buea."   MOULD, 4 (1980),
        1-3.

MUTISO, GIDEON-CYRUS M.

Criticism

5620.   Wanjala, Chris.   "African Literature and the Social
        Scientist."   SUNDAY NATION, 4 June 1978, p. 13.
            Also discusses Palmer briefly.

MUTLOATSE, MOTHOBI

Interview

See 3390.

MUTSWAIRO, SOLOMON M.

Criticism

See 3545, 3773.

MUTWA, VUSAMAZULU CREDO

Biography

5621. Scott, Leslie. "Credo Mutwa Wins Heart of Red Indian Girl."
        BONA, August-September 1976, pp. 88-89, 91.

Criticism

See 4022.

MVULA, ENOCH TIMPUNZA

Criticism

See 4080.

MWANGI, MEJA

Biography

5622. Anon. "Kenya: Meja Mwangi." LAAW, 40-41 (1979), 120-22.

5623. Anon. "Meja Mwangi." In Eckardt, 4995, p. 108.

Interviews

5624. Anon. "Audience, Language and Form in Committed East African
        Writing: An Open Discussion with Meja Mwangi."
        KOMPARATISTISCHE HEFTE, 3 (1981), 64-67.

5625. Lindfors, Bernth. "Meja Mwangi: Interview." KUNAPIPI, 1, 2
        (1979), 68-76; rpt. in Lindfors, 3387.

See also 3389.

Criticism

5626. Barrett, Lindsay. "Liberation War Is Brought to Screen."
        WA, 20 April 1981, pp. 858-61.
            Ola Balogun's CRY FREEDOM is based on CARCASE FOR
        HOUNDS.

5627. Imfeld, Al, and Gerd Meuer. "Meja Mwangi: Life Among the
        Slum Dwellers." AFRIKA, 21, 5 (1980), 24-26.

5628. Naipaul, Shiva. NORTH OF SOUTH: AN AFRICAN JOURNEY. London:
        Deutsch, 1978; New York: Simon and Schuster, 1979;

Harmondsworth: Penguin, 1980.

Includes brief discussion of GOING DOWN RIVER ROAD, pp. 40-42.

5629. Palmer, Eustace. "Meja Mwangi's THE COCKROACH DANCE."
FBSSL, 2 (1981), 50-68.

5630. Parasuram, A.N. MINERVA GUIDE TO MEJA MWANGI: <u>KILL ME QUICK</u>.
Madras: Minerva Publishing House, 1977.

See also 3478, 3514, 3544, 3686, 3728, 3740, 3813, 3834, 4420, 4488.

MZAMANE, MBULELO

Biography

See 4965.

NAKASA, NATHANIEL NDZIVANE

Biography

See 5904.

Criticism

See 3490, 4574.

NAZARETH, PETER

Autobiography

5631. Nazareth, Peter. "Development and Wellbeing: The Confessions
of an African Bureaucrat." PanA, 8 (1979), 49-53; AFRISCOPE,
9, 4 (1979), 31-33.

5632. ____. "Practical Problems and Technical Solutions in Writing
My Two Novels." AFRISCOPE, 10, 9 (1980), 49-52; CALLALOO,
11-13 (1981), 56-62.

Interviews

5633. Moss, Jim. "Ugandan Exile: Amin Timetable Unpredictable."
CEDAR RAPIDS GAZETTE, 1 April 1979, p. 2B.

5634. Winett, Michael S. "From Uganda, Reluctantly: The UI's Writer
in Exile." DAILY IOWAN, 6 December 1978, p. 5.

Criticism

5635.   Amur, G.S.   "Peter Nazareth's IN A BROWN MANTLE: Novel as
        Revolutionary Art."   In Narasimhaiah, 3593, pp. 111-17.

See also 3498, 3595.

NAZOMBE, ANTHONY

Criticism

See 4080.

NCHWE, MANOKO

Interview

5636.   Boitumelo.   "Women Writers Speak."   STAFFRIDER, 2, 4 (1979),
        60-61; rpt. in House, 3327, pp. 19-21.
            Unpublished writer interviewed.

NDEBELE, NJABULO S.

Criticism

See 4168.

NDOVI, VICTOR.

Interview

See 4736.

NDU, POL NNAMUZIKAM

Biography

5637.   Nwoga, Donatus.   "Obituary: Pol Nnamuzikam Ndu (1940-1976)."
        OKIKE, 12 (1978), 89-91.

Criticism

See 4072, 4122, 4159.

NEOGY, RAJAT

Interview

5638.   Hall, Tony. "Liberalism...the Toughest Creed There Is."
        SUNDAY NATION, 11 July 1967, pp. 15-16.
            Interview with editor of TRANSITION.

Criticism

See 3498.

NGONGWIKUO, JOSEPH ANGNAYUOH

Interview

5639.   Butake, Bole. "Guest Artist." MOULD, 5 (1981), 1-6.

NGUBANE, JORDAN KHUSH

Criticism

5640.   Nazareth, Peter, "USHABA as an African Political Novel."
        ENGLISH IN AFRICA, 5, 2 (1978), 57-65.

See also 4087.

NGUBIAH, STEPHEN N.

Criticism

See 3728.

NGUGI WA THIONG'O [James]

Bibliography

See 3315.

Biography and Autobiography

5641.   Adagala, Seth. "The Long, Hard Battle to Stage Kimathi
        Play." SUNDAY NATION, 10 October 1976, p. 15.

5642.   Anon. "Ngugi wa Thiong'o." In Eckardt, 4995, p. 108.

5643.   Anon. "Novelist James Ngugi Turns Lecturer." DAILY NATION,
        13 September 1967, p. 15.

5644.   Anon. "Why the Play was Banned." DAILY NATION, 22 November
        1977, p. 3.

        NGAAHIKA NDEENDA (I will marry when I want).

5645.   Anon. "Ngugi Wants DC to See Play." NAIROBI TIMES, 11
        December 1977, p. 3.

5646.   Anon. "No Official Word on Ngugi." NAIROBI TIMES, 8 January
        1978, p. 1.

        After his arrest.

5647.   Anon. "Ngugi wa Thiong'o: Writer in Trouble." WEEKLY
        REVIEW, 9 January 1978, pp. 5-6.

        Kenyan police pick him up.

5648.   Anon. "Ngugi Detention was 'over his activities, not
        writing.'" NAIROBI TIMES, 15 January 1978, p. 1.

5649.   Anon. "Ngugi wa Thiong'o is Detained." WEEKLY REVIEW, 16
        January 1978, p. 5.

5650.   Anon. "One Step Over the Line." AFRICA NEWS, 30 January
        1978, p. 6.

        Detention.

5651.   Anon. "Ngugi's Detention." VIVA, 4, 1 (1978), 3.

5652.   Anon. "Ngugi Detained." AFRICAN PERSPECTIVES (Nairobi), 2
        (1978), 14, 35.

5653.   Anon. "Ngugi wa Thiong'o Detained." POSITIVE REVIEW, 1, 1
        (1978), 21.

5654.   Anon. "African, West Indian Students Link Arms to Win
        Freedom for Kenyan Novelist." CARIBBEAN CONTACT, May 1978,
        p. 19.

        Protest meeting in London, 21 March 1978.

5655.   Anon. "Verhaftung des kenianischen Schriftstellers und
        Kollegen Ngugi wa Thiong'o." ACOLIT, 2 (1978), 10.

5656.   Anon. "No Playing Matter." WEEKLY REVIEW, 15 December 1978,
        p. 5.

        On banning of NGAAHIKA NDEENDA (I will marry when I
        want) and detention of Ngugi.

5657.   Anon. "Ngugi Picked Up: Drinking Charge Denied." WEEKLY
        REVIEW, 16 March 1979, pp. 21-22.

5658.   Anon. "Ngugi Cleared Drinks Charge." DAILY NATION, 28 April
        1979, p. 24.

5659.   Anon. "Ngugi Found Not Guilty." DAILY NATION, 5 May 1979,
        pp. 1, 24.

        On drinks charge.

5660.   Anon. "Ngugi Set Free: Magistrate Flays Police." WEEKLY
        REVIEW, 11 May 1979, p. 23.

        Acquitted on drinks charge.

5661.   Anon. "Ngugi Issue: President Petitioned." WEEKLY REVIEW,
        20 July 1979, p. 13.

        University Academic Staff Union requests reinstatement
        of Ngugi to teaching position.

5662.   Anon. "Reinstate Ngugi--MPs." WEEKLY REVIEW, 3 August 1979,
        pp. 5-6.

        To University of Nairobi teaching post.

5663.   Anon. "The Final Word: Ngugi Refutes Wanjigi's Claims."
        WEEKLY REVIEW, 24 August 1979, p. 11.

        Ngugi denies his contract with University has expired.

5664.   Bardolph, Jacqueline. "L'écrivain Kenyan Ngugi wa Thiong'o
        est libéré." AFRAMN, 7 (1979), 21-22.

5665.   Bentsi-Enchill, Nii K., and Kojo Bentsi-Enchill. "For an
        Afro-Asian Literature." WA, 22-29 December 1980, pp.
        2604-05.

        Report on talk given at Africa Centre in London.

5666.   Cabezas, Miguel. "Ngugi wa Thiong'o." INDEX ON CENSORSHIP,
        7, 6 (1978), 78-79.

        Letter concerning his detention.

5667.   Hill, Lawrence. "Ngugi wa Thiong'o." NYTBR, 16 April 1978,
        p. 37.

        Letter to editor from Ngugi's American publisher urging
        further protests against his arrest and detention.

5668.   Hower, Edward. "Kenyan Writer Detained." NYRB, 4 May 1978,
        p. 50.

        Former classmate of Ngugi urges readers to write letters
        to Kenyan authorities expressing concern about his
        detention.

5669. Kahiga, Miriam. "Ngugi on Language: For Literature that is National, not Merely 'Afro-Saxon.'" DAILY NATION, 27 July 1979, p. 13.

> Talk at Press Club luncheon in Nairobi. See response by Mzee wa Kiswahili, 4355.

5670. Munene, Fibi. "The Last Word." DAILY NATION, 14 December 1977, p. 19.

> On revocation of license to perform NGAAHIKA NDEENDA (I will marry when I want).

5671. Nation Reporter. "Permit for Kikuyu Play Cancelled." SUNDAY NATION, 20 November 1977, p. 3.

> NGAAHIKA NDEENDA (I will marry when I want).

5672. ____. "Ngugi Sacked 'by act of state.'" DAILY NATION, 21 August 1979, p. 20.

5673. Ngala, Joseph. "Kenya's Foremost Author Detained." S AFRICAN OUTLOOK, 108 (1978), 47.

5674. Ngugi wa Thiong'o. DETAINED: A WRITER'S PRISON DIARY. London: Heinemann, 1981.

> Excerpts from this book were published in INDEX ON CENSORSHIP, 9, 3 (1980), 20-24; SOUTH, April 1981, pp. 38-39, POSITIVE REVIEW, 1, 4 (1981), 28-31.

5675. Nkosi, Lewis. "A Voice from Detention." WA, 20 February 1978, pp. 334-35; abridged and rpt. as "Campaign to Free Ngugi wa Thiong'o" in AFRICAN CURRENTS, 12-13 (1978), 34-35.

5676. Ochieng, Philip. "Ngugi, the Writer, Extends 'Exile.'" SUNDAY NATION, 12 July 1970, p. 14.

5677. Rajab, Ahmed. "Detained in Kenya." INDEX ON CENSORSHIP, 7, 3 (1978), 7-10.

5678. Robinson, David. "Arrest and Detention of Ngugi wa Thiong'o." AFRICAN STUDIES NEWSLETTER, 11, 2 (1978), 26.

5679. Soyinka, Wole. "An Open Letter to Arap Moi." DAILY TIMES, 7 November 1978; WA, 20 November 1978, p. 2312.

> Urges Ngugi's release from detention.

5680. Standard Reporter. "Professor Thiong'o Denies Drinks Charge." STANDARD, 9 March 1979, p. 1.

5681. ____. "Ngugi Issue a Matter of Public Security." STANDARD, 21 August 1979, p. 2.

> On University of Nairobi's refusal to reinstate him to teaching post.

5682.   Sunday Nation Correspondent. "'Criticism is a Very Healthy Thing....'" SUNDAY NATION, 8 January 1978, p. 5.

> On Ngugi's opinions on literature, drama and society.

5683.   Sunday Nation Reporter. "Ngugi's Wife Reveals How He Was Picked Up." SUNDAY NATION, 8 January 1978, pp. 1, 5.

5684.   ____. "Ngugi was Taken Away after Two-hour Search of Home." SUNDAY NATION, 8 January 1978, p. 5.

> On his arrest.

5685.   Tejani, Bahadur. "Social Responsibility of the African Writer: Background to the Detention of Ngugi wa Thiong'o." CHIMO, 2 (1980), 19-23.

5686.   Walmsley, Anne. "Ngugi wa Thiong'o: Free Thoughts on Toilet Paper." INDEX ON CENSORSHIP, 10, 3 (1981), 41-42.

> On DETAINED.

5687.   Wanjala, Chris. "Dilemma that Ngugi Faced." SUNDAY NATION, 31 July 1977, p. 14.

> On choosing a publisher.

5688.   ____. "Where is Ngugi?" BLACK PHOENIX, 2 (1978), 23-24.

> On Ngugi's arrest.

5689.   ____. "Ngugi and the National Language Issue." SUNDAY NATION, 5 August 1979.

See also 3315, 3405, 3988, 4873, 4948, 5904.

Interviews

5690.   Amooti wa Irumba. "The Making of a Rebel." INDEX ON CENSORSHIP, 9, 3 (1980), 20-24; POSITIVE REVIEW, 1, 4 (1981), 28-31; STAFFRIDER, 4, 2 (1981), 34-36; DRUM (Nairobi), April 1982, pp. 47-48.

5691.   Anon. "An Interview with Ngugi." WEEKLY REVIEW, 9 January 1978, pp. 9-11.

5692.   Darling, Peter. "My Protest Was Against the Hypocrisy in the College." SUNDAY NATION, 16 March 1969, pp. 15-16.

> On his resignation from University College Nairobi.

5693. de Villiers, John. "The Birth of a New East African Author."
        SUNDAY NATION, 3 May 1964, p. 10.

5694. Dolfe, Mikael. "Intervju med Ngugi wa Thiong'o." PERMANENT
        PRESS, 13-14 (1980), 74-76.

5695. Esibi, John. "'Open Criticism is Very Healthy in Any
        Society.'" SUNDAY NATION, 17 July 1977, p. 10.

5696. Gacheru, Margaretta wa. "Ngugi wa Thiong'o Still Bitter over
        his Detention." WEEKLY REVIEW, 5 January 1979, pp. 30-32;
        rpt. in SUNDAY NATION, 28 January 1979.

5697. Lampley, James. "'Resistance is the Only Choice.'" AIBEPM,
        114 (1981), 69-70.

5698. Magina, Magina. "People Have a Right to Know." AIBEPM, 90
        (1979), 30-31; AFRICA CURRENTS, 14 (1979), 5-7.

5699. Martini, Jürgen, Anna Rutherford, Kirsten Holst Petersen,
        Vibeke Stenderup, and Bent Thomsen. "Ngugi wa Thiong'o:
        Interview." KUNAPIPI, 3, 1 (1981), 110-16; 3, 2 (1981),
        135-40.

5700. Omari, Emman. "Ngugi wa Thiong'o Speaks!: 'I am not above
        the contradictions which bedevil our society.'" STANDARD, 28
        August 1981, pp. 11, 15.

5701. Parker, Bettye J. "BBB Interviews Ngugi wa Thiong'o." BLACK
        BOOKS BULLETIN, 6, 1 (1978), 46-51; corrections noted in 6, 2
        (1978), 14; FIRST WORLD, 2, 2 (1979), 56-59.

5702. Shreve, Anita. "PETALS OF BLOOD." VIVA, 3, 6 (1977), 35-36.

See also 3383, 4509.

Criticism

5703. Abdelkrim, Christine. "PETALS OF BLOOD: Story, Narrative,
        Discourse." ECHOS DU COMMONWEALTH, 6 (1980-81), 37-51.

5704. Albrecht, Françoise. "Blood and Fire in PETALS OF BLOOD."
        ECHOS DU COMMONWEALTH, 6 (1980-81), 85-97.

5705. Alot, Magaga. "The Massacre of Hopes." AFRICAN PERSPECTIVES
        (Nairobi), 1 (1977), 23-25.

            PETALS OF BLOOD.

5706. Andrews, Barry. "The Novelist and History: The Development
        of Ngugi wa Thiong'o." NLRev, 2 (1977), 36-43.

5707. Anon. "Quiet Revolution in Kenyan Theatre." AIBEPM, 78
        (1978), 72.

            NGAAHIKA NDEENDA (I will marry when I want).

5708. Anon. "A Voice from Detention." WA, 20 February 1978, pp. 334-35.

Political elements in Ngugi's writings.

5709. Anon. "Dedan Kimathi is a Dramatic Winner." WEEKLY REVIEW, 23 May 1980, p. 43.

5710. Babura, Ahmed Sa'i'du. "Betrayal and the Quest for Self-Preservation: Ngugi wa Thiong'o's A GRAIN OF WHEAT." KAKAKI, 1 (1980-81), 15-24.

5711. Balogun, F. Odun. "Ngugi's PETALS OF BLOOD: A Novel of the People." BA SHIRU, 10, 2 (1979), 49-57.

5712. Baraka, Amiri. "Ngugi." LitR, 23 (August-September 1980), 6.

5713. Bardolph, Jacqueline. "Fertility in PETALS OF BLOOD." ECHOS DU COMMONWEALTH, 6 (1980-81), 53-83.

5714. ____. "Le Romancier Kenyan Ngugi wa Thiong'o: Le texte écrit en anglais peut-il dire l'oppression?" In OPPRESSION ET EXPRESSION DANS LA LITTÉRATURE ET LE CINÉMA: AFRIQUE, AMÉRIQUE, ASIE. Ed. Jacqueline Bardolph, François Desplanques, Richard Feray, Jean-Pierre Jardel, Claire Laurent. Paris: L'Harmattan, 1981. Pp. 33-56.

5715. Chesaina, Jane C. "Who is on Trial in THE TRIAL OF DEDAN KIMATHI? A Critical Essay on Ngugi wa Thiong'o and Micere Githae Mugo's THE TRIAL OF DEDAN KIMATHI." BUSARA, 8, 2 (1976), 21-37.

5716. ____. "East Africa Ngugi wa Thiong'o's THE RIVER BETWEEN and the African Oral Tradition." In Gachukia and Akivaga, 4799, pp. 62-76.

5717. Chileshe, John. "PETALS OF BLOOD: Ideology and Imaginative Expression." JCL, 15, 1 (1980), 133-37.

5718. Cochrane, Judith. "Women as Guardians of the Tribe in Ngugi's Novels." ACLALSB, 4, 5 (1977), 1-11.

5719.* Connelly, John J. "Analysis of the Themes of Protest and Conflict in James Ngugi's Novels: THE RIVER BETWEEN, WEEP NOT, CHILD, and A GRAIN OF WHEAT." Master's thesis, Duquesne University, 1971.

5720. Dada, Segun. NOTES, QUESTIONS AND ANSWERS ON JAMES NGUGI'S WEEP NOT, CHILD. Ibadan: Aromolaran Publishing Co. Ltd., 1975.

5721. Dolfe, Mikael. "Ngugi wa Thiong'o, Kenya: Östafrikas störste berättare. [East Africa's Greatest Storyteller]." FOLKET I

BILD, 27 March-10 April 1980, p. 9.

5722. Durix, Jean-Pierre. "Politics in PETALS OF BLOOD." ECHOS DU COMMONWEALTH, 6 (1980-81), 98-115.

5723. Gachukia, Eddah. "The Novels of James Ngugi." In Gachukia and Akivaga, 4799, pp. 102-13.

5724. Gitau, Karugu. "The Play That Got Banned." WEEKLY REVIEW, 9 January 1978, p. 13.

      NGAAHIKA NDEENDA (I will marry when I want).

5725. Glenn, Ian. "PETALS OF BLOOD and the Intellectual Elite in Kenya." ECHOS DU COMMONWEALTH, 6 (1980-81), 116-25.

5726. ____. "Ngugi wa Thiong'o and the Dilemmas of the Intellectual Elite in Africa: A Sociological Perspective." ENGLISH IN AFRICA, 8, 2 (1981), 53-66.

5727. Gurr, Andrew. "The Fourth Novel." HEKIMA, 1 (1980), 13-21.

      PETALS OF BLOOD.

5728. ____. WRITERS IN EXILE: THE IDENTITY OF HOME IN MODERN LITERATURE. Harvester Studies in Contemporary Literature and Culture, 4. Brighton: Harvester; Atlantic Highlands, NJ: Humanities, 1981.

5729. Haynes, John. "The Notion of Education in PETALS OF BLOOD." NSAL, 2, 1 (1979), 134-48.

5730.* Hennings, Almut. "Ngugi wa Thiong'o: PETALS OF BLOOD--Eine Analyse." Master's thesis, University of Bremen, 1978.

5731. Iga-Basajjabaaze. "On A GRAIN OF WHEAT." UMMA, 6, 2 (1976), 152-59.

5732. Jabbi, Bu-Buakei. "Conrad's Influence on Betrayal in A GRAIN OF WHEAT." RAL, 11 (1980), 50-83.

5733. Kamau, Ngethe. "PETALS OF BLOOD as a Mirror of the African Revolution." AFRICAN COMMUNIST, 80 (1980), 73-79.

5734. Killam, G. D. "A Note on the Title of PETALS OF BLOOD." JCL, 15, 1 (1980), 125-32.

5735. ____. AN INTRODUCTION TO THE WRITINGS OF NGUGI. London: Heinemann, 1980; Exeter, NH: Heinemann, 1981.

5736. Kirinyaga, Muhoi wa. "Kenya: Trying to Silence the Truth." AFRICAN COMMUNIST, 73 (1978), 69-73.

      On works that led to his detention.

5737. Lindfors, Bernth. "Ngugi wa Thiong'o's Early Journalism."
       WLWE, 20, (1981), 23-41.

5738. Maloba, O.W. "THE TRIAL OF DEDAN KIMATHI by Ngugi wa
       Thiong'o and Micere Githae Mugo." UMMA-N, 5 (1977), 19-20,
       22.

5739. Martini, Jürgen. "Ngugi wa Thiong'o: East African Novelist."
       In Massa, 3571, pp. 5-11.

5740. Masilela, Ntongela. "Ngugi wa Thiong'o's PETALS OF BLOOD."
       UFAHAMU, 9, 2 (1979), 9-28.

5741. Maughan-Brown, David. "'Mau Mau' and Violence in Ngugi's
       Novels." ENGLISH IN AFRICA, 8, 2 (1981), 1-22.

5742. Mezgebe, Alem. "The Class Enemy." NEW AFRICAN, September
       1978, p. 65.
           THE TRIAL OF DEDAN KIMATHI in Britain.

5743. Mnthali, Felix. "Continuity and Change in Conrad and Ngugi."
       KUNAPIPI, 3, 1 (1981), 91-109.

5744. Nagenda, John, et al. "Ngugi wa Thiong'o." In Popkin, 3638,
       pp. 323-29.
           Extracts from selected criticism.

5745. Ojo-Ade, Femi. "Mugo, the 'Strange' Hero: Madness in Ngugi's
       A GRAIN OF WHEAT." PQM, 6, 3-4 (1981), 133-45.

5746. Palmer, Eustace. "Ngugi's PETALS OF BLOOD." ALT, 10 (1979),
       153-66; rpt. in Palmer, 3813.

5747. Parasuram, A.N. MINERVA GUIDE TO JAMES NGUGI: THE RIVER
       BETWEEN. Madras: Minerva Publishing House, 1975.
           Rpt. of 1970 ed.

5748. Peicke, Sigrid. IN DEN FRAUEN LIEGT DIE ZUKUNFT:
       FRAUENGESTALTEN IM WERK DES KENIANISCHEN SCHRIFTSTELLERS
       NGUGI WA THIONG'O. Frankfurt am Main: Nexus, 1981.

5749. Petersen, Kirsten Holst. "Birth Pangs of a National
       Consciousness: Mau Mau and Ngugi wa Thiong'o." WLWE, 20
       (1981), 214-19.

5750. Rangan, V. "THE BLACK HERMIT as a Tragedy of Love." In
       Srivastava, 3677, pp. 217-27.

5751. Reed, John, et al. "Ngugi wa Thiong'o." In Ferres and
       Tucker, 3467, pp. 76-80.
           Extracts from selected criticism.

5752.   Richard, René. "History and Literature: Narration and Time
        in PETALS OF BLOOD, by Ngugi wa Thiong'o." ECHOS DU
        COMMONWEALTH, 6 (1980-81), 1-36.

5753.   Robson, C.B. NGUGI WA THIONG'O. London and Basingstoke:
        Macmillan; New York: St. Martin's Press, 1979.

5754.   Sander, Reinhard W. "Two Views of the Conflict of Cultures in
        Pre-Emergency Kenya: A Comparative Study of James Ngugi's THE
        RIVER BETWEEN and Elspeth Huxley's RED STRANGERS." IKORO, 3,
        1 (1976), 28-42; LHY, 19, 2 (1978), 27-48.

            Rpt. of BALE 2871.

5755.   Sarvan, Charles Ponnuthurai. "Conrad's Influence on Ngugi."
        KUCHA, 1, 1 (1977), 39-44.

            Rpt. of BALE 2872.

5756.   Schild, Ulla. "Ngugi wa Thiong'o." AFRIKA, 19, 8-9 (1978),
        37-38.

5757.* Segla, M. Kouassi Barthélémy. "Engagement politique et
        création artistique dans les romans de (James) Ngugi wa
        Thiong'o." Ph.D. dissertation, University of Dakar, 1976.

5758.   Seymour, Hilary. "Pedagogical Politics in Ngugi wa
        Thiong'o's PETALS OF BLOOD." JLSN, 1 (1981), 7-25.

5759.   Sharma, Govind Narain. "Ngugi's Apocalypse: Marxism,
        Christianity and African Utopianism in PETALS OF BLOOD."
        WLWE, 18 (1979), 302-14.

5760.   _____. "Ngugi's Christian Vision: Theme and Pattern in A
        GRAIN OF WHEAT." ALT, 10 (1979), 167-76.

5761.   Singh, Malkiat. JAMES NGUGI'S THE RIVER BETWEEN. School
        Certificate English Literature Companion Series, 5. Nairobi:
        Highway Press, 1970.

5762.   Sole, Kelwyn. "Art and Activism in Kenya." AFRICA
        PERSPECTIVE, 8 (1978), 26-31.

5763.   Speares, I.J. "THIS TIME TOMORROW by Ngugi wa Thiong'o."
        BACKGROUND NOTES, 9 (1975), 7-11.

5764.   Stratton, Florence. "Cyclical Patterns in PETALS OF BLOOD."
        JCL, 15, 1 (1980), 115-24.

5765.   Vaughan, Michael. "African Fiction and Popular Struggle: The
        Case of A GRAIN OF WHEAT." ENGLISH IN AFRICA, 8, 2 (1981),
        23-52.

5766.   Vogt, Elke. "The Heroes of the Mau Mau Movement: A

Self-critical Appreciation of the Kenyan Liberation Movement by Ngugi wa Thiong'o." AFRIKA, 20, 11 (1979), 25-26.

A GRAIN OF WHEAT.

5767. Wanjala, Chris. "Portrait of a Writer: A Pioneer in the Literary Field." SUNDAY NATION, 8 January 1978, p. 4.

5768. Yohanna, M. Karienye. "There is More Than Politics in the Making of a Nation." KENYA WEEKLY NEWS, 4 August 1961, p. 30.

5769. ____. "THE BLACK HERMIT." KENYA WEEKLY NEWS, 2 November 1962, p. 21.

See also 3412, 3419, 3437-38, 3455, 3467, 3473, 3478, 3499, 3508, 3513-14, 3544, 3555, 3566, 3572, 3574, 3580-81, 3585, 3605, 3608-09, 3619, 3628, 3637-38, 3642, 3644, 3655, 3681-83, 3686, 3702-03, 3706, 3710, 3719, 3725, 3728, 3740, 3745, 3751, 3758-59, 3764-70, 3774-75, 3778, 3789-91, 3793, 3806-07, 3810-11, 3813, 3815, 3837-38, 3842, 3916, 3938, 3990, 3993-94, 4028, 4035, 4058, 4187, 4215, 4333, 4345, 4355, 4375, 4388, 4394, 4409, 4420, 4435, 4471, 4476, 4488, 4494, 4500, 4531, 4725, 4851, 4972, 5868, 5871.

NG'WENO, HILARY

Interviews

5770. Hall, Tony. "Local Bookmen Meet Our Needs Better." SUNDAY NATION, 19 February 1967, pp. 15-16.

Ng'weno speaking as East African Director of the Franklin Book Program.

5771. Lindfors, Bernth. "Interview: Hilary Ng'weno." ABPR, 5 (1979), 157-61; rpt. in Lindfors, 3387.

5772. Roberts, John Storm. "Hilary Ng'weno: Publisher and Editor of the NAIROBI TIMES." AfricaR, 23, 4 (1978), 22-24.

Criticism

See 3544, 3703.

NICOL, S.W.H. DAVIDSON [Abioseh]

Criticism

5773. King, Bruce. "Abioseh Nicol." In Petersen and Rutherford, 4467, pp. 73-75.

See also 3756.

NJAU, REBEKA

Interviews

5774. Irungu, Robert. "False Report on Girlfriends Saddened Us..."
       SUNDAY NATION, 20 February 1977, pp. 14-15.
            Interview about FESTAC.

Criticism

See 3728, 3992, 4028, 4488, 4494.

NKOSI, LEWIS

Bibliography

See 3315.

Biography

See 3315.

Criticism

5775. Magel, Emil A. "Theme and Role-Change Motifs in Lewis Nkosi´s
       THE RHYTHM OF VIOLENCE." JAAAA, 3, 1 (1979), 80-90.

See also 3438, 3490, 3602, 3910, 3920, 4028, 4479, 4574.

NNOLIM, SIMON ALAGBOGU

Criticism

See 5205.

NORTJE, KENNETH ARTHUR

Bibliography

5776.* Woolley, H., and S. Williams. A BIBLIOGRAPHY OF KENNETH
       ARTHUR NORTJE 1942-1970. Pretoria: Unisa Sanlam Library,
       1979.

Biography

See 5904.

Criticism

5777. Brutus, Dennis. "Two Poems by Nortje with a Note." ALT, 10 (1979), 231-32.

5778. Chapman, M.J.F. "Arthur Nortje: Poet of Exile." ENGLISH IN AFRICA, 6, 1 (1979), 60-71.

5779. Davis, Hedy I. "Arthur Nortje, A Forgotten South African Poet." REALITY, 11, 4 (1979), 5-7.

5780. ____. "The Poetry of Arthur Nortje: Toward a New Appraisal." UES, 18, 2 (1980), 26-31.

5781. ____. "Arthur Nortje: The Wayward Ego." BLOODY HORSE, 3 (1981), 14-24.

5782.* Lefevere, André. "Arthur Nortje's Poetry of Exile." RESTANT, 8, 2 (1980), 39-45.

5783. Leitch, R.G. "Nortje: Poet at Work." ALT, 10 (1979), 224-30.

5784. Nkondo, Gessler Moses. "Arthur Nortje's Double Self." AfrLJ, 12 (1981), 105-21.

See also 3602, 3652, 4063, 4088, 4092, 4479.

NTIRU, RICHARD

Criticism

See 3655, 3702, 4090, 4092, 4147, 4164, 4435.

NTSHONA, WINSTON

Biography

See 3874.

Interview

See 4019.

NTULI, DEUTERONOMY BHEKINKOZI ZEBLON

Interviews

5785. Garb, Gil. "Artist in Exile." NEW AFRICAN, May 1980, pp. 66, 68.

5786. Rajab, Ahmed. "Pitika Ntuli: Sculptor in Prison." INDEX ON CENSORSHIP, 9, 3 (1980), 33-37; AFRICA CURRENTS, 23 (1980),

30-31.

NWAKUCHE, FLORA (See **NWAPA, FLORA**)

NWALA, T. UZODINMA

Criticism

See 3743.

NWANKWO, ARTHUR AGWUNCHA

Interview

See 4655.

NWANKWO, NKEM

Biography

See 3373.

Criticism

See 3520, 3720, 3743, 3754, 3826-27, 3837, 4340, 4477, 4488.

NWANKWOR, IRECHUKWU

Criticism

See 4083.

NWAPA [NWAKUCHE], FLORA

Bibliography

See 3317.

Biography

See 3373.

Interviews

5787. Uwechue, Austa. "Flora Nwakuche, nee Nwapa, a Former Cabinet
        Minister and One of Africa's Leading Women Writers Talks to
        Austa Uwechue." AFRICA WOMAN, 10 (1977), 8-10.

See also 3378.

Criticism

5788. Githaiga, Anna. NOTES ON FLORA NWAPA´S EFURU. H.E.B.
       Student´s Guide, 16. Nairobi: Heinemann Educational Books,
       1979.

5789. Ogunsanwo. "NEVER AGAIN." AFRISCOPE, 11, 1 (1981), 37-38.

See also 3408, 3432, 3520, 3727, 3743, 3754, 3796, 3830, 3833, 3837,
       4315, 4473, 4488.

NWOGA, DONATUS I.

Criticism

See 3710, 4187, 4383.

NYABONGO, PRINCE AKIKI K.

Biography

5790. Langlands, Bryan. "´Prince´, Dr. Akiiki Nyabongo." UGANDA
       JOURNAL, 38 (1976), 120-25.
           Obituary.

NZEKWU, ONUORA

Criticism

5791. Gleason, Judith Illsley, et al. "Nzekwu, Onuora." In Ferres
       and Tucker, 3467, pp. 80-83.
           Extracts from selected criticism.

5792. Horton, Robin, et al. "Nzekwu, Onuora." In Popkin, 3638,
       pp. 329-33.
           Extracts from selected criticism.

See also 3467, 3520, 3567, 3638, 3743, 3754, 3830, 3837, 3843, 4340,
       4509.

OBENG, R.E.

Criticism

5793. Saint-Andre-Utudjian, E. "Un pionnier littéraire de la Côte
       de l´Or: le romancier R.E. Obeng." AUBTL, 4, 1 (1977), 75-90.

See also 3777.

OBI, ADA D.

Criticism

See 4083.

OBIECHINA, EMMANUEL

Bibliography

See 3315.

Biography

See 3315.

Criticism

See 4187.

OCULI, OKELLO

Interviews

5794. Atta, Victoria, and Ode Ogede. "Okello Oculi: Exclusive
       Interview." KUKA, (1978-79), 63-72.

5795. Mulei, Christopher. "Writer Who is Proud to be Called
       Ugandan." SUNDAY NATION, 23 May 1971, p. 13.

Criticism

5796. Wanjala, Chris. "Okello Oculi: He Qualifies as a Thinker."
       SUNDAY NATION, 21 August 1977, pp. 14-15.

See also 3438, 3538, 3580, 3655, 3683, 3702, 4111, 4476.

ODAGA, ASENATH

Criticism

See 4312.

ODAMTTEN, VINCENT OKPOTI

Criticism

See 4072.

OFIEMUN, ODIA

Criticism

See 3584, 4099, 4136, 4240.

OFORI, HENRY

Criticism

See 4336.

OGALI, OGALI A.

Bibliography

5797. Sander, Reinhard W. "A Checklist of Works by Nigerian Popular
       Writer Ogali A. Ogali." RAL, 9 (1978), 445-48.

Criticism

5798. Ayers, Peter K. "Ogali A. Ogali and COAL CITY: The
       Pamphleteer as Novelist." WLWE, 18 (1979), 99-113.

5799. Haruna, Matthew. "A Critical Analysis of the Speeches of
       Chief Jombo, Bomber Billy and Mike in the Play VERONICA MY
       DAUGHTER, a Play by Ogali A. Ogali." KUKA, (1980-81), 1-6.

5800. Sander, Reinhard W. "Foreword." In Ogali A. Ogali, COAL
       CITY. Enugu: Fourth Dimension, 1976. Pp. 1-15.

5801. ____. "Foreword." In Ogali A. Ogali, VERONICA MY DAUGHTER
       AND OTHER ONITSHA PLAYS AND STORIES. Ed. Reinhard W. Sander
       and Peter K. Ayers. Washington, DC: Three Continents Press,
       1980. Pp. ix-xix.

5802. Sander, Reinhard W., and Peter K. Ayers. "Foreword." In
       Ogali A. Ogali, THE JUJU PRIEST. Enugu: Fourth Dimension,
       1978. Pp. ix-xix.

5803. Sander, Reinhard W., Peter K. Ayers, and Helen O. Chukwuma.
       "Foreword." In Ogali A. Ogali, TALES FOR A NATIVE SON.
       Enugu: Fourth Dimension Publishers, 1977.

See also 3754, 4344.

OGBUAGU, O.A.

Criticism

See 4083.

OGIEIRIAIXI, EVINMA

Criticism

See 3945.

OGOT, BETHWELL

Interview

See 4608.

OGOT, GRACE AKINYE

Bibliography

See 3317.

Biography

5804. Anon. "Grace Ogot." VIVA, 2, 11 (1976), 19.
            Profile.

Interviews

5805. Dolfe, Mikael. "'Afrika är det förflutna, nuet och framtiden
       [Africa is the Past, Present and Future]." FOLKET I BILD,
       8-21 November 1979, p. 15.

5806.* Ganjuly, Shailaja. "An Afternoon with Grace Ogot." FEMINA,
       8-22 September 1979, p. 39.

5807. Lindfors, Bernth. "Interview with Grace Ogot." WLWE, 18
       (1979), 57-68; rpt. in Lindfors, 3387.

5808. Mulei, Christopher. "A Writer Who Prefers Pleasing to
       Preaching." SUNDAY NATION, 28 November 1971, pp. 15-16.

5809.* Sharma, Veena. "In Search of a New Identity." EVE'S WEEKLY,
       12-18 July 1980, pp. 10-11.

See also 3389.

Criticism

5810.   Bede, J. "La donna e la terra natale in LA TERRA PROMESSA di
        Grace Ogot." In LA LETTERATURA DELLA NUOVA AFRICA. Ed. Lina
        Angioletti and Armanda Guiducci. Rome: Lerici, 1979. Pp.
        117-65.

        Translation of BALE 2906.

5811.* Mukayiranga, Callixta. "The African Woman in Grace Ogot's
        Work: THE PROMISED LAND (1966), LAND WITHOUT THUNDER (1968),
        THE OTHER WOMAN (1976)." Thesis for Licence d'Enseignement
        en Lettres, University of Burundi, 1978.

5812.   Wanjala, Chris. "Superstition, Magic and Writing of Prose."
        SUNDAY NATION, 16 October 1977, p. 10.

        THE OTHER WOMAN.

See also 3419, 3513, 3655, 3686, 3702, 4473, 4476, 4483, 4488, 4609.

OGUNBIYI, YEMI

Criticism

See 4256.

OGUNNIYI, LAOLU

Criticism

See 3916.

OGUNYEMI, WALE

Criticism

5813.   Adegoke, 'Yemi. "THE VOW -- a Drama of Conflicts." SPEAR,
        August 1978, pp. 14-15.

See also 3857, 3891, 3989, 4028.

OGUTU, ONYANGO

Criticism

See 3655.

OJAIDE, TANURE

Interview

See 3378.

OKAFOR, DUBEM

Criticism

See 4159.

OKAFOR-OMALI, DILIM

Criticism

See 3769.

OKAI, JOHN ATUKWEI

Biography

See 5904.

Criticism

5814. Anyidoho, Kofi. "Atukwei Okai and His Poetic Territory." In
        Ogungbesan, 3617, pp. 45-59.

See also 4070.

OKARA, GABRIEL IMOMOTIMI GBAINGBAIN

Biography

See 3373, 3377.

Criticism

5815. Ashaolu, Albert Olu. "A Voice in the Wilderness: The
        Predicament of the Social Reformer in Okara's THE VOICE."
        IFR, 6 (1979), 111-17.

5816. Egudu, R.N. "A Study of Five of Gabriel Okara's Poems."
        OKIKE, 13 (1979), 93-110.

5817. King, Bruce. "The Poetry of Gabriel Okara." CHANDRABHĀGĀ, 2
        (1979), 60-65.

5818. Niven, Alastair. "Okara, Gabriel (Imomotimi Gbaingbain)."
       In Vinson and Kirkpatrick, 3377, pp. 178-79.

5819. Obiechina, Emmanuel, et al. "Okara, Gabriel." In Popkin,
       3638, pp. 334-39.
       Extracts from selected criticism.

5820. Soyinka, Wole, et al. "Okara, Gabriel." In Ferres and
       Tucker, 3467, pp. 83-85.
       Extracts from selected criticism

5821. Webb, Hugh. "Allegory: Okara's THE VOICE." ENGLISH IN
       AFRICA, 5, 2 (1978), 66-73.

See also 3467, 3520, 3545, 3566-67, 3582, 3586, 3602, 3604, 3608,
       3638, 3658, 3681-82, 3731, 3735, 3743-45, 3757, 3769, 3827,
       3837, 4078, 4084, 4097, 4109, 4117, 4120-21, 4143, 4154,
       4181, 4185, 4363, 4370, 4374, 4382, 4460, 4509, 4814.

OKIGBO, CHRISTOPHER

Bibliography

5822. Anafulu, Joseph C. "Christopher Okigbo, 1932-1967: A
       Bio-Bibliography." RAL, 9 (1978), 65-78.

Biography

5823. Achebe, Chinua, and Dubem Okafor, eds. DON´T LET HIM DIE:
       AN ANTHOLOGY OF MEMORIAL POEMS FOR CHRISTOPHER OKIGBO
       (1932-1967). Pref. Chinua Achebe. Enugu: Fourth Dimension
       Publishers, 1978.
          Biographical preface.

5824. Ottah, Nelson. "The Truth about Christopher Okigbo." TRUST,
       1, 6 (1971), 9.

See also 3373, 3377, 5904.

Criticism

5825. Azuonye, Chukwuma. "Christopher Okigbo and the Psychological
       Theories of Carl Gustav Jung." JACL, 1, (1981), 30-51.

5826. Beier, Ulli, et al. "Okigbo, Christopher." In Ferres and
       Tucker, 3467, pp. 85-89; Popkin, 3638, pp. 339-44.
          Extracts from selected criticism.

5827. Bouyssou, Roland. "LABYRINTHS ou la quête initiatique de
       Christopher Okigbo." ANNALES DE L´UNIVERSITÉ DE TOULOUSE: LE

MIRAIL, 13, 1 (1977), 61-70.

5828.   Gomwalk, Philemon Victor. "The Stages of Style and Thematic
        Pre-occupation in Okigbo's Poetry of LABYRINTHS." KUKA,
        (1978-79), 46-54.

5829.   Heywood, Annemarie. "The Ritual and the Plot: The Critic and
        Okigbo's LABYRINTHS." RAL, 9 (1978), 46-64.

5830.   Lindfors, Bernth. "Okigbo as Jock." ENGLISH IN AFRICA, 6, 1
        (1979), 52-59; rpt. in Parker, 3630, pp. 199-214.

5831.   Maduakor, Obi. "Creative Process as Ritual: Okigbo's
        HEAVENSGATE." KIABÀRÀ, 3, 2 (1980), 159-69.

5832.   Nazombe, Anthony. "Meaning in Okigbo's Poetry." ODI, 3, 1
        (1978), 34-42.

5833.   Ngate, Jonathan. "Two African Prodigals: Senghor and
        Okigbo." DAI, 40 (1980), 4021-22A (Washington).

5834.* Okafor, Dubem. NATIONALISM IN OKIGBO'S POETRY. Enugu:
        Fourth Dimension, 1980.

5835.* Provinciael, Annie. "An Introduction to Okigbo's
        LABYRINTHS." RESTANT. 8, 2 (1980), 57-67.

5836.   Thomas, Peter. "An Image Insists." GREENFIELD REV, 8, 1-2
        (1980), 122-26.

5837.   Tibble, Anne. "Okigbo, Christopher (Ifenayichukwu)." In
        Vinson and Kirkpatrick, 3377, pp. 180-81.

See also 3467, 3499, 3511, 3562-63, 3567, 3609, 3638, 3769, 3837,
     4065, 4078, 4085, 4091-93, 4107, 4111, 4116, 4118-20,
     4122-23, 4135-36, 4142, 4154, 4159, 4162, 4187, 4215, 4217,
     4380, 4435, 4455, 4460, 4525.

OKOLA, LENNARD

Criticism

See 3580.

OKORO, ANEZI

Criticism

See 4301.

OKPAKU, JOSEPH OHIOMOGBEN

Biography

See 3373.

OKPEWHO, ISIDORE

Interview

5838.   Smith, Mary C. "Interview with Isidore Okpewho." INTERLINK, 9, 1 (1973), 8, 10, 12.

Criticism

5839.   Johnson, Alex C. "Language and Character in Isidore Okpewho´s THE LAST DUTY." FBSLL, 1 (1980), 27-49.

See also 3743, 3827, 3837, 4363, 4488, 5505.

OKRI, BENJAMIN

Autobiography

5840.   Okri, Benjamin. "Fear of Flying." WA, 3 November 1980, pp. 2177-78.

OLE KULET, HENRY R.

Criticism

See 3728.

OMOTOSO, KOLE

Interviews

5841.   Adeniyi, Tola. "Writers´ Search for Audience in Africa." DAILY TIMES, 14 March 1974, p. 12.

See also 3389, 4675.

Criticism

5842.   Dash, Cheryl M.L. "An Introduction to the Prose Fiction of Kole Omotoso." WLWE, 16 (1977), 39-53.

5843.   Vignal, Daniel. "Littérature nigériane d´expression anglaise: Quoi de neuf?" PEUPLES NOIRS/PEUPLES AFRICAINS, 14 (1980), 50-58.

See also 3584, 3595, 3743, 3765, 3809, 3811, 3827, 3837, 3949, 4136, 4435.

ONIBONOJE, G.O.

Biography

5844. Akano, Remi. "Onibonoje, Author and Publisher." SPEAR, August 1976, pp. 25-27, 29.

ONYEAMA, DILLIBE

Biography and Autobiography

5845. Anon. "Old Etonian's Black Mark." OBSERVER, 21 December 1980.

5846. Onyeama, Dillibe. THE RETURN: HOMECOMING OF A NEGRO FROM ETON. London: Satellite Books, 1978.

    Autobiographical.

See also 3373.

Interview

5847. Anon. "Nigeria's 'Nigger at Eton' Speaks to DRUM." DRUM (Lagos), February 1973, pp. 8-10, 13, 15.

Criticism

5848. Onyeama, Dillibe. "Nigerians are Masochists." WA, 18 December 1978, pp. 2551-52.

    Reaction to review of THE RETURN.

OPOKU-AGYEMANG, KWAJO

Criticism

See 4069, 4072.

OSADEBAY, DENNIS CHUKUDE

Criticism

5849. McLeod, A.L. "Colonial Canticles: The Poetry of Dennis Chukude Osadebay." WLWE, 16 (1977), 25-37.

OSAE, SETH K.

Criticism

See 4336.

OSAHON, NAIWU

Biography

5850. Simmons, Michael. "Where is Osahon?" GUARDIAN, 11 August
       1980, p. 19.

Interview

5851. Anon. "Conversation with Naiwu Osahon." THIRD WORLD FIRST,
       1, 2-3 (1978), 9-11.

Criticism

See 3743.

OSINYA, OLUMIDI

Criticism

5852. Nazareth, Peter. "The Fiction of Idi Amin." RIKKA, 4, 3-4
       (1977), 96-101.

       THE AMAZING SAGA OF FIELD MARSHAL ABDULLA SALIM FISI, et
       al.

OSOFISAN, FEMI

Interveiws

5853. Enekwe, Ossie Onuora. "Interview with Femi Osofisan."
       GREENFIELD REV, 8, 1-2 (1980), 76-80.

See also 4675.

Criticism

5854. Balogun, F. Odun. "KOLERA KOLEJ: A Surrealistic Political
       Satire." AfrLJ, 12 (1981), 323-32.

5855. Osundare, Niyi. "Social Message of a Nigerian Dramatist."
       WA, 28 January 1980, pp. 147-50.

       "Once Upon Four Robbers" and "Morountodun."

See also 3584, 3743, 3808-09, 3811, 3827, 3886, 3948-49, 4234.

OSUNDARE, NIYI

Interview

See 4675.

Criticism

See 4069.

OWUSU, MARTIN

Criticism

See 3769, 4028.

OYEKUNLE, OLUSEGUN

Interview

5856. Drame, Kandioura. "Oyekunle on Africa Film Industry."
       AFRISCOPE, 11, 2 (1981), 27-30, 33.

OYÔNÔ-MBIA, GUILLAUME

Interview

See 3389.

Criticism

See 4371.

PALANGYO, PETER K.

Criticism

5857. Cochrane, Judith. "The Significance of Death in Peter
       Palangyo's DYING IN THE SUN." CRIT, 22, 1 (1980), 65-78.

See also 3438, 3655, 3728, 4476.

PALMER, EUSTACE

Criticism

See 4187, 4218, 4246.

PATEL, M.M.

Criticism

See 3498.

P´BITEK, J.P. OKOT

Bibliography

5858. Lindfors, Bernth. "A Checklist of Works by and about Okot
       p´Bitek." WLWE, 16 (1977), 300-03.

Biography

5859. Wanjala, Chris. "The Examination Controversy: Where Okot
       Blundered in ´Feeling´ Literature.´ SUNDAY NATION, 26
       February 1978, p. 27.
          p´Bitek´s views on teaching.

See also 3377, 4806, 4948.

Interviews

5860. Darling, Peter. "Relevance: A Must for Our Culture." SUNDAY
       NATION, 1 June 1969, pp. 11-12.
          Correction of BALE 2999.

5861. Esibi, John. "Africa Is Full of Bogus Types Who Are Fools."
       SUNDAY NATION, 18 December 1977, pp. 8, 29.

5862. Hall, Tony. "Great Dancers, Great Poets Are Left Out."
       SUNDAY NATION, 19 November 1967, pp. 18-19.

5863. Lahui, J. "Okot p´Bitek...to Sing ´Song of Lawino.´" PAPUA
       NEW GUINEA WRITING, 23 (1976), 12-13.

5864. Lindfors, Bernth. "An Interview with Okot p´Bitek." WLWE,
       16 (1977), 281-99; rpt. in Lindfors, 3387, pp. 134-49.

5865. Petersen, Kirsten Holst, et al. "Okot p´Bitek: Interview."
       KUNAPIPI, 1, 1 (1979), 89-93.

5866.* Živančević, Nina. "Intervju sa Okotom p´Bitekom." KNJI, 72,
       7-8 (1981), 1471-73.

See also 3389.

Criticism

5867.   Anon.   "Okot p´Bitek: ´Karibu.´"   OPON IFA, 1, 2 (1980),
        36-39.

5868.   Asein, Samuel Omo.   "Okot p´Bitek: Literature and the
        Cultural Revolution in East Africa."   WLWE 16 (1977), 7-24;
        JAfrS 5 (1978), 357-72.

        Includes comments on Liyong, Ngugi, Rubadiri.

5869.   Cook, David, et al.   "p´Bitek, Okot."   In Popkin, 3638, pp.
        350-55.

        Extracts from selected criticism.

5870.   Ejrnaes, Anne Marie.   IMPERIALISMETEORI OG AFRIKANSK
        LITTERATUR [Theory of Imperialism and African Literature].
        Skriftraekke fra Institut for Litteraturvidenskab, 7.
        Copenhagen: GMT, 1975.

5871.   Heron, George.   "Okot p´Bitek and the Elite in African
        Writing."   LHY, 19, 1 (1978), 66-93.

        Includes comments on Achebe, Kibera, Liyong, Ngugi,
        Soyinka, et al.

5872.   Heywood, Annemarie.   "Modes of Freedom: The Songs of Okot
        p´Bitek."   PA, 113 (1980), 235-57; JCL, 15, 1 (1980), 65-83.

5873.   Moore, Gerald, et al.   "Okot p´Bitek, J.P."   In Ferres and
        Tucker, 3467, pp. 89-91.

        Extracts from selected criticism.

5874.   Mwasaru, Dominic.   "Okot p´Bitek and Religion."   AFER, 17
        (1975), 280-89.

5875.* Ogunyemi, C.O.   "In Praise of Things Black: Langston Hughes
        and Okot p´Bitek."   ConP, 4, 1 (1981), 19-39.

5876.   Tanna, Laura.   "Notes towards a Reading of Okot p´Bitek´s
        SONG OF LAWINO."   ASAWIB, 8 (1977), 18-31.

        Expansion of BALE 3026.

5877.   Tibble, Anne.   "p´Bitek, Okot."   In Vinson and Kirkpatrick,
        3377, pp. 189-91.

See also 3467, 3473, 3478, 3508, 3514, 3538, 3545, 3555, 3557, 3572,
        3580, 3582, 3585, 3605, 3608-09, 3638, 3644, 3655, 3681,
        3683, 3702, 3706, 3769, 3940, 3990, 4078, 4090, 4092-93,
        4111, 4130, 4136, 4164, 4187, 4333, 4420, 4435, 4460, 4476,
        4488.

PETENI, R.L.

Criticism

5878.   Rice, Michael.   "THE HILL OF FOOLS: A Worksheet."   ELTIC
        REPORTER, 5, 1 (1980), 24-26.

See also 3544.

PETERS, LENRIE [Leopold]

Biography

5879.   Anon.   "Lenrie Peters."   In Eckardt, 4995, p. 109.

Criticism

5880.   Egudu, Romanus N.   "´The Colour of Truth´:   Lenrie Peters and
        African Politics."   In Ogungbesan, 3617, pp. 60-70.

5881.   Jones, Eldred, et al.   "Peters, Lenrie."   In Ferres and
        Tucker, 3467, pp. 95-97.
            Extracts from selected criticism.

5882.   Ohaeto, Ezenwa.   "The Predominant Themes and the Nature of
        the Poetic Style of Lenrie Peters in SATELLITES."   KUKA,
        (1980-81), 19-25.

5883.   Pajalich, Armando.   "Africa e Africanità nella poesia di
        Lenrie Peters."   AFRICA (Rome), 33 (1978), 69-96.

5884.   Tolson, Melvin B., et al.   "Peters, Lenrie."   In Popkin,
        3638, pp. 355-58.
            Extracts from selected criticism.

See also 3467, 3518, 3638, 4091, 4097, 4115, 4117, 4165, 4187, 4377.

PHIRI, MASAUTSO

Interview

5885.   Kapumpa, Mumba.   "´Ideology of Fear.´"   AIBEPM, 92 (1979),
        81, 84.
            Theatre in Zambia.

PIETERSE, COSMO GEORGE LEIPOLDT

Criticism

See 3910, 4063, 4106.

PLAATJE, SOLOMON TSHEKISO

Biography

5886. Anon. "Pages from History: Solomon Tshekisho Plaatje, First
       ANC Secretary-General (1876-1932)." SECHABA, December 1981,
       pp. 23-32.

5887. Lindfors, Bernth. "Sol T. Plaatje's Date and Place of
       Birth." AFRICANA N&N 23 (1978), 66-68.

       See response by Willan, 5889.

5888. Willan, Brian. "The 'Gift of the Century': Solomon Plaatje,
       De Beers and the Old Kimberley Tram Shed, 1918-1919." In THE
       SOCIETIES OF SOUTHERN AFRICA IN THE 19TH AND 20TH CENTURIES.
       Collected Seminar Papers, 22. London: Institute of
       Commonwealth Studies, University of London, 1977. Vol. 8, pp.
       77-93; rpt. in JSAS, 4 (1978), 195-215.

5889. ____. "Sol T. Plaatje's Date and Place of Birth." AFRICANA
       N&N, 23 (1978), 172-74.

       Corrects Lindfors, 5887.

Criticism

5890. Couzens, Tim. "Sol Plaatje's MHUDI." In Parker, 3817, pp.
       57-76.

       Rpt. of BALE 3035.

5891. ____. "Introduction." In MHUDI. By Sol T. Plaatje. London:
       Heinemann, 1978. Pp. 1-20.

       Rev. of BALE 3036.

5892. ____. "MHUDI: The Passing of Information in Literature."
       SPEAK, 1, 5 (1978), 16-17.

       Comments on original typescript of novel.

5893. Couzens, Tim, and Stephen Gray. "Printers' and Other Devils:
       The Texts of Sol T. Plaatje's MHUDI." RAL, 9 (1978),
       198-215.

5894. Futcha, Innocent. "The Theme of Freedom in Two Early

Southern African Novels: FESO and MHUDI." NGAM, 3-4 (1978), 202-32.

5895. Gray, Stephen. "Sol Plaatje's One Hundred Years." LANTERN, 26, 1 (1976), 32-35.

5896. ____. "Plaatje's Shakespeare." ENGLISH IN AFRICA, 4, 1 (1977). 1-6.

>   Shakespeare's influence on MHUDI; rpt. of portion of BALE 3038.

5897. Jacobson, Marcelle. THE SILAS T. MOLEMA AND SOLOMON T. PLAATJE PAPERS. Historical and Literary Papers: Inventories of Collections, 7. Johannesburg: Library, University of the Witwatersrand, 1978.

5898. ____. "The Personal Papers of Silas Thelesho Molema and Solomon Tshekisho Plaatje." RAL, 11 (1980), 224-34.

5899. Mphahlele, Ezekiel. "Plaatje, Sol T." In Popkin, 3638, pp. 358-61.

>   Extracts from selected criticism.

5900. Ogungbesan, Kolawole. "The Long Eye of History in MHUDI." CARJAS, 1 (1978), 27-42; LHY, 19, 1 (1978), 139-80.

5901. Ravenscroft, Arthur. "African, Boer, and Indian Attitudes to an Imperialist War." In Narasimhaiah, 3593, pp. 315-26.

5902. Tibble, Anne, et al. "Plaatje, Solomon T." In Ferres and Tucker, 3467, pp. 97-99.

>   Extracts from selected criticism.

See also 3467, 3493-94, 3631, 3638, 3738, 3769, 3786, 3817.

QUAYE, COFIE

Criticism

See 4336.

RAHUBE, JOE

Criticism

See 3976.

RASIK

Criticism

See 3836.

RIBEIRO, HUBERT

Criticism

See 3498.

RIVE, RICHARD

Biography and Autobiography

5903. Rive, Richard. "Caledon St. and Other Memories."
       STAFFRIDER, 2, 4 (1979), 46-49, 61; S AFRICAN OUTLOOK, 110
       (1980), 6-8; rpt. in Rive, 5904.

5904. ____. WRITING BLACK. Cape Town: David Philip, 1981.

       Includes comments on Abrahams, Achebe, Brutus, Clark,
       Gwala, Kariara, M. Kunene, La Guma, Matshikiza,
       Matthews, Modisane, Motsisi, Mphahlele, Mtshali, Nakasa,
       Ngugi, Nkosi, Nortje, Okai, Okigbo, Sepamla, Serote,
       Soyinka, et al. Rpts. 5903.

Interviews

5905. Anon. "Interview--Richard Rive." WIETIE, 2 (1980), 10-13.

5906. Lindfors, Bernth. "Interview with Richard Rive." GAf, 18, 2
       (1980), 45-66.

Criticism

5907. Wright, Edgar, et al. "Rive, Richard." In Ferres and
       Tucker, 3467, pp. 105-07.

       Extracts from selected criticism.

See also 3393, 3467, 3615, 3650, 3652, 3910, 4356, 4407, 4479.

ROTIMI, OLAWALE

Biography

See 3373.

Interviews

5908. Adeniyi, Tola. "The Unife Theatre: An Experiment in African
       Tradition." DAILY TIMES, 8 October 1973, p. 26.

5909. Odiase, Joe. "Rotimi on His New Historical Tragedy: ´I´m
       Satisfied I´ve Done Ovonramwen Justice.´" NIGERIAN OBSERVER,
       20 January 1972, p. 7.

See also 3378.

Criticism

5910. Adedeji, Joel. "Recherche d´un théâtre africain: Ola Rotimi
       et son activité au Centre Culturel Ori Olokun á Ile-Ife en
       Nigeria." THÉÂTRE EN POLOGNE, 11-12 (1972), 64-67.

5911. Nasiru, Akanji. "Ola Rotimi´s Search for a Technique." In
       Ogungbesan, 3617, pp. 21-30.

5912. Neverson, Yvonne. "A Tortured Hunt for the Truth." AIBEPM,
       81 (1978), 95-96.

       THE GODS ARE NOT TO BLAME.

5913. Ogaba, Ogorry. "KURUNMI--The Need for Flexibility and
       Adaptation." KUKA, (1979-80), 44-48.

5914. Olu, Marcos. "Oralité et écriture: Le cas de la littérature
       écrite (d´expression française et anglaise) de la République
       Populaire du Bénin et du Nigéria." EDUCATION BÉNINOISE, 3
       (1980), 41-57.

See also 3852, 3857, 3885, 3891, 3911, 3916, 3948, 3980-81, 3989,
       4007, 4014, 4021, 4028, 4036, 4053, 4458.

RUBADIRI, JAMES DAVID

Biography

5915. Anon. "David Rubadiri." In Eckardt, 4995, p. 109.

Interview

5916. Tejani, Bahadur. "African in Corridors of Power." SUNDAY
       NATION, 5 October 1969, p. 13.

Criticism

5917. Shadle, Mark. "Polyrhythms of Love and Violence in NO BRIDE
       PRICE: Music of African Spheres." PQM, 6, 3-4 (1981),
       123-32.

5918. S[onuga], G[benga]. "David Rubadiri: Poet, Dramatist and

Scholar from East Africa." NEW CULTURE, 1, 8 (1979), 64-66.

See also 3683, 4121, 4126, 4143, 4435, 4476, 4488, 5868.

RUGANDA, JOHN

Biography

5919. Klicker, Jochen R. "John Ruganda: Biografische Notiz." In
       Eckardt, 4995, p. 39.

Interview

5920.* Dolfe, Mikael. "´I Want to Share the Truth with Others.´"
       NEW AFRICAN, December 1980, pp. 51-53.

Criticism

5921. Gikandi, Simon. "Kenyan Theatre Comes of Age." AIBEPM, 95
       (1979), 84.

       Yugoslavian production of THE FLOODS.

5922. Kitonga, Ellen. A STUDY GUIDE TO JOHN RUGANDA´S PLAY, THE
       BURDENS. Nairobi: Oxford University Press, 1977.

5923. Parasuram, A.N. MINERVA GUIDE TO JOHN RUGANDA: THE BURDENS.
       Madras: Minerva Publishing House, 1977.

See also 3862, 3939-40, 3990, 4028, 4058, 4090, 4435.

RUHENI, MWANGI

Criticism

See 3719, 4476, 4488.

RUKUNI, CHARLES

Interview

5924. Seroke, Jaki. "´We are up against colonial hangovers.´"
       STAFFRIDER, 3, 4 (1980-81), 19.

SALLAH, TIJAN M.

Criticism

See 3547.

SAMKANGE, STANLAKE J.T.

Biography

5925.   Sithole, Gordon. "Stanlake's Castle." DRUM (Johannesburg),
         March 1979, pp. 63, 65.

             On his return to Zimbabwe.

Criticism

5926.   Brancaccio, Patrick. "The Origins of Rhodesia: Myth as
         History and Fiction in the Work of Stanlake Samkange." BA
         SHIRU, 9, 1-2 (1978), 124-33.

See also 3545, 3619, 3773.

SANCHO, IGNATIUS

Biography

5927.   Edwards, Paul. "Ignatius Sancho." HISTORY TODAY, 31
         (September 1981), 44.

5928.   Wright, Josephine. "Ignatius Sancho (1729-1780), African
         Composer in England." BLACK PERSPECTIVE IN MUSIC, 7 (1979),
         133-67.

See also 3458.

Criticism

See 4272.

SANKAWULO, WILTON

Criticism

See 3545, 3824.

SEBUKIMA, DAVIS

Criticism

See 3538.

SEGUN, JOLAOSA

Bibliography

See 3317.

SEKYI, KOBINA

Biography

5929. Asante, S.K.B. "The Politics of Confrontation: The Case of
       Kobina Sekyi and the Colonial System in Ghana." UNIVERSITAS
       (Legon), 6, 2 (1977), 15-38.

Criticism

5930. Langley, J. Ayo. "Introduction to Kobina Sekyi's Play, THE
       BLINKARDS." NDAANAN, 3, 1 (1973), 10-18.

            BALE 3055.

5931. Yirenkyi, Asiedu. "Kobina Sekyi: The Founding Father of the
       Ghanaian Theatre." LEGACY, 3, 2 (1977), 39-47.

See also 3930.

SELLASSIE SAHLE BERHANE MARIAM

Criticism

See 3420, 3696, 4710.

SELORMEY, FRANCIS

Criticism

5932. Coustel, J.-C. "Un Enfant noir à la recherche de son
       identité." ANNALES DE L'UNIVERSITÉ DE TOULOUSE: LE MIRAIL,
       13, 1 (1977), 47-54.

See also 3830, 4488.

SENTONGO, NUWA

Criticism

See 3916, 3939.

SENTSO, DYKE

Criticism

See 4530.

SEPAMLA, SYDNEY SIPHO

Bibliography

See 3315.

Biography

5933. Ozynski, Joyce. "Writing is a Painful Exercise--Sepamla."
       SOUTH, 1 (1980), 46.

See also 3315, 5904.

Interviews

5934. Gray, Stephen. "Sipho Sepamla: Spirit Which Refuses to Die."
       INDEX ON CENSORSHIP, 7, 1 (1978), 3-5; PQM, 6, 3-4 (1981),
       257-62.

5935. Meuer, Gerd. "Sipho Sepamla--Poet and Novelist from Soweto,
       South Africa." DEUTSCHE WELLE TRANSKRIPTION, 22 November
       1980, pp. 1-10: 29 December 1980, pp. 1-10; 2 January 1981,
       pp. 1-12; 10 January 1981, pp. 11.

See also 3384, 3390.

Criticism

See 3416, 3652, 3711-12, 4063, 4081, 4095, 4132-33, 4148-49, 4168.

SEROTE, MONGANE WALLY

Biography and Autobiography

5936. Serote, Mongane. "Feeling the Waters." FIRST WORLD, 1, 2
       (1977), 22-25.
           Autobiography.

See also 5904.

Interview

5937. Seroke, Jaki. "Poet in Exile: An Interview." STAFFRIDER, 4,
       1 (1981), 30-32.

Criticism

5938. Gardner, Colin. "Jo´burg City: Questions in the Smoke--
       Approaches to a Poem." BLOODY HORSE, 5 (1981), 38-45.
           On "City Johannesburg."

5939. Langa, Mandlenkosi. "Review of Mongane Serote´s NO BABY MUST

WEEP." PELCULEF NEWSLETTER, 1, 1 (1978), 24-27.

See also 3393, 3608, 3652, 4063, 4081, 4104, 4106, 4132-33, 4148-49.

SERUMA, ENERIKO (See KIMBUGWE, HENRY SERUMA)

SERUMAGA, ROBERT

Biography

5940. Anon. "Daring Playwright: Fighting to Free Uganda." WEEKLY
       REVIEW, 27 April 1979, p. 48.

            Political activities as member of Uganda National
            Liberation Front.

Criticism

5941. Gilbert, W. Stephen. "Uganda/Serumaga." PLAYS AND PLAYERS,
       22, 7 (1975), 11-15.

5942. Rubadiri, David. "Serumaga: Dramatist Who Has Descended to
       Grassroots Level." SUNDAY NATION, 22 January 1978, p. 20.

5943. White, Bill. "Towards a Theatre of Africa: Uganda's
       Olivier." SUNDAY NATION, 30 January 1972, p. 28.

            Theatre Limited.

See also 3608, 3655, 3706, 3728, 3806-07, 3887, 3939-40, 3990, 4058,
       4722.

SITALI, JEFF

Biography

See 3979.

SITHOLE, NDABANINGI

Interview

See 3389.

Criticism

5944. Day, J. "Sithole, The Politician as Author." ZAMBEZIA, 7
       (1979), 93-98.

See also 3773.

SMALL, ADAM

Interviews

5945.   Anon. "SCENARÍA Interviews Adam Small." SCENARÍA, 9 (1978), 30-31.

5946.   Fourie, Lorraine. "Poet-philosopher Adam Small Talks to Lorraine Fourie." SOUTH AFRICA DIGEST, 19 January 1979, p. 12.

See also 3384.

Criticism

5947.   February, Vernie A. "Een stem in de wildernis: de dichter Adam Small [A Voice in the Wilderness: The Poet Adam Small]." KREATIEF, 11, 4-5 (1977), 50-61.

See also 4479.

SOFOLA, ZULU

Interviews

5948.   Adamolekun, Wole. "A Chat with Zulu Sofola, Playwright, University of Ibadan." EMOTAN, 3, 1 (1980), 18.

See also 3389.

Criticism

5949.   Medjigbodo, Nicole. "Zulu Sofola." EUROPE, 618 (1980), 59-64.

5950.   Sonuga, Gbenga. "Christian FESTAC ´77: ´Christianity and African Culture: Which Way Forward?´" NEW CULTURE, 1, 8 (1979), 37-43.

       On KING EMENE.

See also 3745, 3857, 3989, 4036, 4051.

SONDHI, KULDIP

Criticism

See 3498, 3990, 4435.

SOYINKA, WOLE [Akinwande Oluwole]

Bibliography

5951. Avery-Coger, Greta Margaret Kay McCormick. "Indexes of
       Subjects, Themes, and Proverbs in the Plays of Wole Soyinka."
       DAI, 42 (1981), 211A (Colorado-Boulder).

5952. Carpenter, Charles A. "Studies of Wole Soyinka's Drama: An
       International Bibliography." MD, 24, 1 (1981), 96-101.

5953. Page, Malcolm, comp. WOLE SOYINKA: BIBLIOGRAPHY, BIOGRAPHY,
       PLAYOGRAPHY. Theatre Checklist, 19. London: TQ
       Publications, 1979.

Biography and Autobiography

5954. Anon. "Wole Soyinka." In Eckardt, 4995, p. 110.

5955. Anon. "Soyinka joue à Paris." BINGO, 312 (1979), 49.

       Interview with Jean-Luc Jeener, director of French
       production of THE SWAMP DWELLERS.

5956. BBC. "Wole Soyinka's DETAINEE Released." RADIO-TV TIMES,
       13-19 September 1965, p. 14.

       Play broadcast on 8 and 10 September 1965. Soyinka
       performs as Konu.

5957. Gibbs, James. "Brook in Nigeria: Soyinka in London." ODI, 1,
       3 (1973), 16-19.

       THE BACCHAE.

5958.* Lapping, Brian. "The Road to Somewhere." GUARDIAN, 13
       September 1965, p. 7.

5959. Larson, Charles R. "The Trial of Wole Soyinka." NATION, 15
       September 1969, pp. 259-60.

       Play by James Gibbs on Soyinka's imprisonment.

5960. McLellan, Joseph. "The Bard of Nigeria: The Ritual and
       Rational Worlds of Wole Soyinka." WASHINGTON POST, 30
       October 1979, pp. C1-C2.

5961. Osofisan, Femi. "Soyinka in Paris." WA, 21 July 1972, p.
       935.

       A DANCE OF THE FORESTS.

5962. Soyinka, Wole. THE MAN DIED: PRISON NOTES. London: Rex

Collings; New York: Harper and Row, 1972.

Autobiographical work. Extract in TRANSITION, 42 (1973), 38-61.

5963. Special Correspondent, A. "Soyinka in America: A Cockerel Ritual Pays Off." AIBEPM, 100 (1979), 77-78.

DEATH AND THE KING'S HORSEMAN.

5964. Yao, Henri. "Des blancs jouent en noir." BINGO, 302 (1978), 54-56.

On Paris production of THE STRONG BREED; includes interviews with director, Jean-Luc Jeener.

See also 3373, 3377, 4806, 4918, 4933, 5904.

Interviews

5965. Anon. "The Writer in Africa Today: Wole Soyinka." AFRICA CURRENTS, 7 (1976), 26-29.

Rpt. of BALE 3088.

5966. Anon. "No Sense of Direction." AFRISCOPE, 7, 1 (1977), 36-38.

On FESTAC.

5967. Anon. "Onward with Ogun." LISTENER, 3 January 1980, pp. 15-16.

5968. Anon. "Tips on Safe Driving, with Professor Soyinka, Special Marshall, Oyo State Road Safety Corps." EMOTAN, 3, 1 (1980), 10, 44.

5969. Dyson, Soyini. "BLACK BOOKS BULLETIN Interviews Wole Soyinka." BBB, 7, 1 (1980), 36-39, 47.

5970. Mahmoud, Doyin. "An Exclusive Interview with Wole Soyinka." SUNDAY OBSERVER, 18 December 1977, pp. 8-9.

5971. Meuer, Gerd. "Interview mit Wole Soyinka: 'Am Puls des Volkes.'" 3 WELT MAGAZIN, March 1977, pp. 181-83.

5972. ____. "AFRIKA--Interview: Wole Soyinka." AFRIKA, 18, 4 (1977), 14-15.

Criticism

5973. Adams, Lois. "The Prison and Post-Prison Writing (1967-1973) of Wole Soyinka." DAI, 42 (1981), 699A (Wisconsin-Madison).

5974.* Adejare, Oluwole. "Wole Soyinka's Selected Literary Texts: A

Textlinguistics Approach." Ph.D. dissertation, Sheffield
University, 1981.

5975. Adelugba, Dapo. "Wole Soyinka's KONGI'S HARVEST: Production
and Exegesis." In COLLOQUE SUR LITTÉRATURE, 3403, pp.
257-75.

5976. Alcock, Peter. "'Something Different': Problems of Cultural
Relativism in Non-European Literature." ACLALSB, 5, 1
(1978), 48-66.

THE INTERPRETERS.

5977. Anon. "A Tale of Two Cultures." TOPIC, 127 (1980), 31-34.

DEATH AND THE KING'S HORSEMAN.

5978. Attwell, David. "Wole Soyinka's THE INTERPRETERS:
Suggestions on Context and History." ENGLISH IN AFRICA, 8, 1
(1981), 59-71.

5979. Balistreri, June Clara. "The Traditional Elements of the
Yoruba Alarinjo Theatre in Wole Soyinka's Plays." DAI, 39
(1979), 6398A (Colorado-Boulder).

5980. Bamikunle, Aderemi. "'Animistic Spells' as a Political Poem:
An Interpretation." KUKA, (1978-79), 36-45.

5981. Banham, Martin. WOLE SOYINKA, THE LION AND THE JEWEL: A
CRITICAL VIEW. Ed. Yolande Cantù. Nexus Books, 2. London:
Rex Collings in association with The British Council, 1981.

5982. Baré. "A DANCE OF THE FORESTS: Wole Soyinka's Latest Play."
AFRICAN HORIZON, 2 January 1961, pp. 8-10.

5983. Barker, Thomas, and Charles Dameron. "The Twilight and the
God: Two Long Poems of Walcott and Soyinka." ACLALSB, 5, 3
(1980), 51-61.

"Idanre."

5984. Beĭlis, Viktor Aleksandrovich. VOLE SOYINKA. Moscow: Nauka,
1977.

5985. Bestman, Martin. "La Technique romanesque de Wole Soyinka."
EUROPE, 618 (1980), 39-48.

5986. Blishen, Edward. THE LION AND THE JEWEL: WOLE SOYINKA.
London: Heinemann Educational Books for the British
Broadcasting Corporation and the British Council on behalf of
the British Ministry of Overseas Development, 1975.

5987. Böttcher-Wöbcke, Rita. KOMIK, IRONIE UND SATIRE IM
DRAMATISCHEN WERK VON WOLE SOYINKA. Hamburger philologische
Studien, 42. Hamburg: Buske, 1976.

5988. Bonneau, Danielle. "Du Mythe au rite: Soyinka et LES
       BACCHANTES D´EURIPIDE." ALA, 54-55 (1979-80), 81-88.

5989.* Brash, Elton. "Wole Soyinka´s Artistic Sensibility."
       Master´s thesis, University of Papua New Guinea, 1970.

5990. Chinweizu, Onwuchekwa Jemie, and Ihechukwu Madubuike. "The
       Leeds-Ibadan Connection: The Scandal of Modern African
       Literature." OKIKE, 13 (1979), 37-46.

5991. Cook, David, et al. "Soyinka, Wole." In Ferres and Tucker,
       3467, pp. 111-18.

       Extracts from selected criticism.

5992. Crewe, A.R. "THE MAN DIED." AIBEPM, April 1973, pp. 64-65.

       Response to review of book.

5993. Dailly, Christophe. "Bonheur et progrès dans le théâtre de
       Wole Soyinka." AdUA, 11D (1978), 309-21.

5994. d´Almeida, Irene Assiba. "From Social Commitment to
       Ideological Awareness: A Study of Soyinka´s THE INTERPRETERS
       and SEASON OF ANOMY." UFAHAMU, 10, 3 (1981), 13-28.

5995. Dash, Cheryl. "The Crisis in Modern Nigerian Fiction: The
       Example of SEASON OF ANOMY." CARIB, 2 (1981), 9-20.

5996. Dingomé, Jeanne N. "Soyinka´s THE ROAD as Ritual Drama."
       KUNAPIPI, 2, 1 (1980), 30-41.

5997. Docker, John. "Wole Soyinka as Novelist: THE INTERPRETERS
       and SEASON OF ANOMY." NLRev, 2 (1977), 44-53.

5998. [Dohan, Oyado]. "A Study of Wole Soyinka: Part Two."
       INDIGO, 3, 7 (1976), 15, 17-18.

       On poetry; continuation of BALE 3123.

5999.* Domínguez Claver, Francisca. "Wole Soyinka: The Nigerian
       Background and the Universal Flavour in Two of His Main
       Plays: A DANCE OF THE FORESTS, THE STRONG BREED." ADI,
       (1979), 85-103.

6000. Early, L.R. "Dying Gods: A Study of Wole Soyinka´s THE
       INTERPRETERS." JCL, 12, 2 (1977), 162-74.

6001. Ebeogu, Afam. "From IDANRE to OGUN ABIBIMAN: An Examination
       of Soyinka´s Use of Ogun Images." JCL, 15, 1 (1980), 84-96.

6002.* Ebong, Inih A. "Wole Soyinka´s Concepts of Theatre: A Study
       of A DANCE OF THE FORESTS, THE ROAD, and KONGI´S HARVEST."
       Master´s thesis, Michigan State University, 1980.

6003.   Egberike, J.B.   "The Carrier-Scapegoat Archetype and the Cult
         of Altruistic Suffering: A Study in the Mythological
         Imagination of HAMLET, THE FLIES and THE STRONG BREED."   In
         Köpeczi et al., 3540, pp. 293-301.

6004.   Egudu, R.N.   "The Idyll Sham: Ezra Pound and Nigerian Wole
         Soyinka on War."   PAIDEUMA, 5 (1976), 31-41.

6005.   Enem, E.U.   "THE STRONG BREED by Wole Soyinka."   NigM, 121
         (1976), 47-49.

6006.   Feder, Lillian.   MADNESS IN LITERATURE.   Princeton, NJ:
         Princeton University Press, 1980.   Pp. 244-47.

         THE BACCHAE OF EURIPIDES.

6007.   Férent, Catherine.   "Le Lion de la tigritude."   JeuneA, 24
         June 1977, p. 94.

6008.   Fido, Elaine.   "THE ROAD and Theatre of the Absurd."   CARJAS,
         1 (1978), 75-94.

6009.   Fiebach, Joachim.   "Wole Soyinka: ZEIT DER GESETZLOSIGKEIT."
         WB, 25, 11 (1979), 142-54.

         SEASON OF ANOMY.

6010.   Fraser, Robert.   "Four Alternative Endings to Wole Soyinka's
         A DANCE OF THE FORESTS."   RAL, 10 (1979), 359-74.

6011.*   Galle, Etienne.   "Le Monde unitaire de Wole Soyinka, fonction
         vitale du symbole."   Ph.D. dissertation, 3rd cycle,
         University of Montpellier III, 1978.

6012.*   Gibbs, James M.   "Nationalism and Drama: An Examination of the
         Interaction of National Mood and National Traditions with the
         Playwright in the Early Work of Henrik Ibsen, John M. Synge
         and Wole Soyinka."   Master's thesis, University of Bristol,
         1972.

         Correction of BALE 3135.

6013.   ____.   "Soyinka's Drama of Essence."   UTAFITI, 3, 2 (1978),
         427-40.

6014.   ____, ed.   CRITICAL PERSPECTIVES ON WOLE SOYINKA.
         Washington, DC: Three Continents Press, 1980; London:
         Heinemann, 1981.

         Rpts. BALE 1586, 3122, 3140, 3143, 3149-50, 3172, 3176,
         3191, 3195, 3207, 3219, 3223, 3230, 3236-37.   Also
         includes 6019, 6028, 6034, 6081, 6083, as well as a
         bibliography and some reviews of books and plays.

6015.   ____.   "Comments on Some of Wole Soyinka's 'Early Verse.'"

LHY, 22, 1 (1981), 47-64.

6016. Githae Mugo, Micere. "The ´Saviors´ and ´Messiahs´ of Wole Soyinka´s Drama." In Gachukia and Akivaga, 4799, pp. 139-48.

6017. Goodwin. K.L. "Invective and Obliqueness in Political Poetry: Kasaipwalova, Brathwaite, and Soyinka." In Narasimhaiah, 3593, pp. 251-60.

6018. Gowda, H.H. Anniah. "Tradition and Talent in Wole Soyinka´s Plays." LHY, 19, 1 (1978), 122-38.

6019. Graham, Robin, "Wole Soyinka: Obscurity, Romanticism and Dylan Thomas." In Gibbs, 6014, pp. 213-18.

6020. Griffiths, Gareth. "Traditional Practices and Contemporary Concerns in the Plays of Wole Soyinka." In Massa, 3571, pp. 45-50.

6021. Harris, Wilson. "The Complexity of Freedom." In Harris, 3506, pp. 113-124.

    On THE ROAD.

6022. Houbein, Lolo. "THE INTERPRETERS: The Whole Soyinka?" ACLALSB, 5, 3 (1980), 98-111.

6023. Humbe, Terkaa. "´Ulysses´: The Artist in Society." KUKA, (1978-79), 25-30.

6024. Ibitokun, Benedict M. "Existential Struggle in Soyinka´s MADMEN AND SPECIALISTS." BA SHIRU, 10, 1 (1979), 20-30.

6025. ____. "Wole Soyinka et la cosmogonie nigériane." ALA, 57 (1980), 34-39.

6026. Ihekweazu, Edith. "Two Leaders on the Stage: Soyinka and Brecht." JACL, 1 (1981), 52-68.

6027. Irele, Abiola. "Parables of the African Condition: A Comparative Study of Three Post-Colonial Novels." JACL, 1 (1981), 69-91.

    SEASON OF ANOMY, et al.

6028. Izevbaye, D.S. "Mediation in Soyinka: The Case of the King´s Horseman." In Gibbs, 6014, pp. 116-25.

6029. Jabbi, Bu-Buakei. "Mythopoeic Sensibility in THE INTERPRETERS: A Horizontal Overview." OBSIDIAN, 7, 2-3 (1981), 43-74.

6030.* Jeyifo, Biodun. "Drama and the Social Order." POSITIVE REVIEW, 1, 1 (1978), 22; NEW CULTURE, 1, 7 (1979), 45, 47.

    On OPERA WONYOSI.

6031. Johnson, Joyce. "'The Transitional Gulf': A Discussion of
       Wole Soyinka's SEASON OF ANOMY." WLWE, 18 (1979), 287-301.

6032. July, Robert W. "The Artist's Credo: The Political
       Philosophy of Wole Soyinka." JMAS, 19 (1981), 477-98.

6033. Kauchali, A.H. "THE LION AND THE JEWEL: A Satire with
       Cerebral and Aesthetic Delight." BACKGROUND NOTES, 9 (1975),
       3-6.

6034. Kinkead-Weekes, Mark. "THE INTERPRETERS: A Form of
       Criticism." In Gibbs, 6014, pp. 219-38.

6035. Klicker, Jochen R. "La Compagnie de l'élan: Wole Soyinka, LES
       GENS DES MARAIS: Die Leute im Sumpf." In Eckardt, 4995, pp.
       42-43.

6036.* Lane, Brigitte D. "Theatre for the Unborn: Analysis of the
       Plays of Wole Soyinka, 1957-1974." Master's thesis,
       University of Kansas, 1974.

6037. Last, Brian W. "Destruction: Some Aspects of Soyinka's
       Poetry." KUKA, 1, 1 (1977), 9-12.

6038. ____. "Soyinka's Poetry: Threats and Violence." LHY, 19, 1
       (1978), 108-20.

6039. ____. "OGUN ABIBIMAN." WLWE, 20 (1981), 191-200.

6040. Lefevere, André. "Translation: Changing the Code: Soyinka's
       Ironic Aetiology." In THE LANGUAGES OF THEATRE: PROBLEMS IN
       THE TRANSLATION AND TRANSPOSITION OF DRAMA. Ed. Ortrun
       Zuber. Oxford: Pergamon, 1980. Pp. 132-45, 168-69.

           THE BACCHAE.

6041. Lindfors, Bernth. "Wole Soyinka, When Are You Coming Home?"
       YFS, 53 (1976), 197-210; rpt. in LE CRITIQUE AFRICAIN, 4178,
       pp. 338-51.

6042. ____. "'Egbe's Sworn Enemy': Soyinka's Popular Sport." NJH,
       1, 1 (1977), 67-76; KUNAPIPI, 1, 1 (1979), 69-84.

6043. ____. "Begging Questions in Wole Soyinka's OPERA WONYOSI."
       ArielE, 12, 3 (1981), 21-33.

6044. Lyonga, Nalova. "The Theme of Sacrifice in Wole Soyinka's
       THE STRONG BREED." NGAM, 1-2 (1977), 140-54.

6045. Maduakor, Hezzy. "Conquering the Abyss of the Crypt:
       Survival Imperative in Soyinka's SHUTTLE." WLWE, 16 (1977),
       245-55.

6046. ____. "Cyclic Determinism in Soyinka's 'Idanre.'" UFAHAMU,

8, 1 (1977), 175-87.

6047. Maduakor, Obi. "Soyinka's SEASON OF ANOMY: Ofeyi's Quest."
       IFR, 7 (1980), 85-89.

6048. Mahood, M.M., et al. "Soyinka, Wole." In Popkin, 3638, pp.
       388-98.
       Extracts from selected criticism.

6049. Maughan-Brown, David. "Interpreting and THE INTERPRETERS:
       Wole Soyinka and Practical Criticism." ENGLISH IN AFRICA, 6,
       2 (1979), 51-62; rpt. in Brimer, 3431, pp. 107-14.

6050.* Mbon, Friday. "Pessimism in Wole Soyinka's Poetry."
       Master's thesis, University of Calgary, 1978.

6051.* Mbughuni, Louis Azaria. "Tragedies of Wole Soyinka: The
       African Content." Master's thesis, Indiana University, 1973.

6052. Melamu, Moteane. "A Possible Reading of Wole Soyinka's THE
       INTERPRETERS." MARANG, 1 (1977), [30-33].

6053. Meuer, Gerd, and Al Imfeld. "Wole Soyinka: A Man for All
       Seasons." AFRIKA, 21, 10 (1980), 25-27.

6054. Modum, Egbuna. "Le Mythe de Chaka." ETHIOPIQUES, 14 (1978),
       49-58.

       In works by Senghor and Soyinka.

6055. Moore, Gerald. "Soyinka's New Play." WA, 10 January 1977,
       pp. 60-61.

       DEATH AND THE KING'S HORSEMAN.

6056. ____. WOLE SOYINKA. London and Ibadan: Evans; New York:
       Holmes and Meier, 1978.

       2nd ed. of BALE 3185.

6057. Morsiani, Jamilè. "Wole Soyinka: Per un teatro popolare
       nigeriano." SpM, 6 (1976), 130-41.

6058. Nandan, Satendra. "Beyond Colonialism: The Artist as
       Healer." In SOUTH PACIFIC IMAGES. Ed. Chris Tiffin. St.
       Lucia, Australia: South Pacific Association for Commonwealth
       Literature and Language Studies, 1978. Pp. 11-25.

6059. Nasidi, Yakubu. "Literature and Politics: KONGI'S HARVEST as
       Political Drama." WP, 3 (1980), 25-33.

6060. Niven, Alastair. "Soyinka, Wole (Akinwande Oluwole
       Soyinka)." In Vinson and Kirkpatrick, 3377, pp. 242-45.

6061. Nwoga, D. I. "Perception, Style and Meaning in Soyinka's
       Poetry." NSAL, 1, 1 (1978), 5-18.

6062. Ogude, S.E. "Professor, the Word and the Problem of Meaning
       in Soyinka's THE ROAD." JLSN, 1 (1981), 52-66.

6063. Ogunbiyi, Yemi. "ÒPÈRÁ WÓNYÒSI: A Study of Soyinka's ÒPÈRÁ
       WÓNYÒSI." NigM, 128-129 (1979), 3-14.

6064. Ogungbesan, Kolawole. "Wole Soyinka and the Poetry of
       Isolation." CJAS, 11 (1977), 295-312.

6065. ____. "Wole Soyinka and the Novelist's Responsibility in
       Africa." In Ogungbesan, 3617, pp. 1-9.

6066. Ogunyemi, Chikwenye Okonjo. "Iconoclasts Both: Wole Soyinka
       and LeRoi Jones." ALT, 9 (1978), 25-38.

6067. Ojaide, Tanure. "The Voice and Viewpoint of the Poet in Four
       Early Poems of Wole Soyinka." UMOJA, 5, 2 (1981), 27-35.

6068. Okafor, Dubem. "The Cultural Validity of Soyinka's Plays."
       NSAL, 2, 1 (1979), 12-29.

6069. Okafor, R.N.C. "Wole Soyinka's THE ROAD and the Faustian
       Dimension." PA, 111 (1979), 80-89; rpt. in Banjo, 3415, pp.
       234-42.

6070. Okonkwo, Juliet. "The Essential Unity of Soyinka's THE
       INTERPRETERS and SEASON OF ANOMY." ALT, 11 (1980), 110-21;
       UFAHAMU, 9, 3 (1979-80), 65-76.

6071. Okpaku, Joseph Ohiomogben Onieyone. "From SWAMP DWELLERS to
       MADMEN AND SPECIALISTS: The Drama of Wole Soyinka." DAI, 39
       (1979), 5212A (Stanford).

6072. Osofisan, Femi. "Tiger on Stage: Wole Soyinka and Nigerian
       Theatre." In Ogunba and Irele, 4005, pp. 151-75.

6073. Palmer, Eustace Taiwo. "Wole Soyinka's SEASON OF ANOMY."
       WLWE, 17 (1978), 435-49; rpt. in Palmer, 3813.

6074. Parsons, E.M. NOTES ON WOLE SOYINKA'S THE JERO PLAYS.
       London: Methuen, 1979.

6075. Pearse, Adetokunbo. "Symbolic Characterization of Women in
       the Plays and Prose of Wole Soyinka." BA SHIRU, 9, 1-2
       (1978), 39-46.

6076. Prasad, T. Swarnalata. "Soyinka--'The Lion'--and the Concept
       of Negritude." ComQ, 2, 7 (1978), 82-95.

6077. Probyn, Clive T. "Waiting for the Word: Samuel Beckett and
       Wole Soyinka." ArielE, 12, 3 (1981), 35-48.

6078.* Purisch, Christine Winter. "Wole Soyinka: A Critical
       Analysis of His Poetry." Master's thesis, Duquesne
       University, 1972.

6079. Rama Murthy, V. "Soyinka and the Language of Drama." In
       Srivastava, 3677, pp. 101-06.

6080. Reggiani, Renee, and Luciantonio Ruggieri. "Autodefinizione
       dell'identità e del destino nero." TEATRO DELLA RESISTENZA E
       DELLA GUERRIGLIA. Venice: Marsilio, 1977. Pp. 237-52.

6081. Relich, Mario. "Soyinka's 'Beggars' Opera.'" WA, 30 January
       1978, pp. 188-89; rpt. in Gibbs, 6014.

       OPERA WONYOSI.

6082. Sekoni, Oluropo Johnson. "The World in Search of Viable
       Leadership: A Study of Structure and Communication in
       Soyinka's Scripts." DAI, 38 (1978), 6697-98A (Wisconsin-
       Madison).

6083. Senanu, K.E. "The Exigencies of Adaptation: The Case of
       Soyinka's BACCHAE." In Gibbs, 6083, pp. 108-12.

6084. Skurjat, Ernestyna. "Ludzie jak bogowie, bogowie jak ludzie:
       Wole Soyinka, INTERPRETATORZY [People as Gods, Gods as
       People: Wole Soyinka, THE INTERPRETERS]." NOWE KSIAŻKI, 8
       (1979), 26-27.

       On Polish translation.

6085. Steinvorth, Klaus. "Wole Soyinka: 'Massacre, October '66.'"
       In Momodu and Schild, 3583, pp. 290-96.

6086. ____. "Poet and Politician: Wole Soyinka's SEASON OF ANOMY."
       In Banjo, 3415, pp. 223-33.

6087. Szántó, Judit. "Wole Soyinka." In WOLE SOYINKA DRÁMÁK. Ed.
       Sára Karig. Budapest: Európa Könyvkiadó, 1978. Pp. 383-93.

6088. Tripathi, P.D. "THE LION AND THE JEWEL: A Comparative and
       Thematic Study." BA SHIRU, 11, 1 (1980), 82-101.

6089.* Umbach, Judith M. "Wole Soyinka: A Satirist as a Creative
       Writer." Master's thesis, University of Leeds, 1977.

6090. Webb, Hugh. "Soyinka's Novelistic Autobiography." NLRev, 5
       (1978), 11-21.

       THE MAN DIED.

6091. ____. AFRICAN FACTS AND AFRICAN FICTION: WOLE SOYINKA'S
       PRISON NOTES. African Studies Working Papers, 7. Murdock,
       Australia: African Studies Seminar, School of Human
       Communication, Murdoch University, 1978.

6092. ____. DRAMA, SOCIETY AND POLITICS: AFRICAN IMPACT. African Studies Working Papers, 10. Murdoch, Australia: African Studies Seminar, School of Human Communication, Murdoch University, 1980.

6093. Wilkinson, Nick. "Literary Incomprehension: Wole Soyinka's Own Way with a Mode." NSAL, 1, 1 (1978), 44-53.

6094. Williams, Adebayo. "The Mythic Imagination and Social Theories: Soyinka and Euripides as Political Thinkers." OKIKE, 18 (1981), 36-44.

See also 3413, 3444, 3467, 3472-73, 3499, 3507, 3511, 3514-15, 3520-23, 3536, 3553, 3557, 3563, 3566-68, 3573, 3581, 3585, 3599, 3604, 3608-09, 3627-28, 3634-35, 3638, 3658, 3681, 3688, 3691, 3695, 3710, 3725, 3727, 3729, 3731, 3740, 3743-45, 3747, 3749, 3751, 3758, 3764-67, 3769, 3798, 3800, 3802, 3806-07, 3809, 3811, 3813, 3815, 3825, 3827, 3837-38, 3842, 3852, 3855, 3884-87, 3891, 3894, 3901, 3911-12, 3916, 3920, 3948, 3950, 3973, 3980-81, 4007, 4011, 4014, 4021, 4023, 4028, 4033, 4036-37, 4052-53, 4072, 4078, 4082, 4084, 4092-93, 4097, 4109, 4115-16, 4118-23, 4138, 4142-43, 4154, 4156, 4162, 4165, 4187, 4199, 4201, 4215, 4217-18, 4235, 4301, 4340, 4344, 4358, 4360, 4363, 4366, 4371, 4374, 4380, 4382, 4388-89, 4406, 4409-10, 4420, 4448-49, 4455, 4458, 4484, 4488, 4498-99, 4509, 4525, 4770, 4814, 4851-52, 5853, 5871.

SUTHERLAND, EFUA THEODORA [Morgue]

Bibliography

See 3317.

Interview

See 3389.

Criticism

6095.* Dibba, Ebou. EFUA T. SUTHERLAND, THE MARRIAGE OF ANANSEWA. London: Longman, 1978.

6096. Okafor, Chinyere. "Parallelism versus Influence in African Literature: The Case of Efua Sutherland's EDUFA." KIABÀRÀ, 3, 1 (1980), 113-31.

6097. Onukwufor, Chika C. "THE MARRIAGE OF ANANSEWA: A Modern West African Drama for the WASC Candidate." MUSE, 11 (1979), 55-58.

See also 3432, 3867, 3885, 3887, 3901, 3930, 4014, 4028, 4051, 4312, 4315, 4609.

SYAD, WILLIAM JOSEPH FARAH

Criticism

See 3421.

TEJANI, BAHADUR

Interview

6098.   Anon.   "Exiled Author Says ´Ugandan Writers Are Faithful.´"
        QUEST, 14 (1979), 133.

Criticism

See 4078, 4090.

THEMBA, DANIEL CANADOISE DORSAY

Biography

6099.   Motsisi, Casey.   "Can Remembered."   In Mutloatse, 5592, pp.
        94-97.
                Rpt. of BALE 3243.

Criticism

See 4531.

THERSON-COFIE, LAWERH

Criticism

See 4070.

TLALI, MIRIAM

Biography

6100.   Marquard, Jean.   "Profile: Miriam Tlali."   INDEX ON
        CENSORSHIP, 9, 5 (1980), 30-31.

Interview

See 3390.

TSARO-WIWA, KEN

Criticism

See 4028.

TUTUOLA, AMOS

Biography

6101.   Ackerly, Nancy. "WLB Biography: Amos Tutuola." WILSON
        LIBRARY BULLETIN, 38 (September 1963), 81.

6102.   Anon. "Cultural Plunder." DAILY TIMES, 15 June 1978, p. 3.
        Editorial prompted by Ogunbiyi´s article, 6105.

6103.   Harding, M. Hassan. "Beyond Upholding Tutuola´s Dignity."
        DAILY TIMES, 28 June 1978, p. 7.
        Response to Ogunbiyi, 6105.

6104.   Lindfors, Bernth. "On Shocks, Sharks and Literary Archives."
        DAILY TIMES, 15 July 1978, pp. 3, 34.
        Response to Ogunbiyi, 6105.

6105.   Ogunbiyi, Yemi. "Tutuola in an Ocean of Sharks." DAILY
        TIMES, 10 June 1978, pp. 20-21.
        Charges that publishers and scholars have attempted to
        exploit Tutuola. See responses, 6102-04, 6106.

See also 3373, 3377.

Interview

6106.   Osikomaiya, Jide. "Amos Tutuola--Victim of Exploitation?"
        SUNDAY TIMES, 2 July 1978, pp. 16-17.

Criticism

6107.   Achebe, Chinua. "Work and Play in Tutuola´s THE PALM-WINE
        DRINKARD." OKIKE, 14 (1978), 25-33; rpt. in Lindfors, 6119.

6108.   Armstrong, Robert G. "Amos Tutuola and Kola Ogunmola: A
        Comparison of Two Versions of THE PALMWINE DRINKARD."
        CALLALOO, 8-10 (1980), 165-74.

6109.* Balvaude, Catherine. "L´Afrique du conte populaire et
        mythique à travers l´oeuvre d´Amos Tutuola." Ph.D.
        dissertation, 3rd cycle, University of Paris III, 1978.

6110. Breitinger, Eckhard. "Amos Tutuola: Von der Oralliteratur
       zur Nationalliteratur?" In Breitinger, 3428, pp. 156-92.

6111. Coates, John. "The Inward Journey of the Palm-wine
       Drinkard." ALT, 11 (1980), 122-29.

6112. Devereux, George. "Fantasy and Schizophrenic Delusion, with
       a Note on the African Novelist Amos Tutuola." PsyculR, 3
       (1979), 231-37.

6113. Ekwensi, C.O.D., et al. "Tutuola, Amos." In Popkin, 3638,
       pp. 419-29.

       Extracts from selected criticism.

6114. Elaho, Raymond O. "L´IVROGNE DANS LA BROUSSE d´Amos Tutuola."
       EUROPE, 618 (1980), 49-52.

6115. Gurr, Andrew. "Tutuola, Amos." In Vinson and Kirkpatrick,
       3377, pp. 260-61.

6116. Jahn. Janheinz. "Nachwort." In Amos Tutuola, DER
       PALMWEINTRINKER: EIN MÄRCHEN VON DER GOLDKÜSTE. Trans.
       Walter Hilsbecher. Munich: Paul List, 1962. Pp. 134-37.

6117. Jay, Salim. "La Magie verbale d´Amos Tutuola." ALA, 44
       (1977), 46-48.

6118. Lindfors, Bernth. "Amos Tutuola´s Earliest Long Narrative."
       JCL, 16, 1 (1981), 45-55.

6119. ____, ed. CRITICAL PERSPECTIVES ON AMOS TUTUOLA. London:
       Heinemann, 1980.

       British ed. of BALE 3284.

6120. Lundkvist, Artur. "Inledning [Introduction]." In Amos
       Tutuola, PALMVINDRINKAREN. Trans. Karin Alin. Stockholm:
       Tidens Förlag, 1961. Pp. 5-8.

6121. Mezu, S. Okechukwu. "The Tropical Dawn (II): Amos Tutuola."
       NIGERIAN STUDENT´S VOICE, 3 (October 1965), 6-11.

6122. Nkutt, Ukpabio. "THE PALM-WINE DRINKARD has More Practical
       Literary Values than the Purists Would Admit." SHUTTLE, 8
       (1980), 36-40.

6123. Ogundipe-Leslie, Omolara. "Ten Years of Tutuola Studies:
       1966-1976." AFRICAN PERSPECTIVES (Leiden), 1 (1977), 67-76.

6124. Ogunyemi, Chikwenye Okonjo. "The Africanness of THE CONJURE
       WOMAN and FEATHER WOMAN OF THE JUNGLE." ArielE, 8, 2 (1977),
       17-30.

6125. Palmer, Eustace. "Twenty-Five Years of Amos Tutuola." IFR,

5 (1978), 15-24: rpt. in Palmer, 3813.

6126.   Schipper, Mineke. "Oralité écrite et recherche d´identité
dans l´oeuvre d´Amos Tutuola." RAL, 10 (1979), 40-58.

6127.   Tamuly, Annette. "Amos Tutuola, surréaliste malgré lui?"
ALA, 57 (1980), 27-33.

6128.   Thomas, Dylan, et al. "Tutuola, Amos."   In Ferres and
Tucker, 3467, pp. 118-28.

Extracts from selected criticism.

6129.   West, David S. "THE PALM-WINE DRINKARD and African
Philosophy." LHY, 19, 2 (1978), 83-96.

See also 3397, 3467, 3472, 3497, 3499, 3507, 3514-15, 3576, 3597,
    3604, 3608, 3638, 3681-82, 3695, 3731, 3733, 3737, 3744-45,
    3757, 3766, 3769, 3800, 3811-13, 3837-38, 4185, 4187, 4199,
    4264, 4340, 4371, 4382, 4449, 4453, 4455, 4457-58, 4485,
    4509, 4765.

UDECHUKWU, OBIORA

Criticism

See 4159.

UKA, KALU

Biography

See 3373.

Criticism

See 3378, 4072.

UKALA, SAM

Criticism

6130.   Ebong, Inih A. "Foliage in Display." OMABE, 22 (1977), 4-9.

ULASI, ADAORA LILY

Criticism

See 3743, 3833, 3843.

UZODINMA, EDMUND CHUKUEMEKA CHIEKE

Criticism

See 3743.

VAMBE, LAWRENCE

Biography and Autobiography

6131.   Shopo, T.D.   "Black Liberalism Revisited."   ZAMBEZIA, 5
        (1977), 91-94.
                FROM RHODESIA TO ZIMBABWE.

Criticism

See 3769.

VATSA, MAMMAN J.

Criticism

See 4301.

VILAKAZI, PAUL

Criticism

See 4153.

WACIUMA, CHARITY

Criticism

See 4312.

WAIGURU, JOSEPH

Criticism

See 3538.

WANGUSA, TIMOTHY

Criticism

See 4078.

WANJALA, CHRIS LUKORITO

Bibliography

See 3315.

Biography

See 3315.

Interviews

6132. Dolfe, Mikael. "Intervju med Chris Wanjala." PERMANENT
PRESS, 13-14 (1980), 78-84.

6133. Lindfors, Bernth. "East African Literature: An Interview
with Chris Wanjala." ACLALSB, 5, 3 (1980), 26-39; rpt. in
Lindfors, 3387.

See also 3389, 4417.

Criticism

6134. Ochieng, William. "End This Dog-Bite-Dog Situation at the
University." SUNDAY NATION, 14 May 1978, pp. 13, 15.
On criticism of the critic.

See also 4822.

WATENE, KENNETH

Criticism

See 3655, 4028.

WAWERU, DAVID MIKE MWAURA

Biography

6135. Wanjala, Chris. "´Renegade´ Author Dies in His Prime."
SUNDAY NATION, 12 November 1978, p. 18.

WERE, MIRIAM

Criticism

See 3702, 4312.

WEREWERE, LIKING

Interview

See 3879.

WONODI, OKOGBULE

Interview

See 3378.

Criticism

See 4078, 4093, 4122, 4159.

WORKU, DANIACHEW

Bibliography

See 3315.

Biography

See 3315.

Criticism

See 3420, 3696.

YEBOA-AFARI, AJOA

Criticism

See 3621.

ZELEZA, PAUL

Criticism

See 4488.

ZEWI, MEKI.

Criticism

6136. Babalola, E.A. "Back to Nature: Meaning of Meki Zewi´s A
        DROP OF HONEY." KIABÀRÀ, 2, 1 (1979), 191-202.

ZIMUNYA, BONUS

Criticism

See 4102.

ZIRIMU, ELVANIA N.

Bibliography

See 3317.

Criticism

See 3538, 3939, 3990.

ZULU, PHUMZILE

Interview

See 3381.

ZWELONKE, D.M.

Criticism

See 4386.

Indexes

AUTHOR INDEX

This index is alphabetized letter by letter and contains references to each author, editor, and translator whose works appear in the bibliography. All numbers refer to entry numbers, not page numbers.

TITLE INDEX

This index is alphabetized letter by letter and contains references to the title of every literary work and scholarly study listed in the bibliography, including theses and dissertations. Titles of articles are not included. Titles appearing within titles have been capitalized. All numbers refer to entry numbers, not page numbers.

SUBJECT INDEX

This index contains references to all subjects treated in the bibliography except those included as genres or topics in part I or as individual authors in part II. It is alphabetized letter by letter, and all numbers refer to entry numbers, not page numbers.

GEOGRAPHICAL INDEX

This index contains references to the regions of the world and the countries
in Africa covered in the bibliography. All numbers refer to entry numbers, not
page numbers.

REGIONS

Afro-Asian World
  Studies 3544, 3568, 4094, 4385,
    4387, 4898, 4944-47, 4985-86,
    5665
Anglophone & Francophone Africa
  Bibliography 3315
  Studies 3463, 3533, 3747, 3753,
    3760, 3769, 3792, 4120, 4174,
    4370
Black Africa
  Bibliographies 3312, 3317, 3323,
    3326, 3328, 3331-32, 3335, 3337,
    3343, 3345, 3347, 3354, 3358-62,
    3364-67, 3846, 4060, 4170, 4542,
    4544, 4748, 4751
  Studies 3406, 3426, 3432, 3459,
    3483, 3555, 3646, 3660, 3670,
    3707, 3742, 3838, 3876, 3887,
    3892, 3904-08, 3911, 3916,
    3923-24, 3941, 3949, 3951, 3953,
    3959, 3961, 3970-72, 3996-98,
    4004-05, 4025-29, 4033, 4048,
    4073, 4075-76, 4078, 4085-86,
    4088a, 4099, 4107, 4111-14,
    4121, 4127-28, 4130-31, 4136,
    4139-40, 4147-48, 4154, 4163,
    4165, 4179, 4187, 4292, 4339,
    4347, 4354, 4570, 4677, 4680-82,
    4688, 4690-92, 4694, 4739,
    4759-60, 4771, 4782-84, 4789,
    4803, 4812, 4868-69, 4881, 4891,
    4910-12, 4917, 4938, 4940-43,

4949-51, 4969-71, 4990-5003,
    5118, 5126, 5147, 5149, 5227,
    5841, 5856
Black World
  Bibliographies 3346, 4469, 4538,
    4775
  Studies 3427-28, 3446, 3449, 3480,
    3490-91, 3499, 3530, 3729, 3731,
    3735, 3802, 3920, 4074, 4137,
    4152, 4224, 4270, 4457, 4472,
    4475, 4780, 4836, 4902-03, 4968,
    4977-79, 4988
Central Africa
  Bibliographies 3318, 3330, 3336
  Studies 3655, 3957, 4151, 4672
Commonwealth
  Bibliographies 3308, 3311,
    3313-14, 3329, 3344, 3351, 3355,
    3363, 4273, 4275, 4537, 4539,
    4543, 4776
  Studies 3377, 3400, 3423, 3467,
    3536, 3541, 3544, 3571, 3593-94,
    3603, 3643, 3661, 3677, 3684,
    3793, 4043, 4064-65, 4101, 4212,
    4222, 4268, 4369, 4787-88, 4791,
    4800, 4805, 4813, 4861, 4872,
    4892, 4897, 4901, 4908-09, 4913,
    4961-64, 4972-76, 4980-84, 4987,
    5125, 5234
East Africa
  Bibliographies 3307, 3318, 3330,
    3336
  Studies 3387, 3411, 3478, 3498,
    3508, 3554, 3557, 3560-61, 3575,